D0504723

FLYING IN DEFIANCE OF THE REICH

FLYING IN DEFIANCE OF THE REICH

A Lancaster Pilot's
Rites of Passage

Peter Russell

Pen & Sword
AVIATION

In grateful memory of
Air Vice-Marshal John L. Barker CB CBE DFC

First published in Great Britain in 2007 by
Pen & Sword Aviation
an imprint of
Pen & Sword Books Ltd

Copyright © Peter Russell 2007

ISBN 978 1 84415 576 7

A CIP catalogue record for this book is
available from the British Library

Typeset in Palatino by
Phoenix Typesetting, Auldgirth, Dumfriesshire

Printed and bound in England by
CPI UK

Pen & Sword Books Ltd incorporates the Imprints of Pen & Sword Aviation, Pen &
Sword Maritime, Pen & Sword Military, Wharncliffe Local History,
Pen & Sword Select, Pen & Sword Military Classics and Leo Cooper.

For a complete list of Pen & Sword titles please contact
PEN & SWORD BOOKS LIMITED
47 Church Street, Barnsley, South Yorkshire, S70 2AS, England
E-mail: enquiries@pen-and-sword.co.uk
Website: www.pen-and-sword.co.uk

Contents

Author's Note

In this account of my life in the Royal Air Force during the Second World War I have for obvious reasons changed the names of some of those with whom I lived. Of course, I have had to assume exactly what was said in some of the conversations when I was not present, but my account describes to the best of my ability what took place.

Acknowledgements

Martin Middlebrook, the military historian, together with his research colleague Chris Everitt, has written a book, *The Bomber Command War Diaries*, (first published by Viking in 1985 – the present imprint is by Midland Publishing) which has become the standard basic work of reference on the campaign of Bomber Command, Royal Air Force, in the Second World War, 1939–45. It is a complete review of all the raids and many background stories to the campaign. It includes information obtained from local archives in Germany, Italy and the occupied countries on the effects of the raids and makes retrospective observations in a scholarly approach to the subject.

I would like to thank Mr Martin Middlebrook for his permission to quote from their book.

I would also like to thank my wife Jane, my son, Christopher, and my daughter, Amanda, for their help and encouragement, which has made this story more enjoyable to write and without which it would not have been written.

Help often came from the clear memory and encyclopaedic knowledge of Derek Evans, our Wireless Operator in 625 Squadron. He and I are the only two now left of our crew of seven, but we remember with fond gratitude Titch, Torry, Colin, Reg and Ken, the other members of our crew, without whose courage and efficiency we should not have survived.

I was a new and very late comer to the task of publishing a book, but Mrs Juanita Rothman voluntarily elected to guide me. Thereby I found a friend.

CHAPTER ONE

Prologue

'Fighter! Fighter! Port! Down!'

The urgent shout from the tail gunner rings through the intercom. It electrifies not only me, the pilot of the Lancaster, but every man at his station aboard the aircraft. Instantaneously I throw the control stick forward and away from me, and pull the aileron wheel down to the left, while my left foot kicks forward on the rudder bar. The left wing drops down and the 20 tons of aircraft plunges toward the ground curving as it goes. A few seconds later I roll the plane the other way to dive now to the right, then roll again, hauling the stick back so that the suction of centrifugal force drains the blood from my face and, blurring my vision, pulls my cheeks away from my teeth, as we climb to the left.

Now the voice of Torry the mid-upper gunner crackles: 'He's gone over us, Skip, up to the right. I can't see him now.' My flying instruments are spinning madly in their gimbals. They are of no help, but the dawn is not far away, and the sky is dimly divided into two, a darker half and a lighter; only a tiny difference in colour but enough to give me the suspicion of a crazily tilted horizon by which I can struggle with the controls and get back into level flight.

At the mid-upper gunner's comforting words, the bomb aimer and the engineer, and I too, as soon as I have got the aeroplane straight and level, all look forward and up and right, into which part of the night sky the attacking fighter has apparently disappeared. Suddenly, where there was darkness there now hangs an orange ball of fire. The fighter has got some other poor devil.

'There but for the grace of God,' I mouth, and but for the vigilance of little Titch in the tail, too, I might well have added.

Then we hear the quiet unruffled voice of the navigator: 'Course Two Six Zero, Skip, and continue climbing back to 15,000 feet.'

'Thank you, Colin,' I say. 'Well done, Titch.' My gratitude echoes in the minds of all the crew for their rear gunner's alertness and because my reaction was instantaneous. We are still over Germany but on our way home towards the French coast, our bombs delivered above the huge engineering works at Krupps in the Ruhr. The trip has been scary enough, a near collision over the target and a lot of flak, and we could have done without this extra excitement, up here in the dark sky.

There is silence now in the aircraft, a silence against the background of the regular heavy drone of the four engines. As long as the sound is regular, none of us will be aware of it, but had the sound become unsynchronised, we would have heard it at once, alert to a possible fault. My hands rest lightly on the controls, my attention divided between my instruments and watching the air before me. The navigator is drawing faint neat lines on his chart, checking and rechecking his calculations. The wireless operator peers at the bright disc of his Fish-pond dial, watching the relative speeds of tiny dots of light that are other aircraft in the bomber stream and for any which are coming up too quickly and might be a German night fighter about to attack. The flight engineer is watching his petrol gauges, ready to change over from a fuel tank in one wing to a tank in another and keep the weight of the aircraft balanced. The bomb aimer, now front gunner, in the nose and both gunners in their turrets quarter the sky all round us in our ceaseless watch.

On we fly, grateful for every mile of progress away from the dangerous pyrotechnics above that inferno that we helped to create.

As we fly on, the light of the sky grows with the coming of dawn. Colour is returning to our surroundings. Below us are the green fields of northern France. We cross the French coast and are over the sea.

'Course 300, Skip, and descend to 8000 feet. We shall be flying up the Orwell soon.'

'Course 300.' I know why Colin has added that information. Colin's home is in the small town of Halstead in Essex, and he knows that a boat in which I often sailed before the war is lying in a mud berth on the shore of the River Orwell. All that Colin himself can see, on his navigator's table behind his black-out curtains, is a large white sheet of paper, but that chart is showing him that he will soon be above his beloved Essex. In his mind's eye, he sees his mother and one of his teenage brothers and another man in their small bakehouse in Halstead's main street. He knows that their forearms are dusted white with flour and their hands gloved, as they pull out of the oven, this early morning, as every morning, the hot trays of new-baked loaves. It is as though he can even smell the new brown-crusted bread, as he has always done, helping his mother after his father died. He doubts they know he is among the pre-dawn drone they hear above them.

I look down at the long finger of the Orwell estuary; Harwich at its seaward opening and the town of Ipswich up at its other end. About halfway, though everything is tiny, I can recognise the hamlet of Pin Mill at the water's edge on the left-hand side, and beyond it, towards Ipswich, a thin white line along the shore. I know that this is a line of yachts in their mud berths, gunwale to gunwale with their bows nose-in to the grass-grown bank, laid up for the duration of this bloody war. At the top of high water at spring tides they will float, then settle down again comfortably in the soft mud as the tide goes down. One of them, though impossible to tell which one in this distant bird's eye view, is my father's boat, *Nancy Blackett*, in which with other members of the family and friends I sailed and enjoyed holidays before the war.

Happy days! When shall we be able to launch her and fit her out, and sail in her again?

But I must not look dreamily down, remembering. We are not yet back at base. Still airborne, we remain in danger of being jumped by an enemy bandit, which might be near the English coast, waiting to attack any one of the British bombers who, tired and perhaps insufficiently watchful, are on their return to one of the many aerodromes of eastern England.

CHAPTER TWO

Pin Mill 1939

It was a halcyon day in August 1939. I was sailing with my father in *Nancy Blackett*. A light breeze no more than rippled the surface. There was not yet a cloud in the sky. Apart from a family of shelducks feeding on a mudflat newly uncovered by the tide's fall, we seemed to be alone on the estuary. With the ebb tide under us we cut through the water towards the sea in effortless silence.

'Gosh, what a day!'

'Perfect: this is the poetry of motion.' I smiled at my father's familiar phrase.

I looked towards the shore on each side, and up over the blue arch of the sky above our tan-red mainsail. Little wisps of early morning mist still lay in quiet creeks, not yet dispersed by the sunshine. It was the epitome of peace and the promise of a lovely day.

'It's going to be like this all weekend.' I spoke more in hope than confidence.

'I think you're right, but Miss Powell might say it was a weather breeder.'

We laughed together at this happily remembered saying. Dear Miss Powell; we had both heard her use that expression, in her soft Essex voice in the front garden of Alma Cottage up beside her brother's sail loft. Come a golden day that looked as though it would last all summer, sometimes her old bones told her that it was the harbinger of wind and rain, 'a weather breeder'. But today's faultless morning looked set to last.

We had spent the night off Pin Mill, a shoreline hamlet some way downstream from Ipswich, the town that straddles the river above its highest navigable anchorage. *Nancy Blackett* had a mooring just off the end of the Hard, on which there were always several Thames sailing barges beached.

Lying on our bunks, snug in the comfort of our sleeping bags, we had heard the 6 o'clock shipping forecast. We had got up, thrown the mooring over the side, threaded our way through the other boats and gone down on the ebb towards the sea. A following breeze filled the sails, and when I went below to put the kettle on, I heard through the planking a happy gurgle running back along the water-line as we gathered speed.

After about 5 miles we were passing the Naval Training establishment, HMS *Ganges* over on our right, built on the point of land that divides the two rivers: Orwell and Stour. Here the confluence of the two estuaries widens out into Harwich harbour and the ebb water of the other, flowing down the Stour from Manningtree, pushed us over to the left, towards Felixstowe Dock, where the grey ironwork of the big crane, used for lifting RAF flying boats out of the water, stood clearly in the morning sunshine. I had the coffee boiling on the paraffin stove of the little galley at the foot of the companionway, leading down into the cabin from the cockpit, as we sailed under the stern of the Royal Navy destroyer that lay there at anchor. Standing on the companionway steps, my father at the tiller, I saw the officer of the watch give us a friendly wave.

'Look it's Martin!' He was one of the naval officers whom we sometimes met in the Butt & Oyster at Pin Mill in those last expectant weeks of peacetime summer.

We had arrived at Pin Mill at about tea time of the previous day; I on my motorbike from Leicester, my father by train from Liverpool Street to Ipswich and thence by taxi, bringing each a kit-bag containing sailing gear – though there was more aboard – and the few items of food that we would want for the weekend that might not be available at the shop. We had changed into sailing clothes, thick flannel trousers, navy blue Guernsey pullovers and deck-friendly non-slip lace-up shoes. We had stowed everything and while daylight lasted had attended to a few things that would have to be done before we left our anchorage in the morning. We had cooked supper on the stove in the galley and eaten it at the folding table between the two bunks. I had sluiced the plates over the side and washed them up in just a little fresh water, which I had boiled on the stove. Fresh water was precious. Not much could be carried in the tank under the starboard seat in the cockpit, so it was used only as a finishing touch. It was almost impossible to get any lather in seawater from the bits and ends of soap in the little wire cage that hung on a hook above the sink on the other side of the companionway.

While my father satisfied himself that everything was shipshape aboard, I lit the oil riding-light and hoisted it with a halyard part-way up the forestay. It was still daylight now, but we should be coming back aboard in the dark and it was better to have some way of recognising *Nancy Blackett* among the other dim shapes of boats in the anchorage. Having made fast two fend-offs on the shoreward side of the boat, I loosed the painter and pulled the dinghy alongside, got down on to the centre thwart and held her steady for my father to get in and sit in the stern. Shipping the rowlocks, I pulled the dinghy away and towards the shore with short, deep strokes of the oars.

Pin Mill was a pretty place. Its ten or a dozen houses were all down at the water's edge and a narrow lane ran down a valley from the village of Chelmondiston with its pub and Baptist chapel a few miles up by the road, which runs from Ipswich to Shotley. A green hill sloped up behind Miss Powell's Alma Cottage to meet the clear bright sky of early evening. On the other side of the lane from the cottage was Harry King's boatyard, smelling of paint and varnish and freshly sawn timber, with a slipway running down to the water. The hamlet was dominated by the Butt & Oyster, an old building

rendered with lime plaster and painted cream. Its base up to a height of about
6 feet, almost to the sills of the lower windows, was coated with black tar, and
at the time of big tides at high water the water crept up the wall towards the
windows.

'Pull on your right a bit,' I responded, and the nose of the dinghy swung a
little upstream to allow for the ebb tide, discernible even here in the shelter of
the anchorage. A wood of tall dark trees framed the building, and continued
on downstream against the water's edge. Now, as we approached the shore, the
low, slanting sunshine of evening bathed the western wall of the pub in a bright
orange light.

Inside, those who sat within, or stood, pint in hand, about the red- and black-
tiled floor of the bar, could watch small coastal steamers, sailing barges and
pleasure boats passing up river to Ipswich or down river to Harwich and the
sea, out in the deep-water channel. Across the estuary from Constable country,
where Essex and Suffolk meet, one looked across to a green, undulating skyline
with little woods and isolated red-roofed farmhouses, and perhaps could see the
round Saxon tower of Levington church.

In front of that happy pub, the broad Hard of sea-weedy gravel projected
over the soft grey mud, right down to the low-water mark. A small stream,
called the Grindle, ran down beside the Hard, bordered by baulks of timber,
and, to a large extent, prevented the mud from encroaching on to it. At times
of big tides, at the bottom of low water, there were a few yards of mud beyond
the end of the Hard before there was enough water to float a dinghy, so one had
to avoid coming ashore, or attempting to get off, in that brief time before the
tide turned and began to flow up river again towards Ipswich. But flow it did,
lifting the several dinghies that sat waiting on the Hard, or sat on the mud,
secured to their small anchors or to something static and, preferably, within
reach. The water of the flood tide would lift all those yachts whose anchorage
or mooring was in shallower water and so had been left aground by the falling
tide. It would lift, or perhaps only surround with seawater, those huge dark-
hulled Thames barges that were always gathered together on the Hard. They
were waiting to be painted, refitted, or in various ways serviced by those Pin
Mill men whose livelihood it was to keep those anachronistic craft from an
earlier age still able to work the tideways and estuaries that ran in from the sea
there in the Thames Estuary.

This evening, though nearly high water, it was a small tide that did not reach
to the wall of the pub, and I was able to bring the bow of the dinghy to ground
on the gravel of the Hard. We pushed it off the Hard and onto the mud close
beside the bordering stream. We laid the anchor at the side of the Hard as far
down as was possible while not having to wade into the mud or block the access
to the Hard for other dinghies. When we should want to use it again that
evening, the anchor would be accessible and we should be able to pull the dinghy
down into deeper water until it could float enough for us to step aboard.
Satisfied, our rubber sea-boots crunching on the wet gravel, we walked to the
side door of the pub and went into the bar.

Mr Watts was behind the bar as usual. He was a good landlord, able to please the local customers and also the increasing number of yachtsmen who came in their boats to Pin Mill. It was said that he had been butler at the Suffolk mansion of Cobbolds the brewers, and it was known that the family tried whenever possible to offer the management or tenancy of one of their pubs to their trusted men when the time came for their retirement from service.

Two customers, sailing men off their boats, judging from their attire, were at the bar talking to Mr Watts; a group of three or four sat at a table near the window and two of Pin Mill's local men sat at a table near the door, as was their custom.

'Evening, Mr Russell.' My father acknowledged the welcome from the landlord with a smile and a wave of his hand, and stopped to speak with the local men at their table. Nearest the door was George Burroughs, harbour master of the anchorage at Pin Mill. He was a man whose face had been altered a few years before when a duck gun had blown back at him as he lay in a punt on the mudflats in the dark-before-dawn on the other side of the estuary. He had been lucky to have been found and brought home. Next to him was Ephraim Sharman, the night-soil man, whose job it was to visit the houses of the hamlet with his little hand-cart and empty the buckets in their outside privies. He called it 'the Business'.

'And how are you both?'

'Well, thank 'ee Sir,' they each replied. George Burroughs added 'I see'd you and your son workin' aboard your *Nancy Blackett* this evenin'. Everythin' all right?'

'Thank you, yes. Not many down to Pin Mill this weekend though. I don't know when I've seen the anchorage so empty, and hardly anyone in here – though it's a good forecast, I understand.'

'I reckon it's all this talk of war,' said George. 'Even last weekend several owners were askin' about a mud berth for their boats. Will you be wantin' one for *Nancy Blackett*?'

'I hope not. But if I do, I hope you'll find one for me.'

'Certainly I will Mr Russell, but, like you, I hope you'll not be needin' one.'

My father now moved across to the bar where the two men were talking to Watts.

'Good evening, Paddy. Mild, Peter?' I nodded. 'A pint of mild and one of old and mild if you'd be so kind.'

The landlord drew the beers and set them on the bar. The two men turned to include us into their conversation. One was Basil Blagdon, a barrister from London. His boat was *Alanna*, a big, sturdy Falmouth Quay-punt, and Basil seemed to be always up his mast. His wife, who was sitting at the table nearby, was a very tall woman with one eye, who hunted in the winter and sailed in the summer. She had lost the eye when a flying block on the jib-sheet had caught it, several years before. She was the indomitable kind. I could not help covertly studying her strong features. I had always felt a little unnerved by her rather masculine presence. They had a sea-going tabby cat, which they always brought down to the boat with them.

The others at the table were Arthur Davis and his wife Freda. They had a small boat in which, regardless of its size and the lack of comfort occasioned by that, they had made long and fearless passages. They were a popular couple at Pin Mill and wherever they visited. Arthur was a most amusing raconteur, but this evening even he seemed to be depressed.

'Hallo Basil, hallo Arthur,' said my father. 'Where are you bound this weekend? I understand that we've got a pretty good forecast.'

'And we'd better make the most of it. I think it will be our last.' This was unlike the Arthur we all knew, but the threat of war, this early August evening in 1939, was getting some people down. For others, it was a reason to show people they met, and themselves, that they could take it in their stride.

Neither George nor Eph' had quiet voices, and from where I was standing I could hear their conversation.

'I hear you had a bit of trouble with that Mr Jones,' said Eph'.

'I did that. I see'd him come up to Mr Pike's moorin' an' pick it up, an' for all I knew Mr Pike would be comin' back here and wantin' it any time this weekend, so I rows out to him an' asks him to choose another moorin' an' I points one out to him which I knew would be free.

' "I know the owner of this moorin'", says 'e, "an' I know 'e won't want it, so I'm staying put. If 'e comes back I can get orf it," 'e says. But it was the way he spoke which riled me, like as though he was too good to be told where to go by someone the likes of me, less of a toff than 'e was, 'arbour master though I am. I'm glad we've not got many like 'im, proud-like.'

Eph' was silent for a minute, thinking about what George had said and about what he himself thought about it. Then in a determined way, Eph' put his pint mug down onto the scrubbed wood table and looking across at the men standing by the bar, said:

'That Mr Jones, 'e's a 'igh twig on a low bough, but that there Mr Russell, 'e's a bonner fiddy gennulman!'

I looked across at my father to see if he had heard this unsolicited testimonial from the night-soil man. I decided he had not.

Eph' was a small man with a large walrus moustache. He had a small rowing boat with a sail, in which he sometimes did a bit of fishing. Arthur Davis had a story about him, and now perhaps feeling a little less depressed, he leaned forward over the table, and the others waited to hear what he would have to say.

Yesterday, Eph' had his boat up on the Hard and when I came by very little of him was visible. Most of the contents of his boat were out on the shingle and he had got his head hidden under the small cuddy up in the bow of the boat, obviously looking for something. His hands were busy pulling out some bits of fish, which had presumably been intended for bait, and they were intensely malodorous.

'Hallo Eph',' I said to as much of our night-soil man as was visible, 'what are you looking for?'

'A mouse,' he told me, 'I know it's here an' I'm going to catch 'ee.'

It looked a pretty hopeless intention, and I asked him, 'Are you sure it's there?'

'I'm quite sure,' said Eph', 'I can smell 'ee.'

A ripple of benign laughter ran around the bar. Eph' acknowledged the story with a nod and a smile, before taking a sip from his mug of mild.

Father and I walked across to the table where Basil's wife and the Davises were now sitting, and soon afterwards we were joined by the two men from the bar. Most of their glasses were charged but Father's pint mug was nearly empty.

'What can I get you, Dad?'

'Old and mild, old chap. Thanks.' I went to the bar and ordered it and one for myself. 'You too, Mr Watts?'

'I'll have a small dark, thank you. Nice to see you and your father down. Not many people here this weekend.'

I was a reservist, RAFVR, and both of us realised that with all this talk of war, my freedom to get away for a weekend's sailing might soon be more difficult. With two mugs in hand I walked to where the others were standing or sitting. My father was talking about the activity around our home in Hertfordshire to make arrangements for the evacuees who were expected.

'My wife's sister Connie seems to be in the thick of it. Last week, I understand, she met a trainload of children from London and was distributing them around the countryside, hoping that no one who had agreed to take in one or two of them would have changed their minds. I got the impression that one little girl from some overcrowded place in the East End had remained in her memory. She saw a look of mild horror cross the face of the lady in whose house the child was to stay when she saw the dirtiness of the poor little thing's clothes and hair as she walked in. It was a home very different from what she was familiar with, but my sister-in-law is confident that she will be well looked after. At the station Connie had taken the girl's hand and led her to the car, rather longing to take a handkerchief to her runny nose. Once in the car the girl reached across to the steering wheel and pressed the button of the horn in a long determined sort of way. It was noisy, but it conquered her shyness and anxiety for a while.'

Father's voice mimicked an East End dialect. 'The child said: "I like ringin' 'ooters" and her voice showed how badly she suffered from adenoids. Poor little things, uprooted and transported to the unknown, but you can understand that London may soon be no place for children.'

'You got any evacuees yet, Rosy?' Basil asked Father.

'I've not heard yet,' replied my father, 'but probably not many 'cos we've only got one spare bedroom. How about you?'

'I think we may be more in danger of having the whole house requisitioned if the rumour is true that I hear about what is planned for elderly lawyers like me.'

'Where did you say you were bound tomorrow, Arthur?'

'I don't think we'll be making a very early start, Arthur wants to take some water aboard and I should like to get one or two provisions; I shall see what the Mayor has got available.' Freda answered for her husband.

'The Mayor' to whom she referred was a small man with a moustache and twinkling blue eyes. He sold vegetables off a trestle table in the open doorway of a shed below Alma Cottage. After a few beers one lunchtime some years before, some young wags from the Naval Training station at Shotley had decided that Pin Mill ought to have a mayor. Taking a short length of light anchor chain and a mug and one or two bottles with which to refresh the man of their choice, they had gone out and performed a simple mayor-making ceremony, draping the bit of chain around his neck. The old boy had liked the idea, entering heartily into the fun of it. The next day he had painted, 'MAYOR'S PARLOUR' over the door of his shed where he sold his vegetables. Since that time everybody had called him 'the Mayor', to the extent that soon there were few people who could remember what his true name was.

'That's right,' said Arthur, 'Ken and Nancy are down this weekend in *Damsel Fly*, though they've not come ashore this evening. This afternoon we agreed that it would be fun to sail in company tomorrow. With this light north-westerly, we thought we'd take the later part of the ebb down to Harwich and across to the Medusa Buoy, round the Naze at slack water and take the flood up the Wallet and hope to go into West Mersea.'

West Mersea, I thought, that was my favourite anchorage, but my father and I had decided to go north tomorrow; still, perhaps if the weather held we could go south on the following day. 'Give my love to the S&S,' I said, annoyed with myself for a slight blush I hoped no one else would notice. The S&S, or Sailing & Social, was a little restaurant at West Mersea with simple premises, but the lady there was a superb cook. She had two daughters who helped her and who, by general consensus and in my hopelessly inexperienced opinion, were really lush. In consequence, someone had renamed it the Sailing & Sexual, and the name had stuck. It was deservedly something of a Mecca to sailing folk.

'Your daughter down this weekend, Rosy?'

'No, she's doing something with her mother.'

'Then Ransome will be disappointed,' Basil replied with a smile. They both knew how often the famous writer came rowing alongside to ask, 'Can I borrow Miranda, please?' And that he had said that Miranda, although only fourteen, was a first rate crew.

Thus, in convivial conversation, we continued to pass the evening, joined sometimes by others who came into the pub, until it was time to leave and return aboard.

*   *   *

There was a moon and it was a clear starlit night. We had no difficulty locating the small anchor, pulling the dinghy down to where there was more water, with the help of the little stream, and getting in and pulling across to our boat. The blades of my oars stirred the phosphorescence as they dipped into the water. We could see *Nancy Blackett*'s riding-light as we rowed through the anchorage in the dim twilight, past boats dark and unoccupied, and a few other boats showing warm light from porthole or cabin-top, among round bobbing mooring buoys not this night in use, which appeared suddenly, streaming with the tide's pull on the rope, which held them to the chain of their mooring. Arriving beside *Nancy Blackett* by the pale sausages of the fend-offs and bow to bow with her, I held the end of the painter and with two hands grasped the gunwale while my father climbed aboard. I followed him and made fast the painter and watched the dinghy stream back behind the boat, carried by the tide. I walked round the deck, checking that all looked as it should be. My father was standing by the shrouds.

'I'll just pump ship before I turn in.' I followed suit. Below, we lit the oil lamp, which hung over the table, laid the sleeping bags on the two berths, put on our pyjamas and got into the bags.

'Want to read?' asked my father.

'No thanks. Pleasant evening. Good night, Dad!' and darkness came as he turned out the light.

Soon, I could hear the quiet whistle of Father's breathing. He must be asleep. I heard too the soft chuckle of the water running along the outside of *Nancy Blackett*'s planking less than a foot from my ear, and occasionally the gentle slap of a halyard against the mast. The tide was turning, and even though we were on a mooring rather than with a long length of chain to an anchor, I heard the dull sound of the mooring chain dragging across the muddy bottom of the estuary below us, as the boat turned head to wind and then head to the tide's new direction.

My sleepy thoughts turned over the discussions in the bar of the coming of war. It must have been disappointing to my father and to those with whom we had spent the evening, to feel fairly certain that war was coming again, so soon after the 'war to end all wars', the conflict in which they had fought and lost friends and companions over in France in the Flanders mud. Of course, they were fortunate to have survived, when so many had not, but it must have been pretty awful. I fell to wondering, as I often had before, how I would behave in the fighting that people said was imminent.

I'd got a hard act to follow in my father, who had been Mentioned in Despatches and had received an MC. As Transport Officer in his battalion, nightly with his team of horses, he had brought up to the Front ammunition, food and all vital supplies, staggering through the mud piled around the rim of each shell-hole. There was mud, mud, and sometimes the unburied bodies of men and horses.

I had only very recently heard about Father's MC. He never spoke of it, but I had met Father's Colonel a few weeks before and he had told me. My father

Rosy had been a student in Chemnitz for nearly a year after leaving school and spoke fluent German. He had not infrequently crawled across no-man's-land, under the wire, and had lain with his head hanging into the German front line, listening to their conversation. He would then crawl back again to report on morale, news of their home front and, possibly, rumours of the next push.

Being in the Air Force, I did not expect to have to crawl through any mud. My idea of what to expect had largely been coloured by a film, 'Dawn Patrol' starring Errol Flynn. It portrayed Mess parties of young men like me in flying clothing, drinking mugs of beer and singing 'Here's to the next man to die', with much laughter and apparent devil-may-care acceptance of what was in store. What very little flying I had so far done had made me realise that I enjoyed it, but I knew that flying against the enemy would be very different from exhilarating dives and tight turns in a Tiger Moth over the English countryside.

Lying warm now in my sleeping bag, I flew over green fields in my imagination, banking the aeroplane and looking down, until sleep claimed me.

In the clear soft light of a lovely morning, with the wind behind us filling our sails and the ebb tide carrying us seaward, we were in the wide bay of Harwich Harbour. The Royal Navy destroyer we had passed was becoming smaller in the sea behind us. Landguard Point lay quite close on our port bow and the blunt headland of the Naze was slightly hazy in the distance and well over to our right. Father and I silently rejoiced that we had this spell of lovely weather and that as I should have Monday off on this holiday weekend, we should be able to take advantage of it.

We hoped to carry the last of the ebb up the Suffolk coast, past Felixstowe, and take the flood into the Deben, the next estuary northward, and put an anchor down at Ramsholt. There, old Mrs Nunn's pub, not advertising its presence save by a finger-board nailed to a tree saying 'To the Tap', was almost hidden among the lilac trees on the northern bank where a steep narrow lane ran down to the shore. Earlier that summer, those lilac trees had been a cloud of mauve blossom above the roof of the old house. Here, in Mrs Nunn's kitchen, customers drew their own pints from the barrels of beer lined along the wall and were trusted to put the money in an old, small drawer left on the counter.

But we had not yet turned up the coast and forward of our tan-red staysail; our bowsprit still pointed eastwards and out to sea. Out beyond the Beach End and Cliff Foot navigation buoys, which marked the deep water channel for the bigger ships and ferries that plied between Harwich and the ports of Denmark and the Hook of Holland, the sea's horizon lay broad and clear. Just out of sight behind Landguard Point was the Cork Light Vessel, and further east was the Dutch coast. Beyond Holland lay Germany. Like most people in those August days of 1939, we felt conscious of the threat of the evil that now ruled Germany, the Nazi bullies who had marched into the Rhineland, Austria, Czechoslovakia and now threatened Poland. Few believed that Hitler could be trusted to honour any treaty he had made. Chamberlain's spoken hope when he had returned from Bonn and from Munich may have been, perhaps, only a bid for more time in a desperate state of unreadiness, but my friends and I thought that Chamberlain's attitude of appeasement was wrong.

Now at last, perhaps too late, the nation was facing up to the probability of war. The goose step-by-step overrunning of the countries of Europe by Germans had to be stopped before Hitler ruled all Europe and beyond, as he had so often declared his intention to do. News films at the cinema had revealed a small figure whose looks had passed into caricature, seemingly yapping at hordes of adulating followers whose cheers always made the sound go distorted. It was a fervour quite unlike any kind of behaviour I had ever witnessed. And it was so foreign.

One country after another had fallen, crushed under Nazi jackboots. Few had much faith in the ability of France, for all its vaunted Maginot Line, to stand up to a German attack, and Holland, Belgium, Denmark and the Scandinavian countries looked even more vulnerable. How long could England survive behind that last barrier, the sea on which we now sailed, and hold out against the onslaught of the *Luftwaffe*, which would prepare the way for the expected invasion of Britain by the German armies?

In Leicester, where I worked, several of my friends and I had joined the RAFVR, the weekend-flying Volunteer Reserve of the Air Force. We could fly at the little airfield at Desford in Tiger Moths, and this, so far from the sea as Leicester is, was a more practical form of Territorial Service than the Navy's RNVR. With my friends, I had known that I must join one of the armed services and be trained to fight against that Power, which, for the second time in twenty-five years, threatened Britain. After the warning of Munich, many of my contemporaries in Leicester had joined the 4th Battalion of the Leicester Regiment, but for some, searchlights lacked the glamour of service in the field against the enemy. I had been to see Mr Jack Barrett VC, a Leicester surgeon, who was forming the 5th Leicesters, a Territorial Infantry Battalion. But for various reasons, perhaps one of them a realisation of the urgent necessity of a stronger Air Force in those dark times, or perhaps because of Errol Flynn, I had chosen the RAFVR.

We had rounded Landguard Point now, and were on a north-easterly course, parallel to the coast, level with Felixstowe and about a mile off-shore. There was more wind out here, but it was off the shore, giving us a comfortable broad reach in quiet water. Father was sailing the boat, his pipe in his mouth, standing with a slight lean against the tiller. His eyes were on a mark ahead of him and occasionally he lifted them to see, and was pleased to see, the set of the sails. I was standing on the steps of the companionway, as I often did. I was enjoying the sunshine, the wind on my face, and the movement of *Nancy Blackett* in Father's capable hands, as she heeled confidently to starboard with a bone of white water in her teeth, and the sheer happiness of this wonderful life aboard a boat under sail.

'You know, it's a strange coincidence. Twenty-five years ago almost to the day I was sailing a boat very much like this and war was threatened – war to hold back the same bullying enemy as faces us now, only that time the war actually happened.'

'Don't you think it will this time?'

'Who knows, dear boy, but I rather think it will. Hitler is a lunatic, and those foolish people who have put him where he is seem to want it – Master Race indeed! We used to say that the only good German was a dead German, and I'm afraid may soon think the same way again.'

'What boat were you sailing that time then?'

'I was in *Tewk*, which I shared with your godfather, Barry. She was hard-headed, but a good sea-boat. We won the Houghton Cup in her, outright, that is, three years running. It was an early and much less ambitious version of what is nowadays called Ocean Racing. We didn't go round the Fastnet, or anything like that, but it was a course among the lightships and buoys of the southern part of the North Sea, where the sand banks and shoals can make the water pretty lumpy as the Thames Estuary tides race over them. We used to say that the most important chap in the crew was the one who managed to remain upright and keep his stomach steady down below and keep supplied with hot food and drink those of us who were having to work pretty hard up on deck in all weathers.'

'And the occasion twenty-five years ago?'

'Well, Barry and I had sailed *Tewk* across to Flushing, and while we were ashore some large vessel must have bumped *Tewk* or squeezed her against the jetty, perhaps loosening a plank. Also, while we were ashore, Barry ate something in some Dutch café that disagreed with him. Then we had learned that war had been declared between England and Germany. We were both Territorials, and had to get back quickly.'

'And you did?'

'Yes, I remember that passage well. I was sailing the boat, navigating, pumping to keep pace with the leak, looking after a sick friend and sometimes grabbing a bit of something to eat myself. All the way across the North Sea all that night, with what seemed like the whole of the Royal Navy charging up and down without lights. I got back to the Crouch, threw an anchor over the side and slept for sixteen hours.'

I had a photograph of my grandfather Russell in the uniform of a Volunteer Defence Force of about 1880 vintage. My father in the years before 1914 had managed to combine Territorial service in King Edward's Horse with sailing almost every weekend. It had been his boast seldom to have failed to see sunrise on a Sunday morning throughout the whole year, winter and summer alike.

In 1938 I had applied to join the RAFVR and fly at weekends, but I had broken my knee on a motorbike riding back from a weekend on the boat one late autumn Sunday evening, which delayed my flying training. It was on a sharp bend. In the dark and in the rain I had hit the end of the parapet of a bridge over a railway line. Or had I fallen asleep? I had woken up and I was lying on the top of a wall in the rain. I had got off the wall, on the right hand side, and found I couldn't stand. If I had got off on the left-hand side I should never have stood again, for it was a long drop down onto the railway lines. I had knelt beside the road and two cars passed me. There were not many cars on the roads, and I despaired of any Samaritans being in those that were. I must have looked most unpleasant kneeling in the mud of the roadside with blood on my face because I'd put a tooth through my lip. Then a car stopped and took me to Kettering station. The AA collected my bike next day, and I spent about two weeks in the Leicester Royal Infirmary and five weeks with my leg in plaster. My leg was still in plaster when I reported for my RAF Medical. They had laughed and said 'Come back another time'.

'I'll be coming about in a minute.' I took up my position in the cockpit ready to hand the jib-sheets, as we would turn to port and come through the wind.

'Ready about. Lee-O!' We turned to line up the marks on shore to lead us through the Deben's treacherous entrance. To the right, at the northerly point of the estuary mouth, stood Bawdsey Manor. We had heard that something very secret was going on there, but never realised the extent to which the survival of England against German airborne attack would depend on those secrets. Also, we did not realise quite how imminent was the outbreak of war. In a week's time I should be 21 and in less than a month England would be at war and I should be in the Air Force full time. So Miss Powell might have been right, this lovely last weekend was indeed 'a weather breeder'.

At the end of August 1939 they called up the Territorials and Reserves. The dread of some was my exhilaration. For a day or two the reservists reported each morning at The Cedars, the RAFVR's Town Centre on London Road, waiting for something to happen. Then Chamberlain spoke to the nation on the wireless and next day we were taken in a bus to Cambridge. We went along the road from Kettering, over that same railway bridge where I had broken my knee a year before. We had thought that the bus was taking us to Marshal's Airfield near Cambridge to start flying, but we were taken to Jesus College to be kitted out. We were accommodated in Trinity Hall, where we dined in the ancient Hall, bought our beer in the Buttery, strolled in the beautifully kept garden and passed in and out through the Porter's Lodge: we were treated like undergraduates, but felt like gods.

I should have loved to have studied at Cambridge or Oxford; but I had left school before I was seventeen. It was not on offer. Now I had got there at last. I enjoyed to the full those lovely, sunny autumn months of 1939, while we drilled on the lawns and fields of the Backs, breathing the smell of dew-soaked grass, or route-marched for miles and miles around the countryside, or learned

Morse code in Cambridge lecture rooms. I was in wonderful company. There were other units of RAFVR in other colleges, and undergraduates too, but in our exuberance and self-confidence we young men of the Air Force dominated the place. As well as friends from the Leicester centre I had several good friends, newly made from London centres. It was at Cambridge, too, that I met Katherine, the loveliest girl I had ever seen, and fell precipitously in love.

CHAPTER THREE

At War

From Cambridge we went to Anstey near Coventry. Anstey was an Elementary Flying Training School (EFTS). We flew Tiger Moths and learned basic things about aeronautics and the sort of carburettors that didn't mind being upside down. Compared with Cambridge, accommodation was crude. Boys like me, and especially boys who had even more recently left boarding school (the more cold baths and open windows the better) found no inconvenience in the conditions in which we had to live. To sleep in a double-decker iron bedstead with another young man in the bed above, his weight curving down the thin palletts on which he lay, was, for me, unremarkable. But some of the men were older; they were married, used to the warmth of a woman they loved as they had cuddled together every night in their peace-time homes. They, I noticed, were finding life more difficult.

Until the snow came we threw ourselves about in the sky and tried to make three-point landings. We didn't often get lost because Rugby's wireless masts were generally visible. I had found that I loved flying and it was all most enjoyable. Except, that is, for the threat to everyone's happiness, to their very existence and status as pilots-under-training, of Squadron Leader Duke. He wore a distinctive white helmet and had very high standards about flying. He did not teach us. He periodically tested us. He failed many of us. There was no second chance. Failure at one of his tests meant OUT. You saw strong, brave men crying when he had failed them. They limped away, their hopes and dreams shattered, to join the Army.

One day, having finished an hour of perhaps rather clumsy aerobatics, I walked into the crew-room, my seat-type parachute knocking on the backs of my thighs. There was Terry Rutter sitting on a bench, head in his hands and tears all over his face. He looked up at my entrance and his mouth was drawn into a straight line of misery.

'Got the chop from Duke,' he croaked in an uneven voice. 'What the Hell am I going to say to my parents? I thought I was doing quite well, too.'

There was nothing to say. I liked Terry, and had got to know him early on because the two of us were next to each other in any alphabetical roll-call.

I could well understand his misery. I dreaded the ignominy of having to tell my parents – and Katherine too – that I had been failed. Not many months later

I realised that the Air Force would have jumped to accept some of those whom Squadron Leader Duke so wastefully threw away.

It was a desperately hard winter. Because of the frequent delays and cancellations in our training programme caused by the bad weather, our time at Anstey was prolonged until the end of April. I passed all my tests and was sent to Flying Training School (FTS). It was my good fortune to be sent to Cranwell out of all the alternative FTSs to which I might have gone.

First, I had a few days' leave. I went home to Hertfordshire and by arrangement took a train to Salisbury. Katherine met me at the station for two happy days and a night, which was all too short. Katherine's home was in a village nearby and she took me to meet her father that afternoon and again the next day. We stayed at a small hotel where Katherine had booked in. The proprietress showed us into our room with a conspiratorial smile on her face, which seemed to reveal both her knowledge that we were not married and also to share with us our happiness. We had never slept together at Cambridge and our excitement was transparent. Katherine had 'the curse', but it was still lovely to be in bed together at last.

In those days Cranwell had two small grass airfields, one on each side of the College and its ancillary buildings. Those who were going to be fighter pilots flew Harts and Hinds; those who were earmarked for heavier aircraft flew Oxfords. I flew Oxfords. The rooms in the College were comfortably furnished; two shared a bedroom and the anterooms had an atmosphere of well-bred tradition. On dining-in nights the College band played in the gallery at the end of dinner, finishing with the Post Horn Gallop.

The course previous to ours had been the last of the pukka courses of permanent commission Cranwell cadets; ours was the first course to be adulterated with amateurs. One-third were seeking permanent commissions; one-third were Australians coming over to England for Short Service commissions who had been on their way when war had been declared, and one-third were RAFVR. Though those of the RAFVR were only Sergeants, hopeful but by no means certain of getting a commission, we received the same treatment and had the pre-war luxury of civilian batmen.

I found that I had been allocated a room with another reservist, called Wills. He was taller than the average, 6 feet 5 inches, and an intelligent and well-balanced young man who had been to a co-educational school in the north of England. A good friendship developed between us and we became friendly also with an even taller young man whom we knew as Sergeant Clive. Clive was 6 feet 7 inches, and his name, in fact, was Viscount Clive. He was a descendant of Clive of India, and when he knew me and SB (by which name we came to call Wills) better, he told us that he also had another title, Baron D'Arcy de Naithe.

'I am a constitutional freak,' he confided in us, 'the title comes down through the female line.' This gave him a seat in the House of Lords. More than once in those difficult times, such as when Chamberlain resigned and Churchill became Prime Minister, Clive went up to London to take his seat and vote.

Clive flew the single-engined training aircraft, for he was determined to be a fighter pilot and defend his homeland, but he was 37. The powers that be had decreed that the maximum age for a fighter pilot was 30. After that birthday, it was considered, a man could not turn his head fast enough to achieve the all-round watchfulness that was essential. He said that he had had to pull every string that his nobility gave him to be accepted for the 'fighter stream' of training. He had great charm, and a remarkably 'stiff upper lip'. It was noticed that he showed enviable imperturbability when one night Cranwell was visited by a German aircraft that dropped a stick of bombs, probably 200-pounders, and everybody had to repair to the air-raid shelters.

We three friends went, whenever we could, to the White Hart in Lincoln. It was a gracious hotel by the cathedral, among attractive old buildings at the top of the hill. We enjoyed the delicious dinners that were provided there at that time and served with such decorum. Sometimes a fourth man joined us, but not for long. Taking off one day, he clipped a wheel on a hedge at the aerodrome boundary and turned the aeroplane over.

'Poor man was hanging there in his straps upside down, soaked in petrol,' said Clive that evening. 'By a miracle he didn't catch fire, but he was cut about a lot, and I doubt if he will be well enough to come back to the course before we have finished.'

I was on my best behaviour at Cranwell. I did not wish to be sent to a squadron without a commission, which quite a few were, but the well-mannered behaviour of my friends was never likely to lead me astray. It was a tradition for each course to produce an entertainment for the whole College on their last night. Some thought it understandable that none of the Australians would want to be involved, but it was perhaps surprising that no talent was forthcoming from the Permanent Commission Cadets, so it fell to SB and to me to write the review for our course. That was fun: what was not fun was finding that most of the appearances on stage would fall into our laps as well. Being so shy, I had never enjoyed amateur dramatics, and the thought of making a speech or performing on stage made me curl up inside. I said afterwards that I expected that it would be the bravest thing I did in the whole war. Worst of all, I had to sing two songs and anyone who knew me would agree that I could not sing a note. The band played a chord for me to sing 'Somewhere over the Rainbow', with different (and we thought amusing) words of course, and I hit the wrong note or the wrong key or something, and stayed wrong all through. It must have been excruciating and it is surprising that I was not lynched.

The appearance before the Commissioning Board had to be reasonably before the end of the course, because those who were now Pilot Officers had to get uniforms. Even more prestigious was getting one's wings, and being able to wear that proud brevet, which was the most enviable cachet of all. Burberry's was the official outfitters and had a shop at the College, but somehow SB learned that our Flight Commander – for we were both in a flight of men being trained on Oxfords – received a commission on any uniforms supplied by the rival outfitters Gieves, a fact that he could not advertise, which must have been frustrating. So we told him that we had heard of Gieves' superiority and were disappointed that the absence of a Gieves shop on the station made it impossible to go to Gieves who were in London. If he realised our subterfuge it did not matter, the important thing was that we both were allowed two days' leave of absence. We stayed at a hotel near Piccadilly Circus, were measured in Bond Street and enjoyed our evening.

Before we were awarded our wings, there were a lot of tests to get through. There were things we had to be able to do with an Oxford in daylight and at night, including formation flying, dropping 11-pound practice bombs, instrument flying, air gunnery, flying on one engine, low flying and cross-country flights. I got lost on one of those. It was from Cranwell, down to Abingdon near Oxford and then to Southampton – and back. It was a day when shower clouds kept blotting out the landscape I was trying to map-read, and at one point I had not got a clue where I was. Then, circling fairly low, I saw an avenue of trees leading up to a very large house. Suddenly, I realised that it was Cirencester Agricultural College, which I had visited with a friend who had been a student there and who probably it was who gave me the impractical idea of becoming a land agent. It was a stroke of good luck. Once recognised, it was not difficult to set a new course for Southampton.

When the 'Points List' came out at the end of the course, I was astonished to see that I had come quite high up. But then, they did not know that I had been lost on a cross-country. And they would have drawn the list up before they had heard me sing.

There were many whose ambition it was to be a fighter pilot. Certainly, it appealed to the more extrovert. Nobody could call me that. The Battle of Britain was about to begin and these weekend flyers would join the small number of career pilots in fighter squadrons and become 'The Few'. Then as many of them were shot out of the sky, they would be replaced by other amateurs now coming through the Flying Training Schools. But I was already destined for multi-engined aircraft, having been trained in Oxfords. I had seen a large photograph of a flying boat, a Catalina, and thought how wonderful it would be to fly one. So I put in a preference for Coastal Command flying boats or 'Reconnaissance'. I got Coastal Command but not flying boats, but thought that perhaps I should be able to aspire to them later. So I was posted to No. 1 COTU, Coastal Operational Training Unit at Silloth in Cumberland, after a week's leave.

Home to Hertfordshire, I, in my new Pilot Officer's uniform with my cream-white pilot's wings proudly on my chest. My wings made me feel happily conspicuous; everybody seemed to notice them. I was most disappointed that Katherine would not see them, but she was now a FANY, having joined the Field Army Nursing Yeomanry, and was too far from Hertfordshire for us to meet within the time available.

On my first evening at home my father, who was commanding a platoon of the local Volunteer Defence Force, which included several of our neighbours with whom I was familiar, asked me to follow him, as soon as I had finished supper, to see their usual drill on the fairway of the golf course at the top of the hill on the other side of the lane. As I approached, my father called the men to attention and saluted me. Now a commissioned officer, I was nevertheless astonished to see my father saluting me and it was with some shyness that I returned the salute.

Next day I was driving down to do some shopping in the local town with my mother.

'I met a very pretty girl the other day,' she mentioned casually. 'Daughter of a friend of mine, they live at Dogget's End.'

Within about a hundred yards we had decided to call there at once and suggest having a bit of a dance at home. Presumably, we must have invited one or two others, but that evening I saw only Sally. She was seventeen and I thought she was lovely.

Deer Leap Swimming Pool, among the beech woods near Amersham, was still open and in the lovely late summer weather we went there together on most of the days of my short leave. Sally was tall and slim, and looked delicious in a bathing costume, her beautiful long legs no longer hidden by her clothing. Sexually, she was no more experienced than I was, or indeed than Katherine was, but her smile, all her body movements, and her costume's delineation of her femininity had a strong effect on me. My thoughts of the lovely Katherine were certainly not swept away, but I began to realise that it would be difficult to separate and quantify in my mind the feelings I had for each of them. It was a very happy leave, spent almost entirely with Sally.

I was, by the standard of my contemporaries, a 'late starter'. It had been Katherine, she just seventeen, when I had reached twenty-one, who had awakened in me strong, physical longings that I had not known before. Now, when two girls had produced in me the same sort of feelings, I was conscious of a more urgent determination to hurry towards putting into action what I was being trained for. I felt an impulse to protect them. I had an impatience to get into the fight.

CHAPTER FOUR

Leuchars

At Euston, I caught a train to Cumberland and found Pilot Officer Douglas Timson, whom I had known vaguely at Cranwell, heading for the same destination. We found that Silloth was a bit back-of-beyond with few actual aerodrome buildings. We learned that we would sleep in tents and Mess in what must have been a small hotel before, probably serving the golf course in peacetime. It was getting dark when we arrived, and horizontal dark grey stripes of cloud layered the fading orange of the western sky. We had been allocated adjacent tent-space and walked together round the edge of the airfield to stand among the sand dunes and look out across the mudflats and emptiness of Solway Firth towards the distant coast of Galloway. We felt a vague excitement – our training was over and we had come here to get acquainted with the Lockheed Hudson, the aircraft in which we would now begin operational flying.

Night flying was in progress. We could recognise by sight and sound the Bothas and especially the Hudsons that we would soon be piloting. We watched each aircraft roar down the runway towards us, lift off the ground and cross the coast, and climbing, bank round in a circuit, across wind, downwind, across wind again, then turn to line up, descending, and approach the far end of the runway to make their landing. The last light of evening had nearly gone and the tiny lights that showed the line of the runway were becoming more visible. Another aircraft was on its approach run – it was a Botha. We got the impression that it was lower than had been its predecessors, but it was hard to tell at this distance away. Suddenly, the far end of the aerodrome was lit by an explosion of flame, a brilliant fireball followed by the deep, terrible sound of it crashing. Black smoke, illuminated by the bright orange of fire, rose from the far boundary of the airfield. One of the night fliers had 'gone in'.

Neither Douglas nor I spoke. We each felt a cold chill at this display of the lethal danger that all airmen must face as they learned their craft and then put it into practice in the operational tasks for which they had been trained. That it was not a Hudson, but was, or had been, a Botha, an aeroplane with a poor reputation made by Blackburn's, was not much consolation. It was not a good start but we were glad that we were to fly Hudsons: two-engined, tubby-looking, all-metal, twin-finned aircraft with a Boulton & Paul mid-upper gun turret.

I had half a dozen short flights with my instructor, Squadron Leader Moll, then some night flying, some bombing and gunnery practice, and the 'conversion course' was over. Moll was a Dutchman, in unfamiliar navy blue uniform, who with Parmentier had won the London to Melbourne Air Race. His English was not good, and his urgent 'more garss!' I knew meant that I must come in faster, with more throttle. But his 'Not so much less spid!' required more fractions of a second to interpret.

There were several Polish pilots being trained there too. Two words of their language would stay in my memory. One, sounding like 'papiross', meant cigarette and the other, something like 'djefchinki', meant 'girls'. 'Girls' was a very important word to a Pole. They were footloose expatriates who had escaped to England to carry on their fight against the Nazis and had had to leave their women-folk behind to who knows what fate. They had a reputation for considerable courage but sometimes for a rather cavalier attitude to women, though many were very happy to consort with them.

There was little to recommend Mess life, except for a small, attractive waitress. My thoughts were embarrassingly divided between Sally and Katherine, but Douglas took the waitress out and reported that they had knee-trembled together while she stood on two bricks – or was it four? However many it was, I thought it an unlikely tale, even if Douglas was so tall that she needed them and so attractive that she had to have him.

'I don't believe it,' I replied, 'but anyhow you ought to have made her more comfortable.'

As it happened, Douglas had only a few months to live.

A few days later we were both posted to 233 Squadron. The squadron had Hudsons and was based at RAF Leuchars near St Andrews on the east coast of Scotland. Leuchars was a peacetime station with a very comfortable Mess. News reached ahead of our arrival of the Station Commander there, Group Captain Pope. Tiger Pope was a very large man who loved Mess parties. He excelled at 'going-round-the-room-without-touching-the-floor'. This boisterous game required circumnavigation of the large anteroom. He would leap from one piece of furniture to another, with loud whoops of triumph and a certain amount of destruction. The Squadron Commander was Wing Commander Purvis, formerly Royal Naval Air Service, the precursor of the Fleet Air Arm. He, too, enjoyed Mess parties, especially when everybody gathered round the piano and sang loud Rabelaisian songs.

There was a Hudson squadron at Wick at the north-eastern tip of Scotland, 150 miles away, and one at Bircham Newton in Norfolk, 250 miles to our south. Along with other Coastal Command squadrons, continuous patrols were kept up between the British coast and the continent in order to guard against any seaborne attack, to look out for German surface raiders like the *Tirpitz*, which sometimes lurked in Norwegian fjords, and to attack enemy shipping should we get the opportunity. Our principal enemy was not Germany but the weather. We had always to fly beneath the clouds and there was not always a lot of room between them and the sea. Each time we made landfall at the Norwegian coast and turned along it for a while before flying back on a parallel track, we were more on the look-out for enemy fighters than enjoying the beauties of the fjords, spectacular though they were. For the Germans had fighter squadrons at Stavanger, conveniently about halfway along the beat allocated to 233 Squadron, which picked quite a lot of us off. We were rather like pheasants and partridges, I thought, which are driven towards the guns of so-called 'sportsmen'. In familiarisation flights that Douglas and I had with more experienced pilots, we learned that as we approached the coast, we must keep as near to the sea's surface as we could in the hope of being below enemy radar or whatever detection devices the Germans had. Hudsons were 'maids of all work' in those early days, but not very fast or manoeuvrable when Messerschmitt 109s or 110s appeared on the scene. There were two Browning .303 guns in the nose operated by the pilot and two in a dorsal turret well aft along its stubby length. In addition, there was an iron peg in a window on each side, onto which a VGO gun could be mounted if a crew member was strong enough and agile enough to manhandle the heavy thing while the pilot was probably throwing the aeroplane about a bit, and he was not otherwise engaged in the 'emergency'. The bomb load was usually a stick of depth charges to be used against a submarine if you could get yourself over it, low enough and slow enough and going in the same direction, after you had sighted it, before it had dived to a safe depth. The aircraft usually carried two pilots, a wireless operator and a rear gunner – a crew of four. Normally the senior pilot flew and the other was navigator and look-out.

About a week after arrival, that September of 1940, I went with F/O Boop Badoux, a Canadian, by way of familiarisation, on one of these sweeps, of which I was to do seventeen in the following month. Having been 'blooded', so to speak, I received a week's leave. At home in Hertfordshire I was much nearer to London; near enough to hear the sound of bombs and guns and to see the glow of fires. The pines and larch trees of Bury Wood across the road from my parents' house were silhouetted against them, silhouettes which grew deeper, momentarily or in pulsating clarity as bombs burst and areas of London flared with unquenchable intensity. Recently, my father had arrived in the City one morning, after hours of delay in the cigarette-smoke filled compartment of the train, to find the old houses of Lilipott Lane and the surrounding streets, in which his office had been, a smoking smouldering ruin in the aftermath of the previous night's raid. He eventually succeeded in making his way home and offered himself as full-time adjutant of the West Herts Home Guard, in which he had been serving as a member of the local unit of the LDV (Local Defence Volunteers).

On one of those seventeen sweeps F/O Piejus was flying when we attacked a merchant ship that was proceeding along the Norwegian coast. We saw no spectacular damage to the ship when our depth charges exploded with great columns of seawater, but they may well have loosened its plates and put it out of action as a carrier of materials for the German war effort (which we must always assume ships were doing) for a while at least. But there was nearly spectacular damage done to Piejus. As we flew low over the ship, those on board loosed off some sort of firearms and a bullet passed between the legs of Piejus, making two holes in the fabric of his Sidcut, the outer garment of his all-in-one flying suit. The bullet missed that part of him that undoubtedly he held dear by little more than an inch as it passed harmlessly on its upward journey. It was an almost laughably narrow escape.

These flights were usually about four hours, not physically too demanding in good weather but fairly stressful in bad, but I was not called on to do anything too hazardous. Most fortunately I had been on my recent leave and not on the station when someone at Group had the foolhardy idea of sending the squadron on a low level dusk attack, on a target near Hamburg, which depleted the numbers considerably.

One day I found myself on the list to do an SA2. This was a straightforward reconnaissance operation. It demanded flying at low level, particularly low when approaching the Norwegian coast because you wanted to keep down below what was thought to be the effective height of German radar. You flew towards a predetermined point on the coast, then parallel to the coast, glancing about in case any enemy fighter was taking an interest, until you had reached the distance along the coast to which you had been instructed. Then you gratefully turned back to fly on a parallel line to the Scottish coast, and so home. Assuming that you saw and encountered nothing that might make you think it necessary to report it back to base, or attack it, an SA2– in fine weather – was uneventful. But this time Purvis took me to one side:

'Group want to be kept informed about the enemy strength and any apparent changes at Stavanger. They think that this reconnaissance could most easily be done if periodically whoever is doing the SA2 which brings them nearest to the aerodrome should climb up and take a photograph or two before turning back. This is to start today. You will be the one making landfall, and leaving the Norwegian coast, at points which will position you best to do it. Photographic Section have been instructed to fit a suitable camera into the aircraft you will fly, and will brief you on the procedure. I suggest that you approach the coast – and be careful to be on course to strike it very close to the aerodrome at as low a level as you can safely manage. Climb up quickly to about 1500 feet, take your photographs and then dive down to the sea as fast as you can and away home.'

My crew and I were not exactly enthusiastic about this idea, but we received the instructions about the camera and set off. Jobs of this kind were normally done by PRU (Photo Reconnaissance Unit) people in a little blue Spitfire; unarmed, unladen, impressively fast and able to climb quickly to a dizzy height. To do these missions at low level in a slow and dumpy aeroplane like a Hudson seemed far from ideal. But Hudsons were thought of as 'maids of all work', and here was new work for the maid to try.

A few hours later we were over Stavanger aerodrome, looking down and preparing to press the camera button. What we saw below us was an awesome sight. I felt my testicles tighten with anticipation at my first close-quarters encounter with my German enemy. The layout of the aerodrome, a perimeter track encircling a grass field with two crossing runways, two or three hangars and what could have been a small village of aerodrome buildings and huts, was such as we had looked down on at various places in England and Scotland on many occasions. This time, drawn up on an apron in front of one of the hangars, however, was a line of Messerschmitt 110 fighters – twin-engined, twin-finned and looking lethal. Taxiing round the perimeter track was a single-engined aircraft, a Messerschmitt 109. A windsock at the edge of the field showed that this plane was approaching the end of the longer runway that one would expect it to use for take-off. It looked imminent. Surely something else was imminent: that all the batteries of short-range Bofors-type guns would open up.

We took our required photographs and I put the nose down and opened the throttles with adrenalin pumping through my whole body, enough to make my legs tremble. I reached the surface of the sea grateful but sweating, and the dear aircraft sped over the water as though it, too, realised how urgent it was to put the maximum of distance between it and Stavangar. A minute or two later Menzies, in the turret, confirmed that we did not appear to be being followed.

Our photographs turned out to be clear and well positioned, but thinking back later I realised how exceedingly lucky we had been. It had been a fairly irresponsible idea to send in a slow, cumbersome Hudson at low level above that scorpions' nest, and one likely 'periodically' to make the Command short of one aircraft and one expensively trained crew. Someone in authority must have thought along the same lines, for no one in 233 Squadron was subsequently required to repeat it. The photographs required by Group were thereafter obtained by PRU in fast, very high-flying and much more suitable aircraft.

Articles by Godfrey Winn appeared on alternate weeks in the *Sunday Express*. To gather material for his articles, he was prepared to stick his neck out and join some arm or other of the fighting forces as they went about their wartime duties.

'He's coming to see us tomorrow,' the Adjutant told me, 'and as you will be Duty Officer you will be in charge of him. See about his accommodation for tonight and arrange for him to do some sort of op tomorrow with someone competent. Have you read any of his articles?'

'Yes, about a fortnight ago, I read about his trip in a British submarine.'

'That's right. Not everybody's idea of a Sunday picnic. He's clearly as queer as a coot but he's obviously got guts.'

Whatever his orientation, I found him most entertaining and we seemed to get on very well. He wanted to go on one of the squadron's 'usual' operations and I fixed him up to go with two Flight Sergeant pilots of whom the senior was Bailey, but both were very competent. I put him into his flying clothing, telling him what to do with his parachute in the unlikely event of him needing to use it at a height when it could be of the faintest advantage to him. I introduced him to Bailey and the other members of his crew and waved to him as he set off on one of the North Sea sweeps. They brought him back safely, but not without some interesting copy for his next article in the *Sunday Express*. Not far from the Norwegian coast they were attacked by a Messerschmitt 110. Bailey brought the Hudson down as close to the sea's surface as he dared and banked left and right in a series of twisting turns, heading hopefully in a homeward direction (for compasses are most erratic in such circumstances). Happily, the German fighter, perhaps not as good at very low flying as Bailey, gave up the chase.

After they had landed, they taxied back to the tarmac apron in front of the squadron offices as befitted an honoured guest. They all got out and we stood talking about their adventure.

'His flying was quite wonderful,' gushed Godfrey. 'Last week I was watching a Hurricane in a dogfight with a German in the sky over Kent. I think our airmen are splendid: I'm sure we'll win the war! This fighter plane came rushing at us and shooting: I could see the flashes of its guns, but Bailey twisted this way and that – so low I thought we should hit a wave-top!'

Then Godfrey noticed that the side of the aircraft low down was wet. Curious, he ran his finger along the wet surface and tasted its tip.

'Good Heavens it's salt! I knew we flew very low but we must have touched the water!'

Not until I happened to meet him again several months later, did I tell him that one of the German fighter's bullets had gone through the Elsan, the on-board lavatory. Whether the salty liquid he tasted was his own urine or someone else's, was a matter of humorous debate in the Mess for days.

The parties at Leuchars were not all rowdy. There were even highly respectable dining-in nights and several officers, particularly of the administrative branches or non-flying people, had wives living close by to be entertained. Officers were often invited to parties given in homes in that part of Scotland. Two friends of mine, Bruce and Campbell, organised Scottish-dancing practices so that members of the squadron would not disgrace themselves when we were entertained by the local gentry. The squadron had a transit van capable of taking eight or ten people to such houses when several were invited, and I was among those in a van load of us going to a twenty-first birthday party for a daughter of Lord Elgin. We danced, to fiddle music as seemed very proper, reels and flings. We stripped willows, dashed white sergeants, and similar, on a vast expanse of marble floor.

The squadron had an Admiral in the Mess masquerading as a Pilot Officer. He had retired from the Navy before the war but was determined to join the Services again. He could not expect to rejoin the Navy as an Admiral, and he might embarrass his senior officers if he was in a lower rank, so sportingly he had come into the junior service in the lowest commissioned rank there was. He was a charming old boy, older than one would expect to find among serving officers, and even Wing Commanders called him 'Sir'. He was employed in the Operations Room.

Sometimes an aircraft would return to base with a crewmember wounded, and having been warned by the pilot before joining the circuit, the 'blood wagon' (the airfield ambulance) would drive out to the end of the runway to meet the landed aircraft. One of the squadron's aircraft came back from a sweep having been shot up. The casualties aboard included one of the air gunners, who had been killed. That evening I was called to the squadron headquarters office. Purvis briefed me for an unusual task.

'Peter, the boy's body has been put into a coffin and I want you to deliver it to his home. It's on the outskirts of Dunbar. You will go by train from the small railway station here at Leuchars. As you know, it is little more than a halt, and the next train will be at 7 o'clock in the morning. Take it to Edinburgh. There you will be met by transport from RAF Turnhouse and go to the house. Here is the address. I have informed the family by telegram, so you are expected.'

Next morning I was up early and wearing my best uniform. I stood on the platform of the little station not far from the gates of the aerodrome. It was a single-line track, the station unattended on that damp, misty, early morning; I was the only person there. Three or four seagulls circled above me, their mournful crying sympathising with the lack of enthusiasm I felt for the gloomy task I had been given. A van approached, which stopped at the other end of the platform, its end doors open to show the coffin inside it. I walked towards it as the train came puffing along the single line and stopped. One of the four men who were standing beside the van opened the doors of the guard's van and they put the coffin in. I wondered if I should travel with it or go along the corridor to a compartment.

'Keep an eye on it, Sir,' was the advice of some wag among the men who had put it on the train. 'You don't want to arrive at your destination and find it gone and hear someone say . . . Coffin? What coffin? Oh yes, one was taken off at Dunfermline.'

So I stayed in the guard's van with the coffin, sitting on a packing case, and endured the funny looks of people as they passed through the van and along the corridor. Although I had been told that transport from RAF Turnhouse would meet me at Edinburgh station, nothing had arrived, so I telephoned and was told that transport was on its way. I had assumed that 'transport' would be a hearse, but what eventually came was a small and rather elderly van with an LAC (Leading Aircraftman) driver. We put the coffin into the van, which was just long enough with the end of the coffin hard up against the backs of our seats, and set off for Dunbar. We were clearly behind schedule but the driver claimed to know a quicker way than the obvious one, though this proved to be very bumpy, with the coffin making a lot of noise on the metal floor of the van behind us. I had been told to go to the house, not to an undertakers', and I was not happy about arriving in this dreary little vehicle. So having identified the house, or so I hoped, we parked the van and I walked a hundred yards or so, and found the undertaker who was looking anxious and wringing his hands.

'I was beginning to wonder if you were coming. The coffin is to go into the house. They want to see the boy. Does he look all right?'

'I've no idea. I think he was shot in the chest.'

'I think we'd best have a wee peep.' The undertaker began unscrewing the lid of the coffin in the van. I chose to think that my help would not be needed and walked towards the house. It was in a poor district and the address we needed seemed to be the upper floor of a house, reached by a wooden staircase outside, at the top of which someone beckoned me to come up. I ascended to the room. The blinds or curtains were drawn across and the room was lit, apart from the doorway when it was open, only by a coal fire. It was hot in there and there were a lot of people, their faces bright in the firelight.

As I entered the room, everybody stopped talking. Only a stifled cough and the faint brittle sound of a coal falling from the fire into the grate punctuated the silence. There was a smell of recently served food. A mothball memory lingered on someone's long-cupboarded funeral clothes. Then the low buzz of conversation began again. I felt accepted, and my embarrassment for my late arrival passed.

'You must be his officer,' said a kind and welcoming voice at my elbow. It made me feel wretched because I realised that I did not know the boy, had never flown with him, and could not even remember his face from among all the air gunners in the squadron. The Minister was there, a large, stern-looking man. Someone showed me where I should sit. There were two stools in front of the fire prepared to receive the coffin. Quite soon it arrived, manhandled with little ceremony up the wooden outside stairs by the undertaker and his men and put, open, before the fire.

The distress of the boy's mother and of his close relations was audible, almost tangible, there in that small, crowded room with the orange glow of the fire lighting up the grief on their faces and glinting in their tears. This was his home-coming. This young boy from a poor family who had joined the Air Force and volunteered to be aircrew, had made them so proud of him. What they had dreaded when they knew what he was doing had come about. And he had come back to them without even the dignity that was due to him – a coffin in a little old van. Two, whom I imagined were his parents, stood looking down at the face they knew and loved as he lay there on his back in the open coffin in the fire-light. The sound of people's grief filled the quiet room.

Then the Minister began. What denomination he was I knew not, but no words of comfort came from him. It was as though the Grim Reaper had come among us in person.

'It is because of our sins that this has come about' was roughly what he was saying; it was a form of service quite unfamiliar to me. 'I am the Resurrection and the Life' was not in his book. Perhaps it was 'I am the Punishment and the Death'. In that hot, firelit room, I felt astonishment and anger as that dark, uncompassionate flagellator pitilessly whipped those about him with his words. Did they go willingly on Sundays, I wondered, to hear him, these people, in his altarless, blackened brimstone chapel on the edge of town? At last he finished. The lid was put back onto the coffin and it was carried down the stairs. One of the undertaker's men must have been sent to bring a hearse and the coffin was put onto it. Then we all walked in solemn procession behind it to a traffic-free main road. Our numbers were increased by mourners who now joined the quiet parade past outlying bus stops and unattended shops, past cold damp toolsheds and half denuded brussels sprouts in wintry allotments, until we came to the cemetery where we laid him in the wet ground.

CHAPTER FIVE

Battle of the Atlantic

Aldergrove lies 2 miles to the east of the large lake, Lough Neagh, which dominates the centre of Northern Ireland. Out of the lough the River Bann flows north between hills on its east and west, about 40 miles to the town of Coleraine and the sea. Here, even more than at Leuchars, the enemy that would deplete our numbers was the weather.

On the same evening as the squadron had arrived, S/Ldr Kearney, acting CO, got us all together to give us an introductory talk. Some, including himself, had done a spell of flying from Aldergrove before, but for most of us it was a new experience, a new kind of work, requiring a briefing about what the job was and what was expected of us. He stood on the platform in the Operations Room, a good-looking man, perhaps a little older than most of the aircrew and perhaps a little younger than most of the non-flying men who were also gathered in that cigarette smoke-filled room. The friendly smile that he gave us as he began had the effect of getting everyone's attention and silence immediately.

'You all know that our towns and cities are still suffering badly from the attacks of German bombers. Thanks to Fighter Command, Hitler has lost the Battle of Britain. The aerial battles of recent months have shown the German High Command that if they continue to send their massed formations of bombers against England, their Air Force will be reduced to insignificant numbers.

But it looks as though Hitler might win the Battle of the Atlantic. The ability of this country to continue its lone fight against Nazi world domination depends on getting supplies of almost every kind across the seas from the countries of the world that are still free. German U Boats, singly and in packs, helped by the air reconnaissance of very long-range Focke-Wulf Kondors, are taking a terrible toll of the merchant ships that are running their gauntlet in the crowded sea lanes towards our ports. Though they are mostly banded into convoys and escorted by destroyers and corvettes, the U Boats are lying just out of range and then coming in to attack the convoys as twilight falls.

Your job is to fly out into the Atlantic. Find your convoy. Search the sea all around its periphery and beyond for lurking U Boats. And stay with it as long as your fuel supply allows. And remember, while you are over or near the convoy, it is vital that you maintain absolute wireless silence.

You will be given an estimated position of your convoy, which we shall be given through Group by the Navy, and your only means of navigation will be 'dead reckoning'. You must never fly over Eire, which in spite of her reputation for sometimes being pro-German, you must consider a neutral country. Donegal, to our north-west, is part of Eire, so you will normally have to fly due north to the coast before you take a more westerly course to the probable vicinity of the convoys.'

He tapped his pointer to a large varnished map as he explained the rudimentary geography.

'Fortunately, we have the River Bann flowing north down to the sea from Lough Neagh, but often the cloud will be down on the hilltops on either side of it so you must be very careful to avoid deviating from the river. When you return, you must try to make allowance for the movement of the convoy while you have been with it and decide what is your position as you leave it, and though you may sometimes get a QDM well after you have left the convoy [he emphasised this strongly] the line of your bearing from base will often pass over Eire and so can be used only as a guide and not as a line of flight. Remember, too, that the mountains of Donegal are high. If the weather is making you fly at a low altitude, your landfall at the coast must be as accurate as you can make it, especially in poor visibility.'

The first convoy escort that I did from Aldergrove was with Phil Piejus, with whom I had been when a ship we were attacking off Norway fired at us and almost did irremediable damage to the South African by nearly removing his wedding tackle.

Bill Kearney had called Piejus over.

'Phil, you have been here in Aldergrove on these jobs before. I want you to take Peter Russell with you and show him the ropes. Remember, young Peter, that navigation is vitally important. When you were at Leuchars you had to get to the Norwegian coast and back again. If you made a nonsense of it you would probably still make landfall on the Scottish or English coast and be able to find your way home or land somewhere. Now, you will be coming back from miles out in the Atlantic, and if you make a cock of it here you may hit the coast of Eire, as they call Southern Ireland nowadays. If you have to land there, or perhaps even fly over it, you will be interned, which will be bad for your record and disappoint scores of women, apart from writing off an aircraft.'

As Phil and I were walking together to the crew-room to collect our kit, Phil went through the routine:

'I know you know how to use the CSC, but as it's the only bit of navigational equipment we've got, I'm going to run through it with you. Now, we'll use your CSC. Make the settings on it as I speak. Let's assume that you have been given the position of the convoy, the wind and the information I've written on this envelope. You set the wind direction and speed you've been given by Control or have decided for yourself. You do this by rotating the dial so it registers against the lubber line and draw a line from the dot, equal in length to the speed on the scale. Now lay off the track you want to make from your last known datum point, say the point where you leave the coast. Now do it – good. You turn the band till the airspeed you intend to fly lies exactly under the dot. That's right. Mark your required track on the dial in pencil and put it to register against the lubber line. Read the drift at the end of the wind vector. Set the track mark against this drift on the drift scale. Now you can read the course on the dial and read the ground speed on the concentric arcs against the outer end of the wind vector. That's fine. Right, I assume that as you can get your course to fly if you know your track and wind, you could know what track you're following and at what ground speed if you know your course and wind. But we'd better get on.'

From Leuchars experience, I knew how to tell the wind direction by observing (if it was daylight) the 'sea lanes', the lines of foam combed back on the shoulders of the waves as they ran before the wind at the surface of the sea. The angle of these lines to my adjusted compass told me the wind direction, and their concentrated whiteness or their faintness told me the wind strength.

Phil explained as he and I and his two wireless operator/air gunners were in the aircraft ready to take off:

'On this runway we shall be heading for the Mountains of Mourne. We shall make a left-hand circuit and come round over Lough Neagh. There are about 150 square miles of the lough with rivers flowing out of it and also into it, so we must be sure we choose the right river. We want the River Bann, which flows out of the north end of the lough and then northwards 35 or 40 miles to the sea at Port Rush. It starts at less than 200 feet above sea level, and then obviously flows downhill, but when the cloud base is low you must keep the river in sight because the hills on each side are 500 feet. They are 1700 feet if you wander off far. Sometimes the cloud is down on the hills and then it becomes rather a tunnel. That tunnel is sometimes the only way home.'

Phil was now heading for the entrance or exit of one of the rivers and I saw that it was the River Bann. I took great care to see that I would recognise it again, as next time it might be I who would have to choose the right one. The cloud was quite low today. The clouds were not much above the hilltops, and I realised how very important this guiding path of the river could often be. Drizzle was now making visibility poor, but as we flew down the valley I could see through the mistiness the grey-green fields. There were no villages, but cows and the occasional bothy seemed to hurry below us.

'As we have already calculated our course for after we have reached the coast, you can enjoy the scenery. Though there doesn't seem to be much of that at present.' Phil called up the two gunners on the intercom, and they both sounded happy enough. In due course we were over the village of Port Rush, having passed the town of Coleraine, and I looked down at the sea, grey and cold-looking and flecked with white wavetops. Phil altered course, now flying approximately north-west. He skirted Inishowen and Malin Head, as they were part of 'neutral' Eire. Within minutes there was nothing to see but the grey rough water below us.

'When is our ETA?' I told him. 'So we've got about an hour and a half.'

It was quite a dull time. There was only the low drone of the two engines and the faint smell of petrol from the priming pumps. I made several checks of the wind strength and direction and the pilot sometimes called up the two gunners to see that they were all right. I noticed that Phil flew very accurately, by speed and height and compass direction. All of us were looking at as much of the sea as was possible in this visibility, which had not improved as more rain was now falling and the sea was getting rougher. The two engines were still running smoothly, praise be! Later, Phil looked at his watch and there ahead could be seen, unmistakably, a ship, and then other ships, well spaced out on the water, vague in the rain.

'Identify,' called Phil. The wireless operator fired the colours of the day. A lean, grey shape of a destroyer signalled back acknowledgement. Then for nearly two hours we circled the convoy, watching the restless surface of the sea for any sign of a lurking U Boat.

Now it was time to begin the flight home, and as we turned and signalled a good-luck message, I thought with pity of all the brave men in those vulnerable ships. The light was fading. The watery light of the end of the day was nearly gone, and for them the darkness of a long night was beginning to enshroud them. Now would be their time of greatest danger, but the Hudson's petrol gauges told us that we must not delay, and we should be of little help to the convoy in darkness.

Phil could not fly at a comfortable height above the waves, the clouds were too low. There was not much room between the cloud base and the sea. I had calculated for him a course home, trying to guess how far from our original position of the convoy the convoy's forward movement would have taken us, but I realised that there was indeed some guesswork needed to decide on a probable datum point for our departure.

The next hour and a half was full of anxiety. We must not climb to any greater height; we would then be in the cloud in darkness. It was unlikely that we could then descend out of it without probably hitting the sea, and water is just as hard to hit as land. Apart from the altimeter, we had no instrument to tell us accurately how far above the surface of the sea we were. The altimeter set on the ground before leaving Aldergrove would undoubtedly now be showing an incorrect reading. In the rain and in the beginning of darkness, and with a display of only an approximate estimate of our height on the altimeter, Phil was having to fly with consummate care and accuracy.

I had experienced poor visibility and low cloud when flying from Leuchars, but this evening there was the added hazard that the coastline we were approaching rose higher than the height at which we were having to fly. Any inaccuracy in my navigation – and in all conscience this was of necessity dependent on quite a lot of guesswork – or inaccuracy in the pilot's flying, could mean chips for all of us. I rechecked several times the calculations on my CSC. Phil was concentrating on his instruments, but also peering through the wet gloom to catch any glimpse of the water that might be allowed to him.

The rain continued to strike the windscreen. The cloud base did not lift at all. Occasional glimpses of the sea's waves seemed to suggest to me that the wind was stronger than before. A change in wind strength would alter the course that I had told Phil to fly. If the pilot was worried, so indeed was I. Looking at my watch and with a small torch at the map, I realised that we were probably now on the seaward side of Malin Head. But were we? If we were not on the seaward side we would hit the hills around it at this height.

Then, over to port, we saw the misty flashing of a light. What was that? The Dutchman read my thoughts.

'I am sincerely hoping that that light is the Inishowen lighthouse. If so, we are about on track.' Even if it was, our watches showed that we were not yet due to turn in towards the coast, just beyond the entrance to Lough Foyle, and hope to be over Port Rush and begin our flight up the river valley. Then, to my surprise, I saw a red light almost dead ahead. What on earth was that?

'Good,' said Phil. 'That's the light on Rathlin Island. I once read an Aldis light signal from one destroyer to another, "Meet you in the red light district!" It was later explained to me that this was a Naval joke, meaning that part of the North Channel which is swept by the red light on the point of Rathlin Island. They spend most of the time desperate for it, those Naval types!' We both smiled.

'Well done, Peter, we're on track but we've gone a bit too far. Probably a change in our wind, or you were a bit wrong about where we were when we left the convoy. Get me a QDM, please, Wireless Operator.'

Back came the answer, the magnetic compass bearing from Base.

'We could not have done that nearer the convoy. Mustn't break radio silence and it would have given us a line to Base right across bloody Eire. But we won't fly on it for another reason. I think your map will show that that line would take us over some hills higher than we want.'

He paused, thinking.

'We'll turn round and fly on a reciprocal course for about 20 miles and then get another QDM, which may give us a bearing to fly up the valley. Please check the sense of what I've said on your map.'

I did that, and the second QDM seemed safe to use for a flight up the 'tunnel'.

Perhaps the rain had eased a little, or the sky had lightened a tiny bit, because it was just possible to discern the vaguely paler colour of the River Bann as Phil flew up it towards Lough Neagh. The colour of the lough, too, was just paler than that of the surrounding land, and Phil turned to port and approached the aerodrome. He called up on R/T (radio telegraphy) and the Chance-light shone down the runway and we landed.

'Thank you Phil, you're bloody good at this.' I heard the other two crew members laughing with a note of gratitude on the intercom.

'Well, it was a bit dicey, but nice of you to say so. Anyhow, we're home now. Let's go and have a beer.'

The next twenty-five or so escort flights that I did after my initiation with Phil Piejus, had me usually as the second pilot/navigator, but after that I was more often the pilot flying with various other men. In due course I teamed up with Alexander, a tall, sandy-haired, methodical chap with whom I got on very well. I usually flew, and Alexander, who was new to the squadron, was second pilot and navigator, at which he was very reliable.

I always managed to choose the right river to fly down from the lough to the coast at Port Rush, but it was the undoing of Douglas Timson. He took off from Aldergrove in the dark before dawn light of a January morning. He turned right over Lough Neagh and took the wrong turning. He flew up the River Main, which flows down into the northern end of the lough through Randalstown from the hills above Ballymena, parallel to the River Bann that flows out of the lough at its northern end and only about 6 miles away from it. So the height of his 'tunnel' was getting lower as he flew up a river valley instead of down one. He ran out of visibility and had no room to turn and crashed. All were killed, but the position of the crashed aircraft and the weather conditions at the time made it fairly clear what had happened, and people in Ballymena had heard an aeroplane flying over, very low, that early morning.

Douglas's death drained a little colour from Mess life – more than most because he was large in life and larger than life. Many felt his absence was a reminder that Death did not spare the jovial and the confident, as much as it was a lesson that error in bad weather was, in that terrain, even more deadly than the enemy. The impact was greater on me as Douglas had been as close a friend as I had in the squadron. I always remembered with a wry smile the episode in Silloth of the waitress on the bricks, an account that had, in a sense, peeled away a layer of my own sexual innocence.

Aldergrove is about 12 miles from Belfast and thither we went when we were free to do so. Mostly we frequented the Grand Central Hotel, the GC, as it was known. At closing time it was customary to repair to a tiny shop where you could get fried eggs, of which there was no shortage in Ireland. It was a plain, undecorated little room, typical of Northern Ireland, just a few yards down a small side street almost opposite the GC. It was kept single-handedly by a small, coloured woman. She offered only one dish: fried eggs and baked beans on a slice of toast, which she cooked to order upon our arrival. Her patter was always the same: 'De eggs is under de beans,' she would say as she handed each one of us our plateful, treating each of us to a wide, infectious grin, with lots of pure white teeth and eye-whites. She was to us an institution, our visits to her a ritual.

Amid the routine of the convoy escorts came an invitation for me and others to a party in Belfast. There was a room full of uniforms (Navy, Army and Air Force) standing with glasses in their hands, shouting at one another through the cigarette smoke and the babble of conversation. Bill Kearney was there and certainly others of 233 Squadron. We had only just arrived and were looking round to see who was there, when I heard a vaguely familiar voice behind me.

'Peter!'

A man was coming towards me, a man with greying, curly hair, dressed in an immaculate dark green corduroy smoking jacket. It was Godfrey Winn.

'Peter, why aren't you in Scotland? How lovely to see you! Now listen. I've been sent to fetch you. A little sweetie I was with said to me "Who's that gorgeous boy over by the door? Get him for me Godfrey!" And I looked and I said, "I know him! I'll bring him at once and give him to you as a present." So you must come this instant; what a lovely surprise!' And he held me by the arm and steered me through the crush and stopped in front of a pretty girl of about 22, with a very vivacious face. Her well-cut, lightweight tailored coat and skirt showed off her young figure.

'Dizzy darling, this is my friend Peter. He looked after me quite wonderfully in Scotland when the Germans tried to kill me. Peter, this is Dizzy Eaton, I know you two ought to get together.'

'It's true they tried to kill him, but they missed and punctured the aircraft lavatory!' I said.

Godfrey gave me a quizzical look and then it seemed the penny dropped. But just then a woman with blue hair claimed him.

'Darling, I've been looking for you everywhere!' And off he went with her.

'He seems to know everyone.'

'He certainly does. Did he really get shot at?'

I told the rather dazzling creature before me briefly of Winn's courageous way of collecting copy for his newspaper articles.

'Did he say Eaton as in Eaton Square?' I asked.

'Peter dearest, we ARE Eaton Square, but we live here because Daddy says that it's cheaper to hunt here, though of course he's with his regiment now.'

Like Godfrey, Dizzy was much in demand. A rather resplendent-looking Army Major appeared and interposed himself between us.

'Hello, old girl! How did you get on with that little filly I recommended to you?' When he saw that she was preoccupied with me he stomped off, muttering some sort of apology. Then two girls, who had not been blessed with her looks, came up.

'Dizzy darling we're giving a party on Saturday. You really WILL come, won't you? Oh gosh, is this your latest? Of course you'll bring him!'

'How does that appeal to you?' Dizzy turned a lazy smile on me.

'Unfortunately, I never know when I'm going to be free.'

'Bother that, I want to see you again. It's a bit crowded here.' She gave me her telephone number. 'Ring me when you can come and see me.'

Dizzy probably spent quite a lot of time in crowds, she would sort of create them.

All February I flew from Aldergrove. Flights escorting the convoys, each usually of between six and seven hours, were routine, rarely exciting though often full of anxiety. The misty twilight air at early morning or in the evening was an unwelcoming place, and sometimes as I fumbled my way to the coast among the hills I would think how bloody silly, or bloody dangerous it was. Then a sense of proportion would return. It was a danger matched or exceeded by that faced by brave men in vulnerable ships in constant danger – men ever expectant of the unseen silent torpedo. The silent wraith tearing into their ship's side to explode, catapulting them or bits of them into the icy water in which, be they the best swimmers in the world, they could not, would not, survive. Or perhaps the torpedo would merely cripple their ship. Leaving them to wallow there. Helpless. Powerless. Each minute anticipating the next torpedo to deliver its *coup de grâce* of raging fire or send her, nose first or stern first, sucking all down with her, under the waves. And though I supposed it is no worse than burning on land or in an aircraft in the air, Death's baptism when a man is thrown into the water, when oil is burning on the surface of the sea, seemed a gruesome way to go.

So banishing such thoughts from my mind I pressed on to the coast and out over the sea, watching its white horses to judge the wind's strength and peering into the winter weather. Sometimes it was a nice day, when I could see the fields and farmsteads on the land, cows grazing in green meadows, the sea's surf breaking on the rocks below the cliffs, white gulls gliding, black cormorants with beating wings, following the ever-moving hollows in the restless surface of the sea. And so onward to find the convoy: merchant ships of tired workworn colours, some large, some small, well spaced-out on the grey-green canvas of the pitiless ocean, its grey, purposeful escorts hurrying beside them with white wake and winking Aldis signal lights. Only very rarely did they below or they above detect the lurking U Boat and attack, but at least, I hoped, our vigilant presence circling in the sky above them all was a deterrent. Perhaps we were a fear to keep the U Boats under water, using up their reserves, wearing down their confidence in their invincibility, giving some comfort to the men in those cargo ships.

Sometimes, flying home, the visibility was good, almost limitless. Even if our navigational reckoning was dreadfully far out we could see and recognise our landfall from a safe distance and alter course to a point on friendly Ulster coast and make our way back to Aldergrove, flying at a comfortable height. Sometimes it was not, and our tired eyes stared ahead of us, watching for the coastline which here, low down, barred our way. Only once, coming back in rain on an evening when grey wisps of cloud dragged their skirts along the wave-tops and ahead of us hung a misty curtain, was I confronted with the heart-stopping sight of a black wall of cliff towering in front of me where Donegal's mountains fall into the sea. I knew I had seen it too late, too late to pull back the stick and throw the wing down in a frantic effort to avoid disaster. But once is enough, and fortunately for us all, the dear aeroplane we flew responded in a flash and by what seemed only yards we showed our belly to the cliff-face and turned along it and out to sea. But if it happened only once in fact, it happened other times in my anticipation and sometimes when the thought of it woke me, sweating, from my sleep.

One March day we found the *Simoloer*, a merchantman, drifting helpless and engineless far out at sea. I flew down near to her decks and we saw that there were men aboard her, to whose eyes we must have appeared like an angel from Heaven. Now was a time when, though it might alert every U Boat in the whole North Atlantic, we must break silence. Probably, if she had any transmitting power, she was already sending out Mayday calls and SOSs. She may have been sending them for hours. Should we make a square search about her for another ship or stay to try to guard her from another attack, this sitting duck below us, and rely on our signals or hers to bring help? Fortunately, visibility was good and my second pilot that day was Sam Murphy, a competent Ulsterman, whose navigation, if I flew accurately enough, should be good enough for us not to lose her. I made circles about her while all of us strained our eyes for the sight of a malevolent periscope. We flashed our Aldis lamp at her to tell her of our intention, then set off on a square search.

I had no way of knowing if we brought the *Clan Cameron* to her aid or if she was already on the way. All that matters is that she came to the rescue of the *Simoloer*, to whom no more harm seemed to have come when we returned to her. We flew back and forth between the two ships as the distance between us lessened. It seemed a long time before we were together, while Murphy made rather nervous calculations of our fuel reserves for our return, but nothing like as long, we were convinced, as it must have seemed to those on board the *Simoloer*. Eventually the two ships were alongside each other. There was a shouting match, no doubt, as well as a discussion in more reliable signalling as to what each should do; who, if anybody, depending on her damage and liability to fire, should stay aboard. Then, to our immense relief, we saw men enter *Simoloer*'s boats and pull away towards the *Clan Cameron*'s side. It would now be a negative effort indeed if we stayed until our own loss in the sea became probable, although no new aerial escort was in sight, so we turned for home. A couple of days later, we were one of a relay of escorts for a merchant vessel being towed back towards a British port by an ocean-going tug. We were disappointed to see that it was not the *Simoloer* but another crippled ship. It would have been good to know if she safely reached her haven, but on such occasions you seldom did.

CHAPTER SIX

Jill

Day escorts, dusk escorts and night escorts followed, and then it was April, but the weather was not kind to us. Spring seemed reluctant to arrive; but one day it came. I was walking past the Cipher Office, where Intelligence Officers, usually WAAF, sifted incoming signals from Group and from the Navy. A window was open. Like most of the buildings at Aldergrove, it was a single-storey wooden building. As I passed, I looked in. The window sill came to my waist, and sitting at a desk was a girl I had not seen before: a WAAF officer one stripe, the same rank as mine. She looked up as I stood at the window, and so also did a senior WAAF two-striper, or Flight Officer, whom I knew and who called to me.

'Oh, Peter, this is Jill Bolton. She has newly joined us. Jill, this is Peter Russell.' I looked at the young girl who sat there.

My eyes took in every visible detail of her. The belted tunic of her uniform emphasised a lovely figure. She got up and came to the window. Her eyes were very clear and blue.

'Would you care for me to show you around the place?'

'Thank you. That's very kind.'

'Tonight I'm on a dusk escort. Tomorrow at six I'll stand outside the Mess, rain or shine, unless I'm flying. Which here at the hub of things you'll know.'

I walked towards my room as though on air. At about teatime P/O Rusk and I took off and climbed up to about 1000 feet and headed north. Below us the fields were green, a green flush had spread through the hedges that divided up the little Irish meadows and shone more brightly, in our bird's eye view, where the whitethorn buds had opened. I felt that down there the birds were singing, and as we crossed the coast the sea looked bluer than it had for ages. Perhaps I was singing too, because Rusk said, 'You sound very happy this evening.'

'I am. Spring has come.'

Next evening Jill and I walked off the aerodrome towards the lough, across the unimportant railway line near to the little station and then along the shore round Ardmore Point. We walked and talked as the lowering sun across the lough turned the water pinky orange. On the airfield the Wright Cyclone engines of the Hudsons roared as they were tested in their dispersals, but we scarcely heard them, as we were concentrating on learning everything we could about each other.

Jill had come into the WAAF after leaving St Andrews University, where she had read Philosophy and Arabic, but she had left before I had gone to Leuchars so I had not seen her there in her scarlet cloak.

The early evening breeze off the lough did not feel cold. It was just strong enough to drive little wavelets to splash on the pebbly beach. Some 5 or 6 miles ahead of us, Antrim's eleventh century round tower was just in sight, not quite obscured by the cluster of trees further along the shore, where rooks were building.

'You must meet Jemima.'

Of course I said I'd love to, secretly hoping that Jemima was not some dull friend to gooseberry our acquaintance. Jill probably read my thoughts.

'She's my little car. I have some old friends in Belfast on the edge of Belfast Lough; I'd like to go to see them, will you come with me?'

She told me all in one breath that Jim Mackie was one of Ulster's captains of industry, director of Harland and Wolf, and had a sweet wife called Marcia and two little girls. Together, we planned to go when Jill could telephone and confirm that our time off coincided with the Mackies being free to receive us. We walked slowly back towards the Mess while some remains of supper could still be on offer. But before we entered camp she put her arms about my neck and lifted up her face. It was a lovely mouth to kiss, her lower lip so soft and full. We kissed and she allowed my hand, as I of course, did hers, to register a claim for rather more than friendship in the days and months ahead. Thus then a while we stood, not speaking, as the dusk fell around us, very close together. That night I hardly slept at all.

Very soon after Jill's arrival on the station and my happy meeting with her, I was called to the office of the Group Captain commanding the station, RAF Aldergrove.

'Next week we are being honoured by a visit from His Royal Highness the Duke of Gloucester in his capacity of a senior Army officer. He will be shown round by myself and some of my senior officers. The Duchess, who holds senior rank in the WAAF, will be shown round by our OC Women's Auxiliary Air Force and some of her ladies of the Administrative branch but I wish you to accompany Her Royal Highness also. Nearer the time you will be given instructions.'

'How on earth did this come about?' horrified, I asked my friend Jill later.

'I understand that the CO asked a few people; including several WAAFs.' There was a great twinkle in her eyes. 'One of the junior WAAFs was listened to, for a change.'

The time appointed came and it happened as the Station Commander had said. I stood near the CO in a group of senior officers and WAAFs as a twin-engined plane circled the field, landed and taxied towards us. Someone disengaged himself from this party and stepped forward to open the door as a small block of steps was put on the ground before it, and then stood aside, saluting. The CO moved forward, saluted, and received the royal party as they stepped down from the aircraft and stood beside it. Officers were introduced, and I, bowing slightly from the waist, shook hands with the Duke. The CO and the royal party moved off to the left and I, taking my cue from the senior WAAF, went in the other direction with her and the Duchess. Dutifully, but struck almost dumb with shyness, I toured those parts of the station in which HRH was interested. Then we adjourned to the Mess for lunch and I was seated near the Duchess in that part set aside for the visitors' reception. For the second course we had cherries, tinned cherries, and for some reason I was fascinated to watch what she would do with her cherry stones. What I had thought that she would do with them I cannot imagine. I can hardly have expected her to swallow them or put them on the floor, and, of course, she put her spoon to her mouth, neatly transferred each stone from her mouth to her spoon and put it on the rim of her plate. Perhaps it was a pity that our plates had rims, it would have been a more interesting enquiry if they had not, for I am sure that I had at some time been faced with that conundrum, which probably unconsciously prompted my interest.

'Well, how did it go?'
'Darling, I was so overcome with shyness that I was virtually speechless.' Jill was laughing at me.
'I did hear that you didn't monopolise the conversation,' she said when she could speak.
'I was a rotten bad choice!'
'Perhaps you ARE just a pretty face!'

For my flying duties, escorting convoys continued. Once, unexpectedly, we came across one of the Navy's biggest battleships out in the Atlantic. Compared with the vulnerable little ships we were used to seeing in the convoys, she looked majestic, leviathan, lethal. Her white wake showed the speed at which she cut her way across the ocean. I imagined all the guns now trained upon us, awaiting the shout of recognition or the order to take no chances – Fire! – shattering our paper-thin aircraft into red-hot flying fragments. As we flew towards her I dredged my mind for any Ship Recognition I had learned. The wireless operator put the proper Very light cartridges in the pistol and prepared to flash her with the colours of the day.
'Jill, darling, if you've not given me the correct codes you'll be looking for a new boyfriend!' But of course they were right, and back at once came the proper signals. But I still did not know for certain who this beautiful monster was: *Rodney*? *King George the Fifth*? *Renown*? I could not when I got back to base tell them that I had seen but failed to recognise a large Naval vessel. 'Are you even sure it was British?' they would ask in amazement. So, somewhat embarrassed, I flashed her: 'May I approach?' I flew low on the water close beside

her. But needless to say she did not wear her name conspicuously like a racing yacht so I flashed again: 'Who are you?' Even if some Naval eyebrows were raised at this my ignorance, she answered promptly and without reproach KG5. Silently, I blessed her for her kindness.

'Jill, today I had to ask our greatest battleship who she was,' I confessed in shame later.

Next evening as I waited for her by Jemima's parking place near the Mess, I saw that she was carrying a book.

'You sweet child!' She had brought me a copy of *Jane's Fighting Ships*.

Though for the ships in the convoys the same dangers lurked in the waters around them, for those of us who flew vigilant above them, the improving weather lessened the hazard of our journey to the coast. Now, because we were less often mantled in rain or snow, even our engines sounded more reliable as we crossed the friendless emptiness of those miles and miles of sea. Back at base around the lough as spring grew into summer, Jill and I delighted in the changing beauty of the lush green Irish countryside. Primroses and celandines gave way to bluebells and the first red campions, then hedgerows were a-froth with May blossom. Wide-spreading chestnut trees bordering the meadows and giving shade to the cattle that stood beneath them munching, bore cream-white candles among their broad-lobed leaves. Soon, poppies were vivid in the growing corn and there were roses and foxgloves in the quiet lanes where Jemima was our friend and confidante.

April, May, June and July of 1941 were filled with happy days. Happiest of all were when our leisure time could coincide and when we knew early enough that tomorrow would be free, for then we could spend a night away from camp.

Five of the six counties of Northern Ireland share a portion of the coast of Lough Neagh and if we circled it we passed through all of them. But to go halfway round the lough southabout took longer than going north. There was no bridge over the Lower Bann River, which flowed into the lough''s southern end from its source in the Mountains of Mourne, or over the Torrent River, which flowed into its south-west corner, unless one drove further to the south than a quick glance at the map might make one think one need. And Jemima demanded bridges. She would, of course, have no truck with little passenger ferries.

I was free, and Jill had finished her shift in the Cipher Office. We both felt an urgency to get off camp and be together.

'Let's go northabout.'

We drove north to Antrim, but we skirted the town and headed west to Randalstown on the River Main, where poor Douglas had made his fatal mistake.

We came to Toome, where the Upper Bann flows out of Lough Neagh northward its 35 miles to the sea. This was the entrance to our bad weather 'tunnel' when the clouds were very low, but not that day.

Toome had the largest eel-fishing industry in Europe. We got out of the car, as we had done before, and stood on the bridge looking down at the fish-traps and the weir and the lock on the short canal.

From Toome we rounded the north-west corner of the lough, far enough away from its shore to cross a bridge over the Mayola River and down its western side. So we came to Ballyronan, a little village hidden from the lough-side by a band of trees, 12 miles across the water from the aerodrome and prying eyes. Never had we seen anyone from over there here in our private place.

Mrs Wilson opened the door of her house in the quiet main street. She was dressed in black and her voice had a musical Irish lilt. She smiled.

'It's your usual room you'll be wanting.' She stood aside in the narrow hallway to let us pass and climb the stairs. Our 'usual' room was the one at the front of the house, and we believed that apart from her own room it was, in fact, the only one. Its lace curtained window looked on to the road, and it was simply furnished with a rather noisy bed and a tile-topped washstand on which was a large china bowl and ewer. There were two small towels, a candle in an enamelled holder and a box of matches. I could bring kettle-hot water upstairs from the kitchen range.

'I'll not start to make your tea till I hear you come down and I know you're ready,' she called as we got to the top and opened the door to the little room.

'Thank you, Mrs Wilson.' I closed the door.

She was right. It was a little while before we came downstairs to the small sitting room at whose cane-legged table we always ate our meals. It was not necessary today, but sometimes we had a fire in the grate under the narrow shelf on which stood two china candlesticks, 'A Present from Portrush', and a photograph of a middle-aged man in a thick serge suit, which we felt certain was Mr Wilson.

She heard us come down.

'Shall I get your tea now?' Soon she returned, her entrance preceded by an appetising smell of hot, buttered toast. Here were boiled brown eggs and home-made jam.

'Thank you, Mrs Wilson, that looks lovely.'

Afterwards, we walked across the empty road, and through an orchard pink with apple blossom, to the shore of the lough. The air was very still, the water near us unruffled except for the ripple of widening concentric circles when a fish rose to the surface, perhaps a dollaghan, a local kind of very large trout.

We wandered in this now familiar peaceful place, where bees were still busy in the apple blossom in the long light evening of double summer time. Not far away a family of ducks paddled in the sandy shell-strewn water's edge.

'Dear Mrs Wilson, she knew that we should need to stay upstairs alone after our arrival,' I said.

'Yes, when we stood on the bridge at Toome looking down at the eel-traps there seemed to be no hurry to get here, but when I saw that little room again I felt an urgent need to have you inside me.

'We are so lucky.' Jill took my hand and turned towards the house and smiled. 'I think an early night, don't you?'

*   *   *

Flying is fun. Like most things it is less fun if one is obliged to do it. But there was one task we had that was pure joy. This was to take off in the very early morning and fly from the north coast of Ireland up the west coast of Scotland. Looking for submarines? Looking for German agents being put ashore? Hoping to intercept the Focke-Wulf Kondor flying from Stavanger to the south of Biscay round the west side of Ireland to report on the convoys in the north-west and south-west approaches? The briefings mentioned all three of these tasks, but I never saw anything of a likely nature.

To fly at four or five hundred feet is to see scenery at its best. Passing to seaward of little fishing villages, lifting the aircraft over promontories that sometimes barred our way, we flew between the islands, between the complicated coast of Scotland and the Outer Hebrides. On each of these flights, if the weather was fine I crammed into a few hours the visual enjoyment of a hundred coast-path walks. Flying like a sea bird, though too fast to identify wild flowers on the cliff tops or the birds whose world I was sharing, which is one of the joys of walking on the cliff top, my crew and I could wonder at the grandeur and delight in the colours in our birds' eye view. Ocean-blue Atlantic waves hurling themselves at the rocky coast threw lacy aprons at the cliffs' dark feet, ringing each island with a fringe of white, bordering each windward headland, invading each seaward inlet with changing patterns of restless surf. When the morning sun looked over the shoulder of the Scottish mountains, the colours of the rocks brightened, and in early summer we could see the yellow gorse and even see patches of wildflowers decorating the cliff top and blooming in clearings in the bracken. Here and there partway down a cliff-face we saw a rock garden planted by the wind, growing in the scree of crumbled rock in the meagre shelter of a boulder, stonecrop, and cushions of thrift and hair-fine rush-grass, clinging to the crevices in defiance of salt-laden gales.

When we came to Cape Wrath we turned for home. There was a speck ahead. Adrenalin flowed into my face and limbs. What is that speck ahead and higher, its shape vague against the background of the mountains but closing us at the rate of our combined speeds? Could it be a Kondor making landfall at Cape Wrath on its long journey behind the British Isles?

'Alex, VGO probably starboard.' (That gun was a cumbersome thing to move hurriedly across from the thole pin in the portside window should starboard prove to be where it was wanted). There was a change of mood, the idyllic pastoral ended, danger might be seconds away. My thumb moved onto the firing button on the steering column in readiness. But all was well. It was a Sunderland flying boat, probably patrolling on a line from Cape Wrath to Iceland. So we completed our turn for home, flying down between the Highlands and the Western Isles.

We passed desolate places with Gaelic-sounding names if any names they had, where fingers of the sea probed between the mountains, and there were flat islands of rock and saltmarsh, inhospitable outposts in the merciless sea. Even here, however, there seemed to be tiny crofters' dwellings and perhaps Christianity had found a refuge there long ago in the Dark Ages.

That April and May, Jill and I had spent together whatever leisure time we could. Happy June and July continued the same. The weather was kind and I had no flying misadventures. There were marshes with kingcups and iris, and meadows ringed with honeysuckle. There were ancient Celtic crosses and a place near a river where a low cliff showed whence china clay had been taken, creamy white and soft like cheese. There was a small seaside town, perhaps it was Portrush, with comfortless misogynous 'Paddys' Bars' and postcard shops selling little presents to take home to those who could not come. The place looked sad and jaded, unpainted, regretting the wartime loss of its summer visitors. We found it a poor alternative to the unspoilt countryside where the beauty of our surroundings and the softness of each other's company was all we seemed to need, and our discreet accomplice, Jemima.

Then, with little warning, at the beginning of August, the squadron was posted to Cornwall. The blow that had had to come had fallen. Jill was station, not squadron staff, and would stay in Northern Ireland. For me, if I had to go, it mattered little where. For the squadron it could have been much worse. There were Coastal Command postings like Benbecular in offshore Scottish islands, where men made rude jokes about putting sheep's hind legs into their flying boots, for there was little other company beyond their fellow airmen on the camp. Indeed, Cornwall might be lovely.

CHAPTER SEVEN

Stopper

I had had the happiest four months of the war, perhaps the happiest of all my life so far, but now it had to end. Jill and I spent our last bitter-sweet evening together and in the morning the squadron flew down the Irish Sea and landed one at a time at St Eval on the north coast of Cornwall, between the towering cliffs of Trevose Head and the sandy beaches of Newquay. The aerodrome had recently been bombed. One bomb had fallen on an air-raid shelter outside the Officers' Mess, killing everyone in it. To our surprise, transport took us to the Watergate Bay Hotel, about 4 miles down the coast towards Newquay, where we were to live. Each time we were required to fly, transport would collect us and take us to the aerodrome to be briefed and then fly. Transport would then take us back to the hotel after we had returned and been debriefed and perhaps given an out-of-hours meal. The hotel was only a few yards from the beach, a lovely place to spend the summer months, if you were not broody as I was.

The work we were doing still included escorting convoys, but now it was as they neared the south-west approaches up from the west coast of Africa or out of the Mediterranean or from across the Atlantic, bound into the Irish Sea or up the Channel or up the west coast of Ireland: or outward bound on the same routes.

But our most regular task, because someone had to do it every night, was called 'Stopper', watching for the expected emergence from Brest of two German battle cruisers, *Scharnhorst* and *Gneisenau*, which had been in there since April.

We were summoned to hear the Intelligence Officer explain this new task and the reason for it.

'Thank you Richard, the floor is yours.' The Intelligence Officer took Kearney's place and began:

'At the beginning of this year the battle cruisers *Scharnhorst* and *Gneisenau* slipped out of Kiel, evaded the Home Fleet at Scapa Flow and got into the Atlantic, where they preyed on our convoys, sinking twenty-two ships in two months to a total of about 100,000 tons. They are fearsome great predators, each around 32,000 tons, 740 feet long and with a complement of about 2000 men. They are capable of 32 knots, having each six 11-inch torpedo tubes and formidable armament.

On March 22nd they arrived unchallenged in Brest for urgent repairs, *Scharnhorst* in particular needing a boiler refit.

On March 30th Bomber Command attacked, and though they did not damage either ship, they hit a hotel housing German Naval staff, killing very many. Agents had passed to England information about these repairs, and from the fragments of armour-piercing shells that the Germans found after the raid, they realised that we knew what our target was. High-level raids continued nightly.

For a low-level attack they looked impregnable, close by a wall and protected by a curving mole, and the hills surrounding the port would make it impossible for a dive attack, as no aircraft would be able to pull out of a dive and climb away without hitting a hill. Also, those hills bristled with anti-aircraft guns and there were three flak-ships in the harbour. Nevertheless, on April 6th from St Eval, this station, [he paused and surveyed his audience as if to imbue in them the gallantry which he was about to relate] F/O Campbell in a Beaufort skimmed over the mole into the mouths of the guns and at deck level fired his torpedo at point-blank range before crashing into the water in flames. His torpedo exploded against *Gneisenau*, almost sinking her at her buoy. Our intelligence suggests that *Gneisenau* will be out of commission for at least six months.'

' . . . You will be pleased, but not surprised,' interrupted Kearney, 'that Campbell was awarded a posthumous VC.'

The Intelligence Officer continued:

'The Huns realised, that the ships would be static for a long time and decided to use them as a training centre. They posted 100 midshipmen to complete their training in anti-aircraft defence aboard the two ships, *Gneisenau* being in dry dock. Four nights later Bomber Command attacked again, hitting *Gneisenau* with three bombs, setting her on fire and killing fifty and wounding ninety, of whom many were of the midshipmen flak crews resting between decks.

After this, the defences of Brest were still further increased. *Scharnhorst* was moved and decoys made, nets were hung over the now-closed lock gates, smoke-screen generators were brought in, and the crews are taken nightly in lorries to barracks further away.

You will have read in your newspapers that in May there was a naval battle with the battleship *Bismarck*, which had been lurking, like the *Tirpitz*, in the Norwegian fjords, in which the old HMS *Hood* was sunk and the new *Prince of Wales* badly damaged. But Lt/Cdr Esmonde in an ancient Swordfish from *Victorious*, attacking *Bismarck* at wave-top height in darkness, scored a torpedo hit amidships from less than 1000 yards. Slowed down, after a three-day chase the Home Fleet sank her.

On June 1st the heavy cruiser *Prinz Eugen*, which had escaped, arrived in Brest with confirmation of *Bismarck*'s sinking. We realise that this loss, and the almost nightly bombing of Brest by the RAF, will make the Germans want to attempt a break-out. Although this might be out into the Atlantic, it might be up the Channel, so Fighter Command have been ordered to make daylight sweeps, and Coastal Command to organise three separate dusk to dawn reconnaissance patrols off Brest and along the Channel, to be code-named 'Stopper'. These, (he pointed at the large wall-map) are from Brest to Ushant, from Ushant to Brehat, and from Le Havre to Boulogne. The first, off Brest, is 233 Squadron's section of Stopper Patrol.'

The Intelligence Officer moved aside and took a chair on the right of the platform. Bill Kearney climbed up into his place and took a paper from his pocket.

'Our Stopper Patrols will begin tonight. I have already briefed F/O Maudsley for this evening's patrol. F/O Jamieson and his crew will be in reserve. Those two crews are at present in the Wireless Section receiving instruction in the operation of ASV Mark 2 Radar. Tomorrow morning at 10 o'clock F/O Badoux and for his reserve P/O Walsh, and their crews, will report for instruction, and patrol tomorrow night. F/O Williams, and Sergeant Barley for his reserve, will report to Wireless Section tomorrow at twelve noon. They will operate on Wednesday night. I myself will patrol on the fourth night. These details, and the roster for other crews, will be promulgated in the usual way and will be on display within the hour.

This piece of equipment, ASV, is calibrated to show a blip on its screen if either of the two big boats emerges from harbour. When it is your turn to patrol, you will be shown the line which you will fly up and down, just to the west of the island of Ushant, not above 2000 feet, and lower if the cloud base does not allow you to fly any higher. There will be no heroics. If you see a blip, you will immediately signal the code letter, which you will be given that night, back here to base. Bomber Command or the Navy will take action at once. The intention is that you should get the urgent information of a ship's emergence back here without a moment's delay, and not that you should be destroyed before you can do so while you are attempting to sink it yourself!'

This instruction was received with a rather apprehensive laugh from the audience assembled.

'Any questions?'

'What sort of reliability can one expect from ASV?'

'About 50 per cent.' Kearney's tone of voice showed that he realised its obvious shortcomings, but was not volunteering to discuss it.

I walked with my crewmen towards the Transport Section. Other crews similarly were discussing, before returning to their Mess hotels, this unexpected duty, which they could obviously expect to come their way quite often, with two crews in effect being required for the duty each evening. As the end of summer advanced and nights lengthened, the watch on Brest would require two crews each night as well as reserves. Crews would then have to do Stopper more frequently.

'It won't be long before we're on,' said Alex.

I nodded. I was also thinking about the gallantry of F/O Campbell, who had achieved his act of astonishing bravery two days before my meeting with Jill. Had he not done so, I realised, had one of the ships, which preferred to hunt as a pair, not been disabled for several weeks, their emergence would have been expected sooner. No. 233 Squadron would almost certainly have been sent down to St Eval by the middle of April, and the wonderfully happy time we had spent together would never have happened.

A few nights later it was our turn to do the Stopper Patrol. During those short nights of August it was not necessary to divide the watch into two. I should be doing about a six-hour trip and be the only aircraft on, though I would have a reserve standing by at base. I had not been looking forward to it at all. It was not so much that I was frightened, or so I claimed in my own private thoughts, of being jumped by a German fighter, though I realised that there was a greatly increased likelihood of this happening when compared with patrols further out into the Atlantic, but I had an even greater fear, that it would be I who would let the ships out. It was an anticipatory guilt of failing to discharge such a responsibility.

There was plenty of light in the sky when we took off. Keeping low to the water, we headed for Brest. Short of the island of Ushant, I lifted the nose of the aeroplane and climbed to 1500 feet. Believing ourselves now to be on the line that we were to patrol and able in the fading twilight to see the shadowy bulk of the island, I turned and flew along the line, then turned again and flew back. It was now mercifully dark. I took over the place that had been occupied by Alex, and bent down to watch the small screen in front of me. Alex moved into the pilot's seat and took over flying the aeroplane. Miller was still at the wireless set, headphones on his ears, ready to send that vital coded message back to base if the looked-for spark of light should appear on the circular screen. Menzies was in the turret, but it had been decided between them that they too, like Alex and me, would change places part-way through. We two men at the front, alternately flying the aeroplane, would rest our eyes from the fixed stare we were keeping on the ASV. The other two, Miller and Menzies, had to keep a continual listening post in case of any instructions that might be received from St Eval, while it was also important that watch should be vigilantly kept for fighter aircraft in all the vast dome of empty sky around them.

Backwards and forwards we flew along the line. No one attacked us. No blip showed on the screen. Alex and I had changed places perhaps three times.

Looking at my watch, the luminous dial told me that we had about twenty minutes left of our patrol. But already, the paler light in the eastern sky was making us feel exposed and even more vulnerable. After all, Brest with its docks, its ramifying estuaries and anchorages, now sheltering three of Germany's most valuable weapons of war, and home base for her submarines, was one of the most heavily defended places in Europe. The anti-aircraft gunners down there, and those who controlled and sent out the night fighters waiting near there, perhaps on Ushant itself, were alert to the danger of British bombers approaching the port. Already, as they knew, Bomber Command aircraft had done great damage to the installations, to one of the ships in particular, and to some of the living quarters of those men whose job it was to defend it. Indeed, it seemed strange to me that so far we had been allowed to continue our patrol unmolested.

But at last we reached the end of the time appointed, and with a feeling of great relief, I, who was flying at the time, turned for home.

In the late summer of 1941, Bill Kearney had left the squadron. He was very popular, managing to maintain discipline without bullshit. He had been replaced by W/Cdr Kidd. No one could call that one popular. He had spent the war so far in Training Command, Chief Flying Instructor somewhere, a sort of S/Ldr Duke of ill remembrance. This was something that put him at a disadvantage. All through the war it was noticeable that men with operational experience, that is, who had flown against the enemy, did not have the same respect for those who had not as for those who had. This did not apply to non-flying men who served in occupations like, for example, Intelligence. But if a man was put in command of an operational squadron, those whom he commanded would expect him to 'have got some hours in', as they would say. But there was no doubt the man could fly. He was to prove it one day soon after the squadron got to St Eval.

Though the Hudson was most unsuitable for any fighter-aircraft role, being neither fast, nor manoeuvrable, nor sufficiently well armed, we were a squadron operating from an aerodrome in Cornwall. It was therefore not surprising that the squadron was scrambled when a fleet of the Royal Navy was being attacked by German aircraft off the south-west tip of neutral Ireland. The Tannoy blared all around the station; in hangars, Messes, crew-rooms, on the field.

'All aircrews report to Operations Room at once!'

Alex, Miller, Menzies and I were in the Operations Room already, for we had just landed, returned from an anti-submarine sweep in the Bay of Biscay. We had divested ourselves of flying clothing, parachutes, and simple basic aids and been debriefed. Briefings on a Coastal Command station were not like those in Bomber Command. There were seldom mass-briefings of all the squadron's crews – no smoke-filled room for all who'd come there in obeyance to a battle order posted everywhere, with time of briefing given, and time, perhaps, of an extra meal before. In Coastal Command, operations were almost always individual affairs: one Hudson to escort a convoy, another one to do a sweep, one or two perhaps to do 'gardening' – laying mines – and here at St Eval there was an added complication, few crews would expect to be on the station. Some were flying, some about to fly, but some were at Watergate Bay Hotel or at Bedruthan Steps 10 miles away, or travelling thence or thither. The normal arrangements were unsuitable for reaction to a 'panic'.

The Station Commander came quickly in, and various 'penguin' people – without wings – like Operations Room officers, Met men, Engineering staff, and several WAAFs with papers in their hands.

'What's the panic?' I asked of someone near me. But now an Intelligence Officer was speaking loudly.

'There is a small force of Royal Navy ships being attacked by German aircraft off the south-west tip of Eire. Each crew is to collect two papers from a WAAF. One is a position of the Naval Force, and one – most vital – your identification details, Colours of the Day – then get away quickly to your aircraft, get airborne, and get there at once.'

Alex took a paper showing where to go, and Miller one with the urgent Colours of the Day – no one would want to fly over Naval ships without means of identification. Then all four of us hurried off, running together by the perimeter track to reach the dispersal where we had left our aircraft, D for Dog. Several ground crew were around her, fitters, riggers, with step ladders up to her engine nacelles, whose covers were off.

'How long will you be?' I asked of the Flight Sergeant.

'Hard to say, Sir. It's not our turn with the petrol bowser yet, and your port engine's not running very smooth.'

'We're Fighter Boys today. We're scrambled. Attack on some Naval ships, south-west of Ireland, urgent stuff.'

'We're doing our best, Sir. And I think I see the bowser coming now.'

'Is there a spare aircraft? Perhaps Q Queenie – Quemby's off on leave.'

The Flight Sergeant looked towards the centre of the airfield.

'The Winco's taken that. There he goes now, racing down the runway. He was in a bit of a hurry, and he's made it.'

'What about the ammunition?' shouted Menzies to an armourer.

'All done, Mick. All guns cleaned and ready. We've got our fingers out here.'

The ground crew worked quickly, and very soon the tanks were full and the port engine, as I tested it, was running smoothly. All at our stations, I saw Winnicott taxiing past in N for Nan. He smiled and waved. Then, Good Heavens! There was the Met plane, a Gladiator biplane, taking off. Richie wasn't going to miss the fun. Next came the little sky-blue Spitfire, the PRU plane, which sat on a dispersal nearest to the Mess. Neither would be armed, I thought, but perhaps the Spitfire, at least, would be a deterrent. Seldom could a more motley band have been scrambled against the *Luftwaffe*.

Soon we, too, were airborne.

'Course 260,' said Alex, 'and any speed you like.'

Over the Irish Sea, heading for the south-west of Eire, I climbed to about

10,000 feet, high for us, but perhaps not high enough to be in as good an attacking position as this job would require.

'Some flak over there,' called Menzies, who had turned his turret to face forward. 'Must be the ships.' We all saw a few black puffs in the sky ahead of us.

The weather was lovely, visibility miles, and the rocky bays and inlets were lined with white Atlantic foam as deep blue rollers threw themselves at the coast. There were the ships, not far from Bantry Bay, and many aircraft, too far away to identify with any certainty. I saw a smoky black trail slant across the sky into the sea.

'Someone going down there. Maybe we are not late for the party after all.'

Even as we looked, the planes were thinning. We could now see a few Hudsons, and Richie's Gladiator climbing to a dizzy height. We hurried on, but before we reached the scene, the party was over. Perhaps the sight of these unusual 'fighters' sent the Germans home. More probably, their fuel gauges provided more compelling argument.

Back at the aerodrome, there was only one thing to talk about; Winco Kidd had shot down a Heinkel 111. The man from Training Command who'd done no operations had been rather resented before. But now his stock now rose triumphantly. People forgot that they had ever disliked the chap! His discipline, it's true, was not Bill Kearney's discipline by consent, but men did as he ordered much more willingly. And the man could certainly fly!

Operating out of St Eval, I and my crew now saw more of the south-west and west coast of Ireland. Sometimes a crew was detailed to patrol from the south-west tip out to sea on a line from the coast perhaps 50 miles, beginning its patrol at first light. The idea was to spot one of the Focke-Wulf Kondors, the very long-range bombers that Germany had been using for a year, not only for strikes against British shipping but for reconnaissance flights to report on the movements of British convoys and call in the packs of U Boats to attack them. It was thought that they were flying out of Stavanger in southern Norway round to one of the airfields on the west coast of France, and sometimes making landfall off south-west Ireland to check their navigation. Days later the same aircraft would make the return flight to Norway. They were a menace and a very worthwhile quarry, though who would win in a confrontation I never had to put to the test, as there was never one to be seen when we were doing that patrol. It is probable that they had heavier calibre armament. Certainly, a Kondor had more men to man its guns than a Hudson had.

In fine weather that coast looked very beautiful, and very varied, from the lovely wooded inlets of some parts of Cork and Kerry to the inhospitable headlands and islands further north. I remembered a film I had seen before the War, 'Man of Aran'. There they were. Bare flat fingers of grey limestone rock pointing out into the Atlantic. All soil had been washed off them by the gales, yet still the stone walls stood, dividing up their naked windswept surfaces to show that once they had been fields. But these bare fingers of rock were part of Southern Ireland, and Eire being neutral, we must not fly over them.

*   *   *

The Watergate Bay Hotel in which the squadron officers lived was very adequately comfortable. The new CO, Kidd, had us out on the beach every morning that we were not flying to bathe and do physical jerks. This was not popular but a good idea, as fitness was most important to keep aircrew alert in their flying duties. There were one or two civilian guests living in the hotel, ancient inhabitants who had been residents there since before the War, or certainly before St Eval was bombed, and the Air Force had had to commandeer some local accommodation. It never occurred to me that anyone could be a spy and, of course, we had no idea what our sortie was to be until we had arrived at the aerodrome Operations Room and been briefed, so while in the hotel we did not have the opportunity for careless talk. I never used the hotel for the purpose of having a civilian friend or relation to stay, but it was possible, for the hotel was not absolutely full. When Harry Rowntree, a Quaker, like many of the chocolate families, wanted to get engaged to his girlfriend, he had her and her parents to stay there for a few days near the end of his time in the squadron. They had returned home some weeks before Harry was killed.

On a golden autumn afternoon I was called with my crew, P/O Alexander and Sgts Miller and Menzies, to the Operations Room up at the aerodrome. We were told that we were to attack 'some shipping' in the port of Lorient, on the French coast between Brest and St Nazaire. We were to wait for further details of our instructions. Looking at a map, I could see that the port was some way up an estuary; it was quite certain that the shores of that estuary, to our left and our right, would be heavily defended. It was, after all, an important base for German submarines. The operation would seem to have much in common with the Charge of the Light Brigade. None of us could imagine any 'further details of instructions' that could make it any more likely that we would return. We waited. Perhaps it was one hour, perhaps two. Either is a long time to have nothing to think about but impending certain death. We sat in a corridor whose walls were painted in a depressing shade of green.

Maybe because the odds were known to be poor, we were apparently the only aircraft to make this attack. I remembered the words in which F/O Campbell's gallant sacrifice had been described when the reasons for Stopper patrol were told to us: 'He skimmed in over the mole at deck level into the mouths of the guns and fired his torpedo at the *Gneisenau* at point blank range before crashing into the water in flames.'

I knew that I was certainly no F/O Campbell. I looked across at Alex, who was sitting with his head in his hands. Was he thinking, trying not to think, or praying? Miller and Menzies were whispering together. Their faces seemed to have lost some of their colour. I tried to imagine how I would fly the aircraft in the last moments of what would be her last flight and our lives. I hoped I would maintain control of the aircraft as well as of myself. Although there would be no one to witness my actions, no one who might later write a citation, I must show no hesitation. It would be better to think of other things, to have totally different thoughts and attempt to hurry these awful minutes of waiting into the inevitable future.

Two airmen passed us in the corridor, talking and laughing happily. So, an hour or so ago, would we have done. A WAAF passed, and, oblivious of the circumstances in which we were waiting there, gave me a friendly smile. Having waited for what seemed to be an interminable time, we were told that 'there is to be a delay'. After another long wait, we were told that the operation was cancelled. We got to our feet, overwhelmed with relief, but all four left that Operations Block several years older.

I wrote to Jill. She had left Northern Ireland and was in Bomber Command. Her reply, in her educated hand, was disconcerting.

I don't know if I can stand it. I find that the losses of so many crews 'gets to me'. People say that I shall become hardened, but being hard is foreign to my way of thinking. They go off into the night, these young men, and so many do not come back. It is not always the flak, not always a burst of red-hot fire from a Jerry fighter, sometimes they do not reach the target at all – ice brings them down. They have to climb to altitude, and if it is through heavy cloud the moment may come when their aircraft seems to lose the will to keep on climbing, and will not answer to the increasingly desperate efforts of the pilot to control it.

One man, still a boy, really, explained 'icing' to me, how in the bitter cold of higher altitude, he said, in the cloud, the still unfrozen super-cooled water droplets strike the leading surfaces of the wings and the kinetic energy of the impact makes the water freeze, spreading a thickening layer of ice until their aerodynamic shape is so altered that there is no longer any lift.

But you must know all this. What it means, to my unscientific mind, is that when flying so high, and in cloud, it creates, dear Peter, a sort of icy, unairworthy sarcophagus. The next night he was listed missing. He was only 22.

But I am due for some leave, and now that we are no longer so impossibly separated by sea as well as distance, perhaps we could meet. It would be heavenly to be with you again, though I realise that the pain of parting, when our little time of being together has flashed by, will be as agonising as before. I need you, to feel you – to know you are still alive.

I also was due for some leave, a precious six days that would almost coincide with that which Jill was expecting. She was able to spend her last few days with me at my Hertfordshire home. I met her train and took her down to Tiled Cottage.

Back at St Eval I settled again to the routines of the job we had to do. I accepted the absence of feminine company and looked forward to my weekly days-off working on a farm. But now, autumn was deteriorating into winter.

Sometimes we set off under a blanket of low cloud, which pressed us down on to the cheerless sea. Sometimes we came back to find the sea-mist rolling in over the coast, forcing us to fumble our way by dimly seen landmarks to recognise the boundary of the airfield. Then, as I made my approach, I offered up a little prayer that I should not make a nonsense of it and have to climb away from this place where I knew where I was and go round again.

It was a season of wind, even gales; out in the Bay of Biscay, French tunny-boats, if indeed they were nothing more sinister, ketch-rigged, well-tried sea boats, carried less sail and sometimes wallowed among the short grey waves. They each hung out a long strong rod arching away from their sides to pull through the water parallel fishing lines to catch and trawl, drowning, behind them, their hapless tuna victims.

On one such routine patrol, on our way back from out to the west of Biscay, we disturbed a U Boat. It was on the surface, well over to starboard and ahead of us. The visibility was good and we were at about 2000 feet. Excitedly, I tried to keep my eyes focused on that soon-to-disappear spot in the distant sea. A rush of adrenaline made my hands tingle. I turned towards our unexpected quarry in a shallow dive to lose height. I gave instruction to the wireless operator

'Make a signal, priority O break A.'

It had seen us, of course. We were a conspicuous silhouette against the sky, so much more visible than it, a small conning tower camouflaged against the changing colours of the restless, wrinkled, surface of the sea. It dived. How difficult it was, without any landmark or points of reference, to keep in my mind's eye, even for only two or three minutes, the point in the sea where some moving object had been. I lined up the aircraft on what I thought was its line of progress, but even that, its angle to our line of flight now, required some guesswork.

'I think this is the line, agree Alex?'

'Agree.'

'Bomb doors open.' Our stick of four depth charges was pre-set for the distance apart of each one's fall and for the depth at which they would explode. But my dive, necessary to lose height, was making me go too fast. I closed the throttles fully and lifted the nose a little, hoping we would not balloon too much. If I thought of putting down some flap I didn't. How far beyond its point of dive would it have gone? We were close on the water now, hurrying over the waves. Now!

'Bombs gone!' I pulled on the stick and turned a little to climb away to starboard; behind me the rest the crew watched the surface of the sea. They saw the four explosions and the hills of white water thrown up to the surface. As I continued on my turn I looked back over my right shoulder and saw the green and foaming water still in turmoil. Circling round, we watched. Watched for oil. Watched for wreckage or any flotsam. None came up.

Then, on our second circuit, it surfaced again. It was within the circle we had described, quite near our drop. We cannot have been very far out. But now, of course, our depth charges were gone. Was it because its captain knew this that it had surfaced again, or because it was damaged? I flew round again to attack and dived onto it, firing with my not very lethal .303 Brownings, hitting its conning tower as it dived again. Again, we circled and quite soon it surfaced for a second time. I lined it in my sights, flying quite close to the water. I fired again. I saw the tracer rodding towards its conning tower, seeming to enter, as tracer does. As I climbed away, turning tightly, banking, Menzies in the turret also got in a burst of fire.

Those aboard must know now that their assailant had no more depth charges. I wondered if some of its crew would come out of the conning tower and fight it out. The U Boat would have better armament than ours. Making another circuit, I came in again in a shallow dive. No one was on deck, and I gave another burst to keep it that way. Once again it dived. We circled around, watching so keenly that patch of empty ocean. Nothing appeared.

We now gave some attention to our fuel supply; we should look pretty silly if we had to try to pancake on the sea and then, should we have been successful, be picked up as prisoners by our quarry. We climbed higher, radioing our signal again from increased altitude and watching the skies towards England for sight of any relief. None came. We circled, watching that area of the sea where the recent activities had been taking place. We had none too much fuel. We had been, after all, on our way home, and I had used a lot of throttle in the last half-hour or so. We made our calculations and reluctantly we turned for home. As we left, while it was still in sighting distance it surfaced again, heading towards the French ports.

We got back, but with little petrol to spare. Our debriefing was longer than usual and Alex had tried to record accurately our track and speed home to give as accurate a fix as possible for the submarine's position when we had left it.

The Admiralty's verdict next day was 'Probable, Damaged'. I and my crew could not know how true their deduction was, or how skilled had been their interpretation of the U Boat's behaviour.

In the days, and more particularly in the long nights, that followed, I wondered how far out our depth charges had been. Were they a little to the left or to the right? Were they ahead of the point the U Boat had reached under the water when I believed we were right over it, or were they just behind? At the time it would have been good to have blown it up, to have rid the sea of just one of those sneaking, evil predators, which had drowned or burned or torn in pieces perhaps hundreds of brave men in merchant ships that could not retaliate. But then I thought I was rather glad that that lonely patch of turbulent water was not stained black with oil in which things floated while we circled overhead incapable of giving any help. That would have been the worst. To have to fly off home and leave behind, struggling in the water, wounded, drowning, men, calling out for help to an emptiness from which none could come. Not that they themselves had probably often stopped, if ever, to help the victims of their merciless torpedoes; but that did not alter my thinking. What I preferred to think was that the Admiralty was right. Perhaps the U Boat's plates were weakened by the blast. All right for limping home on the surface but with joints not watertight enough to stand the pressure if submerged. Or perhaps there was some trouble with its generators on which so many of its functions depended. Generator trouble or buckled plates would tie it up in dock and use up precious shipwright man hours, and keep just one U Boat out of the hunt for Allied shipping for weeks.

An early November day dawned fair. There was no cool wind off the sea, and autumn sunshine gave a promise even of spring. It was warm enough for me to sit against a sand dune. A tussock of marram grass formed my lectern. I watched the waves breaking on the yellow sand. They provided the only sound; a gentle crash and then the small shingly hiss as the water of each wave was drawn back, taking with it pieces of seaweed and powder puffs of foam, glittering in the low sun. I was composing my thoughts for a letter to Sally. I felt a lonely sadness. I loved three girls. Had I lost Jill? She was far away in Lincolnshire. I sensed it was unlikely that we would meet again.

Had I lost Katherine? Our separation, she in London, I in farthest Cornwall, was not of my making. Those who decided such things, it seemed to me, took pleasure in uprooting me. Since I had come to St Eval I had not been very happy. It was my day off, but I had no girlfriend to share it with, no one there to love. Those whom I had loved, who had loved me, were far away and probably loved some other. I thought of Katherine. She was lovely, but she was driving senior officers about London and beyond. Each one of them would fall in love with her. They would have her often close, close enough to press their suit upon her and wear down her resistance. Senior officers, men in authority, offering her their adoration. She had once said that power was an aphrodisiac.

There was still Sally. Her home and my home were near together. It had become almost expected of me to take my short periods of leave at home, to see my mother, and my father too if he also had leave. Often Sally, bless her, took leave when I was at home if she could, but because of the journeys involved there was little time. She was at a Fighter Command station in south-east England, moving the plots of our fighters and of incoming German bombers about on a great table under the anxious eyes of controllers. 'Angels Twenty – Red Leader.' I imagined the voice of the controller. 'Can you see them now?' There would be a tense atmosphere in the room. The plots came together, and, she had told me, she could imagine the twisting, turning flight, the stutter of gunfire, the trail of flames and black smoke of someone going down. It was the world in which she lived. She would think my world very dull. She had written to me – I took her much re-folded letter from my pocket.

'I worry about you, Peter dear, when I think of your lonely aeroplane miles out on the empty sea. Are you lonely? Are you bored?'

So she thought my world, my work, boring. Perhaps it was, compared with hers.

Two seagulls on the sand, picking over pieces of flotsam, looked up as a crow flew over them, and putting up their heads, called a sad, mournful mew. Maybe she was right. My work was dull, without the spice of danger or the glamour of her fighter boys.

But how ridiculous! Why should it matter if she thought my work dull? How absurd to think that if a man's work was dangerous, very dangerous, she would love him, more! But then, if power was an aphrodisiac, perhaps danger, bravely faced, was also. On leave, in pubs and restaurants, I had seen the admiring looks of girls towards a man with the white and purple ribbon of a DFC or an MC above the pocket of his tunic. Yes, that was an aphrodisiac too.

I pulled a pad of paper from my pocket, and a pen.

You ask me, darling, if I am lonely or bored. Lonely sometimes, yes, but never bored. Even as I walk towards the Operations Room wondering what's in store, and especially, what the weather's going to be, there is a stirring in my stomach. That is not because of boredom. Soon I shall lift my aeroplane off the ground and cross the coast and head out to sea. Soon there will be no land in sight.

There are four of us in the aircraft, but still it can feel very lonely. Sometimes low cloud and rain will press me down on to the surface of the sea. It will be difficult to see forward or to either side of me: then I shall be too busy flying the thing and keeping it from crashing into the water to notice if I'm lonely or bored. If you had heard an engine cough when far out to sea, and wondered if it's going to fail; if you had seen a whale smack the water with a tail as big as both my wings; if you had come home to find the sea-mist blotting out the land, or seen the sunlight twinkling in the rock-pools of a Cornish cove, you would know that I am never bored.

The days grew shorter. Evening and darkness came sooner out at sea as we finished our details and headed back to Cornwall to land in the dusk or by the dim lights of the airfield. Nothing much happened. Perhaps I was becoming a little tired. I had been flying with the squadron for over fourteen months and many of those I had known at Leuchars, even at Aldergrove, had gone, posted away on rest. Some had been killed. Like Douglas, with whom I had come new to the squadron in September of the previous year. Like Watson, who had not returned from escort duty – probably visibility was too poor and the cloud base too near to the sea's surface for him to see where he was going. Like Jenkins, whose burnt out remains had been found at the base of a Donegal cliff, which presumably he had hit. There were others, too. With only a few days of the month to go, my lethargy was broken by news that I was to be posted, to go on 'rest'. This meant going into Training Command.

The alternatives for my future employment included being a flying instructor, becoming some senior officer's PA, or going back to school to learn something. I thought I had become quite a competent and reliable pilot. Certainly, I had had enough practice at flying low over land and sea, peering ahead of me through rain and drizzle close to the hedges or close to the hurrying waves under the cloud base without flying into a tree or into the water, or so I thought. I knew I was too shy to be a good PA. Being 'escort' to the Duchess of Gloucester had showed that. So I thought I would take the opportunity to learn something. I had known, definitely I had assumed, that it was almost certainly poor navigation that had so often been the undoing of crews that had not made it home, so I would go on a navigation course. There was a 'Long N', really leaving no stone unturned, but I knew that my mathematics would be too weak. I put in for a 'Short N', and wondered where it might lead me.

At first I was delighted to be leaving the squadron, possibly proving how much I needed a change. And I had never been very happy at St Eval. After those wonderful months in Ireland with Jill anywhere else would be second-rate. Leuchars had been fun too, perhaps for being my first taste of operational flying. I realised, though these things are hard to quantify in retrospect, how lucky I had been. I had completed a tour of operations but had almost never had cause to be shit-scared. There had been times, of course, when things had looked a bit dicey. Enduring in my mind's eye was the view when I was photographing Stavanger aerodrome at low level, looking down at all the Messerschmitts in their dispersals and wondering how quickly they could scramble and teach my prying eyes a lesson. There had been the day when we had been provisionally briefed to go up the estuary at Lorient for a low-level 'shipping' strike, a job from which there would have been no coming back, and then, quite unexpectedly the cup had passed from me. It had been anxiety rather than fear those last fourteen months.

The day of my departure came closer. I must not make a mistake now and write myself off in my last few days. On my last night I went to bed perhaps a little tight. I had downed more glasses with well-wishing friends than was my custom. I was feeling, too, perhaps, that I did not want to leave. Harry Rowntree, who had had his girlfriend, now fiancée, and her parents, down to the Watergate Bay Hotel, took over D for Dog, the aeroplane I had most frequently flown for the past four months, and flew it that night. In the morning, everyone awoke to hear that coming back from the Bay of Biscay, he had flown into the Falmouth balloon barrage. There were no survivors.

At breakfast that morning I said goodbye at the Watergate Bay Hotel. There was an atmosphere of gloom. Although we had learned to come to terms quite quickly with the loss of friends, Harry's death, made known to us at the psychologically vulnerable hour of early morning, meant that we had lost a very jolly companion. No doubt there was similar gloom that morning in the Sergeants' Mess, for Harry's new-formed crew had been three sergeants. Everyone had liked Harry, and liked, too, the young girl he had brought down so recently to Cornwall, for the declaration of their engagement. The telegram they had perhaps dreaded would not yet have arrived at his parents' home, so not yet the shattering 'phone call to the girl with whom he had chosen to spend the rest of his life.

I could see in my imagination the twisted crumpled metal of Hudson D for Dog, blackened by fire, lying near the foot of the steel hawser that tethered the barrage balloon on the outskirts of Falmouth, which had cut off her wing and hurled her down to hit the ground and burn. Of all the squadron's losses, 'own goals' like this were so sadly wasteful.

I said goodbye to Alex. I had bidden farewell to Miller and Menzies in the carefree atmosphere of the previous evening. They were not leaving. I had been much longer in the squadron than any of them, but they were to stay together. Now Alex would be captain of aircraft with a second pilot to join him.

'Good luck, Alex. You'll be all right. Your methodical bloody carefulness will see you through. I owe to it the fact that so far I've avoided a fate like Harry's, and I thank you.'

A serious-minded chap, Alex, he was neither a real party man nor the loner that I was. His responsible manner had kept us out of trouble often in the recent months we had flown together as a team. We had all got on well together, but they had not expected me to go on the razz with them, pubbing and clubbing as a happy inseparable drinking partnership as some crews were. Nor would they be with Alex.

In an hour or so I should be boarding a train. I cast my mind back to another train journey more than a year before. Would someone have to take Harry's charred body back to his home as I had had to take the young dead air gunner from Leuchars to Dunbar? Nowadays I doubted it but someone would probably go to the funeral.

CHAPTER EIGHT

Katherine

As transport took me to the station to begin my train journey, I looked back at the blue sea, at the golden sand, at the green grass and yellowing bracken on the cliff tops. I had been spoilt for colour and crystal-clear air at the coastal stations of Coastal Command: Silloth, behind the Cumberland sand dunes; Leuchars, washed by North Sea winds; Aldergrove; neighbour to the Atlantic but for the pure green meadows of the Irish countryside and the 150 square miles of Lough Neagh; and St Eval. Now it would be different.

I had a series of train journeys, changing at Bristol and several other stations. As I travelled up through the Midlands to the industrial north and to smoke-grimed Cheshire, which was to be my destination, the difference became more and more apparent. It was raining now, out of a leaden sky. A grey, sun-excluded afternoon was darkening into evening. After the tanned country folk of seaside Cornwall, the people who hurried by my carriage window at wet, gas-lit stations looked pale and ill. I remembered a letter my father had written describing a train journey through northern towns in this same drab month of November. Seen through his dirt-grimed window in the damp mist and in the cold light of dimmed, black-hooded gas mantles, tired white-faced people, their shoes wet from platform puddles, pushed past one another to peer into the crowded carriages for a vacant seat 'like codfish swimming in a sea of graphite'. So it was now.

Finally, the train stopped in a hiss of steam near Middlewich at Holmes Chapel, a name evocative of dark Satanic mills. I got out and enquired how I should get to RAF Cranage.

I dreamed that I was still in Cornwall. The view from my window quickly dispelled such images. Hereabouts there was much chemical industry. I saw, through the smoke-dirtied air, steam issuing from a vertical pipe among gaunt factory chimneys. The smell of sulphur hung, rank. At breakfast I had my first look at my fellow students on this 'Short Navigation' course. About half were navigators, wearing the half-brevet, which had one wing clutching a circle containing an N. Just one or two had the old 'observer' brevet, which had no N, leaving the circle empty, known as a 'flying arsehole'. This badge was proudly worn by those entitled to it, as many things are if they show that the wearer was qualified well before his fellows. The other half were pilots, like me, with the full, two-winged, brevet. SN Instructors' Navigation Course at No. 2

School of Air Navigation Cranage, for this was where I was, had only one course going through at a time, so we were all grouped into one class, and back we all went into a day made up of 'periods', one subject at a time.

From RAF Cranage I was dispatched to the Elementary Air Observer School, at Eastbourne, to be an instructor and course leader of air navigators coming into the Air Force for flying duties.

The greatest delight of Eastbourne was being able to go up to London by train every second weekend. One Saturday, I went up with two or three friends and we stayed, as usual, at the Cumberland Hotel. Late on Sunday afternoon, we were passing through the hotel lobby, about to leave for the station to catch our train to return to Eastbourne. I saw three girls in FANY uniform walking upstairs. My eyes were drawn to the tightly tailored uniforms. One of the girls turned her head to speak to one of the others and I saw her profile. It was Katherine – Katherine of the copper-beech-in-spring-sunshine hair. Katherine of Cambridge and, so briefly, Salisbury. I was at the foot of the stairs in three bounds and was hurrying up after them.

'Katherine!' I got her attention and she dropped back.

'Darling! Oh, how wonderful!' For a moment, we each drank the other in. I seemed to lose the power to speak. My mind was racing. I must, I must, see her again. If I delayed and was late back for duty I might forfeit the privilege of coming to London next time. She was even lovelier than before. I wanted to hold her, to pour out to her the fierce emotion, the longing, which suddenly ran like fire through my whole body.

'Katherine, please, darling, hear me! We've got to leave now to catch a train, but I can come to London again in a fortnight's time. Please say that you'll see me, see me here – exactly here – at 4 o'clock on Saturday in a fortnight.' She looked at the watch on her wrist, it was 4 o'clock, then up at me and smiled that lovely smile.

'Yes,' she said happily, deliberately.

The two weeks passed slowly, but then, I was on my way. My train was running late. In an agony of anxiety I looked at my watch, looked again, and again. She would think that I was not coming. But she was there, on the stairs at the Cumberland as I had asked her to be. There, on the stairs, I took her in my arms, squeezing to me this lovely girl in her FANY uniform.

'We've got rooms at the Savoy. Let's get a taxi.'

On my return to Eastbourne two weeks ago, I had written to the Savoy and booked two rooms. I had booked a double and an adjoining single, for propriety, with a bathroom between. The price in those price-regulated days would be 48 shillings, which included breakfast being brought in on a gate-legged table on wheels by two waiters when one telephoned down for room service.

Afternoon tea was brought to the privacy of our room. In that interval of refreshment we looked at each other over our porcelain cups, the names of all others forgotten in our excitement at our reunion. I rang for the tea-things to be taken away and the door was closed. We sat together on the large bed in the bigger room. More than a year had passed since I had seen her. If it were possible, she was even lovelier than before. She lay back across my lap, her head on the pillow, and looked up at me. Her face was pensive, even wistful.

'Darling, you were my first. And I promise no one has touched me since.' Her lips were parted, and she paused. 'I was your first, wasn't I? I want us so much to have been each other's first.'

'You were, my sweet, you were the first girl I ever touched. You were the first girl I ever went to bed with. But you look troubled.'

'I've been wondering. You remember that I had "the curse", that time. Does a wet tummy count?'

'Yes darling, I'm sure it does.' We both laughed happily at this decision, rolling on the bed together and kissing. 'This will crease your immaculate uniform. I think we are both a bit overdressed. Will you have first bath, or not bother?'

'You go first. Then sit here on the bed and wait for me.' I left my clothes in the smaller bedroom and when I had finished in the bathroom I called her. After a minute or so I went into the other room and sat on the bed.

Not long after I had heard the sound of water running away the door opened and there she was. She stood in the doorway, hands level with her shoulders, holding each side of its frame, and she was naked. It was as though a goddess had suddenly appeared, and I leapt to my feet. I was speechless, but I held out my arms and with a shy smile she walked towards me. I took one step forward and fell on my knees before her. Even from lower down she looked tiny. My forehead was against her tummy and my hands, behind her bottom, pulled her close to me. She too, pressed me to her body with her hands behind my head. So, I on my knees, she standing, with her legs a little apart, I worshipped her.

She was conscious of feelings inside her body that she had never felt before. Her head was back, her eyes were screwed tight shut, her breath came quickly. I felt the thrill, the yearning, swelling inside me. I got to my feet. I picked her up and gently laid her on the bed.

I must have dozed off, because later, with returning wakefulness, I knew that she was beside me, and she was sleeping. Oh, dear God she was beautiful! Then she stirred, and opened her eyes and smiled. She looked so happy.

'Are you hungry, darling? I mean, in the ordinary way? 'Cos I've booked a table at Hatchetts in Piccadilly. You know – where Stephan Grapelli plays.'

'Oh Peter, I'd love that, I've heard him on the wireless, with the Hot Club de France.' So, as evening came, the bath was filled again. I dressed quickly so that I could watch her, and then we went downstairs and got a taxi.

Every two weeks while I was at Eastbourne Katherine and I met on Saturday afternoon in London, usually at Gunter's Tea Shop in Curzon Street. I tried to get there before her and secure a table. I would watch for this gorgeous creature to arrive, see her look around the room for me, see her recognise me as I stood up to beckon to her, and see the delight on her face as she walked towards me. We always stayed at the Savoy and we went to the theatre or to Hatchetts. She enjoyed the ballet, but most of all she enjoyed Hatchetts. Everyone was in uniform except, of course, the waiters and the band and Stephan Grapelli himself. He often came on to the floor and danced with some of the girls, he in his shirt and Mediterranean-cut trousers and cummerbund. He seemed to like the look of Katherine and quite often asked to dance with her. Certainly, she looked an attractive little bundle with a lovely smile and eyes that twinkled.

It was wonderful for me to hold her as we danced together, remembering our times together at Tiffin's at Cambridge. But dearest of all were the times at the Savoy. She looked delicious as she stepped out of the bath and tumbled into bed.

On Sunday mornings, we would take a Green Line bus to Hertfordshire, out to the end of the lane where my parents lived, and walk up the lane and have lunch at Tiled Cottage. Then in the late afternoon I took her back to Victoria, where I saw her off on her train to Camberley and I caught mine to Eastbourne. They were happy times, which I in my new, safe job sometimes felt that I did not deserve. My parents approved of Katherine, and liked it that we brought them into our happiness. That summer went quickly, and with regular meals and hours, and a girl to adore and to look forward to, seaside sunshine and plenty of exercise, I was very fit.

We were very lucky that on every one of the precious alternate Saturdays that I was at Eastbourne we were able to meet. Never did anything prevent us, though one Saturday Katherine related a near disaster.

'Oh darling, I was so worried yesterday. I thought I was not going to be able to come today. We have this large and really masculine-looking woman called Pam, who is the CSM. Last evening, she was having a big blitz about the hair of some of us being too long. She was shouting angrily. She even cancelled today's weekend leave for three poor girls. I knew that my hair was rather beyond the permitted length. As she came along the line I was convinced I would be gated too. I really trembled! But when she got to me she touched my hair and said 'I know it's very pretty hair, but you must cut it a little shorter.' And then she passed on and I breathed again. I think she rather likes me, and some of the other girls call me 'Pam's Pet'. They say I get away with murder.'

The next time we met after Katherine had related this incident I could tell by her appearance of contained excitement that something had happened and that she was eager to confide in me as soon as we were in the privacy of our bedroom.

'Darling, the most awful thing happened on Thursday. I was in the room where we can go to wash our smalls. I was just about to wash a pair of knickers, and in came the CSM.[Katherine put on a gravelly voice.] 'So there you are darling.' She came towards me and pinned me against the wash basin and started kissing me. I was so astonished that I suppose I did not show soon enough how disinclined I was. She went down on her knees on the floor and tried to lift the hem of my skirt. I think she was about to – you know — I was horrified, and tried to push her away but not very successfully, so I stepped sideways – and she fell over! I have been dreading since that she would be angry and try to punish me in some way, but she's as nice as pie whenever we meet, or else she behaves as though she has not seen me.'

Not long before the time had come when once more we were to be separated – after nearly a year of being able to look forward to the Heaven of being together every second weekend – Katherine told me in some alarm that she was being moved to Cardiff. She was at that time allocated as driver to a Brigadier, and he was going to take up some appointment there. She had already been embarrassed by his insistence that she come into the Officers' Mess with him, she a non-commissioned FANY. 'You are my driver and you go where I go,' he had said. Then one day in the car he was all over her, saying that he was madly in love with her and wanted to marry her, and she had great difficulty repelling his advances. Fortunately his interest in her was quite apparent to some of his fellow officers. Someone must have dropped a hint to those in even higher authority, and she was moved back to Camberley. It was a reprieve.

I knew that Katherine was driving senior Army officers about in London, and was always worrying myself sick about her being in the air raids there, which, though nothing like as bad as they had been, were still happening. One time we were together, at the Savoy, there was a warning. We were asleep when the horrible wailing siren began. Waking, I asked her if she would like to dress and go down to an air raid shelter.

'What? . . . Goodness me, no. If I'm going to die, it's going to be in your arms, not on some dreary tube-train platform.' So I gathered her more closely to me. She was warm-smelling and divinely cuddly and trying to arrange that she was as much underneath me as possible – a situation with which I had no quarrel. In the morning neither of us could remember having heard the all-clear.

CHAPTER NINE

Shropshire

One evening we marched to the station and filled a special train, travelling by night to Shropshire. Once again, I was heart-broken to know that I would be so far away from Katherine's Camberley, but that was service life in wartime. We arrived at a large camp of Nissen huts and larger wooden buildings and two or three parade grounds, and the Navigation School was joined there by an Initial Training Wing, at which newly volunteered aircrew were drilled, hardened and taught discipline.

The camp was a few miles from the pretty old town of Bridgnorth, a town cut in two by the River Severn. On one side was the 'lower town', down by the river. Across the water was the older half, where narrow, ancient streets climbed between houses built centuries before, many of them half-timbered, firmly founded on a rocky hill. The camp was within walking distance, certainly within cycling distance, of some beautiful woodland country. My friend Hugh and I did some fishing in woodland pools, at first surreptitiously, but then we met the owner of the local great house, a retired Colonel, and it was legalised. He bred beautiful black retrievers, and it was rumoured that his home housed some of the Nation's art treasures for wartime safekeeping.

In a narrow wooded valley on his land there was an assault course laid out with fallen trees and rope ladders and awkward walls to climb, used by Army units and occasionally by Air Force people. I witnessed with horror the sad waste of a soldier when he had his calf blown off by the over-enthusiastic use of gun-cotton mock hand grenades as men ran through a muddy pool.

As well as being a Course Instructor, I was given the job of Station Entertainments Officer.

I got together a band, with some excellent players, by no means all of them drawn from the changing population of airmen under training. They were primarily a dance band. One Sergeant Williams with characteristically widely blown-apart teeth was a splendid trumpet player. They were also, after a while, able to march reasonably well, providing drum-beat and oompah-oompah for parades. They co-operated well because I got fixtures for them off the camp. People requiring a good dance band were prepared to pay good money. It augmented the grant I got for instruments and paid for transport with enough over for distribution to the players. I always went on these 'away fixtures' with them to keep control of the situation, which, apart from one thing missing, was fun.

I craved female companionship. I'd been on the station for nearly six months; I'd written to Katherine and had received letters back, but this was not enough. I had never much enjoyed all-male company. Singing Rabelaisian songs around a beer-soaked piano and overstraining my stomach's fluid capacity with pints of stuff of which I did not even like the flavour had no appeal for me. I had always preferred the company of a girl, not necessarily for sex – though an attractive girl's generosity in that direction was usually most grate-fully accepted – and the sight of many very desirable WAAFs about the station increased my need. I felt this particularly strongly when I accompanied my 'dance band' on the fixtures that I had arranged. I mentioned this problem to my friend Hugh who had a ready explanation.

'Some of us need crumpet more than others. Your desire for yet another but locally available girl is Nature's way. Males produce millions of sperm, with the potential to fertilise many more eggs than can grow into little boys and girls. So males instinctively know that they must have access to females to make the most of their extravagant production. Eggs, produced by a female, each require a lot of energy to make and only a few can be produced in a girl's lifetime. The limit on how many babies can be reared does not lie with the males, it is the number of eggs that females can make available. So males have a strong desire for girls – almost any girl who attractively offers herself – while for the benefit of the race, girls need to be, and can afford to be, choosy. They accept only the fittest males – though you will agree that they often seem to have difficulty in telling which they are. Frankly, I do not believe this 'company of a girl not necessarily for sex', statement of yours, I think that you are just a danger-ously randy flight lieutenant, and probably glibly persuasive.'

What he had begun with a straight face ended with a broad grin as he realised I had started to be taken in by his biological analysis.

'Thank you. I assume that you are making excuses for me and that it is not too awful of me now to want to make some mutually beneficial arrangement.'

'That you say "mutually" means that you believe yourself to be one of the "fittest males" but I think that every poor little WAAF on the station ought to be warned to avoid your advances and beware your conceit.'

As often before, it bothered me that I was in love with three girls. 'How are the Three Graces?' Hugh would sometimes tease me. 'Has Paris made his judge-ment?' The strength of my affection swung uncontrollably from one to another. When I felt most in love with one I was unable to shrug off a feeling of guilt that I was neglecting and in some way being unfaithful to the other two. Anyhow, it seemed most unlikely that I could expect to see in the forseeable future any one of them. Yet I felt a very strong need for feminine company. Sometimes I had to admit to myself that my need was in fact more than that. If

I was now to form an attachment with some other girl, I realised that I would be being unfaithful to all three of them at once. There were several WAAF officers in the Mess, but though two in particular had fairly openly shown an interest in me I found it impossible to reciprocate. Outside the Mess, though there were several mouth-wateringly desirable people whom my friend Hugh would call 'crumpet', Katherines, Jills and Sallys were nowhere to be seen even as dim reflections of their originals among the girls on camp.

Dand did not make objection to discreet liaisons between officers and airwomen. It was not difficult to find convincing employment for decorative but unmusical WAAFS when the band was playing away. One such was Audrey, whom I asked to accompany us on our next and imminent 'away fixture' of the band, on the quickly invented explanation that I needed someone to be 'Secretary to the Band', keeping details of bookings, payments, etc. It did not convince even myself, but no questions were asked, so no explanations were necessary. That first fixture, at a private party in Bridgnorth, was much more enjoyable for me than any of those previously. One of the guests enquired about the band's availability for a similar party, which was of course entered in a suitable-looking book by Audrey with every show of application and efficiency. We danced together, and Audrey left me in no doubt about her affection for me. Other away fixtures followed, and very quickly a bond developed between the two of us.

Audrey and I began to meet off the station for evening walks. Down a narrow way perhaps a mile and a half from the camp, a deep lane ancient as the trees which overhung it, ancient as the trees which had grown there before them, ancient when early Mercians went that way, we came upon an isolated cottage where an old woman lived. Her only neighbours were her own few chickens, which we found her penning into the safety of their shed as the sun went down behind the elms at the end of her cottage garden. We stopped to talk to her and she made us very welcome.

It was the first of many meetings, because for a reasonable fee most gladly given, augmented sometimes by a little gift we brought her, she would cook for us a supper of fried potatoes and an egg with tea and her home-made bread. We would eat this while she chatted with us in her low-beamed room. When we had finished she would take away our plates and tea cups and then return, settle herself in her chair and turn down low the wick of the oil lamp so that it was almost dark except when the embers of the wood fire sometimes flared and tiny red-hot sparks, like soot-goblins' eyes, made widening circles and outline pictures for our imagination on the lampblack surface of the old fireback. And there she sat, a kindly, unobtrusive voyeuse, knitting almost silently while we cuddled happily on the floor near her feet.

'I like you coming here,' she said on one such occasion. 'It warms me to see that you love each other.'

Staring into the embers, wrapped around Audrey, I would hear, or thought I heard, ancient voices in an ancient place. I heard the teams of draught horses that passed there in the mornings, perhaps even the teams of oxen on their way to plough their carucate* in the open field; small bands of soldiers, in leather jerkins and helmets, confident and laughing in their companionship; Gray's ploughman plodding home to his half cottage in his hamlet; and down the slope of time pairs of lovers walking slowly, pausing in the dusk and in the starlight, loitering in the sunshine of Sunday afternoons long gone, looking for somewhere to make love.

We went there often, and no one was any worse for our ritual; in fact, three people were made much happier. When service postings took Audrey and me away from Shropshire, I liked to imagine that we would remain a tiny part of the old woman's happier memories as she sat alone knitting in the lamplight, or dug a root of potatoes from her garden in that little bit of England where not much happened.

Dand was to go and set up a Leadership Course at Banff in the north of Scotland. There was talk of me going with him, but it came to nothing and I was posted to No. 7 Air Observer School (AOS) at Bishops Court in County Down in Northern Ireland, where the training of air navigators would take on a more practical form, in the air.

The thought of returning to Northern Ireland fanned the dormant fire of my love for Jill to a degree that was almost unbearable, even though she was still in England, at a Bomber Command station on the borders of Leicestershire and Lincolnshire, where mounting losses were distressing for her. I was allowed a few days' leave between Bridgnorth and Northern Ireland and I had already told my mother that I should be coming home to Hertfordshire. Sally was the main reason why I was heading in that direction. But I now felt also an inconsolable longing to see Jill again. Studying maps, I could see that it would be difficult but not impossible to get to Birmingham and thence to Coventry, Leicester and then Grantham, which appeared to be the nearest railway station to her aerodrome, without using up in travel almost all of my leave. I telephoned home, hoping to learn when Sally was expected, and hoping, too, that the dates would give me time to call at Bottesford on my way to Hertfordshire without missing her. There was no very clear answer to my question, but I now telephoned Jill.

'Of course, Peter dear, I should love to see you, but I cannot take any leave at present and the situation here is rather fraught. I will explain when I see you.' She sounded so woebegone, not at all like the happy, loving girl I had known.

I made the awkward journey to Bottesford, and got there not long before the squadron began taking off on the night's operation. I found a sad person, much affected by the awful losses being sustained by bomber crews whose misfortune it was to have to do their tour of operations in Manchester aircraft. As well as having many other vices, the Manchester fell out of the sky as often because of

---

* A carucate was a medieval measure of as much land as a team of oxen could plough in a season.

engine failure as because of enemy action. The two-engined Manchester was underpowered and not up to the formidable task of the long night flights into the heart of a fiercely defended Germany that these young men were being required to undertake. Bomber crews averaged only a one in three chance of completing their thirty trips. Only once did anyone succeed in bringing a Manchester home on one engine.

Jill had attended the briefing that day. The target was Hamburg. There were clear skies and a big moon; ideal conditions for German night fighters to pick off the clearly visible aircraft that were probably struggling to get up to the height called for by Group plan. Jill's welcome to me was warm, but there was something held back compared with former times. I could see that her mind was wholly occupied by her anxiety for these young men among whom she was living and working.

> 'It's awful. We lost four crews last night, including B Flight Commander, who was a dear man who had less than five ops to go to finish his tour; such terrible bad luck, when he was so near to reaching the safety of going on rest. In the Mess at lunchtime today there was such a shadow of gloom, and that bodes badly for tonight. I can't keep away from the Flying Control building when there's an op on. I feel I must be there tonight too. Bless you, you've come all this way to see me. Will you sit with me there? I'm sure the Controller will allow it. I know him quite well.'

I saw that there was nothing I could do to help her. Any attempt to console her would be counterproductive. So I sat beside her for five hours that evening, in the upstairs room of the Watch Office. The wide windows faced the darkening airfield. On the opposite wall a large blackboard was ruled in paint with vertical lines to make columns, into which were chalked each aircraft's letter, the name of its captain, and the time of its take-off. The last column was still blank, for none were yet due back. In due course, the time of landing of an aircraft's return would gratefully be chalked in by a tall, fair WAAF, whose duty this was tonight. Jill and I sat together at a small table in a corner. We were talking quietly. Three WAAFs sat at another, larger table. Two of them wore headphones and one of them was turning the pages of a magazine. These were the girls who, speaking on R/T at landing time, would give the instructions to each aircraft when it called up before it entered the circuit, giving it permission to join, perhaps to land, or stacking it among others above the circuit at 500-foot intervals. At another table sat the senior Flying Control Officer (FCO). In front of him were several telephones. One was green, the conversations and messages that passed through its wires were usually scrambled. Other phones were directed to the Fire Station, to the caravan at the end of the runway, or to similar places that might have to be alerted with great urgency.

A phone rang. The FCO answered it. His replies and slight deference suggested that it was a senior officer at Group. A junior officer at another table, with papers spread before him, was completing United Kingdom airfield serviceability forms. A door on to the balcony outside the wide windows opened and a wireless operator came in whom Jill recognised. His crew were not on tonight's battle order, but he had volunteered to be the one who would send and receive messages by Aldis lamp with aircraft in their dispersals before take-off and their requests for help would be passed to the relevant Section according to their need. It was imperative that no one used W/T (wireless telegraphy) or even R/T until much nearer to landing time. Once or twice the Station Commander called in.

The time when the squadron's aircraft could be expected home was approaching. The sound of engines could be heard and one of the WAAFs in headphones became alert. A small loudspeaker relayed a pilot's words.

'Humble *R Roger* downwind.' The WAAF acknowledged. Then about two minutes later, the pilot spoke again.

'*R Roger*, funnels.'

'*R Roger*, pancake.' When the aircraft had accepted her consent and landed safely, another tall WAAF chalked its time of landing into the last column on the blackboard.

It was quite a long time before another aircraft called up, but then one did, and after further delay, a third. I could sense the apprehension, sometimes excitement, sometimes dismay, in Jill's attitude. There was a longer delay. Jill's anxiety became almost tangible.

The atmosphere of tension in the room increased. Jill, a sensitive and soft-hearted girl, sat watching the blackboard from the shadows, as she had been doing night after night, for news. For aircraft that did not return, the column into which she longed to see chalked-in the time of their safe arrival home, remained blank. At the end of her vigil, there were five blanks. Five aircraft. Thirty-five faces from Station life. Missing. Believed killed.

I had hardly spoken throughout her vigil. When the ordeal was over and hope abandoned I took her hand.

'Darling, you can't go on like this. Your nerves are shot to pieces by your worry. You must know that there is very little you can do.'

'I know, Peter, but I'm a woman. Long before history began, women waited in the cave for their men folk to come back from hunting. There was nothing they could do to keep them safe, but when they returned the men would expect their women to welcome them and show them that they cared, that they worried for their safety. Nothing has changed, you see.'

Next morning I made an affectionate farewell to Jill and continued on my journey to Hertfordshire. I felt dejected and in a grey mood. I loved her, and was miserable to see her so unhappy and taking upon herself so big a share of the sadness of this bloody war. I hoped that she would be posted to another station, another job, where she could shake off this depression and become again her joyful, efficient self whom I had known before.

So I went back to Northern Ireland; not in a Hudson but on the night ferry from Stranraer. It was a very different Northern Ireland to which I was returning, one without Jill. But at least I would be flying again. At Eastbourne and at Bridgnorth I had done almost none. I did not know it, but I was now to spend nearly twelve months instructing navigators here at Bishops Court. It was to prove a particularly happy year, largely because I was to meet and spend it with another pilot, in probably the greatest friendship, with another man, of my experience. His name was Cyril Morris.

CHAPTER TEN

Cyril

The aerodrome was in County Down, close to the Irish sea coast, 5 or 6 miles to the south of the small village of Strangford and the sea-entrance to Strangford Lough; the town of Downpatrick lay about 7 miles west and the Mountains of Mourne rose away to the south-west. In almost traffic-free days it seemed very remote.

Among those who gathered in the Officers' Mess before lunch on that first day, there were mixed feelings about the fact that the aerodrome was not finished. It was not ready to be the home of No. 7 Air Observer School, its staff of pilots like Cyril and me and men of other professions and trades, or of course the young navigators who would there complete their training and be posted on to squadrons. Being plucked quite suddenly from one community and put down in another was commonplace, but if you were neither married nor too much in love and the posting did not mean separation, it was acceptable. You made new friends, developed new interests, and got on with whatever the job was. But to many, Downpatrick and its cinemas and dance-hall, its many bars and urban entertainments, seemed a long way away. There appeared to be very little transport, as yet, going in any direction to enable the young men posted there to spend their leisure time in ways preferred by most of them.

But to Cyril and me it seemed a paradise. We had been allocated, with a third officer, a Nissen hut at the furthest point from the centre of the station, only a few yards from the edge of a low cliff. The sea and rock pools were just below us, and a few hundred yards offshore there was a small island inhabited by several cows. We had found that we shared a number of interests. Among mine were sailing, whipping-in to a pack of foot hounds, and an untried enthusiasm for many activities of the countryside. I had other enthusiasms of a more bookish kind, but it was our enjoyment of country things that brought us together. Cyril was married with two very small boys, and the family had been living in the Isle of Man where he had been stationed. Apart from his family and enthusiasm for his pre-war job with Cable and Wireless, his greatest love was rowing, but sailing and rugby were close behind. He seemed to delight and excel in things that required the greatest physical effort.

We were talking together, that first lunchtime in the Mess at Bishops Court, when the station commander, G/Capt Alford, came up to us. We quickly learned of his love of sailing and of his delight in finding that two of his officers shared it. It seemed as though an idea was suddenly born.

'Many of the men we shall send out from here will one day find themselves in the middle of the sea in an inflatable K-Type Dinghy. None of them will be able to sail it. We will teach them how to, and you will be my instructors. Have you seen Strangford Lough yet?'

We admitted that we had not.

'It's a splendid piece of water, about 20 miles long by 4 or 5 miles wide, and it's said to have as many little islands in it as there are days in the year. There's a small sailing club towards the northern end, at White Rock. I'll lay on Air-Sea Rescue to take us up there after lunch. Be ready here at 2 o'clock.'

His staff car took us to the tiny fishing village of Strangford, a sleepy, pretty place on the western side of the narrowest point of the 5-mile long entrance to Strangford Lough from the sea, where tides of 6 or 7 knots boil through and the small open boat that was the ferry between there and Portaferry on the Ards Peninsula had to steer a course that was an almost semi-circular bow, certainly not a straight line, to allow for the tide race. We boarded the Air-Sea Rescue launch and with a high bow wave and a long white wake we went at great speed up the lough.

Grass did not grow under Alford's feet. He had telephoned the little yacht club, and in the enthusiasm of the moment we had quickly chartered, for an indefinite period, two of the club's Viking Class sailing dinghies, one for the station commander and one for us. It was a wet ride back down the lough to Strangford. That it was raining was immaterial; Cyril sat in one Viking and I in the other and we were towed behind the Air-Sea Rescue launch faster than those narrow little tall-masted boats had ever travelled before. We bailed furiously, and we arrived safely – wet, salty and exhilarated.

Alford and his wife had a house just round the corner in the lough, by a calm backwater accessible by road, and his Viking lay offshore on a mooring. Our Viking sat in a sheltered bit of the little harbour at Strangford on two anchors, and especially as it was now June, looked snug enough. The Vikings looked rather like hard-chine Dragons, but smaller, and ours was an emerald green. Soon we were all back at the station, very pleased with the day's events.

Sadly, the idea of learning to sail a K-Type dinghy, if that could ever have been possible, never materialised. The Group Captain had enemies as well as friends and soon afterwards he was court-martialled, it was reported, for making available an RAF flying suit 'outer and inner', to his son who was in destroyers.

We never liked his successor. And he did not like us.

Cyril and I had discovered Strangford. Something that I could not understand, was that no one else seemed to bother to do so. We alone, for nearly a year, enjoyed the charm of that little fishing village and the friendship and hospitality of its natives. Our Nissen hut was nearest to Strangford of any building on the aerodrome. An uneven path ran beside the water from our end of that north-easternmost dispersal towards the village, hugging the coast, climbing and descending with the contours, and our two bicycles went thither, back and forth, with every bit of spare time we had. We knew every clump of cranesbill, gorse and sea pinks along its route. It began as a path, was sometimes a track and for part of the way was a narrow, unfrequented road on which we were once stopped by a pedalling Royal Ulster constable and admonished for having no cycle lamps.

The fact that the aerodrome was not ready and our favour with our initial station commander, enabled us to establish our position. But soon the courses of trainee navigators began to arrive, the work of the station got underway and we did our share of what had to be done. This largely comprised flying Anson aircraft round the Irish Sea navigated by trainees, and trying to ensure that however foul the weather and low the cloud base, we did not fly into any of the walls of cliffs and mountains with which the Irish Sea is surrounded, or find ourselves over the hostile 'neutral' airspace of the Republic.

As flight lieutenants, rather than flying officers, pilot officers or sergeants, we were often 'duty officer' or 'briefing officer'. We not only flew round the Irish Sea, or wherever the training routes lay, but took responsibility for each day or night's exercises. We made the decision, based upon the Met forecast but bearing in mind the necessity for each course to finish on time and make way for the next, of whether flights would take off or whether it would be prudent for the men not to attempt it. No pilot flying in poor visibility and heavy rain at night towards the next turning point just short of Snowdonia, with his courses, speeds and heights given to him by a trainee navigator, thinks kindly of the duty officer who sent him forth in conditions that, to his own way of thinking, should have dictated a cancellation. Cyril and I almost always flew separately. One pilot to an aircraft with one or more trainee navigators was enough, but on the rare times when I had the opportunity to form an opinion, I had a high regard for Cyril's competence.

Of course, we had no idea of how long this posting would last for either of us: how long it would be before we would be sent away to other places or other duties. Photographic reconnaissance was my own stated preference. We were conscious that Bomber Command must be hungry for pilots as their losses, about 60 per cent over the whole period, required continual replenishment. Not that PRU offered a safe job. The enemy knew you were coming and where you would be. That, too, was usually quite a short life.

1943 was a good year not to be in Bomber Command, but, from a safety point of view, no year was. The year wore on. Summer became winter and the weather was worse. Although there is no great pleasure in bogging round the sky so that trainees can learn to make fewer mistakes and eventually go on to join the 40:60 win or lose lottery of the operational flying for which they were destined, our leisure time, our life whenever we could escape to Strangford, was very happy. We volunteered for as much night duty as possible. Thereby, particularly if one could forego some of the time allocated to sleep, we had more daylight hours for other pursuits. And we found that if we spent the maximum amount of time in the fresh air, well exercised, we needed less sleep.

The third member of our Nissen hut, a nice enough fellow but with interests more urban than ours, made arrangements to go to another hut quite early on, about the same time that we began to hang bait up to dry in its vicinity. We were left very much undisturbed, and so long as we were always available for whatever duties we were required for, no one cared when our two bicycles, generally without lights, came back along the path by the shore.

At first we had only the Viking. Then, somehow, we acquired two rowing boats, and later, 'the fishing boat'.

Speaking with Cyril once, I recalled:

When I was in Northern Ireland about two years ago, my girlfriend, Jill, had some friends, the Mackies, with whom we spent happy times in their garden, which ran down to the shore of Belfast Lough. They introduced us to friends of theirs who lived in Belfast but who also had an island on Strangford Lough on which they spent part of the summer. It was a dream place, where the two children, both boys, could lead a truly Bevis-like existence. I remember being a little shocked when their father sent them out to bring a chicken back to the kitchen, and they shot it with a bow and arrow. With Jill's little car Jemima, Belfast was accessible from Aldergrove, but now we shall need an alternative to Jemima.

Cyril's answer to the logistical difficulty was immediate. 'We'll sail there next time we have time off. Probably weekend we'll be more likely to find them at home on the island.'

We had no chart, but by taking frequent soundings with a lead-line and, in shallower water, with a pole, Cyril and I sailed up the lough to the inhabited island and renewed my acquaintance with the people there. They could not have been kinder. Their welcome when, out of the blue, the Viking arrived off their little jetty was memorable. They told us where to anchor, gave us a delicious chicken lunch and most generously lent to us 'the fishing boat'.

She was a sturdy, rather tubby, boat with a big working well aft and a small cuddy forward in which we could, at a pinch, sleep and cook on a primus stove. She had apparently worked in some South American port taking mails out to ships at anchor. She had the most unreliable four-cylinder petrol engine. Once we drifted on the ebb all night down the length of the lough and somehow managed to make over to starboard and into the tiny Strangford harbour before we were swept out to sea by the tide-race through the narrow exit from the lough. We found that the only way we could start it was on one cylinder. Then we would insert and screw in the other three sparking plugs as they pop-popped and jumped in our fingers. We were also able to borrow an 'otter' trawl, which eventually we lost when foolishly we had it out in the swirling tide in the lough's sea-entrance.

We made long-lines and we fished at night. We made lobster pots. Not that we ever caught any lobsters, probably because we had the bright idea (or so we thought) of making them by welding together four iron hoops and four iron bars as longerons. The noise they must have made on the seabed almost certainly frightened away lobsters, but we sometimes caught crabs. The bait that we had hanging up outside our Nissen hut helped to keep the hut ours and ours alone. Making the netting for the pots kept us busy for hours, having first made two netting needles out of shards of Perspex.

We occasionally made a contribution of fish or crabs to the Mess, but we had more friends in Strangford. Strangford, where no holidaymakers came, its little harbour retired through wartime disuse, was a place of wild flowers and peace. We enjoyed our fishing very much, even if it was not 'commercially' successful. Cyril had skill, quick reactions and considerable strength. I was grateful for that once when turning the boat through ninety degrees in an effort to get out of the tide-race, I stupidly got (for seconds only) on the wrong side of one of the trawl's warps. But for Cyril's quick action, I should have been virtually cut in two by the warp against the cockpit coaming. His peacetime rowing and international rugby had left him arms like hawsers.

Eventually early winter gales made us return 'the fishing boat' to her owners and the Viking to White Rock and to lay up the little boats. We were being called out too often because our anchors were dragging. But during the time we still had the Viking, by happy coincidence Cyril's wife Joan, without the boys, came for a short holiday to Strangford at the same time as my father decided to spend in Strangford a short spell of leave. Though aged 55 in 1943, Father, having been a full-time battalion adjutant to the Home Guard, with a good and gallant 1914–18 war record, had been given a General Service Commission and was able to come to Northern Ireland in uniform. He loved messing about in boats but it was something that he had had to forego for four years, because he had been forced, when war broke out, to put his *Nancy Blackett* into her mud berth at Pin Mill. He much enjoyed his leave. His praise of Joan was eulogistic, and understandably so. The two of them were able to sail together whether Cyril and I were there or not, and in the background was the wonderful kindness and hospitality of the Sharvins and Murphys.

The village was divided about 50:50 Catholic and Protestant. There was Castle Ward, seat of the earls of Bangor, and two other bigger houses, probably Protestant, also perhaps Mr Macdonald the ferryman, and others, but the nucleus of the place, and our especial friends, were the Murphy-Sharvins. The Sharvins were staunchly Catholic, and so was Jim Murphy, who had married Winnie Sharvin. They owned the only pub, a farm, and the taxi. The dregs of the Guinness were fed to the pigs, who permanently looked unconscious, dreaming and being fattened up in a sort of alcoholic suspended animation. Jim kept the pub, a plain single room with a bar and matchboarding walls, which was never full; Winnie ruled tirelessly over the kitchen; old Mr Sharvin was theoretically the farmer; and other members of the family would arrive from Dublin, stay, holiday, be happy and return.

I and one little niece who sometimes came with them were noticeably conscious of each other's presence. She was seventeen and a pure sweet colleen with a figure that would make the man of her choice very happy. The family was keen that she should be my wife and make me a good Catholic. The wages of being won over to the Faith could have been very agreeable.

There was no Protestant church but there was the Catholic one, and a picture-book priest who played Gaelic football quite fearlessly on the hillside field beside the grey stone church. Cyril and I took most of our meals in Winnie's kitchen. We were members of the family and her hospitality would have been embarrassing had it not been transparently clear that she would have it no other way. We sometimes had great teas at a house on the other side of the short broad roadway, which ran down to the shore past the pub. The road ended at the flower-grown slipway into the little harbour and at the short quay where Mr Macdonald took aboard or put off anyone brave enough to risk the sluicing eddying tideway of the crossing to or from Portaferry on the Newtonards Peninsula in his small open crab-boat. It was an elderly lady who dispensed the teas to us. We never saw another customer, and she did not charge enough for her good. It was there at Cyril's suggestion and to her amusement, there being no shortage of eggs, that we once ate a dozen each to no ill-consequence. Almost everyone we met in Jim Murphy's bar was Catholic, but there was a great friendliness, and no one ever threatened to burn down any of the bigger houses whose owners were of the other persuasion.

When autumn had turned to winter and we had laid up the boats, we under-took long walks. Particularly when a week's leave was imminent and we were about to return to England and our families' food shortages, we began to collect comestibles to take with us. It was pleasantly energetic to visit quite distant farms for eggs, which we vaselined and wrapped in lots of RAF lavatory paper for preservation and the journey. Rural Northern Ireland flowed with milk and honey compared with England. At the same time, to augment the meagre rations of our families in England, we took up shooting. We could get 12-bore cartridges from the station armoury, intended for clay pigeon shooting. The hospitality of local landlords, particularly the aristos of Castle Ward, gave us a wide country to range over: shore, woodland, hills and marshland. We took hares, plover, partridges, anything edible, back to Fort England, though I, increasingly averse to the killing of any animal, was forced to smother my conscience.

Our walks were a delight. It was a place of ruined castles, standing stones and circles, hills, woods and fields, ponds, streams and marshland, widely scattered little farms, and miles and miles of foreshore. The fauna, and as the spring of 1944 came, the flora, were full of variety. That part of the British Isles saw unusual seabirds, waders and migrants. We both enjoyed the challenge of pushing our endurance to the limit, and the feeling of healthy tiredness at the end of those walks, especially when one of Winnie Sharvin's fry-ups or a great tea across the road was the prize at the end. Though we ate well, neither of us drank more than a modicum of anything stronger than tea. We were both exceedingly fit.

We were not good RAF officers. We did our job, but we avoided Mess life. Probably our confidential papers showed a critical opinion of the way we kept ourselves to ourselves as far as the life of the station was concerned. The attitude to us of the station commander, Alford's successor, G/Capt Batson, was cool. On one occasion when on a wet and blowy night a fire hose with its heavy brass coupling had to be taken to the top of the station water tower, he sent for us. We liked climbing masts and things like that, he said (incorrectly) and we were to do it. I did not enjoy that long climb up the wet iron ladder in the dark.

'As he stood below with other watchers I think the bastard hoped we'd both fall off,' said Cyril.

'But to his disappointment we didn't,' I laughed, 'but there were moments when I thought that we would!'

Later Batson called us, separately, to his office and said that we should contribute more to station life. Of course, he was right. He told each of us that we were a bad influence on the other. Certainly Cyril had a strong personality, a ready smile and an engaging way with man or woman. He was able easily to be an influence, but the depth of our friendship made us together self-sufficient and kept us apart from the rest of the Mess except in our daily, or nightly, duties. Our home was the Sharvins: Winnie's kitchen; the piggeries, where sometimes we carried food and Guiness dregs to the quietly sleeping occupants; the plain but friendly bar with Jim Murphy; and the long green-painted room upstairs where, sometimes, when their Sharvin friends came up from Dublin, there was a party and dancing.

But the time was coming when we would be separated. Cyril went first, into Bomber Command through conversion courses on to Wellingtons, Halifaxes and Lancasters in Yorkshire, Nottinghamshire and Lincolnshire. I was glad to follow. Life at Bishops Court without Cyril would have been very empty.

CHAPTER ELEVEN

Bomber Command

In May, I went to the Beam Approach School at Watchfield near Swindon. For five days I flew Oxfords again. We flew by day. Although not actually blindfolded, we were required to wear spectacles that made it impossible to see anything but the instrument panel in front of us. It was rather like being in a Link Trainer, and through our headphones we heard the dots and dashes, which told us if we were on the beam or to the right or left of it as we came in to land

I did decompression tests. We entered a sort of diving bell and sat round a table wearing helmets and oxygen masks. The air was sucked out of the capsule in which we were sitting as though we were climbing to altitude, our bodies adjusting to the much-reduced pressure and our lungs dependent upon the oxygen coming through the masks. Someone in charge looked in at us through thick portholes of glass and maintained verbal contact with us by R/T. Then the pressure was allowed to return to normal atmospheric, the door was opened and there was an exit to a more normal world. But not for me. I had volunteered to remain in the capsule while the others made faces at me through the portholes. The pressure was reduced again and I was told through the R/T to play patience with the pack of cards that lay on the table before me. I was also to sign my name on the pad of paper there. I was a guinea pig. The difference from the first time was that there was no oxygen. I began to feel more and more drunk. At first it was the sensation of being pleasantly drunk but then I became increasingly anxious, then desperate, at my inability to concentrate. I was making a complete nonsense of my card playing. Now when I tried to write my name I could not get it right. I began to have doubts what my name was. Through the portholes I could see those idiot faces laughing at me. I felt terribly tired. My eyes would not stay open. I had no wish to continue with this ridiculous business of writing my name. I now couldn't remember what it was anyhow. Then I passed out. I had demonstrated to those present, and to myself, the folly of not putting on your oxygen mask and ensuring that oxygen was available to your crew and to yourself, before it became apparent that you were going to need it, which would be always. This was the case whether you were in a bomber aircraft at an altitude at which you could hope to avoid at least some of the lighter flak or were trying to be an invisible speck in the sky in a little pale blue PRU Spitfire or Mosquito.

*   *   *

I was not at Watchfield for very long. Rumour spoke of the imminence of the long-expected invasion of the continent. There were a number of men who were going to be 'ambulance drivers' flying Ansons, and Oxfords, to help in the evacuation of wounded. I still had hopes of getting into Photographic Reconnaissance and should soon know, because the Watchfield course was short.

Bomber Command's insatiable appetite for replacement crews disregarded my request for PRU, and I followed Cyril's path. On D-Day, I arrived at Finningley, a few miles to the south-east of Doncaster, and went back to school. Mainly, I was learning about Bomber Command procedures and about the Wellington aircraft that we were shortly going to fly. It was a remarkable aeroplane. Built on a principle invented by Barnes Wallace, the inventor of the bouncing bomb of the Dam Raids, it did not have longerons and ribs to form the skeleton of its fuselage and wings, like the hull of a small boat, but a framework of criss-crossing metal laths like the lattice that holds the diamond panes of a cottage window. Compared with other aeroplanes I had flown, it felt strangely flexible; you almost felt that the wings were flapping like a bird's as they took the stress of a banking turn or bounced in the uneven upcurrents of unstable air. You felt, too, that flak could blast holes in it and yet it would not break up.

Most importantly, we were beginning to form the crews in which we would fly when we got to squadrons. I met Colin Richardson in the Mess. He was a pilot officer navigator, an Essex man and proud of his county. I liked him at once. Sailing with my father before the war, I probably associated Colin's slight East-Anglian accent with holidays and pleasant times and people I was fond of. Quite quickly we both resolved that we would fly as a team. Together we decided to ask a young sergeant wireless operator, Derek Evans, to join us. Like Colin, he was nineteen.

Temperamentally, both Colin Richardson and Derek Evans were excellent aircrew material. Because I had flown a tour of operations I wore a ribbon beneath my wings brevet and this probably helped, as less experienced crew members might well think that if I had survived one tour I might survive a second, and they with me. Soon afterwards we collected another sergeant, Titch Aldred, a diminutive Lancashire boy, as our tail gunner. Being small, he probably had more room for his legs in the turret than many others. Ken Darley, another pilot officer, became our bomb aimer.

We moved to RAF Worksop, an aerodrome between the small towns of Worksop and Retford, and began to fly Wellingtons and to learn our various functions in the crew. We seemed to get on well. I did not do anything disastrously stupid in the pilot's seat to undermine their confidence in me as their pilot and captain of aircraft, and I was well pleased with their abilities and attitude to the job they had got to perform. They, or three of them certainly, were in their places in the aircraft while I was familiarising myself with flying a Wellington. We made countless 'circuits and bumps', in daylight and at night. In the two months that followed, we dropped practice bombs, fired our guns at towed targets, made cross-country flights, and did all the exercises that every one of the other crews on the course were similarly doing, which experience had shown were necessary or desirable if they were to go to a squadron, fulfil their task well and enhance their chances of survival.

Though we worked together and sometimes enjoyed time off together, I was grateful that they did not, to my knowledge, feel any disappointment that I was never one to seek opportunities for 'going on the jag' together as a crew. Drinking beer and singing rude songs round a piano were not my favourite form of fun. When I was 'stood down' or had an evening at leisure I was always happier in female company than in Mess life, the 'club life' of all-male company that most of my contemporaries seemed to enjoy. My year with Cyril showed that there could be an exception to my preference for a girl's company, but it certainly was an exception, and friendships like that are rare. Some crews, I noticed, always kept together in their evenings or days off. It was never my way.

In those almost traffic-less days, I rejoiced in the independence my bicycle gave me. On it I could escape to enjoy my own solitude or the company of a chosen friend. Aerodromes were, of necessity, in parts of the country where fairly flat terrain made the bicycle an ideal means of getting about. As my bicycle carried me along roads in those early summer evenings of 1944, I saw ahead of me grey, featureless lines of tarmac. Occasionally, there was another bicycle, much less often a service truck in camouflaged livery, sometimes someone walking, but mostly the road was mine for as far as I could see. The verges were wide and green, and alive with wild flowers.

Cyril was just ahead of me in our passage through the conversion courses that were our life in our first weeks and months in Bomber Command. We were posted from Finningley to Worksop, to Blyton or to Sandtoft, to Hemswell and so to a squadron. They were all in Lincolnshire or those parts of Yorkshire and Nottinghamshire that are nearby, but sometimes we were too far apart for cycling when free time was scarce. But during that time Cyril and I sometimes met, cycling over from our respective stations to some small village in between. One was Epworth, where John Wesley preached standing in the churchyard on his father's tomb. In the pub we played not darts but 'ring the bull', in which we took turns to swing an iron ring, suspended from the ceiling, on to an iron peg on the nose of a bull's head fixed like a trophy to the pub wall.

It was July, and we flew every day, and often at night, learning our individual and co-ordinated duties as a crew. Whichever Wellington we were allocated to use climbed without mishap into the sky and 'flapped' in that inimitable way of a Wellington's unique geodetic construction, while we performed and p-ractised our various exercises and unconsciously built up that ease of communication between us as crews who fly together must. Derek from his position amidships maintained that the wings really did flap, and on our first flight he was horrified by what he saw. He had heard tell that when the

Wellington was tried out as a glider tug the airframe stretched about 3 feet. We learned to recognise instantly each other's voice on the intercom so that we could detect at once a sound of stress or urgency, to be familiar with each other's slang, to share each other's sense of humour. The importance of this made men dislike having to fly in 'scratch' crews. In the same way, everyone strove to avoid, even apart from the element of superstition, having a stranger in the crew on an operational sortie as a substitute, though this was sometimes necessary.

It was customary for aircrew going through the conversion courses of Bomber Command to be sent on 'Nickels', sorties of not too hazardous a nature over enemy territory. These were not only valuable experience for them before they were required to fly deeper into Germany. The line they took over occupied France would also act as a decoy and make the enemy defences think that this probe pointed in the direction of the night's main attack. Usually these aircraft carried loads of paper leaflets to shower down on the French population and on the German occupation troops or the soldiers held there in readiness to be thrown into the attack against the invading Allied armies. It was ammunition in the propaganda war, which was intended to give hope to the French and sow doubt among the Germans.

As the swansong to our course at Worksop, in fading evening summer light we climbed our Wellington into the air and set off for the skies over occupied France. It was at the time when the early successes of the Allied invasion had slowed to a halt. Panzer divisions had been withdrawn from defensive positions that had proved to be the wrong ones and had been hurled against the British and American invading forces. I and my crew's target for all the propaganda with which we were to litter France was Angers, a town about 90 miles in from the west coast about level with St Nazaire, between Nantes and Tours. As we flew over Caen, we were able to look down on a landscape in which towns displayed their street-plans as what looked like a reticule of red-hot lines. So many of the houses that lined the roads were still burning. Among them, flashes of light were the guns, the shells, and the mortars of the battle going on.

We left the fires and gunflashes behind us as we flew on over Normandy and Maine and into Anjou. Below us was only darkness, a countryside quiet but doubtless alert and anxious, its people able to hear the distant gunfire and see on their northern horizon the red glow of battle. Sometimes lines of faint light picked their way along the unseen roads, kinking and slowing when, as I imagined, the truckfuls of reinforcement troops passed through a village that tried to sleep. Away from the coastal fires, where flames, glowing embers and the evil orange breath of guns made the background seem blacker by contrast, the blue-black velvet of the summer night was not really dark; up in the dome of the sky there was a faint opalescence as the last of today's daylight, now far out over the Atlantic, could reach us for a few moments longer round the curvature of the turning earth.

Titch in the rear gun turret kept his eyes roving, watching every part of the sky behind us. Though this was only a Nickel, over occupied France, it was the sky over enemy territory, where German night fighters would be patrolling. They would be waiting for the signal from their base in a captured French aerodrome to vector them on to any one of that night's approaching bomber streams or lone aircraft heading for the tideways outside the Biscay ports to sow their load of mines in the sea. Similarly Ken, in the nose, watched, as I did, the apparent emptiness of the sky ahead, and peered down at the almost featureless ground below, hoping to see the nearly imperceptible change of grey where a river wound its way through the landscape and perhaps give the navigator an accurate pinpoint. Behind me, surrounded by black-out curtains, Colin drew fine pencil lines on his chart, noting neatly in his log every detail of change in our present progress and plotting forward even to our planned return. He calculated and re-calculated our course and the time of our arrival and from each known ground-position laid off that third side of his triangles-of-velocities which was the deflecting wind, to plot our air-position and tell me of any change in course, however small, he wanted me to fly. Not far from Colin, Derek sat at his table, headphones on his ears, listening, changing channels, absorbed in the mysteries of his craft.

Each of us was at his station, learning the tasks we must perform and most of all gaining experience in the quiet combination of our duties to make a team whose quick and automatic response to each eventuality would help us to improve the chance of coming through a tour of operations with our lives intact – so far as our skills, our reactions might save us. Statistics showed that in every squadron losses were highest among crews at the beginning of their tour, in the first five or six operations before that teamwork had become as perfect as it could be. It was for this reason that crews hated change, hated the occasional necessity of a substitute, and perhaps why flight commanders and the most experienced captains not infrequently 'bought it', in contradiction of this statistic, when they had to fly with inexperienced crews to give them initial confidence on 'second dicky' flights.

We had come about 400 miles; we had perhaps another 100 to go. There was an occasional word from Colin on the intercom.

'Turn a fraction to starboard, Skipper, course 178, speed as now.'

Otherwise, all was quiet. Once, Titch broke intercom silence.

'Night fighter astern of us, passing port to starboard.'

'Watch it Titch. Derek, watch the rest of the sky astern.'

'OK Skip. I'm in the astrodome.'

Unnecessary chatter on the intercom was of course a sin we must all avoid. Then it was the voice of Ken the bomb aimer.

'I can see the Loire now, Skip. And the confluence of the rivers. We seem to be tracking in perfectly, steady as you go.' I glanced at my instrument panel and concentrated.

'Well done Colin.'

Then Ken again. 'Bomb doors open. Steady.'

'Bomb doors open.' I moved the lever as I repeated my bomb aimer's words. 'Come up and watch forward please Derek.' The wireless operator was beside me in an instant. Absolute accuracy with leaflets was not necessary as it would be with bombs, but for the benefit of practice Ken had the town of Angers tracking down the wires of the bomb sight.

'R-i-g-h-t, steady. Left-left. Steady, steady. Bombs gone! No hang-ups. Close bomb doors.'

'Close bomb doors.' As I repeated the instruction and pulled the lever to close the doors, Colin gave instructions for a new course.

'Course 320 degrees, Skip.'

I turned the wheel down to starboard, pushed the right hand pedal on the rudder bar and pulled back a little on the control column, watching the direction indicator turn through 135 degrees as the Wellington raised its port wing and banked round to starboard on to the new course. I checked the compass.

'On course 320. Are you on watch now, bomb aimer?'

'Bomb aimer on watch front turret, Skip.'

'Right. Derek, thank you, you can go back now.' The quiet figure beside me moved back to renew his W/T watch. Each of us now, except Colin still bent, as ever, over his chart, had a new view. We flew on almost north, aiming to pass between the German-occupied Channel Islands and the Cherbourg peninsula now being fought over by the Americans. Needless to say, some humorist at Briefing had gauged the hazards as about equal.

'Crossing the coast now.' Ken, in the nose, had seen it first. There below us were the burning battle-remains of St Malo. A little light flak was coming up from somewhere on the peninsula, someone shooting at something, and very soon on our port side a heavier gun on Guernsey made some fireworks rather nearer to us. Derek checked that our IFF, the radar device, identification friend or foe, which would give us safe passage over our own air defences, was on just before we crossed the south coast of England. We made our way up the country to Nottinghamshire and landed at Worksop.

We had completed our Nickel. We now were ready to be posted to Heavy Conversion Unit, to learn the intricacies of four-engine flying and acquire two more members for our crew, a mid-upper gunner and a flight engineer.

We did not together fly in a Wellington again, but a few days were filled with various administrative matters like collecting signatures to prove, should anyone ever be interested, that we had done what we should have done and we returned to their custodians on Worksop camp anything that we had borrowed from them and should now render back. We also handed in our log books to the appropriate sections: Derek to the Signals section; Colin to the Navigation; the other two to Gunnery and Armament; and I to S/Ldr Earthrol who gave me, I was glad to see, an 'above average' assessment.

In a few days' time, we were due to be at Blyton, for conversion on to four-engined aircraft. Strictly, our posting was to Lindholm, but RAF Lindholm had two satellite aerodromes, Blyton and Sandtoft, and crews on the four-engine conversion course went to either of these. All three places were too far for cycling to Retford in the sort of time that would ever be available to me. It was also too far for me to meet up again with Cyril, who, being ahead of me, had been at Blyton and was now at Hemswell. The only hope of being with him again would be for us both to be posted to the same squadron. That would have been good news indeed.

Lancasters were too precious to be used by pilots going through Heavy Conversion Course, so we should now first learn to fly the four-engined Halifax, an older and less efficient aeroplane, though plenty were still in service in operational squadrons of Bomber Command. The Halifaxes we were to fly were all aircraft that had been withdrawn from squadrons and not in their first flush of youth, but if we were to have the misfortune to bend one it would be less serious. Less serious for the Command's strength of bomber aircraft, that is, but probably comprehensively fatal for the crew of the pilot who bent it. Indeed, the number of these old Halifaxes that crashed, or 'pranged', was quite large. The reputation of Sandtoft for nasty accidents was worse than that of Blyton, and the station was always called 'Prangtoft' in consequence. We were glad that our posting was to Blyton. The Sandtoft engineering people of course said that the bad name of the one and crew's preference for the other was just bad luck, and certainly not because of any less efficiency by a dedicated maintenance staff.

We were to be at Blyton for two weeks and then we would go (if still in one piece) to RAF Hemswell for a quick conversion course on to the Lancaster. But first we were to add two more members to our crew. One was a flight engineer to stand or sit beside the pilot and be responsible for keeping a watch on the fuel consumption and as necessary change over from one of the several petrol tanks in the aircraft's wings to another, balancing the weight. He would also assist the pilot as necessary with the four engines' propeller pitch levers to get the optimum 'bite' at the air, and in such activities as helping with the spring-loaded throttle levers on take-off. His would also be another pair of eyes. Thus Sergeant Tim Cordon joined us.

The other man we needed was a mid-upper gunner. In the Lancaster, and indeed in the Halifax, there were two gun turrets, one in the tail and another about halfway along the roof of the fuselage, unlike the Wellington, which had only a tail turret, though all three aircraft had also a front turret, which was manned by the bomb aimer when he was not aiming bombs. The Gunnery Leader at Blyton drew me to one side.

'I hope you'll have Torry Large, he's as queer as a coot but he's a damn good gunner. Other crews have fought shy of him. A bit frightened he might take a fancy to one of them, I expect! Poor chap's having a bit of trouble getting into a crew. Have a look at him anyway.'

So I did. He was an officer gunner, a tall, fresh-complexioned young man, quite good looking in a rather effeminate sort of way. Those with a commission had the usual officer's uniform jacket and trousers made of the familiar fine barathea material but when we wore battledress, the trousers and blouse-shaped top, in which we mostly lived, was made of a coarser, rougher-looking material like the uniforms of all other-ranks. You bought the commissioned officer's uniform but the battledress was issue, given to you free. Torry Large, however, had, at his own expense, had his battledress made bespoke in the finer material, and very much smarter it looked. I sought the opportunity to have a chat with him and found him intelligent, distinctly charming and well mannered. I sensed no feeling of threat of the kind the Gunnery Officer had mentioned. Most important, I had been told that he was good at what he had been trained to do.

I had a word with each of the crew, and, finding nobody voicing any objection, went back to Torry and invited him to join us. Thus we gained Torry Large. No one was ever any the worse for our decision, and in fact on more than one occasion, as so often it will be in a crew formed of men who are all necessary parts of the whole, we owed our lives to his being alert. One link, one of seven links of a chain, each reliant on the others for strength and survival.

Now we were a crew of seven who would fly together in various of Blyton's Halifaxes, settle in together as the original five of us had done in the Wellington, and learn and practise our individual and communal tasks. Before we began, we were apparently to have a few days' leave. I had not expected leave at this stage. I had thought that it would be after Hemswell, or perhaps after doing a few operations in a squadron. Perhaps there was a bit of a log jam in the flow of aircrews through the conversion courses.

So I went home to Tiled Cottage and the rest of the crew went to home or holiday. Derek and Ken had not far to go as their homes were in Doncaster and Grimsby. Titch was off to Manchester. Colin returned to his beloved Essex. I did not yet know the other two well enough to know their destinations. Not unexpectedly Sally was captive on some RAF station so I did not see her, but most surprisingly I saw Cyril.

He had finished at Hemswell, and, now conversant with the beauties of the Lancaster, would in a day or two be going to a squadron. We had been keeping in touch and Cyril had phoned Blyton, learned that I was on leave, and he and Joan, without the boys, came over to Tiled Cottage. My father was not at home to renew his acquaintance with them, but I was glad that Mother could meet them. My sister Miranda was at home too, and we met her boyfriend of the time.

Cyril's posting was to 12 Squadron at Wickenby, a few miles north-east of Lincoln. I asked him and Joan not to divulge to my mother that I, too, was heading for a bomber squadron, for though I had told my father and Miranda, I had decided, rightly or wrongly, not to tell Mother, with the intention of saving her worry. It was good indeed to see Cyril again. He loved the Lancaster and was full of enthusiasm to get going on a tour of operations, which he had not yet experienced. The anticipation of danger would, I knew, appeal to him.

All too soon I was back at Blyton, reunited with the rest of the crew. Having been instructed in many things about four-engined aircraft and the Halifax in particular, I was given two short flights of 'dual' circuits and bumps, that is getting it off the ground and back again. Then on the next day I did a circuit and bump to check me and hey presto we were off on our own as a crew. We practised bombing on a range. We played with friendly fighters while the two gunners warned their pilot of the direction from which were coming and I threw the cumbersome beast about in the sky: more cumbersome, anyhow, than anything I had thrown before. Then we did it all again, but at night. Finally we flew two night 'cross-countrys' of about seven hours each, including in them some bombing practice, and it was considered that I, and Colin the navigator, Derek the wireless operator, Ken the bomb aimer, Tim the engineer, and importantly the two look-out gunners, Torry and Titch, knew what the score was.

During the next few days we got to know the new two, Torry and Tim. I never got to know Tim Cordon well, but the others said that his hobby seemed to be drinking beer, a pastime that does not mix well with efficient conduct as an aircrew member. Torry lived in Dublin, so he rarely went home when there was a short spell of leave. Instead, he liked to go up to London 'to meet friends'. These usually were American officers. He would come back and show off a silver cigarette case, or similar present, with which friends had shown their appreciation of his company. It seemed that his parents were wealthy and he had never had, or needed to have, a job. But he was most amusing company and we were all good friends. Very much an extrovert, he loved an audience. When a small 'entertainment' was put on in the camp Torry did a strip-tease, which nearly brought the house down. Torry loved every minute of the adulation. He was billed as 'Miss Dillis Fixey', and was very cleverly made-up. His impersonation of Phyllis Dixey was brilliant. Garment by garment he stripped off down to only a bra and panties to whistles and catcalls. Then the lights went out. After about thirty seconds they came on again and there he stood, on stage, 'stark bollock naked' as it was reported afterwards, but across his midriff was a notice 'Not Tonight, Darling'. The place was in uproar, with shouts of 'More! More!'

There was another man on the camp called Ivan. He was an officer and a gunner, not one of the 'converting' aircrews but on the permanent staff. He had the same sexual orientation as Torry. He had a DFC, not awarded so easily to gunners as to pilots, so clearly he had done something gallant. He, too, was most amusing company and the leading light in the concert party. He was popular, not only with the men who were his fellow officers, but with the WAAF officers in the Mess too. They told me that it was most welcome to them to be able to talk to someone very intelligent about the sort of subjects that normally interested their male Messmates less than it did themselves, like fashion, the arts, and things that would be boring to average airmen.

Once I went into Scunthorpe with Torry and the entertaining Ivan. We were laughing together in a pub when Ivan asked us to excuse him for a while.

'I have just spotted someone I need to see. Pick me up in three quarters of an hour's time outside the White Anchor.'

Arriving there at the time appointed Torry and I found Ivan outside, standing on the pavement, in the company of a sailor. He was swaying about a bit and so was the sailor. The sailor's trouser front was down. Until then I had not realised that sailors' trousers did not have 'flies' like those of other men. As we came up to them Ivan, with his arms hanging indefensibly at his sides, was saying 'Hit me, hit me' and offering himself in a masochistic attitude. We realised that the sailor would be putting himself on a serious charge if he were to be observed hitting an officer and we pulled Ivan away despite his protest.

'I've given him money, of course. He's a lovely boy.'

Ivan, in drink and in lust, was overpowered by the two of us, relatively sober, and escorted back to the bus that brought us to within walking distance of the camp.

I was talking to Ivan in the anteroom the following day when I was told I was wanted on the telephone. It was Joan Morris.

'I've been told that Cyril's missing. They say they can't tell me any more, but that there's always hope he might have baled out. Do you know how I can find out any more?' She sounded very brave. My heart felt clutched in ice.

'I'll go over to Wickenby and see if I can learn anything, then I'll ring you back. What is your number going to be tomorrow?'

I did not feel very confident of learning anything that they had not already told her. I felt numb. Of any one else I could have believed it. But not Cyril. Cyril was so strong, so vital, so quick and alert in all his reactions.

I got leave of absence and told my crew. I got myself over to Wickenby. I met the remaining members of Cyril's crew, his navigator and his rear gunner – a couple of decent New Zealanders, now looking for a new crew. The other four, wireless operator, bomb aimer, flight engineer and the other air gunner were missing with Cyril. I learned that Cyril had not been flying the aeroplane. It was customary in Bomber Command squadrons for a new pilot, and some of his crew, to fly on one operational sortie with a target-hardened pilot to learn the ropes. I too, if I reached a squadron, would similarly be taken, with some of my crew, as a supernumery on my first operational bomber operation. In due course, if I survived long enough to be sufficiently experienced, I might similarly be the target-hardened pilot and take other new crews, but in the same way I would retain Colin and Titch as navigator and tail gunner.

So Cyril had failed to return from his first operational trip, and he had not even been flying the aeroplane! The target had been Brunswick. The Command had lost 27 aircraft, seven per cent of the force. Crews had reported a lot of trouble from searchlights, so aircraft that did not get back could have been picked off by night fighters as they gleamed, blinded, in the lights, or been hit by coordinated flak. No news could really be expected, perhaps for quite a long time, and though Joan had been told that 'he might have baled out' I knew that the chances were not very good. I knew how difficult it was to get along to an escape hatch and get out, hampered by a parachute and the probable need to help other members of the crew, particularly the gunners, out of their turrets, even in a practice outside the hangars on the ground. If you had added to those difficulties the problem of slipstream, and, perhaps, if the aircraft was spinning, centrifugal force, movement in such a confined space was exceedingly difficult. In addition the aeroplane might be on fire or in an accelerating dive. Or both. It was no surprise why such a high proportion of prisoners-of-war were fighter boys. In a fighter, assuming that the pilot was not physically too damaged to exert himself, and if the aeroplane was able to react to at least some of the controls, the pilot could turn upside down and drop out. But not from a heavy bomber.

No one knew what had happened to Cyril. The factors most affecting survival were luck, alertness of look-out, and split-second reaction. The last two of these Cyril had in good measure, but he was not flying the thing himself and there were others, some of whom were inexperienced, on whose alertness of look-out they all depended. Of course, the man who was in the pilot's seat was experienced, so probably it was just bad luck. Alertness and quick reaction applied most to fighter attack, but no amount of it could help if an anti-aircraft shell arrived in the same bit of airspace at the same time as you did. It was luck, very bad luck, if another aircraft's bombs fell on your back, and so it was with mid-air collision. There must have been a lot of those occasions as so many pilots – and their crews too – had at one time or another terrifying experiences of near misses of collision and of 'being bombed'. There were some that were not near misses. You never heard about them.

When I got back to Blyton I telephoned Joan and wrote to her. But I could not be of much help. I was glad that she could presumably expect help from both of the families. Though she had been left with three little boys, she had a strength of character that would enable her to surmount the most appalling difficulties.

I had to admit to myself that Cyril's probable death had shaken me. If the seemingly indestructible had been destroyed, an anchor in my own self confidence had dragged. Thoughts of Cyril filled most of the days that followed, but two days later I and my crew were posted to RAF Hemswell for a quick conversion course on to Lancasters.

Truly it was a lovely aeroplane. On the ground it had a beauty, a purposefulness, more than any I had seen before. In the air it was a delight. I signed a paper in my log book to say that I had completed lectures in, and was fully conversant with, its petrol system, oil system and ignition system. As a crew we practised, on the ground, dinghy drill, Abandon Aircraft drill, Crash Landing drill, and Fire drill. As on the Halifax, on one day I did some circuits and bumps dual, then immediately did two solo. On the next day in the morning I was checked by a member of staff and then took off and landed it again with just my crew aboard. That night we repeated the process in the darkness and on the following day played for an hour with a friendly fighter. Three days flying and the course was over.

CHAPTER TWELVE

Second Dicky

RAF Kelstern was up on the Lincolnshire Wolds; lovely country in the warmer months but desperately cold in winter. The camp had been built and finished (or rather thrown together as some thought) less than two years before. It consisted almost entirely of Nissen huts. Only the Watch Office, or Flying Control building, made to a sealed pattern like them all, and the Operations Room, a rather grim, flat-roofed camouflaged biscuit-box of a place partly hidden by young trees, were built of brick.

The hub of the camp was a place where five narrow country lanes met, and not far away squatted the three camouflaged hangars. They were always the most conspicuous buildings on an aerodrome, with their aprons of concrete in front of their doors, facing in a slight curve the perimeter track which encircled the field and led to the six ends of the three broad runways and to the many aircraft dispersal sites.

The Officers' Mess was a very large Nissen hut with an open fire placed centrally in the anteroom with a brick chimney rising up through the corrugated iron roof. The fire faced four ways, four arched fronts like something made from a child's play-bricks, throwing out its warmth from its four sides. It burnt large logs and in the colder months it never went out, its accumulating mound of ash a grey source of welcome heat quivering with fiery red beneath the great logs if it was disturbed. The bar was in the anteroom and the Nissen huts which were the dining room and kitchen, etc., joined up to it by some architectural subtlety. In front of the Mess there was a large area of rough grass on which lay a pile of fallen trees, our fuel supply.

It was a one-squadron aerodrome, and home to 625 Squadron. The device in the squadron's coat of arms, recognising the importance of every member of the crew, was a chain of seven equal links, surrounding the red rose of Lancaster. There were three flights, each of nine or ten Lancaster bombers, which were dispersed about the airfield on dumb-bell-shaped concrete hard-standings, slightly protected by curving mounds of blast-deflecting turf-grown earth and reached by taxiways off the tarmac perimeter track, which encircled the field.

We began our time in 625 Squadron as members of C Flight, which Woodie Hammond commanded. Each flight had a Nissen hut that served as office for any administration purposes and also as somewhere for aircrew to assemble, though this was principally the pilots, as the other crew members had also their separate Sections: Navigation Section, Signals Section, and similarly Gunnery for the gunners, Bombing Section for the bomb aimers, and Engineer Section, each presided over by a 'Leader'. Alec Flett, once of Scotland Yard, was the Navigation Leader; Jack Bullen, Leader of the Signals' Jock Orr, an artist and late of the London Fire Brigade, Leader of the Gunners and so on. All were 'screened' aircrew who had completed a tour and flew now themselves only occasionally, picking carefully the crews they flew with!

Additionally there was the Parachute Section, always a tall building so the parachutes could hang. Here, WAAF girls packed and re-packed the chutes with careful folds, which would unfold without a hitch if they were needed to save a wearer's life. Further down one of the five converging country lanes there was the MT Section, where there were a few cars maintained, but more tractors to tow aircraft or bomb-trolleys, several buses for taking crews out to their aeroplanes on distant dispersals, ambulances, fire tenders, and every kind of ground vehicle. Where two hedges met there was the Hospital/Sick Quarters, with a doctor on duty and medical orderlies. In the hangars and in various places about the camp were the all-important domains of the engineers, whose ground crew fitters kept serviceable the aircrafts' engines and whose riggers maintained their bodywork. Another section had as its responsibility the radar and wireless equipment, and yet another every one of the complicated mechanisms, parts, and requirements of these darkly painted Lancasters, which crouched waiting in their dispersals.

Then there were the Armoury people with their long articulated lines of tractor-drawn trolleys bringing the bombs from the earth-and-concrete banked-up bomb dispersal stores, to fit them and fuse them and hang them in the bomb bays of the aircraft. Accidents were not unheard of, and these people, in the charge of the Armaments Officer, also supplied the ammunition for the air gunners' .303 Browning machine-guns. There were the fuel store people with their petrol bowsers on an aerodrome where every aeroplane might want more than 2000 gallons of petrol pumped into its tanks before each bombing trip. The petrol came underground, piped from Liverpool by way of Doncaster. Derek, ever inquisitive, had seen pipes being laid along the A1 in 1940 and had asked what they were for. There was a well-like hole in the ground through which it was delivered: without it there would have had to have been an almost continuous convoy of petrol tankers converging on each and every aerodrome in 'Bomber County'. There were even people whose particular responsibility was the great tyres on the wheels, nearly six feet high, and vulnerable to a bad landing.

There was Station Headquarters for the administrators, clerks and pay-clerks. There was also the Equipment Section, a labyrinth of shelf-lined corridors, a stock-taker's nightmare. Closer to the scene of the action was Squadron Headquarters, for the Squadron Commander and his Adjutant and their clerks. All these sections needed WAAFs for many of the duties, so there had to be a WAAF section, separately officered and administered. There were the Messes and the Cookhouses and those whose job it was to keep the station clean and tidy.

The Operations Room, really a series of rooms, in touch by scrambler telephone with Group at Bawtry and Base at Binbrook, employed Intelligence officers, Cipher officers, Met officers, and people to produce the charts, the flimsies, the changing code-books and all the kit that the different aircrew sections needed. Men and women there briefed the crews before they set off, and debriefed them when they came back.

Beside the perimeter track at the edge of the airfield stood the Watch Office. Those within controlled the comings and goings of aircraft taxiing towards the runway in use for take-off. They policed them in the air as they approached the aerodrome and made their circuits prior to landing, stacked them up above the field, noted when they were on their downwind leg, when 'in the funnels' pointing at the beginning of the runway, and were careful to see when an aircraft, having landed, was clear of the runway. They must never fail to give priority to any aircraft in trouble, desperate to try to land.

So aircrew were numerically only a tiny part of all the people on the camp. Though perhaps understandably they thought they were the most important part, there was a veritable town of specialists and dedicated men and women who were needed to send the aircrews into the air at any time to carry the war into Germany when no one else could do so.

As with Cyril, it was now the time for me to go, with some of my crew, in an aircraft piloted and captained by an experienced member of the squadron. F/Lt Treherne took his own navigator and tail gunner and us on a bombing trip for us to to learn the ropes for real. Derek, Ken, Tim, with Titch flying as mid-upper gunner for a change, and I flew on this 'second dicky' trip. I took my place that evening in one of the rows of seats in the Briefing Room in the Operations building. That morning, as we had assembled in the Flight Office, Hammond had come in and told us that the petrol load was 1850 gallons. There was no word of what the target was, but that load, others told me, meant that it was probably somewhere in the Ruhr, about a six-hour trip, so at least it was not Berlin or somewhere distant like Leipzig or Nuremberg.

Now we knew. For up on the large wall-map facing us at the back of the platform the red tapes marking the track to the target and home changed direction at a pin in the sprawl of Essen, part of that huge industrial area of the Ruhr made up of Essen, Bochum, Bottrop, Duisburg, Dortmund, Gelsenkirchen, Mulheim, Wanne Eickel and several other towns. Lots of red crayon showed how great were the belts of flak through which we should have to fly.

The Squadron Commander, W/Cdr MacKay, mounted the platform and called a roll. Each captain answered for his crew. He did not say much, but called the Senior Intelligence officer, a large, rotund, grey-haired, avuncular-looking man who told us the reason for attacking this target, and the ways in which it would be marked by Pathfinder aircraft in fair weather or in foul. With his marker he pointed to the areas of defensive flak that we should probably find giving us most concentrated attention if recent reports could be believed.

The Navigation Leader took the stand and talked about the route, touching lightly on the reason why it had been chosen. By his watch we reset our watches. Treherne's navigator, as would be the case for Colin when he would be flying in my crew, would at the end of briefing go along with other navigators on the raid to the Navigation Section for further briefing. He would be supplied with charts and expected wind speeds at the different heights at which they must fly. He would then know our exact take-off time, particularly if there was to be more than one wave, the time we must be over the target, places where we should cross the coast and points at which we should alter course, now visible on the wall-map, which it was hoped would leave the enemy in doubt for as long as possible what the target was. He would be given flimsies, with information about colours of the day and similar secrets.

Next it was the turn of the Met man. He gave us the general synoptic situation and spoke of the amount and depth of cloud we could expect here at base, *en route*, over the target, on the way home, and for coming down and landing, as well as the very important information about icing conditions we could expect as we climbed and descended through cloud. The weather over the target was expected to be clear, but we had been told of the sky markers we should expect to see if there was cloud cover below our proposed bombing height of 18,000 feet.

The Signals Leader delivered some technical-sounding stuff, but Derek also would shortly receive his specialist briefing in the Signals Section, and the Leader urged the absolute necessity for radio silence. Any message we had to convey to the Watch Office while on the ground or when in the air after take-off must be by Aldis lamp.

After him, the Flying Control man told which of the three runways the wind direction would allow us to use for take-off and later for our return. Always, it was hoped it might be the long one. He spoke briefly about the stacking procedure he would use when we rejoined the circuit. He repeated the Signals Leader's warning of the necessity for W/T silence on return and absolute silence for take-off and the rest of the trip.

Finally the squadron commander dismissed us with best wishes. We rose from our seats and made our way to the sections or to our lockers in one of the hangars and donned our flying clothing. We were meant to empty our pockets of all personal and unnecessary things, not only in case we should become prisoners but so that they could be sent back to our next-of-kin if we did not return. For the same reason also we were meant to give our locker key to the NCO in charge of the locker room so that it would not be necessary to force the door open. We were supposed, on the other hand, to have in our pockets the small aids provided to help us in any attempt to escape capture: a compass and cloth maps.

We boarded one of the aircrew buses and were driven round the perimeter track to the dispersal where the aircraft awaited us, its dedicated ground crew in attendance. Earlier that day we had already visited and tested the aircraft. So, one at a time, we boarded her through the narrow doorway, climbed along to our different positions, and took our places. I watched Treherne follow the careful procedures of all the pre-flight checks. As watchful supernumerary I stood behind the flight engineer noting in my head all that the pilot did. Twenty feet below us, on the concrete ground, the ground crew manhandled the starter trolleys, as the pilot checked the settings of his various levers. His gloved hand waved his readiness. One of the four engines coughed, the propeller turned, turned faster, seeming by optical illusion to rotate backwards, and roared into life. One at a time he started the four engines, revved them up to check them and pulled back the throttles to a quiet tick-over.

During this time the bomb aimer had been checking his bomb release panel and his bombsight; the navigator, surrounded by black-out curtains, had been arranging his charts and all his navigation equipment; the wireless operator, silently, had been checking his transmitter, his receiver, the screen from the navigator's H2S, which was his 'Fishpond', and all the switches and electric leads that fed into or emanated from his compartment. Both gunners, tail and mid-upper, had checked their guns and ammunition chutes and the movement of their turrets. Each member of crew had so many checks to make to ensure working efficiency in every piece of equipment, any of which could, in routine use or in emergency, make the difference between life and death for all of us.

The pilot looked at his watch. He called up each of us on the intercom, checking that each was ready. From our dispersal, in the fading light, we could see other aircraft close to us and far away across the airfield, black silhouettes against the grey of early evening, waiting, tense. Now there was a movement, aircraft were moving out of their dispersals and beginning to taxi out on to the perimeter track and along towards the downwind end of the main runway. Some were on this side of the field, some were on the other; two lines of grey-black Lancasters, each one a few yards behind another, converging on one point.

Treherne raised his hand. At his signal, the ground crew pulled away the chocks from under the fronts of the two great wheel-tyres. With the throttles of his two inner engines providing the power for forward movement, he steered the aeroplane by manipulating those of the two outer engines, so that we moved out of dispersal and joined the queue of aircraft on our side of the field, taxiing towards the eastern end of the runway. Soon, I could just see that the first aircraft had turned on to the runway. It paused for only a moment and then a green light shone from the black and white caravan. It moved forward, gathered speed, bumped a little, rose just clear of the ground, sped on down the mile of concrete and passed out of my view over my left shoulder. In rapid succession and with seemingly clockwork timing, one aircraft followed another: from left, from right. Each one, receiving a green light from the caravan, roared towards the brighter light of the western sky.

Then it was Treherne's turn. The starboard engine roared as it turned us, a brake squealed, and we faced the aquatinted autumn colour-wash of the west.

The Lancaster in front of us was a vague silhouette, wheels up, about to climb into the light above the far boundary's trees; the one in front of that was clear black against the sky, banking, turning left, climbing. The green Aldis winked. All four black pitch levers on the pillar by Treherne's right knee were at fully fine and his gloved hand pushed all four red throttle levers fully forward in their slots. The flight engineer followed, with both hands, the pilot's pressure on the throttle levers upon Treherne's command.

'Full power.'

Treherne brought both hands now to the wheel of the control column. Nearly 66,000 pounds of Lancaster, 30 tons of aircraft, fuel and bomb load, were hurtling down the runway towards the further boundary. The pilot was pressing the control column forward. The tail came up but for a few moments longer he denied the great aircraft's strong urge to fly, keeping it on the ground. Then he eased clear of the ground but kept close to it, until we had enough speed to begin our climb. Now we had achieved lift-off, and our speed was adequate.

'Wheels up,' he reported. With level wings he allowed the aircraft to rise over the hedges and trees and climb away. Then left wing down, right wing up, centrifugal force pressing us into our seats or on to our feet, we banked round in part of a left-hand circuit. Below us the faint lights that marked the runway and the edges of the perimeter track were tiny pinpoints of amber and blue, and the green light, about every two minutes, flashed from the caravan at the runway's downwind end as the remainder of the nineteen aircraft of 625 Squadron on the night's battle order followed.

We were to fly south, down England, climbing as we went. It was preferable to climbing in a circuiting spiral over base. As we flew, to our left and our right and ahead of us, visible against the grey light of the evening sky, other aircraft were climbing with us. There were 561 Lancasters from all over Lincolnshire, mostly from our No. 1 Group, 463 Halifaxes mostly from No. 6 Group in Yorkshire, and thirty-one Mosquitoes, many from Pathfinder Force who would mark the target's aiming points. It was not mentioned at Briefing, but this was to be the heaviest raid on Essen so far in the war and the greatest number of aircraft so far despatched to any target. So many towns and villages of England were now hearing the steady drone of this great force of bombers. We flew down above the Midlands and passed over Reading. Here the whole stream turned left and flew east, to the south of London.

In previous years, when Britain was weak, Londoners had heard the drone of German bombers approaching, heard the scream of falling bombs and the terrifying nearness of sticks of high explosive. Each one nearer, each one the one that could destroy their house, their air-raid shelter, their children and loved ones, themselves. Then it had been London's guns that had barked with tongues of flame and sent balls of savage light into the night sky as buildings crashed and fell around them, as the fires enveloped them, as the smoke choked them. Then it had been London's searchlights that had groped about the sky among the German armadas of bombers that dropped their loads, turned and droned away, leaving chaos, rubble, fire and smoke and cries of the hurt and dying. This evening the people of the capital would look upward and feel safe, knowing that up there were men and planes who were taking the war back to Germany, into the heart of the evil empire, which had caused their sons and husbands and boyfriends even now to be over in France fighting for their lives. They would know that those planes would destroy the factories and steel-plants, the coal-mines and railways that were making and taking to the front the shells and ammunition destined to kill their menfolk who were fighting out there over the Channel. And what, they would have felt, would it matter if German civilians were hurt or killed? The 'front' was not just where the tanks operated. Civilian casualties on both sides were part of one scene in a theatre of war that left almost no one unaffected by its progress.

Approaching our altitude ceiling now, nearly 4 miles up, we flew on in the bomber stream. We crossed the Kent coast and then the Dutch coast, climbing up through cloud, a muffling darkness all around us. Sometimes I glanced at Treherne's instrument panel as he flew on, dependent on his instruments alone – faintly luminous dials with which he kept the aircraft level, straight, at the correct speed, at constant height, with the needle on his repeater-dial, wired to the master DR (dead reckoning) compass at the back of the aeroplane (where it was away from most of the magnetic deviation caused by the bomb load), steady on the course that his navigator had most recently given him. But most of all, as we all did, I strained my eyes into the grey mist that surrounded us. Out there, beside us, above us, below us, were other bomber aircraft, just as blinded in the cloud as we were. Collision, or a destructive touch, wing-tip to wing-tip, was a real danger.

There was a silence. Somehow the steady roar of the four engines did not break that silence, it was too much part of the background. Only if the note of the engines were to change would the sound impinge upon our consciousness. Every now and then Treherne would call up members of the crew, just to make sure that all was well with them; especially the gunners, for as they swung their turrets in their ceaseless survey, it was possible for them to disconnect their oxygen supply. Up there, well above the critical ceiling of 10,000 feet, if one of them was not getting oxygen, inattention, drowsiness, unconsciousness, brain damage and death would follow.

We were lucky that in Lancasters we had H2S. It was capable of showing the navigator on his small screen a rather crude representation of some ground features, so that he could report to the pilot when we crossed the coasts, even if cloud had hidden them from our view in any little light that then remained. The wireless operator also had a small screen led from the same revolving aerial in a fat blister beneath the fuselage, on which blips of light showed up every time the cursor reached that part of the screen's circumference that were to warn him other aircraft were within about 2000 yards of us. Derek was expert in his handling and interpretation of that screen which was called 'Fishpond'. He could tell, and report to the pilot, if any of those little blips of light looked like other aircraft on a dangerously converging course. But now we must not use it, for German detection devices could home on to it. Its use must be delayed until there could be no secret about where the stream was going. The navigator's specialist briefing would have told him, and he would have marked on his chart, when that stage would be.

Quite suddenly we were out of cloud. We were above the now dimly seen grey-white quilt of the cloud-tops. Above us and around us was a different blackness, not quite so opaque to our night-vision-adjusted eyes. Treherne now had a horizon, of a sort, to see, where the top of the cloud layer met the domed enormity of the clear night sky. This was better than the tiny luminous horizontal line, representing our wings, inclining or steady against the fine fluorescent line of the artificial horizon of one of his instruments. For us the watch was the same, but with a better chance of seeing something perhaps, as we strained our eyes out into the darkness, roving, this way and that, never staring steady. Now we were over Germany, heading on a course that might make the defences think we were pointing to Bremen, or Hanover, or who knew where. We had been flying for nearly three hours, breathing into our oxygen masks, which made our mouths dry; warm enough in our flying clothing but none too warm, up here with the outside temperature this autumn evening reading about minus 30°C.

If cloud conditions demanded it we could hope to get up to 20,000 feet, but our briefed bombing height was 18,000 feet, and now the navigator gave Treherne another change of course, to starboard, to bring us on to target from about the north-west. The pilot confirmed it and turned, dipping his wing down a little more than necessary so Titch in the mid-upper gun turret could take the opportunity to look more under the belly of the aircraft, that blind area below a Lancaster from which fighter attacks often came. Then we were straight and level again, on course, at height, unspeaking and watching.

We saw what we knew was our destination from quite a long way off. It was dead ahead now but how many miles away I was not experienced enough to know. There was no cloud now, around us or below us. Some way ahead at about our height white and yellow stars were twinkling: the leading aircraft of the bomber stream must be reaching the airspace over the huge area of industrial Ruhrland and the German guns were coming into action.

As we came nearer, the flashing-star filled arc of the sky broadened like a curtain and its white and yellow pattern, with orange too now, filled more of its space. From the wings of this vast proscenium searchlight beams now arose and groped about the sky above the target, swinging to left and right, crossing and opening like giant scissors. Still nearer now, the curtain of exploding shells was not only in front of us, but to each side as well. They flashed at our height, just below us, just above us, lighting up the other aircraft nearby. Surely there was no possible way through. In the light of the explosions of the nearer ones I could see the puff of black smoke that followed instantaneously the white shell-burst. Suddenly, not far from us, an orange ball of fire appeared, then hung, then slowly fell. An aircraft had been hit.

If the chaos in the air around us was like an evil fairyland, the scene below was fantastic. Fire raged over a large area, peppered with white explosions and lit every few seconds by a greater flash, obliterating in its vicinity all other sight of the red and orange conflagration as 4000-pounders, 'cookies', one from almost every aircraft, fell into the target area.

The sight was mesmeric, but I could not allow it to claim my attention. German night fighters, directed by radar and pencilled on to their quarries by the roving searchlights, were among us. I must watch, and watch, and warn. And learn. I heard Ken's familiar voice on the intercom.

'Left-left a little; . . . steady as you go; bomb doors open.' Treherne's voice echoed in answer.

'Bomb doors open.' I saw the pilot's hand move to the lever as mine had so often in training. Then Ken again.

'R-i-g-h-t, steady, steady . . . steady, Bombs gone!'

I felt the aircraft lift as the weight of our load fell away, one 'cookie' and six 1000-pounders. We were 5 tons lighter, as well as now having used up about 3 tons of our petrol load.

There was a pause before Ken spoke again, 'No hang-ups, close bomb doors!' I imagined Derek ducking down from his look-out in the astrodome to feel with his hand through a hole in the floor to satisfy himself that the 'cookie', at least, really had gone.

'Close bomb doors.' Treherne's hand moved again to the lever as he repeated the instruction. Then it was the navigator's voice.

'Turn to starboard on to 225 degrees, Skip. I'll give you another change in a minute.'

Treherne pulled the right-hand loop of the aileron wheel down, pulled back a little on the column and I saw his feet move on the rudder bar. We banked, and I looked down on my side at the flickering glow below us. With wings level once more, the churn of the instruments settled. Treherne confirmed the new bearing.

'On course 225 degrees.' Very soon afterwards, the navigator spoke again.

'New course starboard on to 285, Skip.' Treherne banked and turned again and I saw that we were about to pass between the flak defences of Munchen Gladbach and Dusseldorf, both of which were throwing up some very un-welcoming fireworks.

'On course 285 degrees.'

I felt no guilt or horror at what we had just done, only relief that the inferno was now behind us rather than in front of us. I imagined Titch now presented with a disappearing view of the battle we were leaving. But the hazard was by no means over. To our right, in what might have been one of the areas of winking shell-bursts, I saw what looked depressingly like another aircraft explode in a fiery ball, but it could well have been on the near side of the flak and been a fighter's kill. Treherne put the nose down a little.

'Increasing speed, Navigator, 260 mph. Height 17,500 feet.' The navigator acknowledged.

'Keep your eyes skinned everybody. We're showing up a bit against that glow.'

The sky was still clear, but a few minutes later cloud enveloped us and the pilot had again to concentrate on his instrument panel.

'Tell me your petrol readings tank by tank, Flight Engineer.' Tim Cordon, stooped beside him, reading them off. Treherne's gloved fingers moved almost imperceptibly on his controls. Almost nothing of his face was to be seen. His head was enclosed in the leather sphere of his helmet and any part not so covered was hidden by his oxygen mask with its blunt mouthpiece of the intercom. His eyes were behind his goggles watching the instruments and making his adjustments as the dials dictated. Treherne looked very relaxed. His competence was reassuring.

So we came home to Kelstern. We made our circuit, landed, and were taken by an aircrew bus from our dispersal to the locker room and thence walked to the operations room for debriefing. The Squadron Commander, W/Cdr MacKay, was there. He greeted each crew as they came in and made their way to one of the trestle tables at each of which a WAAF was handing out mugs of cocoa laced with rum. How lovely to see a girl's face, pretty, smiling, after the ugliness of what we had been seeing, been anticipating, during those last five and a half hours in the sometimes flame-shot darkness.

The room was abuzz with conversation. Men with often strained faces, their mouths ringed by the mark made by oxygen masks and their foreheads lined by the edge of their helmets, greeted one another, and compared what they had witnessed. When one of the interrogation tables was free we moved towards it and answered the questions put to us by an intelligence officer. It was just after 3 a.m.

Colin our navigator, bless him, had waited up to see us in.

'How was it?'

'A bloody dangerous way to spend a Monday evening.' I smiled in relief at our safe return.

When we went off to bed, and in the morning, S/Ldr Hamilton, CO of A Flight, and his crew of six more men, had not returned.

Monday 23rd OCTOBER, 1944 – ESSEN

1055 aircraft – 561 Lancasters, 463 Halifaxes, 31 Mosquitoes. The heaviest raid on Essen in the war to date. More aircraft despatched to this target than to any other target thus far. 4538 tons of bombs dropped: 90% high explosive including 509 4000 pounders because most of the burnable buildings of Essen thought to have been already destroyed in earlier raids. 5 Lancasters and 3 Halifaxes lost.

Local reports 607 buildings destroyed, 812 seriously damaged; 662 killed, including 124 foreign workers and 569 injured.

In this raid, and that which followed 2 days later, the Krupps steel works was particularly hard hit. The firm's archives record 'almost complete breakdown of the electrical supply network' and 'a complete paralysis'. The Borbeck pig-iron plant ceased work completely. There is no record of any further production from this important section of Krupps. Foreign worker casualties were higher because the air raid shelters provided for them were inferior to those for local inhabitants.

(*The Bomber Command War Diaries*, Middlebrook and Everitt)

Was I horrified at the thought of all the suffering of people down there on the ground? Was I appalled at the monstrous violence in which I had taken part? Often I thought of the dogs and cats. Often I thought of the prisoners-of-war in camps in target areas; but of the Germans, no.

Twice within living memory, my father had said, that nation had marched against their neighbours and dragged the world into war. That nation had taken as their leader a power-crazed lunatic. They had sycophantically indulged his every whim. They had applauded his every evil deed. Pathe' news films had shown Hitler going among an apparently fawning German population accompanied by the evil clique who carried out his wishes. Women, old men, and young men hailed him, screaming in hysterical reverence and calling him 'Father'.

Reports were beginning to emerge that their young men had kicked and beaten, starved and delivered into 'camps' the children, the women and the men of whole sections of the community. Those whom it pleased their chosen leaders to say did not conform to a fair-haired prototype that their dark-haired 'Father' told them was the standard of the Germans who must be the Master Race, were expendable and could be disposed of. Even in the last few years they had used the inhabitants of undefended Spanish towns to practise and perfect the aerial bombardment that they would shortly use in their subjection of their neighbouring states. Young men in their thousands had joined the ranks of his bully-boys. Even before the war, I knew, power had been usurped entirely by Hitler's Nazis. The few dissenting voices had been silenced by death. Thousands of the most sadistic of the German race were banded together as the *Gestapo* and encouraged to crush and rule by fear the peoples whom their assenting soldiers had overrun.

My father, who had seen the cream of a generation slaughtered or maimed by Germans, had told me as a boy that the only good German was a dead German. Now I was grimly minded to agree.

I hated the Nazis and all they stood for. I did not hate the German people, the pawns in the Nazi dream of world domination, but they had shown that they could not be separated for different treatment. I certainly did not hate those who flew against me, who shot at me and tried to kill me.

But they must be stopped. I knew, with a deep conviction, that they must be stopped.

CHAPTER THIRTEEN

Cologne

On the Monday following my 'second dicky' trip to Essen with Treherne, we were on the battle order. It was posted up in Flight Offices, Sections, and the Messes. It listed the aircraft letter to be flown and the names of everyone in each crew, and was signed by the Squadron Adjutant. Only this time, of course, the crew for which our eyes first looked was our own. This time Colin would be the one behind the black-out curtains navigating us there and back, Titch would be in his rightful and important rear turret and Torry would have his first operational trip in his mid-upper turret. I would not be a watchful supernumerary but would be flying the thing. If I had any 'butterflies' about this I was determined not to show it. We were to fly J2, *Jig 2*.

That morning, like other crews, we went out to our aircraft's dispersal, met and chatted with the ground crew, climbed aboard and carried out all the ground tests that our training had taught us. Then we had lunch in the Messes and experienced a certain amount of apprehension through the early afternoon. We had our pre-briefing meal, which included an egg as we should be flying operationally, and in due course reported to the Operations Room at the time stated on the battle order.

We sat together in a row of seats looking towards the 'stage' and the white sheet hanging in front of the wall-map. We knew that the petrol load was 1850 gallons, as for Essen, so anticipated a trip of similar length. The sheet was rolled up, and the Senior Intelligence Officer pointed his stick at the map.

'Cologne. Your target this evening is Cologne. Cologne, on the River Rhine, south of the great industrial complex of the Ruhr cities is an important industrial city and a vitally important centre of communications, rail and road, particularly now that the Germans are having to rush reinforcements up to their fronts which are facing our armies. Many of you have been there before. Tonight you are being asked to direct your attention to two districts, Mulheim, to the north-east, and Zollstock, to the south-west of the centre respectively. [His long white pointer patted the map as his explanation continued.] The latter area includes important dock facilities on the Rhine. Because of this, the bombing will take place in two waves – you, navigators, will soon have your times to be on the target. About 700 aircraft are taking part, and you already know that we are contributing eighteen of them.

Now, as to the expected concentrations of flak. Those of you who went to Cologne last time told us on your return that it was thickest here, here, and here. [He made three arcs on the red crayoning on the map with his pointer.] I am afraid that we can do little to avoid all of those by altering the proposed route, though we have kept you away from Aachen where many of you had trouble last time. Also, of course, you will be on your guard as you come across France against the boxes of radar-controlled packs of fighters, particularly those which are working in cooperation with searchlights.

Now, Target Marking. If the target is clear, bomb the red markers. But these will be backed up with greens; I have shown these details on the blackboard here.'

Thus he went on, ending by reminding us of the best way to head if we were to be brought down and trying to escape. He was followed by the Met man who told us we could expect pretty clear conditions for the target area though there might be some mist about over parts of Northern France and southern England for our return. The Navigation, Signals, and Gunnery Leaders had their say, followed by the Flying Control man and finally the Squadron Commander. It was very rare for the Station Commander, G/Capt Donkin, to speak at briefing, but he always attended. Strictly he was an engineer, but he had pilot's wings and had on several occasions proved, to the satisfaction of anybody who happened to be watching, that he could fly as competently as the rest.

After donning our flying clothing in the locker room we were taken by aircrew bus to *Jig 2* in her dispersal. Soon afterwards, having completed our cockpit checks and moved out and joined the taxiing procession round the perimeter track to the downwind end of the long runway, we turned into wind, pausing for a moment until we received the green Aldis light from the caravan.

I selected fine pitch, released the brakes, and pushed the throttle levers forward. It was the first time I had done a take-off in a fully loaded Lancaster.

'She'll swing to the left, be ready to correct it.' The mantra of training repeated itself inside my head. In a few moments the aeroplane was hurtling down the runway, all 60,000 pounds or more of it, gathering speed. I was feeling her wanting to lift off but was holding her down, feeling the tiny bumps as her wheels kissed the ground a few more times. Then she was clear of the ground, airborne and speeding towards the far boundary.

'Wheels up.' The routine was ingrained from training. 'Let her lift off more, keep the wings level, start to climb, bank a little to the left.' The standard instructions filled my head. I could see the aircraft in front of us higher and over to the left, black and clear against the bright late evening sky. Turning, climbing, on to the crosswind leg. Below my port wing-tip were the grey-green nearly colourless fields of Lincolnshire. It was 19.45 hours local time. Colin's voice: 'Steer course 200 degrees Skipper, continue climbing.'

Down the length of England we flew, over Lincolnshire, Rutland, Bedfordshire, Northamptonshire, Hertfordshire and so to Reading. Was it a conceit of those at High Wycombe that they must hear the stream passing over Bomber Command Headquarters? Probably not. We had given the German radar no indication yet of which way we were coming. And now we turned, flew across Sussex and crossed the coast at Dungeness. Northern France, Belgium. Looking to be going more north than we should soon divulge. It was quite dark now; there was no moon, no apparent cloud, no lights down below us but the faintest suggestion of a horizon to make the flying less tiring. Otherwise, there was just the dim luminosity of the instrument panel and of the repeater dial from the DR compass hanging in its gimbals at the rear of the aircraft.

Colin was perhaps still able to get ground positions from his Gee equipment, but very soon now it would be useless, its frequency jammed by the enemy. We had not yet reached the point when he could use H2S. Now there was a new course from Colin.

'Continue climbing to 17,000 feet.' I made intercom checks with the members of the crew.

'You alright Torry?'

'Mid-upper answering, fine Skipper thank you, lovely night!'

'It is. Keep watching, keep your eyes roving, everywhere, never still. We're over enemy territory now. You all right, Titch? You, Derek? You, Ken?' Tim was beside me so I knew he was all right, watching his gauges and instruments and occasionally changing over fuel tanks in the wings to keep our weight balanced.

So we climbed on into the darkness, watching all around us and seeing nothing, though somewhere out there there were over 700 aircraft like us. Every now and then I heard the click of someone's microphone switch and knew if it was one of the gunners from the scream of the slipstream or if it was Derek, Colin, Ken or Tim from the absence of background noise louder than that which was already filling my ears from the roar of the four engines. We reached 17,000 feet and levelled off. Soon afterwards Colin gave me a new course, heading more southerly. We had been flying for nearly three hours. The intercom crackled. It was Colin again.

'After we've bombed, please turn to starboard on to two five five degrees'. I confirmed his message and knew from my watch that we had not long now to go to the target. All was quiet. Then Ken spoke.

'I think I can see the river, over on our left a bit and ahead and running in the same direction as we are.' The navigator agreed.

'That's right. Keep on this course.'

I thought I could see it too, but Ken lying on his stomach in the nose searching the darkness would have his eyes more acclimatised. We should now be somewhere between the Ruhr and our Cologne target. After a few minutes Ken spoke again.

'I can see the red markers going down, almost dead ahead.' So could I now, and plenty coming up too. The sky pyrotechnics were beginning.

Now Ken took over the directions.

'Bomb Aimer to Pilot, tracking in nicely, steady as you go.'

I glanced at my instruments. 17,000 feet; speed correct. Now it was up to me.

Concentrate. Fly very straight and level. Hope for no emergencies. Well done, Colin. Bang on! In among the marker flares I could now see the bombs bursting, sometimes a big one. The ground of the target area was reddening. Momentarily I thought of Torry, seeing it for the first time.

'Hello, mid-upper. Try not to look at the target, Torry. Keep your eyes in the sky. Search the sky, but including the sky underneath us, as well as you can. Here be fighters.'

'OK Skipper.' Ken took over.

'Left-left a little – steady as you go. Bomb doors open.'

'Bomb doors open.' Once again I was confronted by that seemingly impassable barrier of flak. There was a curtain of it in front of us; and now to each side too, enveloping us.

'Steady, steady. R-i-g-h-t, steady.'

Out of the corner of my eye I could see flashes. Orange balls of light. Instantaneous. Concentrate. This is what we've come for. Straight and level.

'Steady, steady. Bombs gone! No hang-ups, close bomb doors.'

'Close bomb doors.' I operated the bomb door lever and put the right wing-tip down. I watched the ring of numbers swing round on to 255 degrees. Straighten up. Wings level. Then it happened. A blinding flash of light on our port side and the noise of stones hitting the aircraft all over. Or was it all over? We were still flying. Nothing catastrophic seemed to have happened. I switched on my intercom to check.

'You all right, Titch?'

'OK Skipper.'

'Torry?'

'Mid-upper OK. But a bit blinded by that flash.'

'Derek, are you and Colin all right?'

'Both OK. But oh my, that was close!'

'Ken?'

'Bomb Aimer all right, thank you.'

'Engineer, one of the port engines sounds funny, how are your temperatures?'

Tim was bent in study of all his instruments. Shells were still bursting around us. Worse still on the ground, no doubt, but I had no time to look there now. Titch, however, was looking, understandably. His voice conveyed his awe at what he was seeing.

'The whole place looks like a furnace.' There was a tone of disbelief in his words. 'And we must be showing up well against it!' This was true, the raid was continuing but we must get away from it.

We seemed to be escaping into the darkness. Cologne and the fires that were turning its river orange were receding behind us.

'Alter course five degrees starboard on to two five zero, Skipper, to avoid Aachen.'

'Two five zero degrees.'

Minutes passed.

'Now starboard again on to two eight five.'

'Two eight five. Thank you Colin. Keep watching everybody.'

I didn't like the sound of the outer port engine. The engine notes were de-synchronised.

'Engineer, what are your temperatures? And can you get the pitch right on those port ones?' That sound of pebbles hitting them could have holed a fuel tank. 'Engineer, watch your fuel gauges: is there any excessive usage?' Could one be leaking? But apart from the rather rough-running sound from the port side they seemed to be all right.

After perhaps twenty minutes it was Derek who spoke.

'Skipper, from my Fishpond we seem to be getting more and more to port of the stream. There are no other aircraft on my screen at all now so we must be more than a mile away from the others.'

Colin obviously thought he was being criticised.

'Who's navigating this aeroplane?'

'Colin, I'm flying two eight five, fifteen degrees north of west. Have I mis-understood you?'

To my enquiry there was silence from Colin. Obviously he was recalculating something.

'Navigator here. Two eight five is correct.'

So we continued flying on that course, but I was puzzled, and so no doubt were the others, too.

'Can you get a fix by any means?'

'Afraid not. They are jamming the Gee absolutely. All I can see on it is grass. And there's no ground detail to be seen at all on H2S. Anyhow, this course should bring us to the coast between Calais and Dunkirk. Piece of cake. Can't see why the others are going so far to the north.'

I looked again at my compass reading. Could I be making some silly mistake? No, it was correct.

Time passes slowly when you are waiting for something to happen and rather fearing that it will not. Fortunately there were no other alarms, the sky seemed empty. But the engine sounds did not improve and I kept asking Tim for readings from his instruments. If an engine was heating up I should have to stop it and feather the propeller, but I had no wish to be down to three engines at any time, let alone as things were. Finally it was Colin who became convinced that there was something wrong.

'Navigator to pilot. We should have reached the coast a quarter of an hour ago, but nothing has shown up on my H2S. I've got to admit that I don't know where we are.'

'Thank you Colin. Derek is certain we were too far to port of our expected track. We've not reached the coast. I suggest we fly due north and hope we find the coast. If we do not, we must assume we are too far to the west because Derek's information makes it unlikely that we shall be flying straight up the North Sea. Then, if we don't recognise a coast crossing, when you calculate that we really ought to have got to the south coast, and we haven't, we must be over the Atlantic, so we'll fly east. Think that over and let me know what you think.'

'I must say that I was thinking along exactly the same lines. Alter course on to three six zero.'

'Three six zero.'

My hands felt clammy inside my flying gauntlets. It seemed the discipline of training and routine was powerless. Here we are, lost. No idea where we are. An engine running roughly, and we've certainly not got petrol for this sort of indefinite flying.

'Engineer, watch that engine's temperature. Don't let it overheat, but we must fly with the very minimum fuel consumption. You believe we are not losing any, so how long do you calculate we can stay up?' After a pause he gave me a figure that made sense but did not make me feel any happier.

Seven men, sitting there in darkness, throbbed their unsynchronised way in a direction that they hoped was towards the coast of England. Time passed very slowly indeed. 'Ken, if we pass over any ground feature which you think any of us could recognise, let me know and we'll circle it. You'll probably see it first.'

It was a very dark night but the bomb aimer's eyes were most accustomed to peering ahead of us through the Perspex as he lay there on his stomach in the nose.

In fact it was he, and Colin watching the screen of his H2S, who saw the dim line of the coast. It was a glad moment. But where the hell was it? Happily no one was denying our right to look at it or showing their resentment by shooting at us. I began to circuit the feature that, for all its anonymity was, to us, a welcome place.

'Colin, come out of your curtains and have a look. Any theories?' The navigator joined me at my shoulder.

'No. It looks pretty featureless. But on my screen I think I saw a feature way along that way.' He pointed down and left. 'Wait, follow the coast along that way when I'm back in my place and note what your course is. Then if we recognise it I'll tell you what the course ought to have been from my chart.'

'Will do. Watch the coastline Ken, I don't want to lose it.'

That little exercise taught us two things: one was that, to our astonishment, the 'feature' was pretty certainly the mouth of the Seine, and the other was that our compass was completely at variance with the people who made the chart.

'Right Colin, give me a course for home. At least it ought to lead us to some point on the south coast of England even if our compass is chock full of gremlins. Then we'll think again.'

'Wireless Operator to pilot. Don't want to add to your troubles but IFF is U/S.'

This was a serious problem. Nothing that he tried would make it work. IFF (Identification Friend or Foe) was the vital bit of equipment which when the wireless operator switched it on, gave out a signal that was supposed to deter British gunners on the English coast from shooting at us. We did not feel happy about crossing the south coast, however welcome in every other way, without it. But we knew that now we were across the French coast. We were already somewhere over the Channel. It was time to use W/T. Derek called UH9, which that night was Binbrook. He called repeatedly. They did not answer him.

We flew on, our anxiety transferred. If our message was not received, English air defences would deal us the fate spared us over enemy territory. At about a quarter to one Derek got a fix. It put us halfway between Cherbourg and the Dorset coast. As we were on a northerly course this showed how much the compass was misleading us and sending us further and further west. It enabled Colin to calculate a compass correction, at least on this heading. He was able to give me a course for home. We could not have complete reliance in the compass, but Derek got two or three more fixes as we flew up the spine of England. Moreover, to our intense relief, nobody shot at us. Binbrook must have heard.

Tim had been giving me estimates of our endurance. They were rather better than I had feared. Thinking that I did not now need maximum height for maximum gliding distance, we now began to descend. In case our estimate of endurance was optimistic, it might be a good thing to see the ground if at all possible, and going downhill would save a little of our precious fuel. Derek reported that the intercom had been U/S, but that he had got it going again on an emergency system. Colin gave me 'courses' based on his calculation of the compass error; we could not of course know if it was constant. Colin's Gee equipment was definitely U/S, even if the German jamming was less interfering, but we were making our way up what we thought was the centre of England, Derek's fixes, passed to Colin, contributed considerably.

At last Colin estimated that we were very near base, but our fuel supply was very near the bottom. It was a happy moment, when Titch said he could see the lights of a car. No question, we were over land! I decided to make a 'Darky' call. Derek put me through on the correct frequency for this variation of 'Mayday'.

'Darky, Darky. Himself *Jig 2*.' I called out into the air. The effect was miraculous. Ahead of us a circle of Drem lights appeared as if by magic. A female voice responded.

'Himself *Jig 2*, this is Folkingham bearing 345, permission to land, over.'

It was music to our ears. We made a rather fast rate of descent. We saw the runway lights come on to make a welcoming path within the Drem circle. We approached the funnel lights. I prayed that I would not make a nonsense of it and have to use up vital petrol making another approach.

'Himself *Jig 2*, funnels, over.'

'Himself *Jig 2*, pancake.' That lovely voice again. We landed.

Folkingham's Watch Office gave us our taxiing instructions. We came into the haven of a dispersal. A Crew Bus collected us and we were taken to Flying

Control. The Controller greeted us with one hand covering the mouthpiece of a telephone.

'I've got Kelstern on the blower.' He spoke into the phone. 'Please tell Wing Commander MacKay Flight Lieutenant Russell is here now.' He passed me the phone. I recognised the voice of my Squadron Commander.

'Well, Russell, glad you're down. Welcome back. Are you all all right?'

'Thank you, Sir. We've been a bit of a long way round.'

'Really? Bit of navigation trouble?'

'I wouldn't put it that way, Sir. We've got a first class navigator but we acquired a few gremlins in the compass.'

'Really, how's that?'

'I think it may have been something to do with a very near flak burst as we were leaving the target.' I detected a change in MacKay's tone.

'So you bombed the target then?'

'Of course, Sir.'

'Good.' He paused. 'I expect you're all tired.'

'You could say that Sir.'

'Well, get some sleep and ring me again in the morning when the ground crew people have had a look at your aeroplane in the daylight.'

Folkingham, though an RAF station, was being used by the Americans. It was in Lincolnshire, between Grantham and the Wash. We were accommodated in tents. I do not know which happened first, my head touching the pillow or falling asleep.

We were called in the morning and breakfasted with a buffet system among Americans. Breakfast was a surprise. Jam, beans and bacon all mixed up together on one plate was unexpected. Dear Jig 2, she had got us back to the right county, even though in the circumstances she did not have quite enough petrol to get us back to the right aerodrome. Nine crews, seven on the Cologne target, that night did not get back at all.

We went out to the dispersal, where several RAF ground crew were attending to the aircraft. A flight sergeant fitter came forward.

'I'm afraid she's U/S, Sir. The CSU of the port outer has been hit and is very shaky. Oh, and we found this in the port inner without looking very far into it.' He handed me a piece of shrapnel on which I could see traces of the rifling marks of the gun-barrel.

'And have you seen your bomb doors Sir? I think you've been quite lucky.' The port bomb door, which perhaps had not yet closed when the shell exploded, was like a colander, full of holes. Colin emerged from the rear of the fuselage. His face bore a broad grin.

'Here's what spoilt my evening.' The DR compass, which in order to be as far away as possible from variable magnetic fields, was hung in gimbals near the tail, with repeater dials that led from it to the pilot and navigator, had been hit by shrapnel and been made unable to do its duty. A detail of particular interest to Colin and Derek was a shrapnel hole, in the floor of the bomb bay, about 6 inches by 1 inches, right between where they both sat. There was a corresponding hole in the roof of the fuselage above the partition that separated them as the foreign object had continued its trajectory. I turned to the Flight Sergeant.

'You mean we can't fly her home?'

'She's U/S, Sir. Our Engineer Officer would not take the responsibility of letting you.'

By now several American aircrew had gathered round. They were astonished at the size of a Lancaster's bomb bay. But then, a Flying Fortress was just that. It was not the carrier of a great load of bombs like the Lancaster.

We returned to Kelstern by road. They sent for us in a lorry.

It was a six and a half hour trip and we were in the air for seven hours thirty-five minutes. *Jig 2*, though a bit wounded, did very well to eke out her petrol.

Saturday, 28th OCTOBER, 1944 – COLOGNE
733 aircraft, 428 Lancasters, 286 Halifaxes, 19 Mosquitoes. 4 Halifaxes and 3 Lancasters lost.

The bombing took place in two separate waves. Local reports confirm that enormous damage was caused. The districts of Mulheim and Zollstock, north-east and south-west of the centre respectively, became the centre of the 2 raids, and were both devastated. Classed as completely destroyed were 2239 blocks of flats, 15 industrial premises, 11 schools, 3 police stations, and a variety of other buildings. Much damage was also caused to power stations, railways and harbour installation on the Rhine. 630 German people were killed or their bodies never found, and 1200 were injured. The number of foreign casualties is not known.

(*The Bomber Command War Diaries*, Middlebrook and Everitt)

Our lorry got us back to Kelstern that Sunday too late to be on the battle order for that night. Twenty-four crews went to Cologne again, the second night running. It was an 'Oboe' marked attack, bombing through thick cloud. No aircraft were lost on that target that night.

The next night, the squadron was stood down. We had 24 hours to calm the shell shock of those flights through barrages of flak. We had a day off to try to forget the horrors that some men had seen – an evening in the company of a girl or friends. We had time off to take whatever remedy each had found could give the therapy needed to relax our jagged nerves, strained by those hours of tension, and make them ready for their next test.

On Thursday a battle order was on the wall again. We were on it. We were one of twenty-five crews furnished by Kelstern. *Jig 2* was still at Folkingham. We were in E2, *Easy 2*. In our line of seats in the briefing room that early evening we watched the curtain roll up as the Senior Intelligence Officer stood with his pointer raised towards the uncovering map. The target was Dusseldorf, an attack by 990 aircraft. Nineteen were not to return.

* * *

Flak was already bursting around us when Colin gave me another change of course, following the feinting zigzag towards our target. Ahead of us now, the brilliant flashes that seemed to fill the sky looked even more dense than I had seen before. I had to fly straight through that lethal barrage, not choosing the more open spaces, not weaving. Absolutely steady, straight and level on the exact course that Colin had given me, and then to the precise directions from Ken on the intercom. I had realised that it would require a double helping of strong nerves tonight, after the experience of three nights before.

'R-i-g-h-t. R-i-g-h-t .... Steady ..... Steady ....'

My whole attention was fixed to follow the guidance from the bomb aimer. I had to keep constant my straight course, my height and my speed. Concentrate, concentrate, but don't seize up; don't stiffen; legs, shoulders and arms, must be sufficiently relaxed to respond to every tiny alteration my brain might dictate as my eyes watched the dimly luminous instruments before me. It seemed so long, so slow. I was sensitised by our experiences. Expecting to hear at each moment the explosion. To feel the pain of red-hot fragments of metal slicing through us. Eyes front; eyes front. The instrument panel was suddenly brightly illuminated, brightly orange, as the side window next to me was hit by something huge. Yet the window did not break.

It was Torry in the mid-upper turret and Derek with his head in the astrodome who saw the other aircraft hit. For seconds it seemed to keep on flying, a torpedo on fire, brilliantly burning, level with us and parallel, over on our left. Then it dipped, below our height. Its flames flared more brightly and pieces of it were breaking off and falling. No one could survive that conflagration. Nor could I afford to let my concentration waver.

'Steady ..... steady .... Bombs gone! ... No hang-ups. Close bomb doors.'

'Close bomb doors.' I flew on. Imminently, Colin would give me a new course to take us away from the target area and begin our journey home. We should not want to turn and cut across the flight path of those aircraft that were now on their bombing run. We had bombed, but the barrage was continuing. I saw two more aircraft hit. One over to my left. One over to my right.

The flak was heavy. Between us at our stations in the aircraft we saw several aircraft hit, but we passed through the barrage, though as we had approached it, to come through it unscathed looked impossible. I did not look at the brilliantly lit target, concentrating on the flying. But Derek standing with his head in the astrodome and Titch in the tail as we left the awesome sight behind us saw a rectangle of fiery red, twinkling with the flashes of bomb bursts. Red except for just one small area, black by comparison. As our bombs fell away, we heard the Master Bomber calling for those who were following to bomb that darker patch. This was 'area bombing'. This was what the Intelligence Officer had spoken of at briefing.

With the benefit of a serviceable compass, Colin had brought us to the target. Now as our bomb doors closed he gave me a new course to starboard, away from the Rhine, to avoid passing too close to Monchen Gladbach, and then another that brought us in due course to the Belgian coast and then north-west towards Suffolk.

'We're flying up the Orwell Estuary now, Skip.'

It was our private communication. He knew that his pilot would realise that we were passing very close to his small Essex market town of Halstead where, before the war, after his father had died, he had although only a teenager kept going the family bakery business, helped by his mother and his siblings. Down below us, too, he knew that I would realise, was *Nancy Blackett*, my father's 7-ton sailing boat. She was lying in her mud berth at Pin Mill, lifting a little at times of higher tides, against the south-west shore, waiting for the bloody war to end.

For me, the thought of Pin Mill and times aboard *Nancy Blackett* – and ashore, perhaps in the Butt, brought mixed feelings: the warm sense of times of fond remembrance and a pang for the separation from regular contact with people and places, I held dear – and for the loss of my self determination and freedom that wartime regulations and service life had brought. It was only a moment's reverie – resolved by a sense of perspective. What was I doing this for, flying this great, dark bird?

'Thank you Colin. God bless Halstead, and all who dwell in her. And keep our *Nancy Blackett* safe too!'

Descending, we crossed Norfolk and the Wash near King's Lynn. Soon, well, it seemed soon compared with the last time, we were stacked up over Kelstern. We were brought down in 500 foot drops by the WAAF R/T operator in Flying Control and we took our turn to make our circuit of the aerodrome and land between the avenue of little lights that marked the runway. Back in *Easy 2*'s dispersal pan I switched on my intercom again.

'And God bless *Easy 2*.'

None of the nineteen aircraft lost that night was of 625 Squadron, we learned as we waited, rum-laced cocoa mug in hand, chatting with those who each day were becoming more and more our friends, our comrades in arms, for our turn at the debriefing tables.

2nd NOVEMBER, 1944 – DUSSELDORF

992 aircraft – 561 Lancasters, 400 Halifaxes, 31 Mosquitoes. 11 Halifaxes and 8 Lancasters lost.

This heavy attack fell mainly on the northern half of Dusseldorf. More than 5000 houses were destroyed or badly damaged. 7 industrial premises were destroyed and 18 were seriously damaged, including some important steel firms. At least 678 people were killed and more than 1000 injured. It was the last major Bomber Command raid on Dusseldorf.

(*The Bomber Command War Diaries*, Middlebrook and Everitt)

CHAPTER FOURTEEN

Area Bombing

Colin and I walked into the Mess together. The anteroom was almost empty. Nearly everyone must have taken the opportunity of the squadron being stood down to go off into town, probably Grimsby or Cleethorpes, by some means or other. Colin was very rarely in one of the carloads that left the station on such occasions. He was seldom to be seen waiting at the pick-up point, outside the gates, of one of the buses that served Kelstern. I enjoyed his company; he was intelligent and had a delightful sense of humour. But he did not seem to have my need so frequently to seek the company of a woman. A religious faith appeared to be more important to him than it was to most of his Messmates. It was the quiet way in which he showed this that had earned him the nickname 'the Vicar' in the crew.

Outside, a cool wind was blowing across the airfield, this autumn evening, and the big central log-fire was giving off a welcome warmth from each of its four arched sides. Several large logs were burning, their red shimmering sides slowly being reduced to a grey ash, which little by little fell onto the mound on which they rested. Colin and I would have sat down in two chairs before the fire front nearest to us as we came in, but we noticed that the Senior Intelligence Officer was at the fireside opposite to us and he gave us a friendly wave of his hand. His chair was drawn up close to the fire and he was leaning forward. In his other hand he had a long, crudely fashioned, toasting fork. Perhaps he had made it himself from one or two wire coat hangers. He had put a slice of cheese on to a piece of bread already toasted and was skilfully managing to melt the cheese on to the toasted bread without letting the bread be burnt. He responded to our polite but quizzical expressions.

'I usually do my cooking in my hut. The coke stove there gets hot enough to allow it. But this evening it seemed rather cheerless in there, so I came in here. Until you two came in it wasn't much more cheerful in here.'

He was a large, grey-haired man, older than perhaps any of his fellow officers, and wore pilot's wings, which showed that although he now had a ground job, he had been a flier. He was a quiet-spoken, friendly man, with an avuncular manner. He was the sort of man whom I felt inclined to call 'Sir'.

'I've recently seen you two sometimes in the Operations Room. How are you getting on?' I glanced at Colin before responding.

'We've not done many ops yet. And perhaps because my previous tour was of a less destructive kind, in Coastal, I sometimes find myself thinking about some of those who are down at the receiving end of the raid, especially prisoners-of-war who may have the rotten misfortune to be in the target area, and also, I must admit it, the dogs, horses, cats and cows down there too.' The Senior Intelligence Officer smiled.

'I do agree. And I think it is to your credit that you do.' I felt emboldened by the compliment.

'Tell me Sir, what did you mean when at briefing for last night's raid on Dusseldorf you said that it was "area bombing"?'

'Ah, perhaps I should not have said that, but unfortunately for those of us who have qualms of conscience, among whom I count myself, it is true. There is nothing new about area bombing. Nothing new about having a Master Bomber. The *Luftwaffe* used one at Coventry. They marked the place with coloured lights. If that was not area bombing, what was? Germany used area bombing against many towns and cities in Poland. London and many other targets in England suffered from it, were burnt by it, were reduced to piles of rubble by its indiscriminate spread of high explosive and incendiary bomb loads'

S/Ldr Barton's Welsh rarebit was now cooked. With a smile of apology to us he began to eat it.

'Rather hungry. Overslept this morning and missed breakfast. Then I had some jobs I had to do. I got in to lunch a bit late and there wasn't much left. But if you'll excuse me talking with my mouth full, let me tell you a few things that led us here in Britain to adopt the same policy. Forgive me if it sounds a bit like a history lesson but it may put into context what you young chaps are being sent out to do.

When the war began our policy was to bomb only targets that could be described as military; warships, naval dockyards, railway 'marshalling yards' being used to deploy and distribute troops and their supplies – that sort of thing. It was a unilateral restriction to our action, which was like fighting with one hand tied behind our back. There was even a reluctance to bomb factories because they were 'private property'! It had to be done in daylight, when the number of losses was shown to be so high that we would soon have had no bomber aircraft left at all. Even under the concealment of darkness there was an increasing toll of aircraft casualties. RAF bombers at night were finding themselves unable to hit the pinpoint targets allotted to them. Through 1941 and into 1942, Bomber Command was achieving very little, although many crews displayed the greatest gallantry and, given the more limited technology at our disposal, remarkable skill and resourcefulness.

We were fighting a defensive war. The Royal Navy and Coastal Command found themselves, with the means at their disposal, unable to counter the threat to our very survival posed by German U Boats and surface raiders. I believe that you, Peter, were involved in the Battle of the Atlantic, so you probably know more about it than I do. [I nodded to acknowledge the reference rather than to accept the compliment.]

Fortunately, for our survival, there were some men in high places, though by no means all of them, who had faith in strategic bombing. They realised the self-evident truth, that the only way to win the war was to defeat Germany. Germany has to be defeated. This is an aggressive and evil nation that is loose in the world. It has overrun its immediate neighbours. We are told by our brave men and women working under cover that it is enslaving millions of people to work in its factories and strengthen its defences, and that they are doing savage and appalling things to huge numbers of men, women and children. The Jewish people of Poland are being wiped out. You have witnessed its attack in mid-1941 on Russia. Russia, with whom it had sought and signed a non-aggression treaty. It must be stopped. But how, and by whom?

Germany lies safe behind the buffer of defeated neighbours. To have attempted to mount an invasion would have been impossible. We could not return, to go back into the continent of Europe from which we had so recently been evicted. Even if it had been successful, which it would not, it would probably, at best, only have led to a stalemate of trench warfare with the astronomical number of casualties of 1914–1918. So how then?'

We waited for him to answer his own question. With a smile he stopped to fix another slice of cheese on to the end of his toasting fork.

'You will remember that our Fighter Command and the men on the ground who directed our planes were throwing back each wave of Germany's aerial strength that came against our land and our cities. But without supplies of every kind we could not carry on. Stretched beyond their strength by German U Boats against which we had found no effective weapon and German surface sea power in the west, by Japanese air power in the east and the Italian and even Vichy French ships in the Mediterranean, the Royal Navy did not even have the ships to stop a German naval force making their way through the English Channel from one end to the other.'

I remembered vividly the Stopper patrols we used to do, and my anxiety that it would be I who would have an unserviceable radar instrument when it was my night on, and be the 'man who let them out'.

'At that same time German surface raiders lurked in Norwegian fjords waiting to sally forth into the Atlantic and harry the ships that were our supply line. Fortunately, there came at last a realisation that there must be a new attitude of mind about what our consciences would allow and what they would not.

In July 1941 the British Chiefs of Staff made a declaration. [He had put down his toasting fork and, grasping his lapels, assumed the caricatured posture of a chief of staff.]

'We must first destroy the foundations upon which the German war machine runs: the economy which feeds it, the morale which sustains it, the supplies which nourish it and the hopes of victory which inspire it. Only then shall we be able to return to the continent and occupy and control portions of his territory and impose our will upon the enemy. For it is in bombing, on a scale undreamt of in the last war, that we find the new weapon on which we must principally depend for the destruction of German economic life and morale.'

[He laughed.] You see, I know that bit off by heart!

For it was realised that the only part of the Armed Forces that could hit Germany in the West and bring some support to the Russians who are fighting so valiantly and unpreparedly on the eastern front was Bomber Command. Only Bomber Command could effectively fight back and take the war into a Germany that stood safe behind the walls of captured territories, armed and supplied by the slave labour of conquered Europe. Germany was waiting, poised, to administer to us in these islands the *coup de grâce* as soon as our lifelines had been strangled and inadequate supplies had crippled our war effort.

While he had been talking, S/Ldr Barton had eaten his Welsh rarebit, cooked another and eaten that. Now he leant back in his chair and smiled.

'When I get the bit between the teeth on this subject of why the bombing we do now is justifiable and necessary I take a bit of stopping! Do I bore you?'

'No, no.'

'We have talked together about this and we are keen to hear what you are saying. Please go on.'

'Right. It was realised that to put into practice so determined and necessary but ambitious a plan would require a tremendous effort, particularly as then, three years ago, effectively we stood alone.

But it would take time. A sufficient number of aircrews, all volunteers, had to be built up. A sufficient force of bomber aircraft had to be produced. This took a massive redeployment of resources. But the goal, the goal was the large-scale bombing of German cities. That would bring about such general dislocation and breakdown in civilian morale that the German home front would collapse. With their cities and their own homes in ruins, it was confidently believed, the German civilians would be unable and unwilling to continue the war.

It had been shown that accurate bombing of specific industrial targets could only rarely be achieved. Once the Air Ministry had clarified that this was indeed War Cabinet policy, they decided that such bombing should be virtually abandoned and most of Bomber Command's effort should now be devoted to the general bombing of the most densely built up areas of Germany's cities. In early 1942 a directive was sent to Bomber Command. Words to the effect of: 'It has been decided that the primary objective of your operation should now be focused on the morale of the enemy civil population and in particular of the industrial workers.'

This would require not only more bomber aircraft and aircrews, but also better navigational equipment. It would also require a new leader. In February 1942, Air Chief Marshal Harris took over the command of Bomber Command. Just a week after the arrival there of the new directive.

Fortunately the new Lancaster was about to come into service. The Halifax was beginning to be available in greater numbers, hugely increasing the potential bomb load. They would replace the ancient Whitley and Hampden and the Manchester of awful reputation. Even the Stirling would make a contribution, though its operational ceiling was dangerously inadequate for the longer-range guns that the Germans were putting into service in devastatingly larger numbers. Of navigational aids, the brilliant British discoveries, Gee, H2S, and Oboe, would soon be available. Things that you and your crew rely on to find the target, hit the target, stay out of trouble, and come home safely.'

He broke off. Another man had entered the anteroom.

'Ah, there you are Bernard!' The Squadron Commander approached the fire. 'I've been looking for you.'

He turned to us. 'Good evening, gentlemen. Not interrupting anything, am I?'

'They were just making sure I ate all my Welsh rarebit, and I was just filling them in on what this is all about.'

Colin and I, who had risen as MacKay had come in, bade our goodnights. MacKay called after us as we made our way to the door

'Well done on that Cologne trip. Can't have been very easy. Jolly good show!'

CHAPTER FIFTEEN

Bochum

Two nights after the Dusseldorf raid, I and my crew were on the battle order for another trip. Some 1850 gallons of petrol were pumped into *Easy 2*, one of twenty-five Lancasters detailed for the operation from the squadron. We learned at briefing that the target was Bochum, another Ruhr city – an industrial area with an important steel works.

As we turned on to the runway and watched for the almost instantaneous green light from the NCO of the flare-path crew at the caravan, I noticed out of the corner of my eye a little crowd of well-wishers standing there in the gathering dusk. I had not noticed before, in my rapt concentration, something that was common to all bomber stations, I supposed: those who turned out to wave the bombers off. Many were WAAFS, some of whom probably had heart-felt wishes for the safe return of special friends and lovers.

We took off at 1737 hours GMT. A westerly wind was blowing. We flew a magnetic course of 165 degrees, which allowing for the earth's magnetic 'variation' of 10 degrees, and a compass 'deviation' on this heading of +2, gave us a true course of 153. We climbed at about 200 mph to a height of 12,000 feet. Half an hour later Colin gave me a change on to easterly as we crossed the Suffolk coast at Orford Ness, well known from my sailing days in *Nancy Blackett* in happier times. We were now at 16,000 feet, still climbing towards 18,000 feet. The stronger westerly wind gave us a speed 'over the ground', a ground speed, of 255 mph. The temperature was minus 22 at this height. At 1808 the heating became U/S. Please God, let this not be another like Cologne!

We had about 115 miles to go to the target. Now, being over the sea, Ken fused and selected his bombs on the little switch panel beside him as he lay on the floor in the nose of the aircraft.

At about 1905 hours, having plotted a 'fix' or actual position relative to the ground, Colin gave me a very slight alteration to our course and asked me to reduce the airspeed a little to 180 mph, which would be 248 mph over the ground by calculation. Derek began 'windowing', that is throwing out bundles of strips of metallised paper to confuse the enemy radar as to the size of the force approaching. Colin was continuing to calculate 'fixes'. By now his Gee was being jammed by the enemy too much to be used. All the time he was also calcu-lating wind speeds and direction and as these changed he was calculating the

Peter Russell sailing with his father on *Nancy Blackett* in the summer of 1939.

Thames barge on the Hard at Pin Mill (low water) drying her sails.

The author in 1939, aged twenty, wearing the RAFVR tie.

22nd October 1939 – No 1 ITW, B Squadron, Trinity Hall, Cambridge..
Left to right – John de Havilland, Clifford Bell, John Barry, Peter Russell and Richard Muspratt.

Elementary Flying Training School at ￼nstey in December 1939. Author back row left.

The Lockheed Hudson was originally designed in the USA as an airliner, the Electra. The RAF took delivery of some 2,000 of the type during the early years of the war, many operating with Coastal Command on long-range Atlantic convoy protection duties. This is a 233 Squadron aircraft photographed sometime during 1940/41.

A Consolidated Catalina. An American amphibious flying-boat that did sterling work for Coastal Command during the Battle of the Atlantic and many other theatres of war.

A typical Mess party at RAF Leuchars. Head of table Group Captain 'Tiger' Pope.

Squadron Leader Will Kearney, kneeling centre, with Peijus at his left shoulder.

A 233 Squadron Hudson from RAF St Eval in typical low cloud found in the area.

A photo of the infamous Fastnet Rock lighthouse photographed by the author from 100 feet in stormy conditions on 29 August 1941.

The author is presented to HRH Duke of Gloucester, the Duchess is 3r from left.

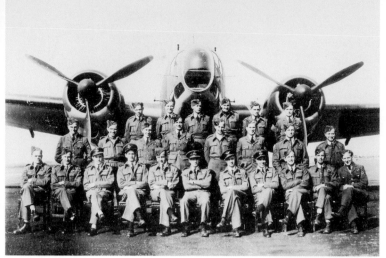

A Flight 233 Squadron, RAF St Eval in 1942. Top Row – 2nd and 3rd from the left Miller and Menzies. Front row from left - ?, Alexander, Harry Rowntree, Peter Russell, Whit, McComb, Haig, Rusk,?,?

French Tunny fishing boats photographed by the author from 100 feet in the Bay of Biscay on 28 August 1941.

A Hudson patrolling over a convoy in the North Atlantic

The author's great friend Cyril Morris. He died in 1944 when the Lancaster he was flying was shot down.

Peter Russell in early 1942, aged 23.

The water tower mentioned in Chapter 9 which the author and Cyril Morris were ordered to climb in rain and darkness with a heavy hose-coupling.

Wing Commander John L Barker who in 1944/5 commanded 625 Squadron equipped with Lancasters. He was also OC Shield Force and after a distinguished career became Air Vice Marshal CB CBE DFC. He died at the age of 93 in 2003.

KELSTON AERODROME has now gone back to being farmland, but this plan shows where some of its Sites and buildings were when it was a Royal Air Force station in Bomb Command from which 625 Squadron flew.

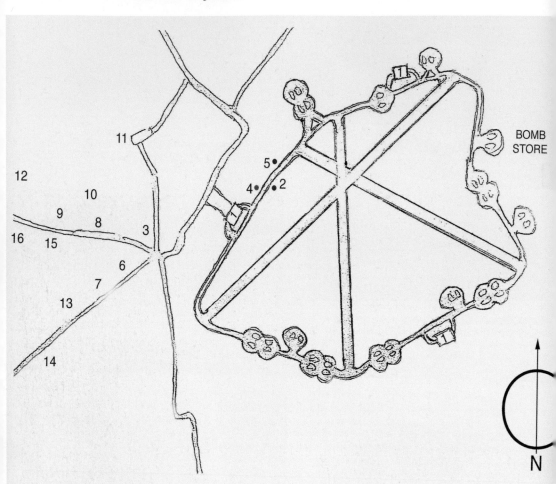

BOMB STORE

N

1 The three hangars	9 WAAF Living Quarters
2 The Watch Office	10 ditto
3 The Operatioms block and SHQ	11 Petrol Compound
4 Squadron Office	12 Hut Site of Living Quarters
5 The 3 Flight Offices	13 ditto
6 Officers Mess	14 ditto
7 Sergeants Mess	15 ditto
8 WAAF HQ	16 Sick Quarters

Additionally there were many Store rooms and Workshops, the Sections of the different Aircrew categories, the NAAFI, Airmen's Dining Hall and Cookhouses, Parachute stores, Equipment Stores, the Armoury, M.T Section and compounds, Photographic section, Squash court, The Guardroom, Latrines, ETC., ETC., On average the population was 100 officers, 300 NCOs, 1190 OR. WAAFs 250 The long runway was 2000 yds X 50 yds Available dispersal sites for 36 aircraft.

625 Squadron Lancaster Himself K for King waits at he hardstanding in dispersal at Kelstern on a winter day in 1944.

The authors Lancaster crew. Back left to right – Torry, mid-upper gunner, Colin, navigator and Reg, flight engineer. Front – Titch, rear gunner, Ken, bomb-aimer and Derek, wireless operator.

Squadron Leader Peter Russell DFC.

'The Vicar' – Flying Officer Colin Richardson, the author's navigator.

Flight Sergeant (later Warrant Officer) Derek Evans – wireless operator.

'Titch' – Sergeant Frank Aldred – rear gunner.

Torry – Flying Officer Torrence Large – mid-upper gunner.

Despatching Officer "C" Flt: F/O VEREX.

A/C LTR	A/C NO.	PILOT	F/ENG	B/A	NAV	WOP	M/U/G	R/G
D2(v)	L.M.579	F/L STEVENS DFM	SGT TAYLOR	F/O BALSER	F/O BOYLE	W/O CLARK	F/S HILL	SGT THORNTON.
H(v)	N.G.394	S/L RUSSELL	SGT WOOD	P/O DALLEY	P/O RICHARDSON	F/S EVANS	F/O LANG	SGT ALLAND.
O(v)	N.M.757+	F/L ALGER	SGT BIRD	P/O DONOGHUE	W/O ZLOTNIK	F/S STEWART	F/S SHEEHAN	F/S AVERY.
L(v)	L.M.747	F/L REYNOLDS	SGT BIRD	P/O HOGBIN	P/O R.EVANS	F/S LUMLEY	SGT DAVIES,V.	SGT DAVIES,R.E.
X(v)	H.D.337+	F/L RUSSELL	SGT ATTENBOROUGH	F/O CHARLES	F/O DRISDALE	SGT GILCHRIST	SGT TUK	SGT COOK.
Z(v)	F.D.376+	W/O CHAMBEY	SGT ROBINSON	F/S MAXWELL	F/S BLACKFORTH	F/S BASSANTE	SGT REED	SGT MILLER,M.
M(v)	L.E.332	F/O BALL	SGT MORTIMER	F/S O'CONNOR	P/O FOOT	F/S McGILL	P/O O'MALLEY	P/S JOE.
V2(v)	Z.B.574	W/O BABNER	SGT MAYNARD	F/S BAIRD	F/L GARDINER, DFC	F/S NAT	F/S NAT	F/L ORR.
J(v)	P.B.500	F/L HENDERSON	SGT RODDICK	F/O BROWN	W/O BULLEN	F/S JAMIESON	F/S MARSH	F/S MAXWELL.
G(v)	H.F.995+	F/O CROCKS	SGT RUSSELL,J.	F/S STARSON	F/O FLETCHER	F/S FOXCROFT	SGT FOWLER	SGT EDWARDS,R.E.
C(v)	N.G.257+	F/O MALONEY	P/O PEARCE	F/O DARE	F/O SHEPHERD	W/O DICKSON	F/S PEARSON	F/S HARDING.
F(v)	P.B.150	F/O PRICE	SGT BENNET	F/S FORBICK	W/O BELLING	SGT WALLACE	F/S CAMPBELL	F/S McROBIE.
Y(v)	L.Z.700+	F/L JENKINS	SGT MILES	P/O COTTRELL	F/S CASSIDY	SGT TELLE	F/S STAPLES,J.	SGT AYERS.
J(v)	H.G.411+	F/L SPENCER	SGT MURRAY	F/S FLANAGAN	F/O O'NEILL	F/O STRASCH	SGT WHARE	SGT TAFFRAIL.
K(v)	H.G.412+	F/O JAMIESON	SGT CUNNING	F/S AITKIN	E/O GRAHAM	F/S SMITH (360)	F/S WHITNEY	SGT WILSON.
W2(v)	N.G.521+	F/L CHARLTON	SGT LYONS	F/O ARCHBOLD	SGT LEE	SGT CROSSMAN	SGT LESS	SGT WALKER,P.
S2(v)	F.L.175+	F/O PARKER	SGT SUTHERLAND	P/O CLOTHIER	F/S COLES	SGT CASEY	SGT BAYLOR,E.	SGT PRESTWICK.
Q2(v)	H.F.596+	F/L GUILLETTE	SGT LUCAS	F/O LUTHER	P/O SLOOTH	SGT WILLIAMS,D.	SGT BASS	SGT HATTON.
B(v)	Z.B.464	F/O RILEY	SGT WILLIAMS	F/O LUSH	F/S GRESWELL	F/S SNOULDER	F/S EVIT	SGT LINDSAY.
A2(v)	N.G.418+	P/O SATTIN	SGT SOEN	SGT DIBBLE	F/O GARDNER	SGT BENNETT,L.	SGT BENNETT,L.	SGT BARRETT.
P(v)	Z.B.536	F/L COUCH	SGT FULLER	F/O RUSSELL,D.T.	P/O ELKINS	SGT NELSON	SGT WHITESON	SGT TAGGART.
H(v)	H.G.240+	F/L WILSON	SGT NICHOLS	F/O COOPER	F/L GARDNER,W.G.	SGT PRATT	SGT STARRY	SGT SLOCOMBE.
S(g)	Z.B.850+	F/O ENGLISH	SGT REDDY	SGT MILLER	SGT MILLER	SGT CLUX	SGT TROWLS	SGT SIGNE.
T(v)	Z.B.176+	F/O GREENSLDE	F/S WHITING	F/O BULLOCK	F/O GODFRIED	F/O LEWIS	SGT ECCG	SGT SKELENKO.
Q(g)	N.G.253+	F/L FORSYTHE	SGT KENNEDY	F/O CHIRDEN	F/O BAKER	SGT HUGHES	F/S LIVERAGE	P/O JONES,DEL.
U2(v)	Z.B.153	SGT COOCH	P/O McQUEEN	F/S BURDETT	SGT PARKER	SGT GREEN	SGT COLLEN	SGT ROBINSON,E.

RES : F/O McFAINT & CREW.
F/O CCCK & CREW.

"A" & "B" Flight : SGT FINNERTY & F/S McGINTEES.
"C" Flight: SGT MOSS & SGT SHEVERS.

M 1/- 182
" 6d nil.

Meal for everyone } Times to be notified
briefing for everyone } later.

[signature] F. B.B... f/t
Wing Commander, Commanding
No. 625 Squadron, R.A.F.

The Battle Order for Zeitz, though of course the target name did not appear.

FIG
1

INSTRUMENT PANEL

See key opposite page.

68. Ammeter.
69. Oil pressure gauges.
71. Oil temperature gauges.
72. Coolant temperature gauges.
73. Fuel pressure gauges.
74. Fuel contents gauges.
75. Inspection lamp socket.
77. Fuel tanks selector cocks.
78. Electric fuel booster pump switches.
80. Emergency air control.
81. Oil dilution buttons.

FIG
4

FLIGHT ENGINEER'S PANEL, LANCASTER X

FIG
4

Key to Lancater's Flying Controls

1. Instrument flying panel
2. D.F. Indicator
3. Landing light switches
4. Undercarriage indicator switch
5. D.R. compass repeater
6. D.R. compass deviation card holder
7. Ignition switches
8. Boost gauges
9. Rpm indicators
10. Booster coil switch
11. Slow running cut-out switches
12. I.F.F. detonator buttons
13. I.F.F. switch
14. Engine starter switches
15. Bomb containers jettison button
16. Bomb jettison control
17. Vacuum changeover cock
18. Oxygen regulator
19. Feathering buttons
20. Triple pressure gauge
21. Signalling switch box (identification lamps)
22. Fire extinguisher push buttons
23. Suction gauge
24. Starboard master engine cocks
25. Supercharger gear change control panel
26. Flaps position indicator
27. Flaps position indicator switch
28. Throttle levers
29. Propeller speed control levers
30. Port master engine cocks
31. Rudder pedal
32. Boost control cut-out
33. Signalling switch box (recognition lights)
34. Identification lights colour selector switches
35. D.R compass switches
36. Auto controls steering lever
37. P.4 compass deviation cardholder
38. P.4 compass
39. Undercarriage position indicator
40. A.S.I. correction card hold
41. Beam approach indicator
42. Watch holder

A Lancaster begins to take evasive action from an approaching Me 110 night fighter on the aircraft's port quarter. (A painting by Ron Homes)

The author looking rather tired on the morning after the Zeitz raid.

The blackboard as it appeared in the Watch Office at Kelstern after 625 Squadron's one thousandth sorties on the evening of 14 July 1944. A short low-level raid on Caen.

| DATE | 14TH JULY · 44 | | | | TARGET - | | CAEN | | | | ZERO - 21·50 | | DEAD |

A/C No	CAPTAIN	TAKE OFF EST:	TAKE OFF ACT:	T.O.T	E.T.A	LANDED TIME	LANDED PLACE	DUR'N	BOMBING TARGET	BOMBING TIME	BOMBING HEIGHT
942	F ROSS	1925	1925	2150	2311	23.07	KELSTERN		P RED TI	2150	7500
031	F TUCK		1928	to		2313	"		P VISUAL	2154	5600
168	F KELSEY		1927	2155		2316	"		P YELLOW TI	2152	5500
	F NANCARROW		1926			2318	"		P RED TI	2155	6000
	F MARVIN		1932			2312	V		P GLOW RED TI	2154	3500
	F SLADE		1937			2380	"		P R+Y TI	2151	6500
	F TORGRIMSON		1929			2317	"		P VISUAL	2151	6800
	F PARKER		1934			2308	"		P RED TI	2152	6000
	F PHILLIPS		1948			2330	"		P VISUAL	2154	4500
	F COLLETT		1933			2326	"		P RED TI	2154	5000
	F MAXWELL		1935	2155		2327	"		P R+Y TI	2158	7000
	F WILSON		1936	to		2322	1		P RED TI	2159	8000
67	F AVERY		1940	2200		2332	"		P RED TI	2156	5600
19	F SHEFFIELD		1939			2329	"		P RED TI	2157	6800
	F MASON		1941			2324	"		P RED TI	2155	7000
566	F SIMS		1942			2337	"		P RED TI	2156	7000
	ATKINS		1946			2334			P RED TI	2159	6500
100			1943			2325			P VISUAL	2155	5500
	ICKE		1938			2334			P	2159	7000
	F MINNIS		1944			2240	FORD		P VISUAL	2154	5000

Happy days – the author's father in 1951.

Butt and Oyster and Alma Cottage at Pin Mill.

ETA, estimated time of arrival on target, which his pre-flight plan told him we must reach at 1944 hours.

At 1913 hours and again at 1925 hours he made another small alteration to course and to our speed. He was then happy about the height and course to get us to the target, and speed to get there on time. Colin's steady voice once more crackled in my ears.

'19 minutes to target.' *Easy 2* surged on. Suddenly, there was a shout from Titch in the tail.

'FIGHTER, FIGHTER, 8 O'CLOCK LEVEL! CORKSCREW LEFT, GO!'

'Going left!' As I responded I threw the control column forward to plunge down, swinging the aileron control to the left, kicking the rudder bar to the left, then to the right, levelling, then pulling the stick back and the nose up. The wings, which were left wing down now rolled to right wing down. The fully laden 29-ton Lancaster responded with a corkscrewing path through the air. With no hydraulic assistance for moving the very large areas of control surfaces of the elevators, ailerons, and rudders, it demanded all my strength. I was hoping that this manoeuvre was proving difficult for the fighter to follow, that it was not just standing off, waiting for me to finish these exhausting attempts to lose it before coming in again for the kill. Then we heard Titch again.

'I think we've lost him Skipper, I can't see him now.' And then Torry's voice.

'I saw him go over us, Skip. He's away now.' The aircraft came back to an even keel. I came back to mine.

'Eight minutes to target.' Colin's intonation was ever imperturbable, as though nothing had happened.

'Right. Ken, can you see the target?'

'Yes. R-i-g-h-t about 20 degrees. That's OK, steady as you go. . . . Left, left, steady . . . Bomb doors open . . . .'

'Doors open, Ken, but I'm afraid we're down to 16,000.' A sudden dart of fear stabbed – 2000 feet under a stream of bombers discharging their loads, perfectly placed for being bombed ourselves.

'No matter. Steady . . . steady. Bombs gone!'

'1944. Spot on Ken.' We had bombed exactly on ETA.

My breathing in the rubber oxygen mask and my heart began to recover normality, or what passed for normality when approaching a keenly defended industrial city that appeared to be expecting us. I was aware that my legs ached from my physical efforts. That and the excitement had almost made me forget the flak, which was bursting all round us.

'Bomb doors closed. No hang ups!' Any minute Colin would give me a new course out of the target. Please come on Colin, let's get out of it.

Suddenly, in a terrifying instant my windscreen was filled with the shape of an oncoming aircraft. Head-on collision! It was huge, lit by the flashes of the flak and the light of the fires below. As I had just done, I threw the stick forward. As we went down I saw its lit-up belly rush over my head. Arrrrgh! A groan escaped me. I heard a chorus of sound from Ken and Tim and from Torry and from Derek in the astrodome. Then there was absolute silence. A shocked silence. As I pulled up the nose again my legs were trembling. Certainly I was sweating, minus 16 though it may have been. In the silence we heard Colin's quiet words.

'Men seeing Death.'

We had gone down. The other aircraft had obviously gone up. But either we or it might not have done. It didn't bear thinking about.

But within two minutes, Titch's shout came again.

'FIGHTER, FIGHTER, CLOSE! CORKSCREW! GO LEFT!'

My arms thrust the stick away from me. I kicked left and turned the wheel left down. Then right – down right. Roll through. Pull back. Left, up, roll. Stick away. Kick right . . . . I was sweating now. My arms ached. My eyeballs felt they were leaving my head from the centrifugal force of my bunt at the top arc of my corkscrew. And we were still driving on away from the target, away from home. Or were we? Heaven knows which way we were going.

'He went under us, to our right I think,' Torry reported.

'Can't see him now,' said Titch.

'When you've had enough of this fun-fair ride, get on to a course about west. 270 degrees.'

'Two seven zero.'

The compass repeater dial was spinning, my instruments were haywire, but after a few moments they steadied enough for me to get *Easy 2* with her wings level and neither her tail nor her nose up in the air. I banked round on to the westerly heading the navigator had asked for. A minute or two later, Colin spoke again.

'Course 288 please, Skipper.'

'288 degrees.' I made my adjustment.

It was nearly half an hour since we had bombed. Half an hour since the nightmare of that near collision, that oh so near collision, followed so closely by the evasion of the night fighter. We ploughed on more or less westward, not attempting to climb back up to our previous height but more anxious to make the best speed we could against what had now become a headwind. About three quarters of an hour later, while we strained our eyes in every possible direction for the sight of more fighters and as the revealing moon was just showing above the horizon, Colin had me turn nor-nor-west on to 346 degrees. We were altering course for Orford Ness and covering the ground at about 200 mph against the wind. Derek was watching his Fishpond. His call was sudden and urgent.

'TITCH! Look port quarter, down!' Immediately we heard Titch's excited voice.

'Bloody Hell! There are four of them. They're queuing up. Go! Go! Corkscrew! Corkscrew right!'

I threw the aircraft down and right, throwing Tim up so that his head struck the rim of the astrodome above him. Kicking with my legs. Hauling and pushing with my arms. Pulling the wheel first one way and then the other. I made *Easy 2* twist and turn crazily through the night air. Almost exhausted, I managed to pull her out of her corkscrew. Then there was silence. I blinked the blur of centrifugal force out of my eyes behind my goggles. As my instruments settled a little, I fought the controls to get on to the right heading. All eyes were searching the sky frantically for any of the other fighters Titch had seen. For the time being there was no sign of them.

'Well done Titch. Well done Derek. Excellent!' Though my heart was beating hard and I was breathing quickly into my face mask I smiled at what I had heard. 'Bloody Hell!' Titch had said. I'd never heard him swear before. In fact, in our crew, none of us swore.

'Crossing the Dutch coast now, Skip. Course 340 and descend to 10,000 feet.'

'Three four zero.'

After a quick glance at my altimeter I was glad to put the nose forward to achieve the descent Colin's calm voice had called for and at the same time to increase my speed to take us away from this dangerous part of the sky. Now over the sea we began to descend more slowly but still further than our evasive actions had taken us.

Two or three more smaller changes of course and then, just before midnight, Ken said 'Searchlight dead ahead'. It was the searchlight guider at Mablethorpe. Fourteen minutes later we were over base, and stacked at 2000 feet, then 1500, then 1000.

The girl in Flying Control gave us a barometric reading to check our altimeter. '*Easy 2* downwind.' Wheels down. '*Easy 2* funnels.' Select flap. Nearer, nearer, to the ground. Nose up a little as I closed the throttles. The little lights of the runway swept past us on each side. The wheels touched the ground, rose a foot, touched again, rolled on down the runway, then squealed a little as I applied some brake. I braked more and slowed as we came to the point where we could leave the runway and turn onto the perimeter track.

'*Easy 2* clear. Over.'

And so we came to our dispersal, to our locker room and to the Operations Room. A nice smile from the WAAF as she handed to each of us a mug of hot cocoa with a little rum in it. Many exchanges of greetings among tired but relieved faces. Debriefing and the usual questions.

I could not remember being so tired.

4th NOVEMBER, 1944 – BOCHUM

749 aircraft – 384 Halifaxes, 336 Lancasters, 29 Mosquitoes – 1, 4, 6 and 8 Groups.

23 Halifaxes and 5 Lancasters were lost; German night fighters caused most of the casualties.

346 (Free French) Squadron, based at Elvington, lost 5 out of its 16 Halifaxes on the raid.

This was a particularly successful attack, based upon standard Pathfinder marking techniques. Severe damage was caused to the centre of Bochum. More than 4000 buildings were destroyed or seriously damaged. 980 Germans and 14 foreigners were killed. Bochum's industrial areas were also severely damaged, particularly the important steelworks. This was the last major raid by Bomber Command on this target.

(*The Bomber Command War Diaries*, Middlebrook and Everitt)

CHAPTER SIXTEEN

Squadron Leader

Next morning was bright and clear. There would be no operation that evening, we understood, and Gerry Wilson and I cycled into the little town of Louth. Gerry and I seemed to have much in common, and had become good friends.

Kelstern is on the Wolds, a ridge of higher ground that runs for about 25 miles, about 12 miles away from the Lincolnshire coast, from level with Grimsby, which is out to the east of it, then south to be level with Lincoln, which is out to the west of it. It is sparsely populated, agricultural downland where small hills fold one into another and in those folds sleepy villages take shelter from the keen icy winds that blow across the Wolds in winter. Driving along the length of this upland Lincolnshire you can often look down to the flatter land to east and west, from the patchwork fields of the Wolds to the larger, more prosperous-looking farms on either side. Here and there on the flanks of the downs men in times gone by have planted woods, and sometimes lines of trees, making a bulwark for a field or meadow from the bitter north-east wind – small gestures against the searing cold.

But now, this November morning, it was a lovely day. The rounded slopes of hills were very green in the autumn sunshine and the narrow road curved down the hill off the high ground where Kelstern aerodrome straddled a grassy plateau and Lancasters in their dispersal pans looked like great long black insects against the pale sky. The airfield was near the seaward edge of the Wolds and could almost look down into the hollow where Louth nestled, its church tower hidden behind the green shoulder of a field but its famous spire rising up out of a stand of ancient trees.

On each side of us was no gradual, even slope of grass fields, but a slope of interlinking gradients. The road, cut between the ancient pastures, followed their winding fall. History had long forgotten how this strange earthwork was made or by whom, but soon we passed a big bowl on our left, which was made much more recently. Earlier that year a Lancaster, fully laden with the night's petrol load and with all its bombs still hanging in its bay, swung off on take-off, went over the edge and exploded.

Our visit to Louth was exploratory. Our first exploration took us into the Masons' Arms, that Sunday morning, a pleasant, small hotel. It was the sort of place at which you would book a room for someone dear, should that requirement ever arise, rather than into any hostelry in Grimsby or Cleethorpes. Those were the destinations you preferred to go on an evening when stood down, perhaps there expect to meet with someone perhaps not so dear but more fitting for your mood.

We ate a simple lunch at the Masons' Arms and then toiled back up the hill to the camp. I was quite stiff after my exertions of last night. Back at Kelstern rumour was soon found to have sound foundation: there were no operations tonight but a briefing was ordered for 5 o'clock in the morning. This could only mean a daylight operation. Accordingly I and also Gerry went that afternoon with our crews to our dispersals and made our usual checks and run-ups on our aircraft, which in my case was again to be the acrobatic *Easy 2*. We were glad to hear from our ground crew that she had apparently not dislocated anything. Soon we knew that the petrol load was 1850 gallons again. Surely the Ruhr would be a rather dangerous place in daylight? Keen to be alert for whatever proved to be in store, we went to bed early.

Though well placed to greet the dawn as early as anyone, Kelstern's buildings were still in darkness as, breakfasted, we approached the Ops Room and took our places. It was to be a large daylight raid on Gelsenkirchen. *Easy 2* was to be one of more than 700 aircraft. The aiming point was the Nordstern synthetic-oil plant. The bombing of German oil supplies was being stepped up in response to intelligence reports that the enemy was finding it difficult to satisfy its enormous appetite for fuel.

As *Easy 2* turned on to the runway in the first light of morning, the little crowd of well-wishers at the caravan was there in spite of the inconvenience of the hour. They waved enthusiastically as each aircraft turned into wind, opened its four throttles and roared down the dim flarepath and up into the cold morning air, gathering its wheels into itself and banking and climbing away to the left. We climbed in darkness, but as we gained altitude we met the first rays of the watery sun as it rose above the horizon in front of us and we scaled the curvature of the earth.

Soon we were bathed in a pearly light. The fronts of our engine nacelles blushed a rosy pink. As minutes passed the real colours, the black of *Easy 2*'s engines and underbelly and the khaki and olive green of her wing surfaces, with indigo and dull red roundels, superimposed themselves on the fairyland colours of dawn and the magic evaporated. We turned southwards and the sun rose higher on our left. We ran into a layer of fluffy altocumulus clouds. Our course took *Easy 2* into the clouds and sometimes between them, so that she was now in sunshine, now in a grey-white mist that shut out all vision, now flying between the sun and a cloud, so that she threw upon it a strange moving shadow, as of a giant winged creature from a distant epoch of the world.

Colin calculated and gave me changes of course. Derek listened out for the messages and information, all in today's code, which came out from England, logging them or passing them on to Colin. Ken fused his bombs and changed the settings on his sight. Tim watched his gauges. Torry and Titch asked for permission to test their guns and did so. I flew on, watching the horizon and all the instruments, which confirmed that we flew at the height, the speed, and on the course that the navigator had last given me. And all the time, each one of us, except the curtained Colin, raised our eyes with urgent necessary frequency from our various tasks to watch, and watch, and watch the sky about us.

The hours passed. Derek confirmed that his Fishpond showed us reasonably in the middle of the stream, individuals of which lay over on our left, and right, and in my own view, there ahead of us. The two gunners spoke at intervals and I knew that they were all right, and on oxygen. The height of other aircraft varied. This was the first time I had been able to see how the stream looked, from one aircraft to all those others near enough to be seen. Being one of about 700, it was surprising to see that we were not in any apparent danger of collision, and yet only two days before, our lives had so nearly ended in an orange ball of flame. It was better to realise that every so often, especially when in cloud, there is another aeroplane, perhaps several, very near indeed and on converging or even collision course, and maintain that nerve-taut ceaseless vigilance, which so much of this bombing thing was all about.

Colin had given us our ETA on target. Now I was watching for any sign that we were really close. It was the bomb aimer who saw it first.

'Target ahead, fine on the port bow.' At that moment I, too, observed the shell-bursts patterning the sky in the distant direction Ken had indicated. At night, flak had been fierce flashes of white and yellow light, muffled to orange by their smoke. They looked like snakes' heads of fire instantaneously poised on lines of tracer, arching upwards, as the big guns far below, aided by radar's invisible antennae, spewed out their deadly shells at a rate of 20 rounds a minute, at a muzzle velocity of 3280 feet a second, and up to a height of 32,000 feet, way above our ceiling. If they were close enough you saw the white-hot fragments tearing through the air around each shell-burst. Now, in daylight, each burst was a black puff, a dirty ball of sooty smoke around a red-hot centre. The result was the same, of course, as sometimes you saw when an aircraft was hit and exploded, usually, in terrible disintegration made silent by distance and the drone of your own engines.

Concentrating on the target, watching the aiming point tracking down the lines of his bomb sight, Ken was no doubt able to get as clear an idea in daylight as at night of the ground and what we were attempting to do. For me, the situation down there, the smoke, the gun flashes and the bomb bursts, seen as I banked and turned away after bombing but of necessity ignored as I concentrated on our bombing run, were, when seen from nearly 4 miles up and in daylight, but a sparkle of pinpoint lights among small mushrooms of smoke and dust. In a daylight raid I was not forcibly made conscious of the fires and brilliant explosions on the ground, or even of the frightening pyrotechnics all around us in the air, or the waving arms of searchlights, as I was at night. So we bombed. We closed the doors and turned away. We flew through a sky made dirty by the black smoke-puffs of flak, which one moment were not there, the next moment hung motionless on our port or starboard bows, and in the next moment rushed past us on the left or right at the speed of our flight. As we made our way from the target area the Master Bomber called the rest of the stream to divert to the town to the east of the plant.

It seemed strange to fly back to an aerodrome we could see, and make our approach down on to the runway's end over trees and quiet lanes and up-turned faces. Strange to see, as we looked across the airfield from about 1000 feet, as we called up on our downwind leg, the Watch Office, the very building from which the girl's answering voice was coming. Strange also, after debriefing and a wash, to walk into the Mess dining room and have lunch, not as tired, unless their last six or seven hours had been particularly straining, as after one of those too-long days that a night trip had lengthened.

6th NOVEMBER, 1944 – GELSENKIRCHEN
738 aircraft – 383 Halifaxes, 324 Lancasters, 31 Mosquitoes.
3 Lancasters and 2 Halifaxes lost.

This large daylight raid had, as its aiming point, the Nordstern synthetic-oil plant. The attack was not well concentrated but 514 aircraft were able to bomb the approximate position of the oil plant before smoke obscured the ground; 187 aircraft then bombed the general town area of Gelsenkirchen.

A Gelsenkirchen war-diarist, who often recorded interesting details, tells of how this Protestant town had celebrated the Reformation Feast the previous day, a Sunday. The celebration had been held back from its proper date, 31st October, so as not to interfere with industrial production. The diarist wrote, 'For many pious people this was their last church service. Catastrophe broke over Gelsenkirchen the following day'. The diary proceeds to give several pages describing the severe damage throughout the town. The number of people killed was 518. The diarist comments, perhaps with some pride, that this was the first time in the war that Gelsenkirchen was mentioned by name in the OKW (German High Command) communiqué.

(*The Bomber Command War Diaries*, Middlebrook and Everitt)

Two days later the battle order was up on the notice board for another dawn briefing. We had *Easy 2* again. So, early on that Tuesday morning, we set course for Germany, changed course, and changed course again, climbing all the time through cloud. The target was another oil refinery, this time at Wanne-Eickel in the Ruhr. As an exercise in instrument flying it had much to commend it, and as a test of pilots' powers of concentration and nervous stamina too, but as an attack on the enemy's oil resources it was a failure. It had been expected that we should come out of cloud before we got to the target, though probably with a layer of lower cloud still persisting, which Pathfinder Mosquitoes would be able to mark with Wanganui flares. Over Wanne-Eickel, however, the cloud was found to extend up to 21,000 feet, which was higher than most of us even in Lancasters could reach with the bomb load we were carrying. The higher-flying Mosquitoes were controlled by Oboe from home stations and although unable to see the target they let fall their sky-markers on signal. The markers were seen to disappear into cloud as soon as they ignited, so our only way of knowing that we had reached the target, for the guns were silent so as not to declare their position, or to leave the sky clear for fighters, was navigators' dead reckoning. After we had bombed, we heard the Master Bomber calling us all on R/T. Those who came later were ordered to bomb any built-up area. After that raid no intelligence reached Air Ministry as to where the bombs fell, and photographic reconnaissance was impossible.

Though the guns were silent, German fighters were in evidence on the way home. In daylight, the .303 Brownings of RAF air gunners were no match, hardly even a deterrent, for the cannon of the fighters. Crews reported persistent attacks.

When my crew and I were in the Operations Room for debriefing, we learned that Wally, the commander of B Flight, who with his navigator and rear gunner had been taking a sprog crew for their 'second dicky' initiation flight, was not yet back.

9th NOVEMBER, 1944 – WANNE-EICKEL

256 Lancasters and 21 Mosquitoes of 1 and 8 Groups to attack the oil refinery.

Cloud over the target was found to reach 21,000 feet and the sky-markers dropped by the Oboe Mosquitoes disappeared as soon as they ignited so the Master Bomber ordered the force to bomb any built-up area. The town of Wanne-Eickel reports only 2 buildings destroyed, with 4 civilians and 6 foreigners killed. It must be assumed that other towns in the Ruhr were hit, but no details are available. 2 Lancasters lost.

(*The Bomber Command War Diaries*, Middlebrook and Everitt)

That evening the Squadron CO called me over to him in the Mess. It was only a fortnight since I had flown my first operational flight over Germany, but it seemed much longer. The CO began by asking me how I was getting on. We had flown six operational trips. In that time the squadron had lost five aircraft and Bomber Command had lost a minimum of 132. The CO and I each had a mug of beer. We talked together and I got to know W/Cdr MacKay, rather better. He had come to 625 Squadron from Training Command, where he had spent the war so far, rather in the same way as W/Cdr Kidd had done when he came to 233 Squadron in the summer of 1941. But MacKay was a humbler man, and I liked him better for it. He told me that when he had first arrived at the squadron he had been astonished at what he saw.

'There appeared to be no discipline, Peter, as I had known it. Fortunately, I realised quickly that there was a discipline, rather better in fact than I had experienced up to that time. It was a discipline by consent. I realised that these bomber aircrew would do anything they were called upon to do. It was the opinion of their fellow aircrew that mattered. In order to keep their esteem they would keep pressing on regardless, even when they themselves knew that they were dangerously tired. All they asked in return was that they should receive recognition of what they were doing: so long as, on the BBC News, there was some mention of the Command's night's or day's activities, however inaccurate that report might be.

And it is the same with the ground crews. You have not yet experienced how bitterly cold it can be up here on the Wolds in winter, yet those ground crews, working almost all the time out of doors, keeping their aircraft serviceable in spite of all the things which can go wrong with them, showing a proud loyalty to their aircrew and to the squadron, and like the aircrews, jealous of their reputation among their fellows, will keep on at it, all night when necessary, even when the metal is so cold that it sticks to their fingers.'

Here was needed something more subtle than leadership by one man, it was something very different from the sort of eagerness to follow (or perhaps readiness to go out in front) such as a man like the Duke of Wellington was said to be able to get from his 'scum of the earth'. And it needed a high quality of man, be he aircrew, every one of whom was a genuine volunteer, or these dedicated fitters and riggers who worked on the aeroplanes, for their corporate pride to make them so efficient a force. I was never able to reconcile as in any way fair or just the fact that some aircrew were commissioned and some were not. They were all doing the same job. Very often in a crew the pilot, who was captain of aircraft and must make the decisions, was an NCO and one or perhaps more than one of his crew was an officer. The commissioned bomb aimer would have slightly more advantages and privileges than the sergeant rear gunner only yards away from him in the same fighting unit, or than the sergeant bomb aimer in the nearby other aeroplane, but no more responsibility in the air or on the ground.

On the morning following my informal talk with the CO I was called to his office.

'Peter, you probably know that Wally did not make it back from yesterday's attack on Wanne-Eickel. There's still no news of him and those who were flying with him. I'm afraid that we must proceed on the basis that he may have been brought down. It is particularly wretched luck if so. He had only five more ops to do before he would have finished his tour. We may yet hear from him, but as from now I want you to take over B Flight. You may immediately assume the acting rank of Squadron Leader, which will be confirmed in due course.'

The news came as a complete surprise to me. Many others were, to my knowledge, more experienced in this sort of operational flying – Treherne for one. As I had so recently been thinking about the illogical disparity of rank between men who were essentially doing the same duties, I was determined to see that the additional contribution which I should make, over and above that of being captain of aircraft in a first class crew, would be commensurate with the extra pay, status, and any other advantages that this change would bring. The information took a few moments to sink in. When I did not respond, MacKay continued:

'I have just returned from the Operations Room. I have been on the blower to Group. We have a target for tonight and I am about to call in the Flight Commanders and the five Leaders, for I have already discussed the proposed route with the Navigation Leader Alec Flett. I expect you know the form. As you are now one of the Flight Commanders, you will remain for our discussion. You will remember that you will then return to what is now your B Flight office and call together the captains of aircraft in B Flight. I am sorry that circumstances have not allowed you to have any time to get to know the men you will now be commanding, for you are of course more familiar with the chaps in C Flight. I'm sure that as the days go by you will be able to remedy that.

Remember, you will tell them the petrol load, but nothing else. You will make out a list of those who will be flying tonight with the letter of the aircraft, subject to serviceability, each will fly. When your list is completed you will take it to the squadron Adjutant for typing and promulgation. At our discussion we shall confirm how many crews each flight will provide. If it were a Maximum Effort you would be flying too. As tonight it is not it is up to you.'

'I shall of course fly, Sir.'

MacKay rose and extended his hand over the desk.

'I expected no less. My very best wishes, Peter. Please come and see me at any time if you have any problem with which you think I could help.'

Very warming was the welcome to their number from the other flight commanders, Woodie Hammond of C Flight and Alan Fry of A Flight, and from the five leaders, which I received. If they were feeling the absence of Wally they did not betray it. I was glad to find that I already knew as friends several of the B Flight pilots, though in the relatively short time I had been in the squadron I did not yet know all of them well, or necessarily know which flight everybody was in.

That afternoon, thirty-six hours after the Wanne-Eickel operation, we were briefed for a night operation on Dortmund. It was a smaller force than several recent ones had been – only fifteen from the squadron and only about 200 from the Command. It was back to the Ruhr against another synthetic-oil plant. On the raid in which 625 Squadron was involved, carried out by No. 1 Group with nineteen Mosquitoes of 8 Group, no aircraft were lost. We heard a similar force of Lancasters of No. 5 Group, however, bombing a synthetic-oil plant at Harburg near Hamburg, had lost seven.

11/12th NOVEMBER, 1944 – DORTMUND
209 Lancasters and 19 Mosquitoes of 1 and 8 Groups. No aircraft lost.

The aiming point was the Hoesch Benzin synthetic-oil plant in the Wambel district. A local report confirms that the plant was severely damaged. Other bombs hit nearby housing and the local airfield. 83 people were killed and 85 injured.

11/12th NOVEMBER, 1944 – HARBURG
237 Lancasters and 8 Mosquitoes of 5 Group. 7 Lancasters lost.

The aiming point for this raid was the Rhenania-Ossag oil refinery, which had been attacked several times by American day bombers. Brunswig's history of the Hamburg/Harburg air raids gives this raid only a brief mention, saying that considerable damage was caused in Harburg's residential and industrial areas but the oil refinery is not mentioned. 119 people were killed and 5205 were bombed out.

(*The Bomber Command War Diaries*, Middlebrook and Everitt)

On the next day, 12 November, and quite without warning to those at Kelstern, W/Cdr MacKay was posted away and his place was taken by W/Cdr Barker. He arrived in the morning and MacKay handed over to him. The squadron was stood down and that evening W/Cdr Barker and I sat together in the Mess and talked. The decision to send him to 625 Squadron must have been sudden, because whereas I and others had left Sandtoft on completion of our conversion course on to Halifax four-engined bombers and gone for eleven days to RAF Hemswell for familiarisation with the Lancaster, he had gone from Sandtoft to Scampton, been given about an hour in a Lancaster and then sent straight to Kelstern to take command of 625, a Lancaster squadron. Certainly no inkling had been given during MacKay's discussion with his Flight Commanders and Leaders on the previous day.

He was a very different man from MacKay, who had seemed rather diffident about his own lack of operational experience. It was almost a humility. Humility was not Barker's strong suit, but I liked immediately his directness and his transparent good-heartedness. My admiration for him was something that would increase with time. In that first conversation in the Mess I learned much about our new CO. Unlike his brother Sandy, a senior RAF medical officer, Barker had not followed his father into medicine but had read law at BNC at Oxford and been called to the Bar. Then he had decided on a career in the Air Force and had come in through Oxford University Air Squadron. Physically a copy-book scrum half, he had played rugby for the RAF and for invitation teams like Leicester Tigers. And he was a good cricketer. He told me so himself. At Oxford he had played for the Greyhounds and for the Authentics, second 15 and second 11 of the university. He had commanded 241 Hurricane Squadron in North Africa, doing mostly reconnaissance and tactical light bombing, and had worked in War Cabinet Plans from October 1943 to August 1944 when Operation *Overlord* was taking shape.

In due course I should know that he was tough – with courage, self-confidence and an engaging though rather sarcastic sense of humour, and he knew the value of the old boy network. That evening marked the beginning of a friendship that I valued very much.

Next day twenty aircraft were required of 625 Squadron by Group. The new CO made out the battle order and put himself on it. It was his second day on a Lancaster and he was on operations in it. His decision commanded the respect of the squadron at a stroke. I and my crew were on the battle order too. We were in *Jig 2*. She was back from Folkingham and serviceable again. *Easy 2* was to be flown by F/O Copland and his crew of six flight sergeants and sergeants. We were down on the battle order as Spare Crew but later, for some reason, F/O Spooner and his crew could not fly and we replaced them. But at least we were all together and not a mongrel crew of substitutes. It turned out to be another daylight operation, with briefing very early on the following morning. Our target was Duren, in support of the American Army. Bomber Command had been asked to bomb three towns near the German lines, which were about to be attacked by the American First and Ninth Armies near Aachen on their slow advance towards the Rhine. Of these towns 625 Squadron's target was Duren. The three raids were carried out in easy bombing conditions, and at debriefing no one spoke of fighters, but there was flak.

We were settled on our bombing run – bomb doors open. Ken was on his stomach in the nose. He watched the approaching aiming point through his bomb sight.

'R-i-g-h-t, steady, steady . . .'

Titch in the tail moved his eyes from left to right behind us, below us. Fighters knew that there, not silhouetted against the bright sky but less conspicuous against the distant, vaguely multicoloured ground, they were less visible. From that direction an attack might come.

I, in rapt attention to my instruments for my direction and speed, keeping my attitude level and height unchanging as we flew through the void of the sky immediately around us, was just conscious of Derek on his feet beside me. He was stretching up to have his head in the clear bubble of the astrodome, as he frequently did on the bombing run.

'LOOK UP! LOOK UP! ABOVE US!' The urgency of Torry's shout from the upper turret made me take my eye off my concentrated flying and look up. There was a darkening above the Perspex of the roof. Something loomed.

Derek, standing beside his wireless compartment with his head in the dome, saw it too. Dead above us, and close, and on our heading, was another Lancaster. Its bomb doors were open. We could see the 4000-pound cookie and all the other bombs on their hangers. There was a total weight of about 14,000 pounds. The bomb aimer above may have seen us. I didn't know. It wasn't possible to ask. My hand shot forward to seize the four throttles and I snatched them back. The jolt of the sudden deceleration threw Derek against the bulkhead in front of him. Tim, the engineer, was nearly thrown down into Ken's department. The higher Lancaster went ahead of us, and as we dropped a little, was now more above us.

It all happened very quickly. I pushed the throttles forward again. I had no wish to stall with a full bomb load and with the doors open. Ken, who must have wondered what was happening, was cool enough to drop his bombs.

Derek was sufficiently recovered from the bang on his head to watch the aircraft above and ahead of us, which had looked about to drop an awful big weight on us and break *Jig 2*'s back. He even claimed to have read the registration number. Certainly, he was as observant as a hawk.

Suddenly there was a blinding flash. The aircraft previously immediately above us, now barely 200 yards ahead, disintegrated. A flak shell must have hit its fused cookie, a shell that had arrived and exploded in the same bit of airspace as Jig 2 and her crew had been about to occupy. There was no question of looking for parachutes. The whole thing and all its contents effectively vaporised. Miraculously, we were just far enough away for the blast to do little more than rock us.

Three Lancasters were lost on that raid. That was one of them and it was so nearly two birds with one barrel. If Derek's reading of the number was correct, it was one of our neighbours of the Australian squadron at Binbrook. When we got home we learned that another of the missing aircraft was *Easy 2*. *Easy 2* had brought us back safely from Dusseldorf, Gelsenkirchen, Wanne-Eickel, Dortmund, and from the horrors of the Bochum adventure, five trips in the first ten days of November. No one knew what her fate had been.

16th NOVEMBER, 1944 – DUREN

Bomber Command was asked to bomb 3 towns near the German lines which were about to be attacked by the American 1st and 9th Armies in the area between Aachen and the Rhine. 1188 Bomber Command aircraft attacked Duren, Julich and Heinsburg in order to cut communications behind the German lines. Duren was attacked by 485 Lancasters and 13 Mosquitoes of 1, 5, and 8 Groups; Julich by 413 Halifaxes, 78 Lancasters and 17 Mosquitoes of 4, 6, and 8 Groups; Heinburg by 182 Lancasters of 3 Group.

3 Lancasters were lost on the Duren raid and 1 Lancaster on the Heinburg raid.

1239 American heavy bombers also made raids on targets in the same area without suffering any losses. More than 9400 tons of high explosive bombs were dropped by the combined bomber forces.

The RAF raids were all carried out in easy bombing conditions and the 3 towns were virtually destroyed. Duren, whose civilian population was still present, suffered 3127 fatal casualties – 2403 local civilians, 398 civilians from other places temporarily staying in Duren and 326 unidentified, of whom at least 217 were soldiers. Heinsburg, described in the British press with other targets as 'a heavily defended town', contained only 110 civilians and a local military unit of 1 officer and a few soldiers: 52 of the civilians were killed. No report was available from Julich.

The American advance was not a success. Wet ground prevented the use of tanks and the American artillery units were short of ammunition because of supply difficulties. The infantry advance was slow and costly.

(*The Bomber Command War Diaries*, Middlebrook and Everitt)

After Duren we never saw Tim Cordon again. He left the station without notice. This was a bit of a mystery, and as W/Cdr MacKay had also left, I could not ask him. Very, very rarely a man's nerve cracked. It was probably an occurrence that any member of aircrew could contemplate happening, but the prospect of it filled him with horror. It was called LMF – Lack of Moral Fibre. Every member of aircrew was a volunteer, and though some might have failed to appreciate what a cumulation of fear and stress some men might have to undergo, the courage and resilience of such men as had offered themselves to be aircrew, backed up by the exceptionally strong spirit of comradeship that existed in every unit, would make each one of them unable to believe that it could happen to them. Men prayed it would never happen to them. Though the engineer had been seen to be more fond of pints of beer than could be expected to improve his efficiency in the team, we preferred to support the theory that he had damaged his ear drums. This could have been at any time when we had had to dive suddenly, particularly if he was flying with a cold. The acrobatics over Bochum in particular had been rather testing for anybody's ears.

Two days later I was on the battle order again, but as Spare Crew for the spare aircraft *Baker 2*. I had Derek, Ken and Torry, but an unfamiliar navigator, F/O Carter, a tail gunner called Sgt Loughran and a flight engineer called F/Sgt Maynard. None of that would have mattered, but for the fact that the spare aircraft was again called upon to fly. There must have been some reason why I could not have Colin or Titch, both vital to my peace of mind, and why those in authority decided, so late on, that one more aeroplane-load was so essential. Knowing his history, I could not be sure if having Maynard to fly with us was something to be glad about or horrified. Was he a talisman or a jinx? Was he a man cursed with bad luck or a man loved by the gods and protected by them? But Maynard was available, and though Derek was not entirely happy about his inclusion, I was of the opinion that the poor chap might think himself shunned if we refused him and that if any man needed his confidence restoring, it was he. It was agreed that he should come with us, and this probably helped him, for he later joined a new crew and they were happy with him.

Earlier in the war, Maynard had been travelling in an aircraft in France that was brought down, and he had survived the bale-out. More recently, coming to 625 Squadron, he was allocated to the crew of Sgt Hannah. Soon afterwards Hannah was taking off on an op, and had the misfortune to have engine failure at about 500 feet. Hannah told his crew to bale out. In spite of the low altitude and consequent considerable hurry, five of the seven survived. Of the other two, the bomb aimer's parachute did not open and poor Hannah, trying to keep the thing up while his crew jumped, did not get out at all. The crater they made was now a fishpond. Maynard wore two of the little gold caterpillar brooches that were awarded by the parachute makers, Messrs Irving, to those who had made a successful bale-out.

The target that night was Wanne-Eickel again, the same town with the synthetic-oil plant that we had attempted to bomb nine days earlier, when there was thick towering cloud over the town and the Master Bomber had realised that it was a non-starter. We bombed with a force smaller than usual.

18/19 NOVEMBER, 1944 – WANNE-EICKEL
285 Lancasters and 24 Mosquitoes of 1, and 8 Groups. 1 Lancaster lost.

The intention of the raid was to hit the local oil plant. Large explosions seemed to erupt in the plant, and post-raid reconnaissance showed that some further damage was caused to it.

The local report does not mention the oil plant but states that the Hannmibal coal mine was destroyed and that 57 people were killed, 35 of them in a Bunkerpanik.

(*The Bomber Command War Diaries*, Middlebrook and Everitt)

At the briefing the Met forecast had sounded a bit dodgy so we were not very surprised when on the way home we received orders to land, not at Kelstern but at Snetterton Heath in Norfolk.

Snetterton Heath turned out to be an aerodrome being used by the Americans, as was our previous 'sleeping around' occasion at Folkingham. But this time we were expected. The unforgettable part of that trip was the early morning tea. Although an American station, there were, as at Folkingham, British WAAFs. It was a hutted camp, we did not sleep in tents, and I was given a room to myself in one of the huts. Having slept very well I was awakened by a trim little WAAF bringing me early morning tea. I could not remember it happening at any other time in the Air Force before. I could have hugged her. Indeed, I should very much have liked to hug her. As we left our huts on the way to the Mess for breakfast a little party of WAAFs, those who had brought us tea, batwomen for Americans, presumably, stood by the path and waved us goodbye. There she was, the one who had brought me my cup, a small, smiling person with dark hair and deep blue eyes. Yes, I should have loved to hug her.

The weather conditions that had required this diversion did not improve enough for a few hours, so it was afternoon before we took off to return to Kelstern. We had lunch there, another of those unfamiliar American meals. We queued up with plates to receive our portion from a cook-lady in a white coat, who cut it out with a fish slice. It was minced meat, about two inches thick in the baking pan, and it was thickly spread with red jam. I of course did not complain; it was only that it was unfamiliar.

A day or two later I and my crew were unexpectedly detailed for some leave. I was ready for it. Leave meant Tiled Cottage, family, and, if there is a God, Sally. It may not seem much but the concentration required for those six- or seven-hour flights, the necessity to fly the thing the required height course and speed and at the same time to keep that desperately important watch on every visible area of the sky, be it dark or light, was quite tiring. The nervous tension of flying through those curtains of flak and at the same time to fly accurately, to keep an eye on those waving fingers of the searchlights, sometimes to have to put everything you had got into throwing up to 30 tons of aeroplane about in a hostile night sky with no assistance but your own arms and legs, took it out of you. The Medical Officer knew this. Knowing I was going on leave he came up to me in the Mess one lunch time.

'You've got a girlfriend at home I expect?'

'I don't know yet if she'll have leave, I've not had time to get a reply back.'

'Well take this anyhow.' He handed me a little phial. I laughed.

'What's this then, Spanish Fly?'

'Call it what you like, but it's for you, and it won't hurt you. Remember that I've been looking after people like you for more than two years.'

I took it, but I managed to lose it. When I found it some time afterwards it had grown furry specks in it, but perhaps water would have done the same.

I had decided not to tell my mother that I was on operations. I had been in Training Command for so long that she presumably thought that I still was. But she said that I looked tired. My answer was mostly honest.

'Too many late nights.'

One evening when neither John Barker, nor I were on the battle order, we were joined by G/Capt Donkin, the station commander, as we were walking back towards the Mess from Flying Control. We had watched the last of the squadron's Lancasters on the operation roll down the runway and climb into the grey evening sky over Lincolnshire and head towards the assembly point, over which the bomber stream would turn and begin their feinting route towards that night's target. It would be several hours before the three of us would return to Flying Control and watch every aircraft, we hoped, return. Something was troubling the senior man.

'John, I'm afraid I've got to complain about the behaviour of one of your officers.'

'Sir?' John's voice was anxious.

'Yes, last night, quite late, I went into the billiard room, and there was your Flight Lieutenant Treherne having Up and Down on the table with Flight Officer Benson.'

'I'm sorry Sir, but these chaps are under a bit of a strain. A little Up and

Down unquestionably helps some of them to unwind. But of course I will . . . '
Perhaps there was a tiny bit more sparkle in Donkin's eye as he continued
deliberately.

'But John, you don't understand. His balls were in balk.'

Donkin had a delightful sense of humour, and in spite of its isolation and
lack of the sort of comforts and facilities that a station built in peacetime could
offer, Kelstern deserved its name of 'Happidrome'.

F/Sgt Reg Wood now joined us as our flight engineer. He had been a bank
manager, we understood, and was older than any of us. He was steady, reliable
and methodical. We had been fortunate. Our next trip, in *N Nan*, was to Bonn.
Bonn was a little further down the Rhine than the Ruhr towns. It was dark when
we climbed up into starlight over Kelstern that evening. I thought that the Met
man sounded hesitant as he briefed us. It was as though, had it been his decision, we should not have gone. I remembered early-winter briefings at Bishop's
Court, when I had had to decide if aircraft should grope their way round the
mountain-encircled Irish Sea. But this man was not required to make a decision, only to tell us what to expect, though it would be a brave man who would
get up and say that of course it was raving lunacy to be going, if his masters had
decreed it so.

There were three raids that night, on Politz up by Stetin, a very long way
away, and on Cologne/Nippes, as well as our Bonn raid. As we flew over France
on our way back, Derek reported that, according to his interpretation of
Fishpond, there were fewer aircraft in the stream than briefing had led him to
expect. Had some squadrons or whole bases been recalled? I had complete
confidence in Derek. He would not have missed a recall signal, however coded.
We had bombed, but the target and that part of Germany had been cloud-
covered. We had had no way of telling if the target had been correctly marked.

Then as we crossed the south coast Derek picked up a signal.

'Change of plan, Skipper. We have been ordered to land at a place called
Sturgate.' Colin knew, even if we didn't, that Sturgate was in west Lincolnshire,
not far from Kelstern. So the trouble at home must be quite local. It was the
weather almost certainly. It was almost inconceivable that someone had
bombed the place but perhaps there had been an accident blocking the runway.
Either that or someone had had such a prang that it had made the place unus-
able. It was Colin who discovered the likely answer.

'Skip, my manual says Sturgate has got Fido.'

We had heard vaguely of Fido, but knew very little. Certainly, we had never
seen it or been trained or even briefed on it. At a Fido station, and I had no idea
how many there were, I understood that earthenware drain pipes were laid
along the runway, on each side, end to end but not joined, and petrol was
pumped through at a pressure sufficient to allow most of the petrol to ignore
the gaps. The vapour was then ignited and became like two enormous almost
mile-long gas burners, one on each side of the runway. I had heard somewhere

how much petrol the thing used; it was an astronomical amount. Fortunately for us, those in authority had decided that this vast expenditure was preferable to losing unacceptable numbers of aircraft and expensively trained crews trying to land in thick fog.

I concentrated on how my landing technique might be affected. Air turbulence as the aircraft came in to land would be considerable. Certainly this would not be a night to swing and run off the runway! I tried to think of any other considerations that could affect my handling of the aircraft. Surely the hot air would be less dense and therefore less buoyant, therefore I should come in a bit faster but remember how near those flames would be, so I must not depart from normal too much, and perhaps I had got the air density theory wrong anyhow.

We were now low enough, losing height as we flew north over England, to get the impression that the entire country was blanked out with fog. Above us it was clear and starlit, but below, the ground was invisible. Then we saw an orange glow ahead of us. As we came nearer it was plain that a blanket of fog indeed covered the land. But the fog above that orange glow seemed to bubble and lift. When I called up, Sturgate gave us a barometric pressure to check our altimeter. We circuited around that strangely lighted cauldron. After a while Sturgate called.

'*Nan*, make your approach.'

I positioned the aircraft to come towards the downwind end of that coloured rectangle. I continued to lose height, watching my altimeter. We were in starlight and then, suddenly, we were in fog. Mist enveloped us. It was as though I was flying towards the sunset, approached through frosted glass. I was totally dependent on instruments. It was like the Blind Approach Course at Watchfield, but this time without the dots and dashes sounding in my ears.

Then the colour brightened and it was like flying indoors. It seemed as if I was flying into a huge vaulted cavern. We appeared to be within a fiery holograph. The walls on each side of us were aflame and the high vaulted roof was smoke reflecting downwards the orange of the walls. Before us stretched the runway. Perspective narrowed it to a point far down this bizarre avenue of hot light. I applied a little brake, but carefully. We should be a funeral pyre if we swung off now. At the end of the runway, where the light was dimmer, there was a lighted arrow to direct us left. And so we taxied cautiously round the perimeter track in the light given us by the flarepath over on our left, and came to a dispersal where circling torches directed us.

The sound was extraordinary. Perhaps because of the roar of the petrol flames our own engines were quiet. An aircrew bus collected us, and the crew of another aircraft too. We were driven from that weird inferno into the cool, damp sightless dark of the countryside. Obviously the driver would know his way well, but it was a slow and difficult journey for him, taking us to an Operations Room and eventually to food, as required, and bed.

21/22 DECEMBER, 1944 – BONN

97 Lancasters and 17 Mosquitoes of 1 and 8 Groups attempted to attack railway areas but thick cloud cover prevented an accurate raid and later reconnaissance showed that the railway target was not hit. No other details are available. No aircraft lost.

(*The Bomber Command War Diaries*, Middlebrook and Everitt)

The great German offensive in the Ardennes had started on 16 December, with the objective of capturing Brussels and the port of Antwerp and splitting the Allied armies into two parts. The attack was launched under cover of poor weather conditions; in the first half of December Bomber Command several times had to cancel operations. Now Sturgate held captive twenty-four Lancasters of 625 Squadron, and doubtless many aircraft from other squadrons, away from home, away from facilities of maintenance and armament, and cut off even by road from their bases.

The next day we were still there, and the day after. I was in touch with W/Cdr Barker at Kelstern. We were wanted back. It was decided on the third day that Sturgate would burn a few more hundred thousand gallons of petrol so that we could take off. We were to land at the now rather clearer Kelstern, but if not, then return to the Fido fires of Sturgate.

It was Christmas Eve. We waited until about midday, but there was no improvement in the weather. So having done our checks in a fog-enshrouded dispersal, I waved the chocks away and followed the circling torches as an aircraftman walked backwards on to the misty perimeter path. I was to take off first. Though quite a recent idea, Fido had been used several times to get aircraft down when conditions of visibility made it likely that many would crash if they attempted to land without benefit of this fog-lifting invention. At the short briefing we had had that morning, I had not been comforted by the news that Fido had not previously been used to enable aircraft to take off. Nobody seemed to know much about it or to be able to give any advice. Before its invention aircraft were hardly ever sent off when the Met people had grave doubts about fog for their return. Had Command gambled a bit on 21 December, knowing that Fido was available? I remembered our Met man's rather hesitant briefing that night. And surely, having got twenty-four of us (and for all I knew many others too of other units) safely down, we should not be going up again into this blind air unless there was indeed some convincing reason!

The roar of the flames as they ignited Fido was again easily heard above the noise of our four engines. Very quickly visibility in our vicinity improved as the fog burned and taxiing became easier. It was just as well, as it was not so much the bill for every minute of all this petrol going up in flames that seemed so extravagant, as the thought of the risk that sailors had taken to bring it here. As I turned *Nan* on to the runway I had again that strange feeling that we were indoors. We were going to career down the length of this great vaulted cavern and fly out through the roof. I released the brakes, opened the throttles and gathered speed. Reg's hand followed mine on the spring-loaded levers.

'Full power.'

Perhaps more consciously than usual I corrected the Lancaster's habitual slight swing to port. I felt her lift off the ground, unladen and eager to climb, but I kept her down a little longer to get up more speed. Then I gave her her head and we went through the roof. Among the eddying smoke of burning petrol the turbulence was noticeable, and then we were above the fog and flying due east in sunshine. Gainsborough behind us to our left and Market Rasen ahead of us lay under that white blanket. But a little further on we could see the hump of the Lincolnshire Wolds lying like a whale basking in white water. We reached Kelstern in fifteen minutes and landed in bright sun.

The twenty-four Lancasters had not been serviced since before they had been bombed up and made ready for our take-off for the Bonn raid. If we had been so urgently wanted back as to justify so expensive a recall, it would not be long before we should be away again. W/Cdr Barker had been busy ensuring that when the call came 625 Squadron's aircraft would be ready.

I walked to my hut in contemplative mood. It was Christmas Eve. Children all over Britain would soon be going to bed and putting their stockings out ready for Father Christmas. Once again it would probably be Mummy Christmas, if one knew about these things, as Daddy was away. Children who had been evacuated to America and Canada, who had made the perilous journey through German submarine-infested seas, probably thought about the Mummy and Daddy they had not seen for a long time, and because of the time-difference they would put out their stockings later than children in England.

And what of the children in Germany? Many of them existed in shattered or doomed towns, perhaps waiting for the siren that would send them once again down to the *Bunkerpanik*. Probably German children had been evacuated too, but where? Nearer to the Russian front? Whither do you evacuate your children when you've declared war on virtually the whole world?

How awful this war was! Now, the newspapers told us that in Russia the Communist armies were driving back the German invaders. For months the German war-machine had fought its way across the whole of Russia. Towns and villages had often been razed to the ground or burnt by the retreating armies to deny them to the Germans. Was there any family there who had not lost loved ones? Be they children or men and women the numbers killed could never be counted, but they would be reckoned in millions. In Poland, that Christmas Eve, it was all happening again as the tide of fighting was reversed. Shellfire and machine-gun fire, anti-personnel mortars and rockets were taking their toll of civilians and soldiers alike. They must be, with the people caught between the Russian advance and the desperate German defence.

In the small Lincolnshire town of Louth children were putting their stockings out ready for Santa as they went to bed. Had the Germans invaded and overrun the British Isles, they were children who would have swelled the numbers of forced labourers, like those who even now, taken from their conquered homelands, were being forced to work in factories all over Germany, slave workers whom my bombs killed every night. But because of those children in Louth, and millions like them, the fighting and the bombing, had to go on, until the Evil was destroyed and the Nazi leaders toppled.

In the lower ground to the east of Louth mist was forming in the hollows but the thick fog had gone, which Louth's soaring famous spire had been trying to pierce. On the higher ground of the Wolds the distant noise of aircraft engines was heard again; people had seen the Lancasters return that afternoon as the fog lifted. Up there it was a clear starry night, but very cold. Frost sparkled on the grass around the dispersal pans and on the Lancasters themselves. It was dark now, but by torchlight and battery light the ground crews were still working on the aircraft. Muffled in balaclavas, their painful fingers protruded bare from their mittens so that they could hold the spanner or twist the wire-end to make a connection. It was one of those nights such as W/Cdr MacKay had spoken of, when the colder than ice-cold metal stuck to their fingers. Barker had said that it was very important to get the aircraft serviceable, and there was still much to do. He in his staff car, flight commanders on their motor-bikes, and some of the aircrews who would be flying their aircraft, yes, *their* aircraft, had been round to see them.

The ground crews worked on into Christmas Day. The fitters and the riggers, the armament crews, those who serviced the wireless sets, the radar sets, all the technical trades into which these RAF men had mustered, were represented among the small groups of men in and around each aircraft crouching on the concrete dispersal pans around the edges of the airfield on that cold night and day.

We heard there was some sort of panic on; it was rumoured that German Panzer divisions were spearheading a determined attack against the British Army who were advancing slowly, oh so slowly, through France and into Belgium towards the Rhine. It was Boxing Day, but very early in the morning, when Group called for a hurried take-off to join at last in the Ardennes battle. 625 Squadron achieved some sort of record by getting fourteen Lancasters off the ground at only two hours' notice. We were among nearly 300 aircraft of 1, 3, 4, 5, 6 and 8 Groups in a daylight attack on German troop positions near St Vith. It was not buildings or installations that I and my crew and all those other crews were bombing this time – Bomber Command was being used as artillery in a land battle.

25/26th DECEMBER, 1944 – ST VITH
The weather at last improved and allowed Bomber Command to intervene in the Ardennes battle. 294 aircraft – 146 Lancasters, 136 Halifaxes, 12 Mosquitoes

of all the bomber groups (not 100 Group) attacked German troop positions near St Vith. This was the first time since mid-October that aircraft from all the bomber groups had joined together in one raid. The bombing appeared to be concentrated and accurate.

(*The Bomber Command War Diaries*, Middlebrook and Everitt)

We returned to find a new battle order already up on the board. Early on the following morning we took our places for briefing, which the Base Commander, Air Commodore Wray (Daddy Wray) from Binbrook, attended. He was a much-decorated airman. His ribbons dated back to the 1914–18 war, and he had a wooden leg. It was to be an attack on railway yards at Rheydt, to prevent reinforcements and supplies reaching German positions. There were to be 200 Lancasters with attendant Mosquito markers. I and my crew were detailed to lead a Vic formation of three Lancasters out in front. As I later told Colin, this was a feather in our navigator's cap. We should be leading 200 and more and they wanted someone who could guarantee to get them there! At the end of the briefing 'Peg Leg' called me up to him.

'Your job is to attract the flak.'

I supposed he was right, a Vic formation of three bombers conveniently grouped together, stuck out in front, was a bit of a gift to a unit of anti-aircraft gunners, who might even get three with one barrel! I did not ask Colin or the rest of the crew to share the stump of anxiety I felt inside at being detailed for such an exposed and responsible position – with over 200 aircraft behind me! 'Your job is to attract the flak': the words delivered so informally, so casually, chased themselves round and round in my head.

We climbed up into the pearly light of dawn towards Germany. By the time we had reached the target the day was well aired. Rheydt, lying between Aachen and Monchen Gladbach, was waking up to the morning sun. The visibility was good.

'I can see the railway yards clearly Skip, steady as you go; bomb doors open . . .'

We bombed. I turned away to the left and made a wide circuit out over brown hills among which I could see many small farms. I was able to look across and see the stream of 200 Lancasters going in to bomb. I saw one hit and go down, a slanting trail of black oily smoke.

'Watch it please Torry – any parachutes?' But there were none.

Back in the crewroom, while closing my locker door, I saw Colin walking towards me. We smiled at each other

'It's you we've got you to thank for this, Vicar. Who else in the squadron – or squadrons of the other groups either – could they choose and be confident that he would get them there? And you did too!'

27th DECEMBER, 1944 – RHEYDT

200 Lancasters and 11 Mosquitoes of 1, 3, 5, and 8 Groups attacked the railway yards. 1 Lancaster was lost and 1 Mosquito crashed behind the Allied lines in Holland.

(*The Bomber Command War Diaries*, Middlebrook and Everitt)

A new crew had joined the squadron. I was to take F/O Greenslade, its pilot, and most of his crew on their 'second dicky' trip. More accurately it should be said that Colin and Titch and I were to take them, for thank Heavens those two were coming with me. F/Lt Treherne had taken me (it seemed such a long time ago) and now I was the 'target-hardened pilot' to take part of a new crew myself. The target was Scholven/Buer. As those four took their seats at briefing and they watched the curtain roll up to reveal the big wall-map, I thought of how I had felt on that briefing for a night operation over Germany when we had gone to Essen and S/Ldr Hamilton, OC A Flight, had not returned to Kelstern, and seven other crews had also not returned to the aerodromes that they called home.

Now it was Greenslade standing beside me as we took off into the darkness.

As we approached and flew through the anti-aircraft barrage over the target and saw the brilliant flashes of exploding shells around us illuminating Lancasters near us in the bomber stream, I was conscious of Greenslade beside me. It was his first experience, and I remembered that first time with Treherne. I remembered how I had wondered how ours or any other aircraft could hope to get through without being hit. But though we were sometimes rocked by explosions, get through once again we did. The glow of fires made orange the blanket of cloud below us and we bombed sky-markers. Presumably bearings from Oboe transmitters had shown Pathfinder aircraft when to release them. I realised that we must be silhouetted alarmingly against that orange blanket of cloud, but that night there was no warning cry from Titch in the tail or from the gunner from Greenslade's crew who was having his baptism in the mid-upper turret. We flew on, ever watchful, into the darkness, though had there been a warning cry, so that I instantaneously had had to throw the aircraft into twisting diving turns, it would have been experience for Greenslade.

29/30th December, 1944 – SHOLVEN/BUER

324 Lancasters and 22 Mosquitoes of 1, 6 and 8 Groups. 4 Lancasters lost.

The raid took place in difficult conditions. There was thick cloud over the target but Oboe sky-markers were accurately placed and the oil-refinery was badly hit. The local report says that 300 high explosive bombs fell within the oil-plant area. There were 2 large and 10 small fires and much damage to piping and storage tanks. The local report records a further 3198 bombs falling in other parts of Sholven and Buer, causing much property and some industrial damage. The surface buildings of the Hugo 1 and the Hugo 2 coal mines were severely damaged. 93 people were killed, of whom 24 were prisoners of war, 41 people were injured and 1368 people had to leave their homes, 1178 through bomb damage and 190 because of unexploded bombs.

(*The Bomber Command War Diaries*, Middlebrook and Everitt)

There was one American in the squadron, Roger Scott. He had joined up in the Royal Air Force and proudly wore its uniform. His compatriots had advised him to transfer to the American Air Force, in which service he would have received an enormous increase in pay, but he had refused. He was in my flight, B Flight, and that week his wife was staying in Louth, taking a holiday from whatever was her war work.

When debriefing from the Scholven operation was finished and the last crews to come in were ready to leave the Operations Room and get some well-deserved sleep, Roger had still not returned. There were no reports from other stations that he had turned up. I sent the others off to bed or whatever was their intention and I myself sat around waiting for some news. It was about 7 o'clock.

The sun was climbing up over the seaward side of the Wolds as Barker and I took a turn outside. It was cold, so that our breath was visible when we spoke.

'She'll be expecting him back now.' John spoke with the resignation of extinguished hope.

'Right, I'll go now.'

I collected my motorbike and sidecar. The chill air and the adrenalin released in anticipation of the task I was about to do meant I was no longer tired.

A remnant of mist hung in the hollow where Louth lay in its fold between sloping fields. The last leaves had fallen from the trees so the church spire no longer looked like a flower's tall grey pistil arising from its lush green calyx as it had in summer. I knew that Roger's wife was staying at the Masons' Arms but I had not met her. I approached a crease-faced woman at reception.

'Would it be possible to speak to Mrs Roger Scott?'

Her eyes did not bother to disguise her reluctance to leave her desk. She was halfway to the stairs before she paused, without turning round.

'Who shall I say?'

'Peter Russell, Squadron Leader Russell.'

Within two minutes she was back. She resumed her post without meeting my eye.

'She'll be down in a sec. You can use the lounge if you like.'

I felt drained as I waited for her. It was not a happy task I had, at any time, and tired as I was, having been flying all night, I felt singularly unready for it. Of course, she knew why I had come.

She was a pretty girl, but now very pale. Shock had already drawn dark rings under her eyes, but she held out her hand to me as she came across the floor of the lounge.

'It's Peter isn't it? I'm Rachel Scott.' She stretched out her hand. A firm hand shake. I noted her voice, trembling a little, had an English accent. Perhaps I was expecting a female version of Scott's American drawl.

'I'm afraid Roger's not back yet,' I said quietly. 'We may yet hear something, but it may be some time.'

'Thank you for coming,' was all she managed to say. I could see that it was hard for her to speak. The tock-tock of an ornate clock behind her made the silence more pointed. I endeavoured to say something.

'You may wonder why Roger had to go when you were here. It was a Maximum Effort requirement from Group, and that means everyone must go, except those actually on leave or ill. I went,' I added, smiling.

'You must be tired. Shall I ask for some tea, or something?'

A waitress brought tea almost at once. Rachel poured, assuming social convention to mask the dread in her mind. We drank it in silence at first.

'You were out there. Did you . . . did you . . . see . . . anything?'

'No.' I could say that truthfully. There was another long silence. 'I was an hour and a half late back once.'

'But it's more than that.' She rose to her feet. I stood up also.

'Shall I come and see you tomorrow? We must keep in touch. Then, if we get any news, we can tell you at once. But I expect now you may want to be alone for a while.'

'Please do. You were a friend of his, I know. He was going to arrange for us to meet. He often spoke of you.' I noticed the past tense

'I am very fond of Roger. Let's keep feeling that we all three soon shall.' I moved towards the door. 'Till tomorrow, then; I'll keep in touch by phone when I know if I'm flying. But if there's anything I can do to help you, you know my number. Keep me informed where I can reach you.'

I kick-started the bike and set off back to camp. She was being very brave, that young girl. I imagined her now, perhaps kneeling beside her bed: 'Please God bring him back to me; please Lord!' And in my thoughts I joined her.

The bike carried me up the hill. As I passed a brown ploughed field some lapwings rose into the air, protesting at the noise. 'Pee-wit, Pee-wit.'

The motorbike, with its mind-of-its-own sidecar, was not my only perquisite when I became a flight commander. I would now fly less frequently, though probably always when Maximum Effort was called for. It meant that I stood a good chanc e, and my crew too, of course, of staying longer in the squadron while we completed our tour of operations. Being in a squadron meant more frequent leave (with petrol coupons), eggs when flying, and most of all, a wonderful comradeship among its members.

About this time Torry moved in to my hut. He did not seem to be happy in the company that he had had. I could guess the nature of the embarrassment, but I never enquired and it was not divulged. It was most likely the homophobic intolerance that fed a wariness when he was around, and muted the conversation when he entered a room. I had a Nissen hut to myself. It was, perhaps, an unnecessary luxury, so Torry moved in with me. We shared a hut, and I never knew him put a foot wrong in the way that I suspected anxiety was troubling his former hutmates and which had made it difficult for him to get chosen to join a crew. In some ways Torry's arrival was a distinct bonus. We each had a small chest of drawers with a stand-up mirror. Torry hung curtains and put pretty cretonne covers on the furniture, which certainly was not issue. Often there were flowers in the hut and in the coldest weather he took charge of keeping the cylindrical coke stove supplied with fuel.

With the start of colder weather the large centrally placed open fire in the Mess anteroom came into its own. Its four arched firefronts meant that people could sit or stand round it in a complete circle of 360 degrees and be 'in front of the fire'. The other focal point was the bar, jutting into the room to offer three lengths of bar-counter for people to sit at or lean against. The anteroom was usually most full at the time of the 1 o'clock news from the BBC. This, I recalled MacKay explaining, was their 'recognition', when men who had flown through very frightening pyrotechnics heard it publicly broadcast to (they hoped) an appreciative nation.

Woodie Hammond's wife came to spend a short holiday at the Masons' Arms. Woodie was a good airman, and getting very near to the end of his tour of operations: we should be sorry to see him go. He was tall, and his face under his dark hair was always pale. He was teased a lot while his wife was staying near; people maintained that he was very much paler.

As he went off down the hill on his motorbike and sidecar when he could snatch a little free time, people would call after him, and Barker was one of the worst, 'Don't overdo it, Woodie!'

CHAPTER SEVENTEEN

Zeitz

Barker was called to the Operations Room in the morning to receive the target for that night. He would have informed Group on the night before of the squadron's strength, when he had known that all aircraft were safely back or if any were missing, so that they would have a rough idea of the squadron's availability for the next night. After the engineering people had reported back on serviceability, later in the morning, he would give Group a more exact figure. The information he received would be the target, the petrol load, the bomb load (the amount of high explosive and of incendiaries) and the route. All of this of course was highly secret. He would discuss the route with Alec Flett, the Navigation Leader, and call in to his office the Flight Commanders and the four other Leaders. He would know the number of aircraft required, and sometimes would have had to tell Group that he could not produce that number. That day twenty-six aircraft were required. The petrol load was 2250 gallons; it was a long operation. The target was Zeitz, just to the south of Leipzig, roughly between Leipzig and Chemnitz. One aircraft was required to be Pathfinder Supporter.

'Now, we want twenty-six crews, that's nine per flight, but we can manage with eight from one of you. Woodie, hasn't one of your more experienced crews got their navigator missing? As it's a long one, about eight and a half hours, we mustn't put any novices on. So shall we say, eight from you Woodie, and nine from each of you, Peter and Alan? Let me know if you strike any snags. We're in only one wave, with an average time on target at 23.30. Alec agrees with me average take-off time 18.30, so briefing 16.30. I'll ask the adjutant to lay on a meal at half past three. Woodie, I'm not going to send you as far as this on your nearly last op, and you, Alan, did Munich last week, so you two will not be going. But I'm going myself. Peter, I want you to be Pathfinder Support.'

Apart from an occasional suggestion sometimes, Barker left the selection of crews to his Flight Commanders, but himself dictated which of his Flight Commanders themselves would go. They would then make out a battle order for the Flight, with aircraft as preferred by individual captains and their crews, if serviceable, which they would take to the Squadron Adjutant for a squadron battle order to be typed out. They would inform captains of the petrol load, but not the target, which was not divulged to anyone else until briefing time. The Armament people were of course instructed about the bomb loads. Captains would then collect their crews and go to their aircraft on dispersal and do the checks, and would report back to Flight if any appeared to require an air test. The timing for all this naturally depended upon briefing time, itself depending on take-off time, time on target, as did whether or not crews would get a pre-flight meal as well as lunch, but it was realised that crews flew better on full stomachs. There were of course differences for daylight operations, when crews would be taking off usually very early in the morning, but the procedure was basically the same.

The target was the Braunkohle-Benzin synthetic-oil plant at Zeitz. It was an oil target night; others in the Command were going to Magdeburg, just to the north-west of where 625 Squadron would be, some to Brux to the south, and some to Wanne-Eickel.

Colin had earned the nickname 'the Vicar'. Whatever qualities prompted that imposed vocation, there was no doubting his reliability to get us there and back again, trip after trip. Sober, never flustered, he accepted every anxiety with a faith that what he was doing was right, a faith too in his own ability and in the efficiency of his crew. His kindness and consideration for others was an example to those who knew him. His opinion on personal problems on which friends and acquaintances sought his advice was greatly valued. That night he did an especially good job. The navigational aid Gee, by which a navigator picked up radar signals radiating from two transmitters in Britain like the ripples sent out by a stone dropped into a pond, using coded tables, which could be interpreted as bearings and thus used to calculate a fix or ground position, had been excellent in the early days. But then the Germans got an undamaged Gee set out of a crashed Lancaster and thereafter were able to jam the transmissions to make Gee useless further east than about the continental coast. H2S had been improved, and a navigator could usually see coastlines, perhaps rivers, even sometimes the vague suggestion of a town on his screen. The wireless operator could see other aircraft even 2000 yards away on his associated Fishpond screen, but enemy radar could detect H2S and so it was forbidden to be switched on further east of a line that excluded its use for very many targets, and most certainly for one such as that to which Colin now had to get us. Anyhow, he knew that our H2S had gone unserviceable that night, when we were due south of the Ruhr, with at least another hour and a half to go to the target and the target still to be located. So for his navigation that night he had to rely on dead reckoning, laying off estimated wind speed and direction against the track and ground speed he wanted to achieve, and from them producing the third side of the triangle of velocities, which was the course and airspeed for me to fly. This required two things, that he should be able to calculate his wind speed and direction or that those estimated by the Met people for more easterly longitudes, should be correct, and that I should accurately fly the compass course, and maintain the airspeed, which he gave me. Needless to say, there are no sign-posts, and for reasons of hoping to keep the enemy guessing about where we were going and by what route, the track from England to the target was a zigzag one.

Pathfinder Mosquitoes were ahead of us, but we, with Colin doing this diffi-cult navigation, and probably a few other aircraft who were Supporters, were in the forefront of the stream in the darkness. The target itself was cloud-covered. As we were Pathfinder Supporters, marking with red flares by Mosquitoes was only just beginning when we got there, in fact we were ourselves carrying green marker flares with which to emphasise the reds or adjust the aiming point if the Master Bomber required it. We climbed and let fall the flares, at 20,000 feet, dead on ETA.

As we were leaving the target area the lights came on! We had no H2S on, of course, but one of those great beams knew where we were all right! Suddenly, instantaneously, we were in its blinding light. It is a horrible feeling, danger-ously close to hopelessness. For we often had seen an aircraft coned, seen it diving and turning, just as helpless as a wounded bird in a cat's clutches, until *flash* a shell from coordinated gunfire, twenty rounds a minute and up to 32,000 feet, blew it to smithereens. We felt helpless, expecting the inevitable.

The light is so bright that it hurts. The body feels ice-cold as though your blood has frozen. But, though blinded, you must try to escape, dive, twist and turn, and yet you cannot see your instruments. You hardly know which way up you are.

Perhaps because of that, perhaps just because I was flying so clumsily, the aeroplane might have been sideslipping fast and temporarily evaded the beam. Or perhaps those below found a better target. The beam swung away and I was left in dazzled darkness. Perhaps because they had kept their eyes shut, because they did not have to try to see, Derek and Torry saw the light's next victim. The beam of the searchlight that had been on us swung away to join two others on some poor devil way above us behind and up to the right. One moment it was a tiny scintillating glitter in the cone of the three beams, the next it was a star's destruction. Then it was nothing, only darkness as the beams moved away to seek their next victim. It must have been a Mosquito, nothing else could have been so high above us. But it was not high enough to escape the guns, which had had it held still for them, like a prisoner bound hand and foot before a firing squad.

We dropped 4000 feet in very few minutes, getting away from those search-lights. We continued on our preplanned route, which was by no means a straight line home, and put in an extra kink to avoid some flak being hosed up over Holland.

We were tired when we got back that early morning. We had been flying for more than eight hours, peering into the darkness for every minute of that time, a darkness that hid many fighters. I felt that those agonising moments in the searchlight's beam did my nerves no good at all. Colin's weariness after so long at a peak of concentration can be well understood. Derek, too, had had a long time to combine his wireless watch, listening for any information base might send us, with an open-eyed look-out in the astrodome. He had more than once made the clambering journey down the aircraft's fuselage and back, relying on a small portable oxygen supply, to make sure that the two gunners, Titch and Torry, were all right, particularly if they were ever slow to answer my call on the intercom. It was easy for them, swivelling in their turrets, to pull out an intercom plug, and easy too, and much more serious, to trap an oxygen tube; the outside air temperature that night went down to minus 27 degrees Celsius. Three minutes accidentally off oxygen could mean a coma from which there would be no return. And Reg, good steady Reg, must make no mistake as he switched from one petrol tank to another, combining his watch of his engine dials with a watch of the sky. Ken in the Perspex nose, like the two gunners at their stations, must be immediately alert, all the time, to the featureless darkness before us, as we flew from one side of Germany to the other and back.

16th JANUARY 1945 – ZEITZ

328 Lancasters of 1, 6, and 8 Groups. 10 Lancasters lost, 3% of the force.

The target was the Braunkohle-Benzin synthetic-oil plant near Leipzig. Much damage was caused to the northern half of the plant.

30 aircraft were lost that night, the above 10 Lancasters, and also 17 Halifaxes, 5.3% of their force, were lost by those who were on the Magdeburg target: also those on Brux and Wanne Eikel lost 1 and 2.

(*The Bomber Command War Diaries*, Middlebrook and Everitt)

For various reasons I had not gone to bed by what one could in normal life call breakfast time, but I had eaten, and someone came to tell me that I was to have my photograph taken by some Air Ministry character who had arrived on the station the previous evening.

'What on earth for?'

'For some Rogues' Gallery.'

The next day and night a young moon brought in a spell of quite different weather. That is how generations of fishermen and shepherds have believed it to be, men who have watched the weather signs and known when most to fear the sea or when to herd their sheep to shelter against the coming of the all-enveloping snow. Low-pressure systems loomed in from the west and fronts, warm and cold, swept across the British Isles. High cloud, lowering and thickening as it came, sloped out across the continent for hundreds of miles as warmer air, laden with moisture, swung round from the Atlantic and mixed with the polar air. Then colder air tried to burrow in under the warm and stirred it so that, unstable, it made great nimbus clouds tower above us. This made for Icing, the phenomenon most feared by airmen. Not the hoar frost, which grew white moss on the bitter cold surfaces of the Lancasters as they crouched in their dispersals, pale pink in the dawn light and flushed to palest orange as the sun went down, but the glazed ice that spread itself on the surfaces as they flew, flowing like sugar syrup over the wings and hardening, thickening, until the aerofoil shape was spoilt, their power to lift was gone, and the heavier aircraft dropped. This was the literal deadweight that had caused Jill such anguish. We knew this danger well in 233 Squadron, for though Hudsons had pulsating 'boots' made of black rubber, along the leading edges of their wings, pulsing to move and break away the ice that formed, sometimes it did not, and futile movement continued on in a space between the rubber and the thickening ice. Icing meant they must fly lower, hoping to get below the zone of the critical temperature, but now as bombers we must climb above that other critical line, the 10,000-foot ceiling of that multitude of 88-mm anti-aircraft guns and be in danger only from the higher reaching ones. Climbing through cloud, descending through cloud, facing the danger of the icing. Some of the Command's worst casualty nights in the years of war had been caused by icing, a ruthless, dreaded, silent killer.

So the next night after the Zeitz trip, 625 Squadron had a target, but the operation was cancelled. It was the same again the next night. Then the snow came. Great flakes of it fell thickly on the land. Even the smallest breath of air eddied it round and piled it up against hedges, banks and buildings, and out in their dispersals the patient Lancasters, if one could see them through the falling snow, were mounds of white. For two whole weeks we had snow, that second half of January 1945, and at Kelstern and at all the aerodromes on the Lincolnshire Wolds operations paused.

On the day before the snow came, our crew was stood down. Derek went home on his motorbike. His parents lived in Doncaster, only about 50 miles away, and he set off next morning back to Kelstern, expecting an easy journey: he did not have the weather forecasting facilities that the Command did. He had not gone far when the snow began to fall, great featherlike flakes of it, filling the roads from hedge to hedge. No one seemed to have gone before him, the virgin snow was trackless. He kept to the road by halving the distance between the hedges. Progress got ever slower. Fear filled him that a battle order would be up. His name would be on it but he would not be there. What was the penalty for desertion?

He never got out of second gear and kept his feet on the ground all the way. There was a village on the way, which lies at the bottom of a hill. Slithering down towards it his bike went on ahead of him and he arrived just after it, sliding on his bottom. An elderly lady paused outside the post office and studied the scene before her.

'Have you fallen off your bike young man?'

'No, I was racing my motorcycle to the bottom of the hill. Just entertaining myself really.' He picked up the fallen motorbike and proceeded on his cautious way.

Back at the camp he found all deserted; huts, Mess, there was not a soul about. Eventually he found somebody.

'Where is everyone?'
'Out shovelling snow. You'd better join them.'

How white it was, that time! Snow filled the lanes and little roads that joined the aerodrome to the outside world. People walking about the camp were silhouettes, printing their footsteps in the snow, while the aircraft waited, and vehicles kept their places in the M/T Section or stayed, snow-covered, where they had last been parked. The BBC news told them of very slow progress by the armies through France and Belgium, the expected assault on the frontier of the Rhine seemed no nearer. We who had been spoilt, able to go into Grimsby or Cleethorpes when we were stood down, to find a girl, to have a few drinks in a pub with friends, or whatever was our fancy, were most of the time cut off by drifts. Those men, or women, with fewest inner resources were the most bored.

Someone had the idea to have a Station Dance. At least for that we needed no facilities outside the camp. Of rooms big enough, the hangars, we had plenty and there was an abundance of talent to form several dance bands. True, there was a preponderance of men, but that was all the better for the WAAFs, though at any dance there was always, to the females, a disappointingly large number of potential male partners who chose to stand around the bar. Standing round the bar was now never my preference; how different I was from the shy boy of before.

I had not been at the dance hall long before I noticed what a pretty girl was standing beside me as I surveyed the dancers. She was small, so I looked down at her. The face that looked up at mine was welcoming. I proposed; she accepted. We danced. It was luxury to feel her little body close. She smelt nice, and I liked her voice. I needed no other partner and her eyes, as I watched, did not rove around, so I thought that she was happy with my monopoly. When, at last, the band stopped for a well deserved rest, I asked her if she would like me to get her a drink or if, though it would be colder outside, she would prefer moonlight. She chose the chill night. It was a fairyland scene. Even the icicles that hung by the walls were not only visible but seeming to hold in their pointed shapes the moonlight that fell upon them. I put my arm about her waist and we walked away from the hangar across the moon-white apron. We heard the band strike up again, but I sensed she was in no hurry to return. We both were enjoying our happy communion as we wandered in the moonlight.

'What's your name?'
'Tricia, and you're Peter Russell; I asked who you were on the first day I got here.'
'You've not been here long, have you?'
'Ten days.'
'Where have they been hiding you these last ten days, that I've not seen you about?'
'They incarcerate me in the Parachute Section: though you've not been flying we keep on packing, and repacking, you see. But I think it's important work. Tell me that it is!'

'It's very important. For though we don't use them very often, thank God, we need to know that if we do, they'll open. And they do! We heard only last week that Squadron Leader Hamilton, who was OC A Flight when I first came, had escaped and got back to this country. His must have opened, though it would have been packed long before your time. And as you know, we pilots sit on ours.' I laughed 'So please make them comfortable!'

What's that place?' We were walking between two buildings. 'It's tall like my Parachute Section.'

'It's the Squash Court.' I opened the door for her to see. We stood just inside the door. She was very close to me. It was clear that she wanted what I wanted, and I pushed the door shut and dropped the Yale lock. She had a lovely little body, with small, firm, high breasts. There was enough moonlight to see that we were alone, and we moved along to a slatted bench by the wall in the lobby outside the court where players would leave a sweater or sit to lace their shoes. She was so cuddly and I needed her. We were kissing, and her lower lip was soft and full. It reminded me of Jill. There was no mistaking her intentions now.

'You're deliciously wet.'

'Come on then, do it!' She pressed herself against me. Her voice was urgent.

You can love someone and desire them: unions then are often made in Heaven. You can love someone but not desire them: there can be lifelong companionship. You can desire someone without loving them: the result can be disappointing, but sometimes it can be so intense, so deeply satisfying that gratitude comes very close to love, temporarily at least. That night it was very intense. Here, in circumstances not particularly comfortable, in a small camouflaged brick building on a snow-bound airfield, having known each other for little more than two hours, we defied King's Regulations. We could have no regrets, only a deeply satisfying restorative happiness.

'You're a wonderful therapist,' I said.

'I really needed it too; I was worried that you might not want to: after all, we hardly knew each other, and I was afraid that you might think that I was too . . . '

'I think you were wonderful. Our nerves get a bit taut, doing what we do in these aeroplanes. We need a therapy to unwind. Each has his way; mine is . . . well, was you: it's some time since anybody gave me this peace I feel. What's your name?'

'Tricia.'

'I know that, silly. I mean your other name.'

'Jones, Leading Aircraft Woman Jones, Sir!' She mocked my superior status, gently, smiling.

'I think it ought to be Doctor Jones,' I said.

'Oh please, yes! Does that mean that I . . . that we can, again, some time?'

'I'd love to Tricia, but off the station would be better. But there's one thing I must ask you: it sounds so ungrateful but don't let me fall in love, I know it doesn't mix with flying.'

'I'll try to stop you.' She laughed. 'But do you mind if I do?'

'I hope you won't, darling. I'm fickle and I may not last long.'

Outside was that silence that hangs over snowy fields, when sound is muted and no footfall can be heard. Outside the cold was anticipated more than real, because it was windless in the silver moonlight. In there, close together, it was warm, as we tried to learn something about each other, a conversation that need had delayed. Then, though it seemed far away, though really it was only a few hundred yards, we heard what sounded like the band playing the last waltz.

'When does Cinderella have to be home?' She looked at her watch in the shaft of moonlight coming from the high window.

'Oh dear, very soon I'm afraid. Please don't fail to pick up my slipper.'

'I won't. But it was a silly metaphor. I'm no prince. I'll walk you to the Waafery. It may be cold, have you a coat in the hangar? No? You'll catch cold, but nor have I. Never mind. Put this jersey on, that someone left behind.'

'That was my pillow. Won't someone come back . . . ?'

'I'll drop it back in here when we've got you home.'

We wandered back to that part of the camp where the WAAF huts were. Many other couples were doing the same, WAAF and RAF, sometimes two WAAFs, keeping a tactful or private distance from the others. Tricia stopped.

'That's my hut.' I steered her into its moon shadow. I held her close and kissed her.

'Goodnight, Doctor. Thank you so very, very, much.' From somewhere against my chest inside my unbuttoned tunic, which I had opened so that she could snuggle in, a voice emerged.

'Goodnight, Peter. My surgery is open twenty-four hours a day for you.' She gave a little chuckle I found enchanting.

CHAPTER EIGHTEEN

Nightmare over Bottrop

For two or three days no more snow fell. With ploughs and much shovelling we got the main runway clear. The engineering people worked hard on aircraft that had lain hidden under snow quite often in the last two weeks, and John Barker was able to give an availability figure to Group. It was said that at Binbrook, the Base aerodrome, from which 460 Squadron flew, they had cleared the runway but could not get off. They'd cleared the short runway!

On 1 February I was called to the Squadron Commander's office, together with the other two Flight Commanders and the Leaders.

'We've got a target. But I understand that although we've also got a runway the weather is not very good once you get away from here. Peter . . . No, Jock, you'd better tell him yourself.'

I looked across at Jock Orr, the Gunnery Leader, wondering what it could be.

'I thought I'd come along with you this evening, Peter, as your tail gunner. Can I?' I glanced at John.

'I recommend him. He's flown with me several times, hasn't he Alec?' said Barker.

Alec Flett nodded. I momentarily weighed up the likely reaction of the crew: the distrust of a change to the regular line-up against the honour of carrying the Gunnery Leader in the tail. As if I had a choice.

'I'd be most honoured, Jock, of course! Where are we going?'

'Mannheim Ludwigshafen. It's about a hundred miles further south down the Rhine than Cologne. Call it halfway between the Ruhr and the Swiss border.'

I went back to the flight office. It was a Nissen hut near the perimeter track, squatting between a semi-circular bank of earth mounded up to give blast protection to a dispersal site where three Lancasters, not too close together, sat looking cold but resigned, with a small silent grove of trees for company. None of the trees were then more than about 15 feet high, but from the direction from which I came, they hid a small farmhouse a few hundred yards away, where lived the farmer, Mr Brook, and his wife. Until three years ago they had farmed the land we flew from. Inside the hut, being the first of the month, pilots of B Flight were entering up their log books. When finished, I would sign them, and then John, the Squadron CO, would sign them too.

'Petrol load 2000, chaps. I'm going, and we want nine more, so that's every-body who's not on leave,' I said.

'I'm on leave,' said one humourist, 'I left the camp yesterday.'

'Excellent, so now you're back, could you very kindly pop over to the Gunnery Section and ask my Titch Aldred and Torry Large if they'd come and see me for a minute. Tell them it's nothing sinister. Then I can write all our names on this battle order. Oh, Tony, *A Able*'s U/S, it'll have to be *X X-Ray*.' And I set about writing the names on a piece of paper for typing, and then got on with reading those log books that were finished. Titch and Torry came in.

'Titch, you've probably heard already. We are to be honoured with S/Ldr Orr's company in the tail tonight, so you've got an evening off, but hang around till meal-time in case there's a change of plan. Torry, I know you'll miss Titch, but the Gunnery Leader is very well spoken of. Sorry to disturb you both. See you later in *Nan* for a run-up.'

Jock watched our ritual of urinating on the port-side wheel, and joined us. To pee was vitally important, to do so on the wheel was for luck; I could not remember who started it. We turned on to the runway. On each side the ploughed and shovelled snow made a low irregular wall dimly seen in the twilight. I looked towards the caravan from where the green light would flash to give us permission to take off. Stamping about on the boot-stained snow beside it was the little band of well-wishers. There among them, waving a gloved hand, then both hands, was Tricia. I pushed Reg's head out of my line of vision and blew a kiss, a green kiss, for it coincided with the light from the caravan, then Reg and I pushed forward the boost levers, a noisy roar rose to a peak, and we thundered away and up into the night.

The bombing conditions were bad. Perhaps the snow-clouds that had kept us on the ground had drifted east, and now obscured the German targets. We aimed our loads at sky-markers and had no idea if they were accurate or not. The coloured lights reflected off the tops of the clouds that covered the ground made an eerie scene. Radar-directed flak shells burst in wicked concentration among us. To any fighter above us we made easy silhouettes. In gaps where the cloud was thinner the light of fires below glowed like an orange haze. We made our run on to the sky-markers Ken had chosen. We passed through the flak-patterned sky and we bombed. I flew on through the shell-bursts, turned and made for home by the kinking courses Colin gave me. I always felt confident that Titch's alert and watchful eyes would see and warn me in time for me to attempt my evasive action; I felt no less confident in Jock.

And so we came home just under seven hours after I had seen those grey-mittened waving hands wishing us well. Jock and the rest of us, once we were on the ground, exchanged grateful remarks.

It was about 3 o'clock when we divested ourselves of our flying clothing before going into the Operations Room for debriefing. Torry, whose locker was next to mine, put his face close to the little mirror that he had hung inside its door and, as he usually did, applied a little make-up to his cheeks and eyes and lips. He seemed happy; he had flown in the other turret with his Gunnery Leader and had acquitted himself well. He had added one more trip to the total that he was expected to accomplish, and he was alive and well. There may have been additional reasons for him to look happy. He returned my smile with a grin.

'I just couldn't face my public looking like that!'

Together we walked to the Operations Room, to cocoa and rum, to meet with friends just as pleased to see us safely back as we were to see them.

Jock was an artist skilled in portraying scenes of the London Blitz with his paints and brushes when he was a London fireman, who could equally well bring to life what he saw from his gun turret when over the target. A few days afterwards he gave me a painting. As soon as I could, I had the photographic section make copies for the other members of the crew.

1st/2nd FEBRUARY, 1945 – LUDWIGSHAFEN

382 Lancasters and 14 Mosquitoes of 1, 6, and 8 Groups: 6 Lancasters lost.

Most of the force aimed their loads at sky-markers and the local report shows that bombs fell in many parts of Ludwigshafen, with much property damage of a mixed nature. The 900 houses destroyed or seriously damaged were the main item in the report but it also states that the railway yards were seriously damaged and one of the Rhine road bridges was hit by 2 bombs and temporarily closed to traffic. 25 people were killed and 6 injured, figures which might indicate that the population either had been evacuated or were extremely well provided with shelters

(*The Bomber Command War Diaries*, Middlebrook and Everitt)

To our crew, and to others no doubt, Bomber Command seemed to try to make up for lost time from that night on. Often the available crews were split on to three targets. That night it had been Ludwigshafen, Mainz and Siegen, railway yards and oil installations being the intention, as similarly the next night it was Wiesbaden, Wanne-Eickel and Karlsruhe.

On the next night twenty-three crews from 625 Squadron went on the Wiesbaden trip already mentioned, but I and my crew did not. Twenty-one aircraft were lost on that night's three raids, and three of the Lancasters on the Wiesbaden trip crashed in France.

On the following night we went, one crew in only nine from the squadron, for crews were not expected to fly three nights running, and the squadron had provided twenty-eight and twenty-three of the force on the two previous nights. My crew had done only one of them so was on the short battle order for this one. The target was in the Ruhr – Bottrop.

The stream flew down England and turned over Reading. It crossed the coast between Eastbourne and Hastings and entered France over the Somme estuary. At Fourmies we stopped pretending we were going back to Mannheim Ludwigshafen again and turned north-east as though for Eindhoven or the battle fronts on the Belgian border. There we turned more easterly and headed straight for the target at Bottrop, almost centrally placed in the Ruhr, joined to

Essen and to Gelsenkirchen and other Rhur towns. After Eindhoven we had
about 80 miles to go. Dortmund, to which the aircraft on the other half of that
night's raid were going, lies about 25 miles further east on the same track, but
they were probably routed to come in more from the north.

We had to fly above 20 or 30 miles of the heavily built up, heavily populated, heavily defended conurbation of the Ruhr complex of industrial towns.
The flak was bad. It seemed a desperately long gauntlet to have to run, and it
looked like being costly. About 190 aircraft beside us were running in through
this unceasing barrage; it was a matter of pure luck if we should get
through without being hit, and of course there was a grave risk of collision. At
such times a pilot's concentration is easily deflected, as is the alertness of those
others whose watchfulness is so vital to survival. German fighter squadrons
would no doubt by now have been vectored on to our approach line. There
were fighters among us, but so far no cry of warning had come from Torry or
Titch to demand my instantaneous action if one might seem to have chosen us
for its attack.

I heard the click of a gunner's microphone switching on and the background
scream of our slipstream. Immediately Titch's voice:

'A Lanc, I think, been hit just astern of us, and up. It's on fire but still flying
pretty much level. . . . .Aarrgh . . . . parachutes are coming out.'

'Count them Titch. Log it please Colin.'

'One, two, three, four. Oh NO, Oh NO!' Titch's voice had become agonised
from what he was now witnessing. 'They're on fire!'

He had seen the parachutes come out, and open, but then the cream-coloured
canopies, faintly orange in the light of the burning aircraft, had flickered and
vanished. They had caught fire from the flames and exploding incendiaries of
the doomed Lancaster's bomb load.

I tried to concentrate on my flying. I had to put from my mind the horror of
what Titch had seen, but from my imagination I could not drive out the picture
of those men. What must it be like? To know your aircraft is doomed; to give
the order to bale out. Would you be calm or with death so large before you overcome by unmanageable fear? To fight to an escape hatch encumbered by your
parachute; to stand by the roar of the slipstream sending your crew into that
abyss before jumping yourself. How many seconds would there be before an
explosion to end your life in an instant, to sever the slender thread of hope that
even from this calamity there might be salvation? Perhaps in unimaginable heat;
perhaps in whatever deaththrows – diving, spinning – the crippled aircraft
would be contorting itself. And then your turn to launch yourself into the icy-
cold black void. The drill. One second, two seconds, three seconds. Fumble with
your right hand for the ripcord. Grasp the last chance for life and pull for
all you're worth. Feeling one moment the relief of the pull of your parachute
straps on your thighs and at your shoulders. Seeing the billowing canopy above
you lit by the aircraft's fire in the darkness. Seeing that canopy burning, feeling
the supporting pull of the straps slacken and vanish. Feeling the quickening
acceleration of your fall. Down, down, down into the annihilating darkness

below. Even at your eventual terminal velocity it would take three or four minutes: it's a long time to fall, certain of the outcome, from three and a half miles up. What must it be like?

We were approaching the target. The heavy flak continued unceasingly.

'Target and markers clearly seen now Skip. There's a big gap in the cloud.' Ken began his routine. 'Left-left a bit, bomb doors open . . . r-i-g-h-t . . . steady . . . bombs gone! That was bang on. Close bomb doors . . . . no hang-ups.'

'Close bomb doors.'

'Fly 350, Skip. Fly left on to 350.'

'On 350.'

The bad flak continued as we flew over Gladbach and on for about three or four minutes. We turned west by north for a little longer, then south-west on another course Colin gave. We were heading for Brussels and descending all the time from the 17,000 feet at which we had bombed. We flew over Eindhoven, close to our turning point of the outward journey, at 9 o'clock, 1959 hours GMT. Half an hour later we turned starboard, still over Belgium, on to about west-north-west. Derek, listening in to possible calls from England, watching from the astrodome, and keeping an eye on Fishpond, could see other aircraft around us proceeding on the same way, little bright flecks of light on the circular screen. But he noticed that one came in to the circle behind us, which was going faster than the others.

'Something coming up behind us, Titch.'

Titch and Torry shouted as one.

'Fighter, fighter 6 o'clock! Corkscrew! Go, go!'

I dived, twisting as I did so. I twisted the other way, then pulled up the nose and where I thought was the top of my corkscrew I twisted back the other way again and down. I tried to tell from the amount of G whether my bottom was being pressed down onto my parachute or was lifting off it, roughly where we were. Then, and I was so glad to hear it, for I was sweating, up there in the bitter cold, came Torry's voice,

'He's gone over us Skip, two engines, very fast.'

There was an orange flash over to the left of us of another aircraft exploding. God! He'd got some other poor devil!

'That was a Messerschmitt 262, German jet.' Titch sounded almost awestruck. 'Cor, he came up fast!'

'Well done, you look-outs. We're all right but I'm afraid he got someone else.'

Just short of the Belgian coast Colin gave me a new course, about north-west, and told me to begin descending to 7000 feet. It was almost 10 o'clock. Derek had passed Colin a warning of low cloud for the last stretch of the journey. We were soon in cloud, flying on instruments, thick sightless darkness all around us.

'Skip, although we've got to break cloud, do not come below 1000 feet. I hope to let you know when we're over the Wash.'

'Will do, Colin.'

We broke cloud just above 1000 feet, circuited the airfield till we were given the OK to make our approach, and landed. Before I got into the Aircrew Bus I patted the side of the fuselage where the companion ladder came down from the doorway,

'Poor girl, you do lead an exciting life.' It was *Jig 2* again, in which we had been so lost, compassless, after Cologne.

At one of the interrogation tables we reported all we could remember. At another table, a gunner was giving his account.

'North of Brussels we saw a Lanc ahead of us and over to the right go into a dive, so we looked pretty hard over that way. Then we saw why it had dived. It was a two-engined fighter; we saw its exhaust flames, and it shot over the top of the diving Lanc. We saw its tracer more than we saw the fighter, it was too dark. Then it did a steep turn left, so that we passed ahead of it, and it came across our tail, just below us. I just blazed away, couldn't see it very well, and it flew straight through my fire. Must have hit something inflammable, 'cos it just blew up!'

So another 625 Squadron Lancaster had accounted for the German jet fighter Me 262 that had attacked us!

We were in bed rather earlier than usual, before 1 o'clock. I was tired, but not inclined to sleep. I was a bit wound up if the truth was known. From across the hut I heard Torry's voice.

'Golly, Pete, that was a dicey night, and I can't help thinking of those poor men falling.'

I was having the same trouble. 'Try to put it from your mind, Torry. It happens, I'm afraid. Just be thankful they were not us.' I wondered if Titch was able to sleep, or Derek either. They had had front row seats for it.

It was indeed the stuff of nightmares. Previously I'd seen men falling without parachutes, long thin black things silhouetted against the bright orange of a shell-burst that had taken a Lancaster with it, but I hoped they were dead. Tonight I had seen men conscious enough to accomplish the superhuman effort of getting out of a burning Lancaster; men who had seen their chutes open and believed they had a good chance of survival; men who had seen with horror the flickering flames of their burning canopies and begun that awful fall.

Not a story to tell Tricia, I thought as I lay there. My limbs still ached from my corkscrewing exertions. My heart was revving with the extra adrenalin my blood had pumped. Sleep seemed a vain hope.

Tricia darling I could do with you now. Please come, little girl, and soothe my nerves. But that was an even vainer hope! 'My surgery is open 24 hours a day for you.' Her words came back to me, with a picture of her sweet, satisfied smile as she had uttered them. Tricia, I want you. I almost said it aloud. But I would have to wait for her therapy.

3rd/4th FEBRUARY, 1945 – BOTTROP

192 Lancasters and 18 Mosquitoes of 1 and 8 Groups attacked the Prosper benzol plant. A local report confirms that severe damage was caused in an accurate raid. 2 people died. 8 Lancasters lost.

(*The Bomber Command War Diaries*, Middlebrook and Everitt)

The squadron had been on operations for three nights and the following evening we were stood down. We were stood down to go and meet someone in town, or take them, or to go to town and hope to meet someone. The night after that we did have a target, but the operation was cancelled and we stood down again.

The next night, the next two nights, 625 Squadron was in action.

At briefing, the senior Intelligence Officer's pointer drew a line close to the German border.

'Gentlemen, your task this evening is to assist a British Army Corps who are operating in this area. The German defence line is very strong and includes the towns of Goch and Kleve. Your target is the first one of these towns here, Kleve. With our own troops perhaps close by, accurate bombing is essential and must be done below cloud. You are therefore required to bomb from a lower height than usual, 6000 feet or as the Master Bomber will instruct you.'

I and my crew were approaching the target at 6000 feet but we were still in cloud, a layer of which was about 2000 feet above us. I was flying on instruments and expecting and hoping to hear the voice of the Master Bomber at any moment.

'Target about 5 miles ahead.'

A clear Australian voice crackled into my headphones.

'Come on down below cloud. There's nothing to hurt you here!'

I put down some flap and allowed the aircraft to sink.

'Bomb doors open.'

Now down to about 5000 feet, Ken could see a few miles ahead of us the red marker flares beginning to fall and to light up the ground of the target.

'R-i-g-h-t, just a little, r-i-g-h-t again . . . . Steady, steady . . . .'

Momentarily I saw that we were down to 4500 feet.

'Steady, steady . . . bombs gone! . . . Bang on! Close bomb doors. No hang-ups.'

'Close bomb doors.'

The exploding bombs, probably those of others ahead of us more than our own, threw us about, making it difficult to control the aircraft, but fortunately not while Ken was aiming and releasing. I was glad when the bomb doors were closed and I had got the flaps up and could climb away into calmer air. I was too busy on the bombing run and afterwards to be able to look down and see what a target looked like from this height.

7th/8th FEBRUARY, 1945 – GOCH and KLEVE

These raids were preparing the way for the attack of the British XXX Corps across the German frontier near the Reichwald. The Germans had included the towns of Goch and Kleve in their strong defences here.

4, 6, and 8 Groups attacked Goch (292 Halifaxes, 156 Lancasters, 16 Mosquitoes). Considerable damage was caused to Goch but most of the inhabitants had probably left the town. Approximately 30 local people died. There were heavy casualties among Russians, Italians and Dutchmen who had been brought in as forced workers to dig the local defences. They were quartered in 2 schools, and 150 of them died. The number of German soldiers killed not known.

295 Lancasters and 10 Mosquitoes of 1 and 8 Groups attacked Kleve. 1 Lancaster lost. 285 Lancasters bombed at Kleve, which was battered even more than Goch. Few details are available from local reports and casualties may not have been heavy (most of the civilian population were absent) but, after the war, Kleve claimed to be the most completely destroyed town in Germany of its size.

The British attack, led by the 15th (Scottish) Division, made a successful start a few hours later, but quickly ground to a halt because of a thaw, which caused flooding on the few roads which had been available for the advance, and also because of the ruins which blocked the way through Kleve. Lieut Gen B.G. Horrocks, the corps commander in charge of the attack, later claimed that he had requested that Kleve should only be subjected to an incendiary raid, but Bomber Command dropped 1384 tons of high explosive on the town and no incendiaries.

(*The Bomber Command War Diaries*, Middlebrook and Everitt)

On 8 February, John Barker put himself on the battle order for a long one. The target was an important synthetic-oil plant at Politz, not far from Stettin, to the north-east of Berlin.

I was not on it; I rarely flew at the same time as John, but I went to the briefing, and I went up to the Watch Office, Flying Control, when the aircraft were coming back. John landed and came up to Fying Control before going into the Operations Room.

'I've been flying on instruments almost the whole bloody way.'

It would not be long before first light. Very soon afterwards everyone was accounted for, except for Warrant Officer Chalkley's crew. Chalkley was an extremely competent flier, and one who seemed to be afraid of very little. I had flown with him once, months before, on some sort of exercise, and had a great admiration for him. He was very good company, 'but he scares the shit out of his crew sometimes' one of my crew told me.

John and I went down to interrogation. There was still no sign of Chalkley. Then a message came through from him, to the effect that he was in some sort of trouble but could be expected shortly. It was first light when he landed. Fire engines and ambulances were at the ready. He was on three engines. There was something very odd-looking about his fourth engine. Being Chalkley, he made a satisfactory landing and came to a stop. Caught in between his wing's leading edge and one of his inner engine nacelles was part of another aircraft. It was found to be part of the tail section of a Halifax. He had collided with another aeroplane, in cloud, somewhere over Denmark. Obviously he had come off best and had been able to keep flying, albeit without one of his engines, which had slowed him down and made things rather difficult. As it was in cloud, he did not know what had befallen the Halifax.

Remarkably, there was a number on that part of the Halifax Chalkley had brought home with him, so John was able to telephone Group, and later also the Halifax squadron, with the details. Soon after that Chalkley went to 617 Squadron. He was that sort of chap. Barker put him up for an immediate DFC.

8th FEBRUARY, 1945 – POLITZ

12 Lancasters were lost, but the raid was a success, accurate bombing in two waves, with a clear sky over the target. Severe damage was caused to the plant, which produced no more oil during the war. Speer mentioned this raid, in his post-war interrogation, as being another big set-back to Germany's war effort. The apparently hard-to-hit oil refinery at Wanne Eickel and railway yards at Krefeld were also attacked that night, and quite a lot of Mosquitoes bombed various targets, including a 'spoof' raid on Neubrandenburg for the Politz raid, and another 5 were lost, making 17 lost that night.

(*The Bomber Command War Diaries*, Middlebrook and Everitt)

There are men like Chalkley, men who seem to enjoy danger and taking physical risks more than ordinary mortals do. Some such heroes are shy, others are equally bold in their social life. The tale of one such put smiles on the faces of the men in the Mess that week. Jimmy Goldie was a rear gunner who flew over 100 operations in Bomber Command. Some of 625 Squadron had met him shortly after he had returned from London. He had been to Buckingham Palace to receive a DFC (after his DFM) from the unfortunately stuttering King George the Sixth.

'And then it was my go. I stood before our King Emperor. There were quite a few others standing about. There was a bit of a pause. I didn't think it was my place to speak first. Then he said, 'I hear you sh-shot down f- five f- f- f- that you shot down five f- f- f- f- . . . . I couldn't help wondering what he was going to come out with. 'I hear you shot down five fuckin' Germans'? Surely not! I could stand it no longer. I'd got to help the man, so though it was not strictly accurate, I thought of something worth shooting down beginning with F. Pheasants? And then it came to me. 'Focke-Wulfs, Sir.' And the King was able to pass on to the next man who stood before him.'

The next three nights, 9, 10, and 11 February, we had a target but the operation was cancelled each time. On 12 February the weather was undeniably awful and no attempt was made to telephone one through. On the 13th the target was

another long one, and John again decided to put himself on it, so I did not go.
He took Alec Flett, the Navigation Leader, with him as before.

The target was Dresden.

13/14 FEBRUARY, 1945 – DRESDEN

The Air Ministry had, for several months been considering a series of particularly heavy area raids on German cities with a view to causing such confusion and
consternation that the hard-stretched German war machine and civil administration would break down and the war would end. The general name given to this
plan was Operation Thunderclap, but it had been decided not to implement it until
the military situation in Germany was critical. That moment appeared to be at
hand. Russian forces had made a rapid advance across Poland in the second half
of January and crossed the eastern frontier of Germany. The Germans were thus
fighting hard inside their own territory on two fronts, with the situation in the east
being particularly critical. It was considered that Berlin, Dresden, Leipzig, and
Chemnitz – all just behind German lines on the Eastern Front now – would be
suitable targets. They were all vital communications and supply centres for the
Eastern Front and were already packed with German refugees and wounded from
the areas recently captured by the Russians. As well as the morale aspect of the
attacks, there was the intention of preventing the Germans from moving reinforcements from the West to face the successful Russian advance. The Air
Ministry issued a directive to Bomber Command at the end of January. The
Official History (Vol IV pp 112–13) describes how Churchill took a direct hand
in the final planning of Operation Thunderclap – although Churchill tried to
distance himself from the Dresden raid afterwards. On 4 February, at the Yalta
Conference, the Russians asked for attacks of this kind to take place, but their
involvement in the process came after the plans had been issued. So, Bomber
Command was specifically requested by the Air Ministry, with Churchill's
encouragement, to carry out heavy raids on Dresden, Chemnitz and Leipzig. The
Americans were also asked to help and agreed to do so. The capaign should have
begun with an American raid on Dresden on 13th February but bad weather over
Europe prevented any American operations. It thus fell to Bomber Command to
carry out this first raid.

796 Lancasters and 9 Mosquitoes were despatched in two separate raids and
dropped 1478 tons of high explosive and 1182 tons of incendiary bombs. The first
attack was carried out entirely by 5 Group, using their own low-level marking
methods. A band of cloud still remained in the area of this raid, in which 244
Lancasters dropped more than 800 tons of bombs, was only moderately
successful. The second raid, 3 hours later, was an all-Lancaster attack by aircraft
of 1, 3, 6 and 8 Groups, with 8 Group providing standard Pathfinder marking.
The weather was now clear and 529 Lancasters dropped more than 1800 tons of
bombs with great accuracy. Much has been written about the fearful effects of this
raid. Suffice to say here that a firestorm, similar to the one in Hamburg in July
1943, was created and large areas of the city were burnt out. No one has ever been
able to discover how many people died but it is accepted that the figure was greater
than the 40,000 who died in the Hamburg fire storm and that the Dresden figure
may have exceeded 50,000.

Bomber Command casualties were 6 Lancasters lost, with 2 more crashed in
France and 1 in England.

311 American B17s dropped 771 tons of bombs on Dresden the next day, with the railway yards as their aiming point. Part of the American Mustang-fighter escort was ordered to strafe traffic on the roads around Dresden to increase the chaos. The Americans bombed Dresden again on the 15th and on 2 March but it is generally accepted that it was the RAF night raid which caused the most damage.

(*The Bomber Command War Diaries*, Middlebrook and Everitt)

CHAPTER NINETEEN

It is a God

W hen my crew reassembled at Kelstern after a few days' leave, we found that the squadron had lost another three crews and aircraft, after the one in our last week there. One of them, sadly, on a trip to Chemnitz, was *Jig 2*. Also, on one night, when the Command lost thirty-four bombers, two 625 Squadron aircraft were damaged by having incendiaries fall on them. Their target had been Duisburg. We heard of a third night, when Pforzheim was the target and was the scene of remarkable (and reported) courage even by the remarkable standard we encountered raid in, raid out. That night the Command lost seventeen.

23/24th FEBRUARY, 1945 – PFORZHEIM
367 Lancasters and 13 Mosquitoes of 1, 6, and 8 Groups and a film-unit Lancaster carried out the first, and only, area-bombing raid of the war on this target.

10 Lancasters were lost and 2 more crashed in France.

The marking and bombing from only 8000 feet were particularly accurate and damage of a most severe nature was inflicted on Pforzheim. 1825 tons of bombs were dropped in 22 minutes. Local records show that an area measuring three Km by one and a half Km was completely engulfed by fire and that 'more than 17,000 people met their death in a hurricane of fire and explosions'. Fire Officer Brunswig from Hamburg, usually reliable, says that 17,600 people died. This was probably the third heaviest air-raid death toll in Germany during the war, following Hamburg and Dresden. The post-war British Bombing Survey Unit estimated that 83% of the town's built-up area was destroyed, probably the greatest proportion in one raid during the war.

Bomber Command's last Victoria Cross of the war was won on this night. The Master Bomber was Captain Edwin Swales, DFC, a South African serving with 582 Squadron. His Lancaster was twice attacked over the target by a German fighter. Captain Swales could not hear the evasion directions given by his gunners because he was broadcasting his own instructions to the Main Force. 2 engines and the rear turret were put out of action. Captain Swales continued to control the bombing until the end of the raid and must take some credit for the accuracy of the attack. He set out on the return flight but encountered turbulent cloud and ordered his crew to bale out. This they all did successfully but Captain Swales had no opportunity to leave the aircraft and was killed when it crashed. He is buried at the Leopold War Cemetery at Limburg in Belgium.

(*The Bomber Command War Diaries*, Middlebrook and Everitt)

I had asked Mother to keep her eyes open for a second-hand car that I could afford, and before the end of the month she told me that there was a Wolseley Hornet for sale in Berkhampstead, not very far from Tiled Cottage. Although she knew nothing about such things she understood that it had a certain charm and character. The price was £70. I asked Gerry Wilson to come with me, and arranged to borrow the Oxford. Sammy Cook agreed to come with us and fly it back. So, with John's blessing we flew down to Halton, the nearest aerodrome to Berkhampstead, and hitch-hiked thither by way of Tring. We met Mother in the Crown for lunch and went to inspect the car. It had a long bonnet, for such a junior car, with two carburettors for swank, and an engine that looked as though it had been bathed in soapy water, which it probably had. Its very sporty body was made of wood, like a de Havilland Mosquito, painted a colour called Eau de Nil, though rather stirred-up Nile water we all had to admit. Its seats, if one could call them that, were of red leather. They once had been pneumatic, though patient mending of innumerable punctures had ceased to make them airtight for very long so that one sat on the floorboards, really, with a layer of canvas, two of partly perished rubber and one of up-market red leather to keep the damp out of your posterior. That said, she certainly had a lot of character. The registration number was ANO 80.

'Ah, the ablative!' was my father's reaction when he saw it.

I paid the money demanded. Gerry and I set off, cut across to the A1 and headed north. It was February, so twilight came early. The advance of nightfall coincided with a noticeable lack of power, which necessitated us getting out and trying to establish the reason. We traced the problem to the petrol pump. We found that if we rubbed the contact points of the pump with a nail file Gerry had on him, there was a temporary improvement. We had to do this quite frequently and a lighted match, which was all the illumination we could muster, was perhaps not the ideal source of light for dealing with part of the petrol supply. We seemed to have come singularly ill-prepared for this journey. Nothing much could be done about the petrol pump and the fuel starvation that issued from it, except continue with our frequent stops and treatment. The time, and the night, wore on.

Eventually we reached Kelstern. It was 5 o'clock in the morning and we were tired. Bed beckoned. We went into the anteroom of the Mess. There on the noticeboard was a battle order. We were on it. Briefing was in an hour, and already people were coming into the Mess for pre-flight breakfast. We had a wash and then breakfast and met our crews at briefing in the Operations Room.

It was a daylight. John had done B Flight's part of the battle order. The target was Neuss, another of the Ruhr towns. John was to lead the Bomber stream with a Vic formation for the gaggle of all the other aircraft to follow. The Vic of course required two more Lancasters, and I was one of them. I was to fly as John's No. 2, on his right; someone else was No. 3, on his left.

The three of us took off first and formed up over base then flew south while all the other Lancasters of 625 Squadron and of other squadrons of 1 Group and perhaps other Groups, tucked in behind us.

It was a fine morning. The sun rose up on our left, and soon it was high enough to throw shadows on the white mattress of cloud that lay below us. Many aircraft were following in the stream. We must have looked conspicuous against that background. I was flying comfortably tucked in on John's right-hand side, my wing tip behind his, close enough but clear of his slipstream. We watched the skies all about us for intruding enemies. Colin plotted his own track and found no fault with John's navigator's course, Ken prepared his bombing arrangements, the two gunners tested their guns, and Derek listened out on the various frequency channels of his wireless receiver. He called me on the intercom.

'We've had a general recall, Skip. All aircraft are to return to base. Operation cancelled. I've checked the code; it's not duff gen.'

Sure enough, the other aircraft were turning away and setting course for home, including the aircraft on John's left. But not John. Wondering, I kept with him. We must have looked brave but foolhardy, two Lancasters flying on alone towards the Ruhr above this revealing blanket of white cloud.

'The squadron commander is flying on. He must have missed the signal. You'd better flash him on the Aldis lamp, Derek.'

Derek appeared beside me, Aldis lamp in hand. In the correct code of the day he flashed our aircraft code to John's aircraft code, followed by the Bomber Command message in code. All very proper. From John's wireless operator he got back one word.

'Why?'

'If he wants plain language he can have it.' Derek flashed the response.

'I don't bloody well know, read your Bomber Command Broadcast.'

The head of the wireless operator disappeared down out of the astrodome and shortly afterwards John turned back and we followed.

Accordingly, I was the last aircraft to reach Kelstern and to request permission to land. I was tired after driving all night. I had a full bomb load and an almost full petrol load. This was something I had never tried before. The Base Commander, Air Commodore Daddy Wray, had suggested, when it had been decided by higher command that on such occasions as this crews should bring their valuable bombs back rather than ditch them over the sea as had previously been the instruction, we should practise landing with full bomb load. However, John had argued that the occasional loss of a complete aircraft and crew on such practice landings would be too expensive. In the same way we never practised parachute jumping. A twisted ankle might keep a valuable member of aircrew out of action for several weeks.

I tried to marshal my thoughts for this new situation. I'm heavier, my stalling speed will be higher; I must come in faster.

I made my approach but I seemed to be dropping too quickly towards the ground. By increasing my speed I was fairly certain that we would overshoot the runway. So pushing all eight throttle and pitch levers forward I kept the aircraft off the ground and staggered over the further boundary, climbed slowly up to circuit height and made another approach, hoping now to correct the miscalculation of my first attempt. It was not a good landing, but we did get down. The undercarriage withstood my clumsy bounce and we stopped before we got to the end of the runway – just. We taxied to dispersal and an aircrew bus took us to our hangar crewroom where we put our flying clothes in our lockers. Colin, Torry, Ken and I walked by way of the Navigation Section to the Officers' Mess and I gave an apologetic grin to Derek, Reg and Titch as they walked towards the Sergeants' Mess.

There was an oval of rough grass in front of the Mess, and I was astonished to see all the squadron officers standing there as though for a group photograph, with the squadron commander W/Cdr John Barker standing in front of them. As I approached, as though from a signal they all fell on their knees. John bowed himself to the ground. Putting his arms in the air he cried out 'It is a God! It is a God! Anyone who could make such a bloody awful landing and get away with it MUST be a GOD!'

Gerry Wilson confided in me the following day.

'A girl I know has just been posted to Scampton. I've had a letter asking me to meet her in Lincoln. Could you drive me over in ANO 80? Today is one of the days she says she could get time off and go there. Could we go there today? It's nearby.'

'Did you call Lincoln nearby? Near her it may be, but from here it's about 25 miles. What am I to use for petrol?'

'You can fix that I'm sure.' I shrugged. It was fixed.

We set off, and reached Lincoln quite quickly, the petrol pump now put right. We went to the White Hart. Gerry met his girlfriend and I made myself scarce.

Wandering into another bar, I was astonished and pleased to meet my friend Hugh.

'What a splendid surprise,' I said, and Hugh looked glad too.

The two of us had become separated since Bridgnorth days. Hugh was now also in Bomber Command, stationed at Waddington, not far away, so Lincoln was a favourite watering place. The barmaid, made up to lie about her age, set full glasses before us.

I saw that Hugh was also a squadron leader, so I assumed that he too was a flight commander. 'How far have you got in your tour?'

'Only five more to go. Fingers crossed. Like you, I expect, I only fly on Maximum Efforts, so it won't all be over next week. In some ways, I suppose, I shall be sorry to leave squadron life. Like I was when I was near the end of my first tour. I was given a flight very soon after I joined the squadron here, so I've been there quite a long time. You too, probably.'

'Yes, but my first tour, you may remember, before Bridgnorth, was in Coastal. It's strange, there one was often anxious, but not as bad as it some-

times is now. Bomber Command can be bloody dangerous! The nervous system
gets pretty wound up, and takes some time to unwind. Still, it's better than it
was a year ago, don't you find?' Hugh paused before answering.

'It can often still be dicey. But I find I can unwind better with a little help.'

'Meaning?'

'You ought to know!' He paused again. 'By the way, how are your Three
Graces?'

'I think I'm still in love with all three of them, but I must admit, there are
sometimes others. The Three Graces, as you call them, are far away so often
when I most need them.'

'History repeating itself!' Hugh laughed. 'Why don't you overcome that by
getting married?'

'You know very well. The cuddly little wife who could cure me would be
away in some women's service, and much more important, it would be unfair
to marry when your life expectancy may be short.'

'Still, sex is the best therapy. Some chaps like to go on the jag, drink lots of
beer, but you and I have never used that course. There's no doubt, a girl is the
only one with the power to soothe away the trembles. There are times, if
you're like me, when you wonder if you can steel yourself to fly again through
those seemingly impassable barriers of flak. And the night before when you
shook off a fighter and regained control of the aircraft with your nerves
jangling and sweating all over, the right girl doing the right things can blot out
horror from the memory and by enchantment make all new the nerves that
channel our reactions and make them ready for their next test.' I nodded in
agreement.

'You always put things well, Hugh. That sounds almost poetic. Are there
many applicants for this job of giving you your therapy?'

'I've got a little sweetie who regularly puts me right, bless her. Without her
I should have found it much more difficult to get this far through a second tour.'

I thought of Tricia. 'For you my surgery is always open.' And I had never
known it closed.

It was a briefing for a daylight operation. I sat with my crew listening. I was
particularly interested in what the Met man had to say.

'You will remember the rain we had last evening. That was a Warm Front,
which has now passed through us, but you may meet it again over the
target. So most of the time today you will be flying in the Warm Sector,
and you may encounter the Cold Front on your return to base this afternoon. After a covering of stratus cloud this morning for take-off, you
should therefore expect to meet increasing cloud and in due course heavy
rain on your outward journey, decreasing for most of your flight home,
before coming into high and turbulent nimbus clouds and rain associated
with the Cold Front over England in which there may well be quite severe
icing.'

The target was Mannheim, which we had bombed exactly a month ago on the night we were at last able to get the aircraft off the ground following the snow of the second half of January.

It was a dull grey morning with a little drizzle as we were taken out to the dispersals. *N Nan* taxied to the end of the runway, and took off, climbing very soon into cloud. As I expected from the forecast, this proved to be only a layer of stratus and we were soon through it and emerged into a clear day, though still grey, as the sun rising in the east in front of us was hidden behind a sloping bank of cloud, which stretched away ahead as far as the eye could see. We were to climb to 20,000 feet, and as we climbed, the slope of the cloud seemed to climb with us. After nearly four hours the cloud was still close below us and we had not seen the ground at all. Had we been in Stirlings or those death-trap Manchesters of our unfortunate predecessors we should have been in it.

With the advance of the Allied Armies across France the Oboe transmitting stations had probably been moved forward, enabling Pathfinder Force aircraft to use the intersecting signals to mark the target effectively. We saw the sky-markers floating down and disappear into the deep, rain-filled clouds below us, but more followed them and we made our bombing run, closed our bomb doors and turned for home. Flak was coming up among us but we saw no fighters, though visibility was not good enough to see anything very clearly in the dull light.

As the Met man had said, as we flew north-west across France the cloud below us fell away with even a few breaks in it, but out to the west I could see a towering wall of nimbus cloud as the Cold Front moved eastward. When we entered that we would probably be thrown about like a shuttlecock. Though *N Nan* was no longer a 30-ton shuttlecock now that we had dropped our bomb load and used up much of our petrol, it would not be a pleasant experience. There was always the danger of one of the large control surfaces being damaged or even ripped off, and if ice was forming on the wings we could drop dramatically or find ourselves without an airspeed indicator if the pitot tube got frozen over. I switched on my microphone.

'Colin, I've no enthusiasm for flying in that weather, which looks like getting between us and our destination. I should like to come down now, over the North Sea, and be well below cloud before we get to the English coast. Could you please give me a course for say Skegness and a sensible rate of descent that will achieve that? How about 1000 feet a minute? Then give me a course from there to base, avoiding any hills or hazards? When we cross the coast I may deviate a bit if we can see clearly the main road to Louth, but I am anxious not to stray westward over the higher ground of the Wolds until I am quite sure where I am.'

'Will do, Skip. Give me a minute or two.'
And so we did. We were under the cloud before we reached the turbulence

of the piled-up nimbus that had loomed, white topped, black-based, blotting out forward visibility, as we had flown towards it. Though the quickening wind as the up-currents of the rain clouds sucking the air up off the sea into its billowing heights way above us drove white horses before it on the wave-tops of the sea, I could see the sea below us. I could judge our height above it and check, to my own satisfaction at least, the reading of my altimeter in this changed meteorological situation to which we were returning. The rain beat upon the windscreen and ran back in horizontal lines around the curved prow of the cockpit canopy and straight back over the Perspex roof above me as we struck into it at 200 miles an hour, as rain or hail always does when seen from the pilot's seat.

I felt at home. This was how it had so often been in 233 Squadron flying back from the North-west Approaches or from the Bay of Biscay. I liked it better than groping down through thousands of feet of cloud, wondering if a faulty instrument reading or an error of judgement I had made while still in the oblivion of cloud could make me break cloud too low and hit an unexpected little hill, or pylon.

We skimmed in over the coast, knowing and seeing where we were, and confirmed by Colin's course saw and followed the main road to Louth, sufficiently high above the rain-drenched countryside to avoid hazards but close enough to it to feel the confidence of sight. Soon, there was Louth, its tall church steeple lashed by rain. We called the Watch Office, circled once, got their OK to pancake and landed.

Three Lancasters were lost over Germany, and though as usual there was no official mention of it, we heard that several of the Command's aircraft crashed on reaching England. Derek made a wry announcement to the Sergeants' Mess.

'We came back by road.'

1st MARCH, 1945 – MANNHEIM

478 aircraft (Lancasters, Halifaxes, and Mosquitoes of 1, 6, and 8 Groups). 3 Lancasters lost.

This was a general attack on the city area. Sky marking was used because of the complete cloud cover. Nothing is known of what happened in Mannheim. The city's recording procedure, one of the best in Germany until now, appears to have broken down completely and, if any report was prepared, it did not survive the war.

The neighbouring town of Ludwigshafen was badly damaged. Public, domestic and industrial buildings were all hit: 424 buildings destroyed, nearly 1,000 seriously damaged. 5 people killed, 17 injured but 6,000 lost their homes.

(*The Bomber Command War Diaries*, Middlebrook and Everitt)

Two nights later, the *Luftwaffe* sent 200 night fighters to follow the various bomber forces back to England. 625 Squadron had no aircraft out, as they had been on operations for two days running

Operation Gisella took the British defences partly by surprise. The Germans shot down 20 bombers: 8 Halifaxes of 4 Group; 2 Lancasters of 5 Group; 3 Halifaxes, 1 Fortress and 1 Mosquito of 100 Group; and 3 Lancasters and 2 Halifaxes from the heavy Conversion Units which had been taking part in a diversionary sweep. 3 German night fighters crashed over England through flying too low.

(*The Bomber Command War Diaries*, Middlebrook and Everitt)

CHAPTER TWENTY

Nuremburg

T he home of Douglas Manns, a young man in my flight, was in Stornoway
on the Isle of Lewis in the Outer Hebrides. Throughout his war service
it had been impractical for him ever to go home on leave. He would have
been long overdue back, well before he could hope to get there. So I cleared it
with John that I should take him home, at least for a '24-hour pass', to see his
family and friends. Having cleared it with Flying Control for Lancaster *Dog 2*
to make this journey, and with twelve aboard because several wanted to make
the trip, we set off. John had had one final order.

'Don't forget to bring some kippers back!'

I flew across industrial northern England, passed to the north of the Isle of
Man, skirted the Mull of Galloway and the Mull of Kintyre, and came down
to a more advantageous sight-seeing height.

I was transported back nearly four years by what I saw to those happy Jill-
filled months at Aldergrove, when, just occasionally it was my turn to have this
treat, I flew from Northern Ireland up the western side of Scotland, inside the
islands of the Hebrides, on an early morning reconnaissance flight. I never quite
understood the purpose, but I did not question it. It was too good to be true.
The weather at this time of year was not so good as it had been then, for we
were only just out of February, but my crew and I and our passengers enjoyed
it very much. There had recently been some pretty rough weather, and a heavy
Atlantic swell was spending itself with determined ferocity against the bare
cliffs, throwing great white breakers into each carved-out inlet, dashing cliff-
high at rugged headlands, and surging forward to submerge beneath their foam
those great rocks that lay broken at the cliffs' feet. It was a testimony to the
times, back through the millennia, when angry storms, beating relentlessly, had
had their way with parts of the cliffs, which had withstood them for so long.

I flew the Lancaster at about 500 feet, and often just below the gale-lashed
cliff tops of promontories whose protecting arms sheltered here and there a
small fishing village. Granite homes and granite lives, or sometimes a green
slope studded with white or grey crofters' cottages in a treeless landscape where
the only windbreak was a line of drystone walling, older than memory.

On our right the highlands of Scotland rose rank upon rank, grey-lined
where burns ran down from the white, snow-capped upper fells through
bouldered, twisting grooves, which patient time had cut in their lower flanks

now dark brown with dead heather and patches of bracken that winter winds had burned.

It all looked so inaccessible and forbidding at this time of year, when the hardened, weathered people who wrung a living from these unwelcoming places, which they doubtless loved, waited for the coming of the spring. Now we were flying over the bare brown moorlands of the Isle of Lewis, a place of dry stony heath and grey-wet marshes whose brackish pools of water reflected back the winter light of the sky, and little crofts that men had made from the stones that lay about them, which generations of men and women called home and met the challenge of so harsh a habitation. At the southern end of the island there are mountains up to 2000 or 3000 feet, while the northern part, and especially the middle, like the neighbouring island of Uist, lies very low, with so many lakes or little lochs reflecting back to us the dull February light that the island looked like a piece of tattered brown lace upon a pewter table.

Now, as I called up for permission to land, we had below us a road, which coming up from the south, snaked among the countless little lochs and came to Stornoway. This was a small town at the neck of a bulb of land projecting east-wards between the harbour to its south, where fishing boats and herring drifters lay side by side at the quayside, and the broad bay, Loch-a-Tuath, to the north. The nearby aerodrome was a peat-brown waste across which ran a grey-black runway, on which we landed. I had heard tell that the land was so spongy that they had had to lay the runway on a series of rafts, but this was a feat of engineering beyond my comprehension. A tractor led *Dog 2* to the Watch Office, perhaps on hand to pull us out if she put a wheel off into the bog.

Having reported in at the RAF Mess, Douglas insisted on taking some of us into the town and introducing us to Mr Macdonald, a man of obvious standing in the community and also his previous employer. I persuaded him to hurry home. He had all too short a time to enjoy with his family, for we should have to return on the morrow. Mr Macdonald showed us round his mill, where looms wove the famous Harristweed, and I bought some lengths to take back. They were coveted materials in those days of shortages.

Mr Macdonald sent me on to a part of the town where the unmistakable smell of kippers pervaded the air. I arranged for several boxes of them to be sent to the aerodrome for us to take back to Kelstern in *Dog 2*, probably the most benign and uninjurious load she had ever carried.

When we got back to Kelstern John gave me the news that I was to go to Blackpool. A Lancaster, returning from an operation, had not come down to its aerodrome in Lincolnshire but had flown on further westwards and then plunged into a marsh between Blackpool and the estuary of the Ribble. I was to be President of a Court of Enquiry. As far as I could understand this was only a formality. Nobody was going to give me the facilities for digging the aircraft up out of its boggy grave. Of eyewitnesses there would be none, and earwitnesses would be able to contribute nothing of useful evidence. But apparently a Court of Enquiry there had to be, and off I went. I was flown to Squires Gate, the airfield nearest to Blackpool.

There were several RAF units there, one of them being a W/T Operators' or Radar School, but it had not been arranged that I should stay in a Mess, though the small hotel was one requisitioned by the Air Force. The first day of the Court of Enquiry took up little time, and I met there one of the pilots I had known in 233 Squadron, though he had not been a particular friend. He was a rather cadaverous looking man called Deacon. He invited me to accompany him to a dance hall in the town to which he was going that evening and assumed the role of tour guide.

'This is an extraordinary place. There are many people here from London who seem to have come here to escape the war. They are bored and often dissolute. Their contribution to the war effort is less than zero.'

I was standing talking to Deacon when a girl, not in uniform, came up and holding on to both of us interposed herself between us in a way that clearly was intended to excite. She was not pretty, but I was conscious of the aphrodisiac sensuality of her movements. She was provocatively attractive, bubbling over with animal magnetism.

'Come and dance with me.' Stepping back on to the dance floor, she pulled me to her and clung to me. Any normal man would immediately be aware of her, roused by her, and I was both of these things. I was excitedly conscious of the quicksilver movements of her body and the way in which she made me believe that I was the one person she had longed to meet and to be with. She was certainly not intoxicated by alcohol. The only drug she might have taken was benzedrine.

Later, walking by the sea in the almost darkness, I thought of my sincerely held belief in my theory of Sexual Therapy. It was wartime, when there were different requirements, for then the nerves of those who flew and fought were sometimes strained, and I thanked God for the gift of sex, which we who operated from home-based stations could thankfully receive, unlike those poor devils who flew or fought in deserts or in the jungle, who could only dream of it. And I thought only of my own experience; others no doubt found other ways to keep their thinking cool and actions instantaneous, to make them ready for the next emergency. I remembered Hugh's words at our recent meeting in Lincoln. For me at least, my dancing partner probably lacked 'the power to blot out horror from the memory, and by enchantment make all new the nerves which channel our reactions and make them ready for their next test'.

My experience in 1944 and early 1945 had not so far been so testing as it had been for some who struck a bad patch in 1942 or 1943. Some of them then could not expect a more than 17 per cent chance of completing a tour of thirty operations. Earlier, in 1940 and 1941 in 233 Squadron I was never really shit-scared, only sometimes very anxious. Sometimes in 625 Squadron anxiety had come nearer to the other thing. And on those occasions I knew that a girl, if she wanted to, could put me right. I knew that the kind of magic that a woman can give a man comes not in the ecstasy but in the peace that follows it, and though

I had no words to make that plainer, I knew that one woman can and one woman cannot. Colour, language, similarity of interests, have no part to play, and nor does the length of time the man and woman have been together. Hugh and I knew this. We knew that it is a severe strain to have to steel oneself to fly yet again, straight and level, defenceless and without hesitation through an anti-aircraft barrage. Let those who disbelieved us try it.

What of the women? Those girls men met at Cleethorpes dance hall, and cuddled in their cars. Those who came to see us off at the caravan as we turned on to the runway and then climbed away into the evening sky. They also had their compelling needs. They must have done, when you consider the risk they were taking. Yet leave was short and infrequent, and their friends for whom they wanted to wait were often far away. When they sometimes snatched the opportunity to gratify that need there was so little time for courtship, a 24-hour pass or even more quickly when the liberty bus would not wait for the girl with that chap on the grass bank near the bus-stop. She knew as she gave herself to a perhaps inconsiderate man how great the price she might be called upon to pay.

My Court of Enquiry established nothing, and I was glad to be home. Marshy places in England were full of British bombers. Many more crashed than people realised – perhaps at least an extra 10 per cent of admitted losses against the enemy – and the numbers were being kept very quiet. If they hit firm ground they usually burned or exploded; many depressions in farming land bore soon-to-be-forgotten witness; but if they hit boggy ground they plunged in and the marsh closed over them. I knew of marshy ground to the east of Doncaster where many lay buried. HCU 'Prangtoft' contributed more than its share, and other Operational Training Stations and Heavy Conversion Units which, because of shortages, had to use aircraft that, truthfully, were past it, worn out, possibly death traps. But most of the unfortunate victims, those who lay in the ooze of East Anglian marshes, were poor devils who had so nearly made it home.

I got back to Kelstern in time to take part in a daylight raid on the unfortunate Ruhr city of Dortmund. A maximum effort had been demanded by Group.

12th MARCH, 1945 – DORTMUND

1108 aircraft – 748 Lancasters, 292 Halifaxes, 68 Mosquitoes.

This was another new record to a single target, a record which would stand to the end of the war. 2 Lancasters lost.

Another record tonnage of bombs – 4851 – was dropped through cloud on to the unfortunate city. The only details available from Dortmund states that the attack fell mainly in the centre and south of the city. A British team which investigated the effects of bombing in Dortmund after the war concluded 'The final raid . . . stopped production so effectively that it would have been many months before any substantial recovery could have occurred.'

(*The Bomber Command War Diaries*, Middlebrook and Everitt)

The next day we had a target again, a night trip, as the Flight Commanders and Leaders learned when we were called to the Squadron Commander's office.

'I know you were flying yesterday, Peter, but what do you think about this new chap you've got, Flight Lieutenant Lennox? Time for his second dicky?'

'I'll take him tonight, Sir, I think it's better to fly through flak at night with someone holding your hand and then do it alone in daylight than it is to do it the other way round.'

So Colin, with Titch in the tail, and I took Lennox and some of his crew that night to Herne. The force was split between benzol plants at Herne and Gelsenkirchen. Lennox's tail gunner Sgt Birkby came too, so of course there were eight, not seven aircrew aboard, Lennox being supernumerary, and Birkby flew in the mid-upper turret instead of Torry Large.

Wally Birkby was engaged to Bessie, a WAAF transport driver at Kelstern. Bessie drove various vehicles. Once, not long before, she had been called to drive the MO (Medical Officer) out to meet a Lancaster, which had returned to base with its bomb aimer wounded. Unfortunately the man was dead when the crew landed. Bessie said that she helped the MO pull the bomb aimer out of the nose of the aircraft, and when they moved him 'his blood ran out and all over me, and it was so warm!' She was eighteen at the time. The bomb aimer was perhaps three years her senior.

Before we set off, I said to the Lennox crew members what I recalled Treherne saying to me.

'Remember that it is alertness by everyone and instantaneous reactions that will most help you to get through a tour, so Be Alert!' Our Herne target was cloud-covered and we bombed sky-markers, pretty hopeless for a pin-point target like a benzol plant, and the raid was not a success, but Lennox and his crew saw flak and searchlights and got 'genned-up' on the procedures.

Three more night targets followed, and the next one for me and my crew was to Nuremberg. The name Nuremberg sounded a note of anxiety in the minds of aircrew after the raid of eleven months previously, the last night of March 1944. That was a night that would normally have been the moon stand-down period, but a raid to the distant target of Nuremberg was planned on the basis of an early forecast that there would be protective high cloud on the outward route, when the moon was up, but that the target area would be clear for ground-marked bombing. A Meteorological Flight Mosquito carried out a reconnaissance and reported that the protective cloud was unlikely to be present and that there could be cloud over the target, but the raid was not cancelled. The disaster had passed into Bomber Command legend. Ninety-five bombers were shot down. The number of aircrew lost on that one target, in one night, was more than all the pilots shot down in the whole of the Battle of Britain. They were easy prey for a concerted force of night fighters. Ill met by moonlight indeed.

So Nuremberg was not a target anyone wanted. As I and other men sat or stood around the bar in the Mess that day before lunch, only a very few knew what the target was, though all knew from the petrol load that it was a distant one. Crews who were on the battle order had been out to dispersal and had run up their engines and done all their checks. A pilot in A Flight, Barry Cunliffe, a glass of beer in his hand, looked tired.

'I feel knackered. Loud cries of chips!'

Some of those about him laughed, but feeling knackered and being alert do not go together, and I was glad that Cunliffe was not in my flight, but Alan Fry's, or I would have felt a frustrated sense of guilt that he had to go. Yet what could Fry have done? It was a Maximum Effort for the squadron, and anyhow, if he had sent someone else instead, and they had 'bought it', 'had their chips', he, and Cunliffe, would have felt worse.

At the briefing when the curtain was rolled up to reveal the wall map, whereon the red ribbons turned upon a pin in the dot that represented Nuremberg, the atmosphere of anxiety was almost tangible. The shadow of the raid of eleven months before fell upon the crews as they sat there in their rows in the Operations Room. Ninety-five aircraft were lost. I heard the quiet involuntary groan from my 175 fellow aircrew, and knew what they were thinking.

When it was the turn of the Met man to speak, I was glad to hear confirmation that there would be no moon. At least there was not a carbon copy of the weather pattern of eleven months ago.

As our crew and another, in one of the crew buses, drove round the perimeter track to the dispersal in which our *X X-Ray* waited for us, the darkening sky was clear. Once aboard we saw that the Lancaster in the neighbouring pan was in Aldis-light conversation with the Control Tower. This was a job that Derek often did when his crew were not flying.

Often then, Derek was out on the balcony of the Control Tower, there to receive and send Aldis signals to any aircraft out on dispersal who wanted to report unserviceability and seek urgent help to put it right. Absolute W/T and R/T silence was demanded so Aldis light was the means of communication, and the Watch Office would alert at once whomsoever was needed to get out there at once. Derek was an energetic fellow, always wanting to be busy, and gladly and efficiently took on this task. But ask him to be a substitute and fly with any pilot but me, and the asker could be certain of a refusal. In his discourse with aircraft across the airfield, A meant Armoury; B Bogged down; C Cancel last message; E Electrics; M Maintenance; O Oxygen; OL Instruments; R Radar; S Signals; T Transport. The sender flashed Vics until a K was received and the letter of the aircraft; the Control Tower signalled R, and acknowledged with a long dash.

As the twenty-five Lancasters of 625 Squadron moved, from left and from right, round the perimeter track to converge on the caravan at the end of the runway, the sky was clear. It was one of those early spring evenings when piled up shower clouds, billowing high but their rain spent now that the warmth of the day had gone, were purple black against the fading orange red of sunset. Round to the north the sky was pale clear green, and further to the north the blue of sky, which was the backdrop to the once-white cumulus clouds now greying in the fading light, was tinged with green in contrast to the orange. It was rather beautiful.

X X-Ray reached the downwind end of the runway from the right, paused, then turned into wind. As usual there was the little crowd of well-wishers there to wave us off, but Tricia was not among them; she was on duty that evening. Nearly always if I was flying she was there in her grey knitted gloves, but not tonight. Perhaps it was the atmosphere of apprehension that had been so noticeable at briefing that caused in me a tinge of superstition. Was it a bad omen that she was not there tonight? I cleared the silly thought from my mind. After all, we had not forgotten to pee on the port wheel. As the green light shone I pushed the four red throttle levers forward, followed by the gloved hand of Reg.

'Full power!'

We roared towards the greying sunset, made our circuit and climbed on the course Colin had given me.

625 Squadron's contingent merged with the other 206 Lancasters of No. 1 Group and the forty-six of 8 Group and we flew out over the continent. The tall shower clouds, which had looked so dramatic at take-off time, were left behind and the stream was flying at about 19,000 feet with stratus cloud spread out far below it. We were not silhouetted against the cloud in bright full moon-light as on the Nuremberg raid of eleven months ago, but we were visible enough. Though our first course had given no indication of the direction in which we should eventually be heading, out there on the way to the target the German night fighters found us.

I calculated that we had probably flown over the Walcheren Islands and the secret waters described in Childer's *The Riddle of the Sands* and were now flying over western Germany. I had recently checked on the intercom that all of the crew were all right and on oxygen, and expected that Colin would soon give me a new course.

Suddenly there was a brilliant explosion beside us. It did not look like flak as I had known it. Ken had had a better view.

'That was a rocket. I think I saw it leave the ground.' Certainly there was no sound of shrapnel hitting the aircraft, as there would have been from flak so close. Then there was another, similar, brilliant red and yellow, on the other side of us. 'Rocket'? Could it be German controllers marking the position of the bomber stream for vectoring their fighters?

Within seconds there was the urgent voice of Titch.

'FIGHTER, 6 O'CLOCK, DOWN!'

Almost at once, Torry took up the warning.

'ATTACKING FIGHTER! PORT BEAM, LEVEL!'

I threw the control column away from me. Streuth, simultaneous attacks! I almost felt the rush of one of the fighters as it nearly collided with us. Out of the corner of my eye I saw an earthwards slanting trail over to the right of us. It was an aircraft going down in flames.

Then to our left, another fighter's kill. But soon in the exertions of my corkscrew it was hard to tell if anything I might see was to the left or right. Torry's next report brought some relief.

'Two fighters gone away right.' I hauled the heavy Lancaster, still with a full bomb load and almost full petrol tanks for the long flight, out of its clumsy manoeuvre and on to an even keel. It was a few moments before my instruments had settled enough to be readable

'We're down to about 16,000 feet, Colin.'

'Climb back up to 19,000 please, Skip. Remember that your course is still 095 until I can give you a correction.'

In a steady climb I in time regained my correct height, but almost immediately I heard with anxiety the sound of the intercom being switched on. There was the scream of slipstream so I knew it was one of the gunners. It was Titch again.

'There's an aircraft been hit dead astern of us. Blown up. An orange ball. I see no fighter yet.'

'There's one been hit ahead of us too.' That was Ken on his stomach in the nose. His prone position probably prevented the blood being drained out of his head when I had pulled out of my dive. It helped maintain his ability to see.

My thoughts were probably the thoughts of all of them. Save us! The fighters have found the stream; this looks like the beginning of a massacre. Was the jinx of Nuremberg upon us all?

It was quiet in the aircraft for a few minutes, while all searched the black dark sky around for more attackers. It was a strained silence despite the roar of our four engines.

Then there was the dull thud of a shell exploding near to us and the sound of pieces of shrapnel peppering the aircraft, a faint smell of cordite and a brilliant light beside us, not too far away. We'd been hit, though not blown up.

'You all right, Titch? You, Torry?' Both gunners replied, in rather shaken voices, that they were.

'You Colin? Derek?' They too sounded all right.

'Ken?'

'Frightened, but still in one piece.' I could see Reg standing beside me, and I myself was suffering no pain as though I had been hit. Then came Titch's shout again.

'FIGHTER! FIGHTER! DOWN RIGHT!'

Once again I hurled the Lancaster into a corkscrew. DOWN right, roll left, right again, then haul back the stick with left bank and rudder. A film before my eyes, the change from diving at who knows what speed to an attempt to pull the kite into level flight and try to begin another climb. God, I mustn't black out! Slowly the blood was pumped back into my head. I was soaked in sweat and near to exhaustion. The weight of those great surfaces was almost more than I could pull up and control. Sanity and a clearer vision returned. I began to climb again and banked right. There was still no word from anyone to suggest that we had lost the fighter. But climb I must. I'd lost a lot of height so might be below the stream, without the benefit of safety-in-numbers, as a lone fish separated from the dense ball of the shoal is vulnerable to predators.

Ken's voice clicked onto the intercom.

'A fighter went underneath us; looked a bit out of control. I don't know where it is now.'

So I carried on climbing, thanking God for my Merlin engines, which allowed me to dive at that speed without failing, unlike what may have been an over driven BMW radial engine in an Fw 190.

I was level and at height again. Then far away across the darkness a red star was born. It grew in brightness then faded. It was some other poor devil. Perhaps it was another fighter's kill.

So many fighters! They are destroying us! Whose turn next? Is this our last trip? Not if I can help it. But it was frightening. Tricia darling, you ought to have been there to wish us well! How long has this massed attack on the stream so far lasted? German controllers have found us and vectored the fighters on to us. How many of us have they downed? Please God they have nearly used up their petrol and must now land and refuel.

They must have done. There followed a period of quiet. I received a new course from Colin. Poor lad, how can he know where on earth we are after all that hectic manoeuvring? Then Ken spoke.

'I think we've got stratus cloud below us now Skip.'

Thank God for no moon. That's what they had eleven months ago, when every aeroplane was silhouetted clear as day against the cloud below. No, they've not all gone home. Nobody saw a shell-burst, but over on our left an orange ball materialised in the darkness, hung a few seconds then dropped away, its brightness fading. Its light illuminated us. It also illuminated another Lancaster on our right, dangerously close, flying parallel. I felt the judder of machine-gun fire and heard its stuttering clatter. From its sound and feel I knew that it was from our mid-upper.

'What are you shooting at, Torry?'

'In the light of that explosion I saw a Lanc quite near on our starboard beam. There was a Junkers 88 just beneath it. I hosed it. I don't know if I hit it, I only saw it for a few seconds, but it went away!' Torry sounded pleased.

'I've got a new ground position, Skip, turn to starboard on to 050.'

'Thank you Colin.'

Not long afterwards Ken called up.

'Target fine on the starboard bow, I can see the markers going down; search-lights too, coming up.'

'Well done, Colin.'

'R-i-g-h-t a little. Good, steady as you go. Open bomb doors. Steady, steady, Bombs gone! No hang-ups.'

We flew on for about half a minute – though it seemed much longer. Then Colin spoke.

'Course 310.'

As we turned I looked down at the burning fires below. They seemed most fierce in the corner that we had approached, and in the right-hand side of the target. Quickly returning my head to look ahead of us, we flew on.

'Keep close lookout chaps, those fighters may be back again.'

But we saw none. It was just a long, watchful, stressful flight. Ken spoke again.

'That low cloud is ahead of us now, Skip, but it looks strangely bright, though there's no moon.' Derek came up again to look from the astrodome. It did look strangely bright; we would show up against it.

'The devils! They're shining searchlights up at the cloud base.'

'That'll be the edge of the Ruhr, Skip. I'll give you a course to the south of it, but north of Cologne. Give me a minute.'

We were all very tired when I was able to call up Kelstern and request permission to land. Back in the Operations Room we compared experiences in weary voices, and were debriefed at one of the tables. I looked about me to see if all were back. After perhaps twenty minutes they all were, except two crews of the squadron's twenty-five. John Barker, Alan Fry, Woodie Hammond and I waited on in the Operations Room after all the others had gone to bed.

One missing crew was from my B Flight, captained by Tony Adams. The other was Barry Cunliffe and his crew. It is a strange thing how men had that feeling of foreboding that so often proved to be right. 'I'm knackered. Loud cries of chips!'

The echo of Cunliffe's Etonian intonation was one that, for me, long sounded as a background to my thoughts. Perhaps because Cunliffe's fatalism had been so offhand, the image of the brave, tired man lingered in the memory – Tall, handsome, fair-haired, battledress unbuttoned, and less than seven hours to live. I had looked at the group of men who stood there at the bar, as they pondered where the day's petrol load would send them on the night's raid ahead, making light of a journey which, for each of them, might be their last.

16/17th MARCH, 1945 – NUREMBERG

231 Lancasters of 1 Group and 46 Lancasters and 16 Mosquitoes of 8 Group.

24 Lancasters, all from 1 Group, lost. 8.7 % of the Lancaster force and 10.4 % of the 1 Group aircraft involved. Most of these losses were due to German night fighters, which found the bomber stream on its way to the target.

The local report (Dr Erich Mulzer) states that the southern and south-western districts were hit, as well as the ruins of the Altstadt which was destroyed in a previous raid. A serious 'fire area' was established in the Steinbuhl district. The main railway station was also on fire and the city's gas works were so badly damaged that they did not resume production before the end of the war. There are no figures for property damage and the only casualty figure given is 529 dead.

(*The Bomber Command War Diaries*, Middlebrook and Everitt)

Both those Nuremberg nights, and many others like them, were nights when the German night fighters did not need guidance from their radar controllers. They could see the stream, pick out their victim, and go in and attack and then choose another. If you were the chosen victim and managed to evade the fighter darting in from the dark side of the sky, you hoped that he had overshot and gone on to another, and was not just holding off and about to come in on another attack. On a clear night, even if it is not just after last light or just before first light, one side of the night sky is often a fraction paler than the other. The experienced fighter would usually come in from the darker side and see his intended victim as a dim silhouette.

The Lancaster had begun its service as an aircraft with an additional lower turret, but this had been dispensed with early on, and this gave it a blind spot. German fighter pilots were known to prefer to try to come up underneath, and with quite a short burst cut off one of the Lancaster's wings between the fusilage and an engine nacelle or between two engines. This put the bomber immediately into a spin. Even if the cannon did not sever the main spar, the petrol from the severed wing's tanks flowed across the red-hot cut made by the cannon shells and the Lancaster burned fiercely. They were, after all, built of an alloy of aluminium and magnesium, and burned like paper. In those circumstances, no one ever got out.

On nights when the fighters were dependent on their radar controllers, the British were using countermeasures that were improving. But the German methods for detecting them and vectoring the fighters on to them were improving too. All through the war, measures and countermeasures were giving a small advantage first to one side and then to the other. One of the many tasks that Derek was nightly performing was listening out to Base at Binbrook and Command at High Wycombe and receiving not only information for Colin, but also, among other things, the frequencies on which the German controllers were transmitting, frequencies that were continually changing. Having been told a frequency, he could quickly transmit on that frequency at 90 watts the sound of his aircraft's engines. Then he would stop and listen, and then perhaps transmit again. It effectively jammed the German transmissions to their fighters in the same way as the Germans were jamming what British bomber crews wanted to hear. Changes of frequency were rapid and frequent, and neither was fully effective; both sides received information but it was all made more difficult.

As you flew up the eastern side of England the circles of Drem lights surrounding each aerodrome, if the night was clear enough to see, were as close together as touching coins on a shove-halfpenny board. 625 Squadron at Kelstern was very close to Waltham and to Ludford Magna as well as to Binbrook. In fact the CO of one of them 'borrowed' a lavatory seat from the White Swan at Grimsby and said he would present it to the next aircraft that landed at the wrong aerodrome. 101 Squadron was stationed at Ludford Magna. Its Lancasters bombed, but some of them also carried out Electronic Counter Measures. They had aboard an extra wireless operator who was German-speaking, and they issued contradictory messages and instructions to the German fighters. Perhaps they, or more often the high flying Mosquitoes of 8 Group or 100 Group, sent back to Command the frequencies on which the controllers were operating.

*   *   *

The Nuremberg raid on which 625 Squadron lost Adams and Cunliffe was on 16 March. Next night the squadron was stood down. But on the night of 18 March they went to Hannau, another maximum effort for which 625 Squadron provided twenty-three aircraft.

Hannau lies to the east of Frankfurt, so is well beyond the Ruhr towns. That night another force was to bomb Witten, home of the Ruhrstahl steelworks and the Mannesmann tube factory, the easternmost town of the great industrial Ruhrland.

After briefing for that Hannau raid on that wet grey evening in March 1945, the crew-buses took crews out to the dispersals, to the bombers that waited for take-off time. They could not see far across the airfield as rain-clouds dragged their misty feet over the grass in little scurries of cold wet showers and wind rocked even the black, 30-ton Lancasters as they stood, bombed up and prepared, on their concrete dumbbell-shaped hardstandings. Made wet even in the short walk from the bus to the door of the aircraft, each member of our crew climbed in through the awkward door and, hampered by parachute and various bits of kit, struggled their way along the fuselage and over the obstacle of the main spar to their several places.

The shower-clouds shut out most of the light that the sky of a March early evening would normally provide. It was a thoroughly depressing scene and you could think of so many better ways of spending the time. One could look forward to about four hours of high concentration of the outbound leg, boring if it were not for the anxiety of what might lie just beyond the limit of one's restricted vision, then the pyrotechnics of the target area, and then the long haul home.

The first hour was just eye-crossing fatigue as I strained my sight on those dim florescent figures and shapes on the panel in front of me. But the Met people had said that we would climb out of the murk well before we got into the airspace of the dangers that awaited us, and so we did, breaking cloud at last and seeing stars above us.

There was no flak, yet, on the far side of Frankfurt. But there were search-lights, and that could mean fighters: keep the skies clear for them, give them a chance at the bombers.

'Looks like there's no flak, everyone. Titch and Torry, expect fighters.'

I myself must not look for them. My job was to fly accurately to Ken's instructions.

'Left-left a little . . . Steady . . . .'

Out of the corner of my right eye I saw something like a comet's tail, orange, slanting earthwards: a fighter's kill. Seven men were diving and burning,

' . . . . Steady . . . steady . . . . Bombs gone. No hang-ups.'

Turn, settle on a new course, then keep watching, waiting for the shout from one of the gunners. Just over three hours more to go. Shouldn't mind a pee, but try to forget it; there's a funnel and tube thing here but 100 to 1 it's frozen. Approaching the Ruhr now, from the other side from usual. Flak going up there, long way ahead. Colin will be giving me another course soon, before we get there; can't believe our course lies through it. But perhaps it does.

'Alter course starboard on to 300 degrees Skip and descend to 14,000 feet.'

'Thank you Colin.'

18th MARCH, 1945 – HANNAU and WITTEN

HANNAU

277 Lancasters and 8 Mosquitoes of 1 and 8 Groups. 1 Lancaster lost

This was another accurate area raid. The local report states that 50 industrial buildings and 2240 houses were destroyed. The Altstadt was completely devastated and, says the report, all the town's churches, hospitals, schools and historic buildings were badly hit. Approximately 2000 people were killed, of whom 1150 were regular residents of Hannau, the remaining dead were presumably evacuees or refugees from bombed cities.

WITTEN

324 aircraft – 259 Halifaxes, 45 Lancasters, 20 Mosquitoes of 4, 6, and 8 Groups.

8 aircraft – 6 Halifaxes, 1 Lancaster, 1 Mosquito were lost.

This was a successful area raid carried out in good visibility. 1081 tons of bombs were dropped, destroying 129 acres, 62% of the built-up area (according to the post-war British bombing Survey Unit). The only German report states that the Ruhrstahl steelworks and the Mannesmann tube factory were severely damaged.

(*The Bomber Command War Diaries*, Middlebrook and Everitt)

Nine British aircraft were lost, though illogically, those on the more distant raid – like 625 Squadron – suffered fewer casualties than those who were on the nearer one. Both raids were successful, for in good visibility much damage was done.

Hannau on the night of 18 March was probably the last raid that could be described as an 'area' raid. From then on targets were strictly 'military'.

The strategic bombing of Germany had achieved its purpose; targets of the next seven weeks were tactical.

A few days after that I and my crew went on leave – gratefully, for we were all tired.

CHAPTER TWENTY-ONE

Peace in Europe

My crew and I returned to find unexpected changes happening at
Kelstern. An effective and popular MO had been replaced by another
man who was generally disliked. That he was apparently homosexual
is irrelevant, though among the men with whom I was living and flying, such
people were treated with suspicion by the majority. But people considered that
he had a mean streak and it was thought by squadron and station officers that
he was malicious when he had made complaint to Group against the Station
Commander. Kelstern, by comparison with many other bomber stations, had
been thrown up in something of a hurry, and though unquestionably it was a
happy station it had shortcomings that were consequent upon the impermanent
nature of its buildings and facilities. As a result of the complaint the Group
Medical Officer made a visit and put in a highly critical report of the Sanitary
Diary. On our return my crew and I were confronted with the fact that Donkin
had apparently been sacked and command of the station had been assumed by
John Barker, in addition to being Squadron Commander. It was not known
where Donkin had gone, but he borrowed a Lancaster from John and flew off
in it, accompanied by whomsoever it was prudent for him to have with him.

On 5 April Kelstern was closed down and 625 Squadron moved to RAF
Scampton. Though Scampton was very near to Lincoln, with a far better bus
service for men and women to enjoy their leisure time among that city's facilities when they were stood down, I was one of many who considered it a change
for the worse. Scampton was a station with peacetime buildings. The squadron
moved out of Nissen huts into rooms in brick-built Messes and were
surrounded with facilities that they had become well accustomed to doing
without. There was already a Lancaster squadron there, 153 Squadron, though
it too had not been there for long. Though we were not made unwelcome, the
atmosphere was not the same as it had been when 625 Squadron had had to
make some effort themselves to make the best of whatever facilities Kelstern
had.

I was not the only one who regretted the change, and it was not only because
some of the station people did not move with the squadron, Tricia among them.
So many others must have had their love life disrupted, as was of course so
frequently the case.

625 Squadron had been at Scampton for only a few days when Tony Adams

returned. He had been in England for a few days. He had been interrogated in London, and had made contact with his family. He had a strange tale to tell, which in part became the buzz of the Mess that week. He had lost an engine as he was running up to the target, but had carried on and bombed. On his return he had been hit again and lost a second engine. He had not been able to maintain height and had ordered his crew to bale out. He still had no news of what had befallen the other members of his crew, though he was apparently the last one to jump, with little enough height in which to hope to do so successfully. The fact that he landed in a tree was, he considered, his salvation. Though somewhat dazed and shocked, he had the impression that he was in a forest, and managed to climb and slither down the tree towards the ground. Though the light was poor, he could see that there was someone or something at the bottom of the tree. Perhaps fortunately, before he had completed his descent, he realised by sight and sound that it was a bear. Also fortunately, the bear was apparently just as anxious as he was to avoid a confrontation, and having waited and watched and listened, Adams eventually decided that there was no future in staying in the tree any longer. Reaching the ground he set off, alone (for there was no sign of any of his crew) in what he believed was the way home, and had the exceedingly good fortune to get picked up at last by friendly soldiers, though not until after some narrow escapes reminiscent of a tale by John Buchan. For the time being he did not want to go into the details of all those adventures to those who sat listening to him in John Barker's office.

But now he came to what – for me – was the most exciting part of his story. Having to pass through a town still in German hands, he saw a party of men whom he took to be prisoners-of-war being marched along the street, and there among them, unmistakably, was Roger Scott. Understandably he did not risk throwing away his hard-earned freedom by shouting his recognition, and continued on his secretive journey.

John and all of us were listening spellbound to his story up until this point, but now I could not contain myself any longer.

'She's in Gainsborough! You must let me take you at once to Roger's wife and tell her this wonderful news yourself. Will you come now?' We both looked to John for approval.

'Take my car.'

As it had been I who had had the awful task of going to Louth to tell her that Roger had not returned, no one wanted to deny me the pleasure of leaping for the phone, telling her that Roger had been seen alive, and that I was bringing the man who had seen him over to Gainsborough at once so that she could hear it from him.

There were tears in my eyes when I saw her happy face as she stood at the open door of the house waiting for our arrival.

'Go and tell her. And tell her that I'm going to wait in the car.'

Later, I went in and joined them, because really there was not much that Adams could tell her, except to tell her over and over again that it really was Roger and that he looked well and was in fact laughing with one of the other prisoners as they marched by. Was this last bit a little embroidery by Adams ? It doesn't really matter. I thanked God that I was given the joy of seeing her happiness, I who had seen her shock and misery on that morning in Louth.

One evening in the Officers' Mess at Scampton I was called to the telephone. I got up and walked out of the anteroom and part way along the wide passage that ran the length of the Mess to where a telephone was mounted on the wall. There was no one else in the corridor. I had an inexplicable premonition that something emotionally compelling was about to happen. As I reached out to pick up the instrument I glanced back to see that no one else had come into the corridor.

It was Jill. She did not preface her news with small talk or padding, but came straight to the point. She was pregnant, she said, by a New Zealander.

'He's a nice chap and I'm very fond of him. He has said that of course he will marry me. He has finished his tour and so is not likely now to become a casualty. But before I take this step, Peter dear, I must ask you – or in time to come I shall never forgive myself – if you, perhaps, before it's too late, wanted to marry me.'

My heart was beating fast at this sudden and so unexpected news. I imagined her standing at a similar telephone, her wonderful blue eyes looking quickly to left and right to make sure no one was overhearing her, those lovely lips I had so often kissed, held close to the mouthpiece, a slight blush on her cheeks as she took me into her confidence. O God, what a decision to have to make! My mind was racing. She had had time to consider what she was saying; but I had had no time to give any thought to this wonderful, moving and flattering offer she was making. Yet I knew that I could not say anything like 'give me time to think about it'. If my answer could be yes then it must be instantaneous and it must be heard to be instantaneous. In the flutter of my emotion my hand shook as nervously I lifted the telephone closer to my mouth. My words, unprepared and unrehearsed, tumbled out.

'Jill, darling, it is wonderful of you to offer to me the greatest gift that anyone could. Forgive my broken voice – I am trembling with such a mixture of emotions. I have never yet in my life considered marriage, except at one time when I thought, wrongly, that I was in the same position of responsibility as your New Zealander. My feeling then was that while I am on operational flying I should not enter into a contract of marriage unless it is really necessary, though I know I shall want to do so when my life-expectancy is better. You know that I have always loved you, and I always shall, and the few months you gave me in Ireland nearly four years ago are, I think, the happiest of my life. I have since had other passionate relationships, as of course you have too, though funnily enough I have none at this present time. Fate was kind then to allow us several months together without the interruption that frequent postings usually so unkindly give.'

I paused, thinking desperately.

'Frankly, darling, I am not ready. You must not let your New Zealander, whom you say is a good chap and whom you love enough to have allowed him to possess your loveliness, know that you ever had any thoughts of a union with anyone other than him. If he should decide to change his mind and withdraw his offer, please tell me at once; that would be another set of circumstances and priorities, demanding that we meet immediately so that you can look at me again and know for sure that you really want what you say you are prepared to give me. I feel now though that as things stand, he is in a position to offer you and your baby stability, while I am only a lottery ticket. Would that I were he, darling, and this war over and free to put down my roots – more and more I long for that.'

At that time, I had little expectation that the war in Europe would be over in about a month. My recent experience on the way to Nuremberg and the total of the Command's losses on that raid did not point to an imminent end. Had I thought it would, I have little doubt that my reaction to Jill's so sweet offer would have been different.

I came away from that phone with everything inside whirring like the wound-up movement of a grandfather clock whose pendulum has been removed. It was some time before I had calmed down.

The last operation on which I and my crew flew together was the daylight raid on the island fortress of Heligoland. It was a lovely clear day, sunshine making the water of the North Sea look unusually blue. Nearly a thousand bombers took part and bombing was accurate on the naval base, the airfield, and the town. In the clear bright golden daylight three British aircraft were seen to go down, but then the defences were probably saturated and I could not help feeling sorry for the gunners whose duty it was to continue firing at the stream of Lancasters and Halifaxes, which must have seemed to them unending. Having added our own brutal delivery to their awful situation, circling round and looking back, I saw a mound of smoke and dust so thick that it looked almost solid, sulphur-yellow upon the blue sea. Members of the crew saw the paler blue lines radiating out from the stricken island, which were escaping submarines beneath the surface of the sea. As we flew home we saw a Halifax flying much lower than the rest of us and went down to enquire if it was all right, but it Aldised to us that it did not require assistance so we did not signal home for air-sea rescue attention and we continued on our way.

18th APRIL, 1945 – HELIGOLAND
969 aircraft – 617 Lancasters, 332 Halifaxes, 20 Mosquitoes of all groups attacked the naval base, the airfield and the town of this small island. The bombing was accurate and the target areas were turned into crater-pitted moon-scapes. The present day Burgermeister was unable to supply any local details; it

is probable that the civilian population had been evacuated long before the raid.
3 Halifaxes were lost.

(*The Bomber Command War Diaries*, Middlebrook and Everitt)

There was a target that was cancelled, and three days later a target that every crew wanted to be on. In fact only twelve aircraft were called for; perhaps it was being 'shared out'! My crew and I were not among the twelve. The raid was on Berchtesgaden, Hitler's 'Eagle's Nest' chalet cut into the mountains, and the barracks of the SS guard not far away.

25th APRIL, 1945 – BERCHTESGADEN
359 Lancasters and 16 Mosquitoes of 1, 5 and 8 Groups. 2 Lancasters lost.

This raid was against Hitler's 'Eagle's Nest' chalet and the local SS guard barracks.

Among the force were 16 Lancasters of 617 Squadron dropping their last Tallboys.

8 Oboe Mosquitoes were also among the bombing force, to help with the marking, but mountains intervened between one of the ground stations transmitting the Oboe signals and the Mosquitoes could not operate even though they were flying at 39,000 feet! There was some mist and snow on the ground also made it difficult to identify targets, but the bombing appeared to be accurate and effective. No other details are available.

(*The Bomber Command War Diaries*, Middlebrook and Everitt)

Berchtesgaden was the last operation undertaken by 625 Squadron. By the end of April, though Berlin had fallen to the Russians, and Allied armies were racing, with very little opposition, to join up with them on the Elbe, much of Holland was still in German hands. The Dutch people were starving. Many old and sick people had already died. Agreement was reached with the local German commander of the occupying force that Bomber Command should drop supplies of food on Holland for civilian use. The first day for this, and the first dropping point, was 29 April, at the Hague racecourse. This was Operation *Manna*. Though it was never thought of as an 'operation', the squadron attended briefing. The Germans had agreed a truce, we were told, and aircraft were to go in at very low level and drop their loads of sacks of food (such things as dehydrated potato and dried milk) on the 'target', which would be marked in the usual way. The Germans had promised not to shoot.

It was an interesting experience. As we came in low over the coast we had crossed before in very different circumstances, we could see the German gun emplacements and the uniformed and steel-helmeted gunners in them. Ken and I were busy ensuring that our 'Manna' should fall from the skies in exactly the right place, but other members of the crew were able to take in more detail of the scene before and below them. Derek and the gunners saw a German gunner swing his gun round as we came over him, keeping us in his sights. 'And I had my bead on him too,' said Titch afterwards. They saw men running out from the sides of the racecourse to drag away full sacks that had fallen, surely a very dangerous occupation. A building a little to the right was on fire and burning well. Marker flares had set fire to the grandstand.

John was on that first 'Manna' trip, but I did not see him when we got back. Next day I heard that he took the Commanding Officer of No. 1 Group, AVM Rice, with him and then on his return found a message telling him to go immediately to London. He must have come back to the station, but I never saw him again at Scampton. The next day the Station Commander sent for me and said that W/Cdr Barker would not be returning and that for the time being I, as senior Flight Commander, was to assume command of the squadron. He added that I was to count on him for any assistance I might require. He offered no explanation, and I had the impression that he knew no more than I did about John's sudden disappearance. It was all very strange and secretive. I went at once and consulted with the Squadron Adjutant, but he was completely in the dark too. So we carried on without him and I did such things as it was now my duty to do. As it was the end of the month I signed all the squadron log books as 'Squadron Leader Commanding 625 Squadron'.

On the next day there was an envelope for me in the letter rack in the Mess. It had an unusual franking and it appeared to have an enclosure. It looked as though it had come from a Government Department. I opened it and saw that it came from Buckingham Palace. Somewhat astonished, I read it.

BUCKINGHAM PALACE
  I greatly regret that I am unable to give you personally the award which you have so well earned.
  I now send it to you with my congratulations and my best wishes for your future happiness.
  GEORGE R

Squadron Leader Anthony Peter Russell, D.F.C.

There, in a small black case was the Distinguished Flying Cross.

My first emotional reaction was one of relief. During five and a half years of war I had continued to have the anxiety that I had first felt aboard *Nancy Blackett* in that last weekend of peacetime. It had been an anxiety that I would be found wanting. My mind went back to lying in my bunk in my sleeping bag, hearing the soft mockery of the water running along the outside of *Nancy*'s planking less than a foot from my ear and occasionally the gentle slap of a halyard against the mast accompanying the quiet whistle of my father's breathing as he slept. I had thought then about the men in the Butt and Oyster with whom we had spent a happy evening, sailing friends of Father's generation. They were men who had fought and lost friends in the war to end all wars, and who had been then imminently to be involved in another war after only twenty-one years.

My father's gallantry had cast a long shadow. He had fought in France and Belgium as early as the beginning of November in 1914. A year later he was Mentioned in Despatches and in the following year awarded the MC. As I had lain there half asleep, aware of the dull sound of the mooring chain dragging across the muddy bottom of the estuary below us, I had wondered, as I often subsequently had, how I could measure up, even if only a little, to the example of courage that my father had set me.

As I held the medal in my hand, a silver medal with the familiar white and purple stripes on the ribbon, I felt that I had done little to deserve it. I had been so lucky. I had only once been hit – so far, I hastened to say to myself. I had never had to try to bring the aircraft back on two engines. I had never had to bale out and swing on a parachute gasping for breath in the bitterly cold oxygen-starved air. I had never had to fly home, weaker and weaker from the loss of blood from an untreated wound. Thank God. I had been lucky. All my war, too, had been here in Britain, never in distant deserts or far-away jungles. I had had leave, been able to go home, and enjoyed the love of girlfriends.

Medals like this were given to men who, like me, had merely survived. Only the occasional rare award of a VC, so long as it had been well witnessed, had been awarded to men who had not survived. Like so many things in life, it was all so damned unfair. I who had given so little and who could hope now to resume a normal life, had received this award. Men like Cyril, tens of thousands of men perhaps like Cyril, and many women too, had given everything, given their lives and died awful deaths, but had received nothing. No one knew how Cyril had died. He had died in his twenties with life barely tasted. Who knows, perhaps Cyril, in terrifying minutes before death took him, had shown courage and self sacrifice worthy of the highest award. If an all-seeing eye wrote all our citations, I thought, most awards would be posthumous.

Though my first reaction to my receipt of the gong had been a sense of relief, a grateful thanks to the Almighty that I now at last had something to show, to give, to my father, this feeling was giving way to a feeling of diffidence, a feeling that it was undue. I said nothing to my crew. When I was with them I was conscious of a guilt that I had received something that should belong to all of them. I should have had one point of a seven-pointed starlike cross, not the whole cross. My father had performed lonely acts of extreme bravery, crawling across no-man's-land at dead of night to eavesdrop upon conversations in the German trenches. I had been rewarded alone with something that rightly belonged, if it belonged to anyone, not to me but to the whole crew. It had been given to me because I was the pilot, the captain of aircraft, the leader of a splendid crew. Was this a good enough reason for it to have been given to me and to me alone?

I kept these thoughts to myself and because of them I did not write to my parents. Father was Welfare Officer to a large transit camp at Clacton, through which passed a continual flow of men with personal problems. As the war was not yet officially over, they were not men demobilised, but men sent back to England (mostly from India and the Far East), often for compassionate reasons. Many of them were broken men. It was a difficult job. Indeed, his predecessor had shot himself because, it was believed, the mental strain of the job had overwhelmed him. I realised that news such as I could give to my father was just the sort of mental relief, the psychological tonic, that he probably needed. Yet, because of this feeling of unmerited reward, for several days I delayed writing.

In due course I received two letters, one from Father and one from Mother. I opened my mother's letter first. It contained a cutting from the local Hertfordshire newspaper.

SQUADRON LEADER RUSSELL WINS D.F.C.

The award of the Distinguished Flying Cross in recognition of gallantry and devotion to duty in the execution of air operations against the enemy has been made to Squadron Leader Anthony Peter Russell, R.A.F.V.R., the only son of Captain and Mrs Russell of Tiled Cottage, Larch Lane, Bovingdon. The official citation, issued by the Air Ministry, states that Squadron Leader Russell had completed, in various capacities, numerous operations against the enemy, in the course of which he had invariably displayed the utmost fortitude, courage and devotion to duty.

Mother's letter read as though she was at a loss for words.

Against the enemy, Dear? You never told me that you were on operations again! I appreciate your consideration for me, and I should have been worried sick if I had known, but well! . . . I don't know what to say. Meda Graves-Pearce told me that she had read it in the paper and brought me a copy. I telephoned your father and of course he is like a dog with two tails!

A letter from Father bore out what Mother had written. He, little knowing the embarrassed feelings of his son, was obviously thrilled. I imagined him proudly telling the news to his fellow officers at Clacton.

Now that the award had been gazetted, I knew that it was no longer information in my sole keeping, and I told the members of my crew. They saw my embarrassment, and each one of them hurried to dispel any misgivings or doubt of their pleasure. They all knew that except in exceptional circumstances the award, though it had been earned by all of them, was always given to the captain of aircraft. They all generously accepted that it was something of which they could all be proud. I thanked them, but I remained unconvinced.

For the next seven days the squadron took part in similar food drops on Holland, sometimes on the Hague, sometimes on Rotterdam, and once on Gouda, when of course some humourist put it about that their load was cheese. The procedures were as for bombing operations; I informed Group of the aircraft availability, Group told me how many aircraft to load and despatch, and the experience was shared out among all available crews who were then briefed with details of where to make the drop. Bombs stayed stacked in their dispersals in the Bomb Dump, and a total of over 200 tons of food (which represented a much larger bulk than our previous consignments) was brought to the aerodrome for 625 Squadron to deliver. My crew and I took part in a second 'Manna' trip on 4 May.

We still did not know how imminent was the end of the war in Europe. But even while we were dropping those sacks of food on Holland on 4 May, German officers were on their way to General Montgomery's Tactical Headquarters of 21st Army Group on Luneburg Heath. Here, they signed a surrender document for all German forces in North-West Germany, Denmark and Holland, to be effective from the following day, and other local surrenders were taking place elsewhere.

On 7 May, when 625 Squadron's drop was on Rotterdam, General Eisenhower, with representatives from Britain, Russia and France, accepted the unconditional surrender of all German forces on all fronts, to be effective from 0001 hours on 9 May.

The war in Europe was over. Indeed, it had really been over two or three days previously. Allied troops had liberated the whole of Western Europe in eleven months of hard fighting. In this period the British Army had lost nearly 40,000 men. Had it not been for the crippling effect by Bomber Command's gallant efforts on the whole German economy, transport system, synthetic-oil production, manufacture of all kinds of armaments, and on the will to fight on by the German population, what would those losses have been? Of the total of more than 60,000 men killed in Bomber Command, more than 10,000 were killed during those last eleven months of the struggle, which they had had to bear almost alone during the long war when no one else could take the war to Germany.

It was May 1945, a few days after the German surrender. The men of the two Lancaster bomber squadrons at RAF Scampton in Lincolnshire and the men and women of the station staff were parading on the tarmac beside one of the hangars for a thanksgiving service for the end of the War in Europe.

It was Victory in Europe, thanksgiving that the horrors of the war were over even though many of the horrors were yet to be uncovered. There was private thanksgiving too from men that their tour of bombing operations, completed or uncompleted, was now over. They had survived and, hopefully, could put behind them the acute anxiety of so many hours in the night sky over Germany and among the alarmingly destructive pyrotechnics through which they had had to fly over their targets.

It was over. A new way of life was beginning, a life without the zest that living so close to danger and oblivion gives, and without the heightened consciousness they had been experiencing while the continuation of their very consciousness had been so uncertain. Many might look back to those times and believe that then the colours had been brighter, enjoyment more intense, even sex more rapturous in those days, each one of which they had known might well be their last.

It was a lovely May day. The tarmac apron on which we stood reflected the heat of the sun and the smell of summer. Though everyone was in battledress the sunshine glinted in the polished brass buttons of men's caps. There was no sound of aircraft engines. Across the green field Lancasters, which would no longer drop death on the good and on the bad in German targets or be a blazing sarcophagus for stricken men within them, rested in their dispersal pans. Their awesome duty was done.

I stood in the position of the CO of 625 Squadron. Beside and behind me were drawn up in ranks the proud and devoted men and women who made up that wonderful force. Standing at ease as the padre was speaking, thoughts were racing through my mind. Many were of gratitude for all the good things that the experience of the war had brought me. Thank God for all the courage that I had witnessed. Surely, especially in wartime, courage is the most attractive of the virtues. Thank God for comradeship, the interdependence of a crew flying together; for the dedication of all those experts whose skills had made the squadron's war contribution possible. Thank God for friendships and the love of so many girlfriends. I had not seen Tricia since we had left Kelstern. That had been interdependence, even if it had been a largely physical relationship, without the mental stimulus of Jill or Sally's home being so near to mine at Hertfordshire. Thank God for both of them and for the love of Katherine.

I was missing Tricia. I felt that same need and emptiness I had felt at St Eval. If I had to stay at Scampton much longer, I admitted to myself, without being blessed with the miracle of meeting with anyone to take her place, I would be tempted to practise the polygamy of Cleethorpes Dance Hall, hoping that an Excuse Me dance or better still a Ladies' Excuse Me would bring to my arms someone I could fall in love with, especially now that I could hope that flying would become a little less demanding.

Jill must now belong to another, yet it was only a month since she had telephoned me. Would I have answered her differently if I had been able to look ahead to the arrival of VE Day?

I had often been very frightened, but in retrospect, and having survived, I had enjoyed my eight months in 625 Squadron. I had flown with an excellent crew and been very lucky. Though the tour had not been as long as the fourteen months in 233 Squadron, that I had stayed with 625 Squadron for as long as I had was due in part to a fairly recent edict that flight commanders should fly only at times when 'maximum effort' was called for by Group, rather than when a specific number of aircraft was called for out of a squadron's 'availability', the number of aircraft serviceable, repaired if necessary, after each raid. This was another piece of my good fortune, for there were perquisites; time in the squadron, time 'on ops', meant normally six days' leave every six weeks, if one survived those six weeks, with petrol coupons to go on leave with. It meant eggs for supper before briefing, or eggs for breakfast when we returned. Most of all, the companionship and atmosphere of goodwill on an operational station, among aircrew and station staff alike, was quite wonderful. The purpose of this edict was to get a better continuation of leadership in a squadron, for a flight commander newly appointed who soon had finished his tour of thirty trips, or perhaps twenty if it was his second tour, or had been posted missing, would have had little time to get to know the pilots and crews in his flight. I understood that I was the first B Flight commander in the history of the squadron to have completed a tour without becoming a casualty.

In my eight months I had done twenty-five trips, though the last one, the 'saturation' bombing of Heligoland was a doddle, or piece of cake as they called it, for after the arrival of the first dozen or so of the lead aircraft (who got a vicious reception) its poor defenders can have had little chance of firing back. Also, I could not of course count my swan songs on 30 April and 4 May when we had swooped in at very low level to drop food on the Hague racecourse to the starving Dutch. They were not operations at all, for the Germans had promised not to shoot at us, and had kept their word.

So now, with John Barker suddenly absent, I found myself in command of the squadron, as I still was at this thanksgiving parade. Of course it would not last long. There were career officers queueing up to have command of a squadron, even for only a short time.

The Group Captain and the padre had turned to walk across the tarmac to Station Headquarters and the VE thanksgiving parade was dispersing. A WAAF, a pretty girl from the station orderly room, came up to tell me that I was wanted on the telephone. I took the call on an extension in Squadron Headquarters in the nearest hangar. It was John Barker. He seldom wasted time in getting to the point.

'Peter, the war here's finished, but there's still one going on in the Far East, I've been given command of an outfit out there, do you want to join me?'

He did not volunteer what the job was, nor did I ask, but in spite of my feelings of relief that it was all over, of only a few minutes before, I did not hesitate for even a moment.

'Yes, please.'

CHAPTER TWENTY-TWO

Shield Force

It was nearly midsummer. Even grimy war-wounded Liverpool was trying to look its best as the *Empress of Australia* left the quayside. She discarded her powerful little tugs, edged out into the Irish Sea and headed for the vastness of the Atlantic. John Barker and I were two of about 3000 men aboard. The boat deck, promenade decks, fore deck and after deck were full of men looking out to get their last view of the British Isles for a long time.

This was the setting forth of Shield Force, leaving Britain, where the war was now ended, and heading for the Far East, where a war was still being fought.

Only a few weeks before, I had left Lincolnshire and 625 Squadron and reported to my old commanding officer at Hednesford in Staffordshire. I found him as ebullient as ever. He was a Group Captain now, and I learned that he had been given command of Shield Force. This was the advance party of Tiger Force, which was to carry out a strategic night bombing offensive against the Japanese mainland from a base yet to be decided. The Americans were winning back Pacific islands and very soon, it was expected, recaptured territory would be within bombing range of Tokyo itself.

As had been seen in the European theatre of the war, the USAF flew by day. They did not have Bomber Command's experience of flying and bombing by night. Their crews lacked, individually, the necessary navigational skills. Consequently they had to fly in large daylight formations, escorted by squadrons of fighters and with their bombers weighed down with defensive armament, armour plating, guns, cannon and ammunition, so that they could deliver only a relatively small bomb load. Bomber Command had developed the skills of individual navigation by night, so that we flew individually and in a loose gaggle, relying on darkness to shield us to some extent, with only modest defensive armament but a very heavy bomb load.

Tiger Force was to be equipped with Lincolns, the successor to the Lancaster. I had travelled with John to Waddington to see the Lincoln from Kelstern. Because rails were being fitted at Kelstern for turning these bigger aircraft sideways into the hangars, I had believed that Lincolns were coming to us for our operations against Germany.

The anticipated destination, where Tiger Force was to be prepared, was Okinawa, an island about 300 miles south of Japan's southernmost tip, on latitude about 25°N. When the *Empress of Australia* left Liverpool the Americans had not taken Okinawa. They were not to do so until 2 July. Officially John was the only one at Hednesford, or later at West Kirby in Cheshire, who knew it was expected to be Okinawa, but I had seen a crate of pink paperback booklets, obviously for eventual distribution, which described with admonitory zeal the dangers of sexual intercourse with Okinawa's native population. That, I was given to understand from the pink booklets, was a sub-race, who had in their loins the gift of two more venereal diseases than any other potential bedfellows in the world could offer.

At least we knew that we would embark at Liverpool, in our 'personnel' ship, the *Empress of Australia*, with eight Liberty Ships for equipment: bulldozers, cranes and the like, which would be accompanied by their drivers and operators and sufficient maintenance men. Two high-speed launches were included in a tally of accoutrements to cover most eventualities.Shield Force was composed mainly of aerodrome builders, led by a Wing Commander – perhaps really a civilian in uniform – but also senior doctors to found and equip hospitals, embarkation officers to prepare for the arrival of the main force, equipment officers, transport officers, and other experts in various fields.

In 233 Squadron on various sorties, I had flown over many empty miles of the south-west and north-west approaches. In my Hudson I had often been not much higher above the sea than we were now on the boat deck of the ship. Now it was interesting to be not only down at sea level, but to be travelling slowly enough to watch seabirds and anything that floated near to us. I saw the Atlantic in many moods, though never very calm. During my days of sailing with my father I had not been particularly bothered by sea sickness, though as we headed west and the ship rolled in and out of the grey deep hollows of the sea or pitched into the foam-capped waves, which ran hurrying eastwards to meet us head on, there were plenty of men aboard who were not so fortunate.

As a Squadron Leader I was in a cabin for four. Two of them were padres, so conversation in our cabin was reasonably intelligent, with a complete absence of even mildly blasphemous adjectives and without any discussion of sexual matters, which so often are preponderant when men only, or women only, are cooped up together for any length of time. We walked the decks for exercise. We had boat drills. We read. We visited other cabins. Time slipped by.

I liked to stand on the boat deck watching the seabirds. In the hedgerows, heathlands and shorelines of the British Isles my bird recognition was quite good, but I had never had the opportunity to get to know the pelagic birds of the ocean. Would I perhaps on this journey see an albatross, with its seven-foot or, in the case of one kind, eleven-foot wingspan? I wished very much that I had brought with me a bird identification book. Some birds I recognised, but many I did not. Sometimes a petrel followed the ship. I knew if it was a sooty petrel, because I remembered that it had a white rump like a house martin, conspicuous against its black wings and body. It flew close to the water just behind us, scooping up small fish brought to the surface by the turbulence of the propellers, seeming to try to quicken its flight by paddling steps as though its feet really touched the white water of our wake. We saw guillemots, and occasionally skuas though I knew not which kind. The skuas were burly brown birds, which swooped piratically on other birds that had fished, to frighten them and make them disgorge their catch. Too far out in the Atlantic to see the pink-footed herring gulls we had seen all around in the Irish Sea, or black-backed or black-headed gulls, I did watch kittiwakes, the most pelagic of gulls, white as fulmars and with jet-black wing tips, which dived like gannets into the sea to fish. I had been brought up to believe that the Navy acknowledges only three birds: the seagull, the shitehawk and the arse-up duck. Even without a bird book I did better than that, but a smile always came to me as I maintained my vigil on the boat deck, remembering my father's tuition on the far-off waters of the River Orwell.

The days of relative inactivity that followed as we ploughed our way across the Atlantic gave me the opportunity of talking with John in his cabin about many things in a more dispassionate way than would have been possible earlier, especially about the happenings of the recent months we had spent together in 625 Squadron. We spoke of our admiration for many of the men with whom we had served. Men who had come through. Men who had been lost. We spoke of men who had shown outstanding courage and flying skill, or skills in any of the other professions whose excellence helped a crew to come through their tour. My own former crew of course were uppermost in my mind.

Soon we saw land on the horizon. Separate lumps represented islands of the Caribbean and we knew we were approaching the isthmus of Panama, which barred our way to the Pacific. Inside the semicircle of islands of the West Indies, which were now sheltering us from the Atlantic swell, the sea was calm. In happy anticipation of our first port of call we drew near to the Panama Canal and the small port of Colon.

No doubt in common with nearly 3000 other men on board the *Empress of Australia*, looking down from the several decks of the ship to the busy quayside below us, I felt a strong desire for some female companionship. I wanted a change from the overcrowded all-male company among whom I had lived and pitched and rolled in the grey troughs of the Atlantic swell, our horizon some-times bounded by the wavetops surrounding us, sometimes almost limitless when the ship was lifted up. Now my surroundings beyond the ship were changed from almost featureless immensity to an intricate diversity of detail in the relatively tiny scene below me. Accustomed to the huge scale of empty ocean and sky, my view was now concentrated into a small kaleidoscopic movement of colours and bustling activity. It was a feast of diversity for the senses.

Quayside buildings shut out the bigger picture. Everything was contained within a few hundred yards alongside the ship's tall side. Men – and women – mostly darker-skinned than in my experience, were trundling sack barrows or filling nets with all kinds of provisions and material. There seemed to be a lot of bananas, heaps of them from palest green to brightest yellow, something few of us had seen for several years of wartime shortages. Unlike Liverpool with its overall backcloth of grey, here was green, clumps of palm trees and growing plants. Here, any bit of space not continually in use had immediately been colonised by fresh-looking green grass, not sooty or dirty like the unused corners of an English port.

Men in pale fawn American uniforms kept tallies, pointed and shouted instructions. But the pace was relatively slow. The objects of their barking were busy but unhurried. Where a group of workers lounged to rest among sacks and crates of the provisions, which were presumably to be loaded aboard the *Empress of Australia*, sometimes a woman lifted a brown arm to wave, showing her white teeth to call to the lines of sex-hungry men on the decks, dressed in the awful babies' diarrhoea-coloured trousers and bush jackets with which we had all been issued. For some reason the men's broad-brimmed cowboy hats seemed to be exciting the women. I was soon to know why.

After the cool winds of the Atlantic and even the onshore breezes of north-west England it was hot, here near the equator. Perhaps that was another reason, as well as the excitement and promise of a visit ashore in this exotic new tropical country, why I craved feminine company. But as the afternoon wore on, leaning lazily over the ship's rail, I was ruminating upon my life as a pilot thus far and in particular my recent experiences in Bomber Command.

I freely admitted that I had probably joined the Air Force because I had long had a fear of somebody coming at me with a bayonet. OTC days at school and 1914–18 War films had made me dread not the pain of a bullet but the horror of a bayonet in my stomach – or indeed being expected to plunge one into another man's stomach. 'In! Up! Out!' had shouted the sergeant major to groups of Army recruits butchering straw-filled sacks hanging before them. It had been all cold steel combat for our forefathers at war, I had thought, but not for me, please, if I can prevent it.

Perhaps, though, the way I had seen many of my companions go was not much better. The searing pain of the bone-shattering bullet or hot steel fragment of anti-aircraft shell or fighter plane's cannon – sometimes it was that way. But mostly it was Fire. Even as men went through aircrew training, when they 'bought it' by 'going in' through miscalculation of one or other of the many factors that must all be correct to achieve a safe landing or take-off, or perhaps because of engine failure, they burned. That dull thud from the end of the field or runway followed by that pall of pewter-coloured smoke and flickering flames – they were burning. And in quite non-belligerent flights that had to be undertaken in bad visibility – when you kept below cloud because the aids for coming down safely through cloud did not exist, or because you had failed to set your altimeter to the reading of your take-off height or to a known datum – a mistake meant Fire. Landfall, after hours of skimming the North Sea or the Atlantic, if it took you by surprise in rain or snow or low cloud, could mean Fire. In the bomber stream, as you strained your eyes through the darkness to see the stealthily approaching night fighter before he saw you, or indeed any other aircraft on a converging course, sometimes a huge expanding ball of orange fire would appear on your left, or on your right, or straight ahead. This was nerve-jarring enough, and it was the things, long, thin, dark, parachuteless things, silhouetted against the orange ball as they fell, that brought home the horror of it all. It's a long way to fall from nearly 4 miles up. Nerve jarring certainly, yet it was the steadiness of nerve, alertness of look-out and split-second reaction, which might make the difference between a crew surviving its tour of operations or not surviving it.

I was watching that woman down there, her lissom body provocatively lolling over a heap of sacks – yes, she somehow knew even at this distance that I was looking at her. She waved. I saw her white teeth as she opened her mouth to call. She made a gesture of invitation that was unmistakable. I was incorrigible – I wanted to be close to her! But my thoughts about life in Bomber Command meandered on.

Losses were high. Crews had had, on average, only a two in five chance of survival. But, they had in the home-based air force one enormous advantage. Unless they were in other ways inclined, they had sex. As a therapy for taut-stretched nerves there is nothing better. I don't mean Love. Love can mean the agony of separation, or pale-faced anxiety lest your passion is not shared by the adored one. There is no therapy in that. I mean the wonderful peace that follows the ecstasy that a girl can give, whatever her colour, whatever her language, background or interests, to the taut-up heterosexual male. There had to be no promises, no plighting of troth, in that kind of relationship. Both partners had to be equally, though selectively, promiscuous, both had just to be satisfying a biological need. Of course, most men and women treasured some long-term love, but for anyone conscious of a poor life expectancy, that needed, ideally, to be kept on a low gas. The monogamous passion of soulmates, which prescribes peccadilloes, could lead to inattention, inefficiency and death.

I had been lucky that during my time in 625 Squadron, following my uncharacteristically asexual year in County Down, I had not had to live and thrive much of the time on a diet of very short-term affairs. I was luckier than most. There were always girls whom I loved, who loved me. Through one or other of them I could channel my emotion, even be allowed to satisfy my longing. Most men, whenever they were stood down, did not curl up with a book, or exercise themselves into exhaustion on the squash court. They headed for Cleethorpes, Grimsby, Lincoln, or wherever they knew their need could mutually be satisfied and peace brought to their nervous system to make it ready for its next test. They went in twos, threes or fours, usually, for some of them had old cars. Though some liked 'a few beers', others, like me, hated the feeling of alcoholic intoxication and preferred to arrive early at the local dance hall or to a dance advertised by some local unit, to which one was always made welcome.

In days when young people were continually being moved about the country, even if not sent abroad, boys and girls were not paired off. They did not usually bring a partner to a dance; they went there to find one. The intention, assuming that an attractive partner was to be found, had to be mutual, and sometimes there was not much time for reconnaissance. The boy had to know that she wanted him as much as he wanted her, and the 'have you seen any good films lately?' sort of conversation could wait until each was certain that he cared whether or not she had, or if she cared tuppence if he had. In this search, there was an institution that was an excellent time saver: the 'Ladies' Excuse Me' dance. On a good night the change of partners was rapid. Her inclination could to some extent be taken for granted if she had opted to interrupt and dance with him, and she did not have to be in his arms for long before he knew if she made him fizz and if he had the same effect on her.

So if pulling a girl was not usually difficult, the next thing was 'to find a roof'. Sex in the car, especially in the days when reclining seats were uncommon, was never satisfactory. The quiet of your parking place could be interrupted by the guffaw of two or three of your so-called friends when some humourist shone a torch into the car. The time taken for your cuddly knickerless girl to regain her composure so that the therapy could continue, was precious time wasted. But usually it was not very long before one of the party danced up alongside with the news 'I've found a roof', or 'Simon's got a roof. Meet after the next dance'. It was surprising how often a couple of bed-sits or the house of a friend of one of the girls was available for them to go there, perhaps make coffee (generally of the 'camp' variety) and then pair off to beds or hearthside rugs for mutual sessions of happiness. Such a person as Tricia had made these means unnecessary. I was so enormously grateful. She gave of herself unstintingly and yet she was never demanding. I was, perhaps, in love with her although I tried to persuade myself that I was not. Looking down from the ship's high deck I could not exaggerate what she did for me by her sexual therapy. She really had the magic – in my friend Hugh's words – to blot out horror from the memory and by enchantment make all new the nerves that channel our reactions. It was a rare and precious gift.

But all that I had left behind in England. What was to come, I wondered, when we reached the further side of the Pacific? How much more trial of the nervous system would there be? How much opportunity – if any – and what need for therapy would there be? These things were quite unknown. I did not even know for certain where we were going. The prospect of launching raids at night into mainland Japan from some recovered Pacific outcrop would be very different to the terrain and associations of high Lincolnshire. This uncertainty and apprehension, and the heat, and the excitement of adventure and the colourful scene below me, made me want to get away from my cabin full of padres, from all these men in bush jackets, and be with a girl.

It was the OC Troops who broke the news.

'The men cannot go ashore.' John was just as surprised as anybody and made some cursory investigation.

'Apparently, Peter, it is because a troopship of Aussie bastards went through Panama a few days ago. They went ashore, and broke the place up. We are not Aussies, but through someone's unfortunate sartorial decision all the men are wearing antipodean-looking hats. Come on, we had better go ashore and see if we can find anyone to cancel this silly edict.'

We went ashore, but the authorities, such as could be run to earth to argue with, were adamant. Someone senior had left an instruction that in the event of any more drunken Australians coming to Colon, they were not to be allowed ashore to take the place apart again. However, John arranged for a lot of beer to be brought to the quayside, and as the captain of the ship would not allow it aboard, a compromise was arranged for the troops to come off to stretch their legs, and all had a beer.

CHAPTER TWENTY-THREE

The Pacific

Next morning we learned that we must wait our turn to go into the Panama Canal. We left the dockside and moved out into the bay and lay at anchor. It was an unforgettable spectacle of pelicans and thunderstorms. All that day and the next, brown pelicans flew around the ship, their heads pulled back into their shoulders, their pouched bills as long as their bodies so that their heads came about halfway along their length. Strong and broad–winged, they flew about us then banked and with half-closed wings guiding their dive, plummeted into the sea among the shoals of fish. There were hundreds of them. It was when they came to the surface that they looked such clowns, holding their heavy, water- and fish-filled pouched bills inclined down to dip in the water, draining the catch, chins held in. Only their eyes moved, roving eyes that made them look humorous and surreptitious, but they were on the look out for frigate birds and boobies, which sometimes chose these vulnerable moments to swoop down and rob them of their catch. Then, the water drained away, they threw back their heads, bills up, and swallowed the fish.

As the *Empress of Australia* waited her turn, great storm clouds, which seemed to cover every hilltop in this part of Central America, flashed with forked lightning. Torrential rain showers blocked out one part of our surroundings or another and when they enveloped us the noise of heavy rain drumming on decks and lifeboats or hissing on the surface of the sea was added to the Jovian rumblings of the thunder. Water was rationed aboard, so everyone was ordered up on deck to stand naked in the rain.

Finally we weighed anchors and came alongside a rural quay, a tree-lined broad pathway beside mown grass, where great bollards accepted the ship's giant-sized warps until a tug took responsibility for our movement and we approached the first gates of the canal. Great gates they were, but the ship towered above them and there seemed to be little room to spare between them and her sides.

The rainstorm had ceased and the ship moved slowly through in brilliant sunshine. The first part of the canal was narrow, and the forest came down to meet it on each side. The noise of the forest was unexpectedly loud.

As we were towed along the straight bright narrow way through the forest, the low hum of tropical insects was as loud as many bumble bees in a lamp-shade magnified a hundred times, and the high screech of tropical fauna too, though this perhaps was mostly tree frogs, who though only thumbnail size and in their leaf-green livery rarely seen, were making in their millions a sound that was indescribable. Birds, tree frogs, cicadas and other insects made a huge orchestra of sound, with solo parts by birds with particularly penetrating voices. And the colour was superb. From one green bank to the other of the lush green trees, which climbed away from the edges of the canal so near to our sides, butterflies flapped and glided across the decks.

I had thought of the Panama Canal as a cutting through rock, overhung by trees, towered over by mountains. I had not realised how much of it is lakes. Now the ship passed into them, followed her course through them, disturbing the beautiful calm of their surface as she ploughed her white-waked way.

Before the end of the day we were through, travelling away from the sunset instead of towards it in a further correction of my weak geography. We were in the Pacific and altering course more northerly. In my bunk among padres I slept very soundly, it had been a wonderful day.

Next day, the Mexican coast was too far away to starboard to be seen. We became once more a tiny speck on an immensity of ocean. Dolphins often escorted us, and sometimes a whale, unperturbed, lifted not far away a huge grey island of a back and shivered a spray of water drops. Day followed day and flying fish came. They emerged from the sea's surface with the astounding speed at which slantingly they had raced towards it, so that their speed carried them through the air on their winglike fins. Some 150 yards or more, or so it seemed, they flew. Faster than the ship they flew, sometimes higher than the ship, sometimes over it. Sometimes they landed on the deck and lay there troubled, glinting in the sunlight and much larger than I had expected, their fate depending on the kindness of whomsoever they crash-landed near.

It was hard to believe that the Pacific, in spite of its name, is usually as calm as it was in those days as we forged on in sunshine or in starlight towards Hawaii. Among the islands of its further, Asian side to which we were travelling, Japanese and Americans still fought, and shot and shelled and bombed and mutilated one another. Innocent indigenous people died in the holocaust of destruction that overcame each of their little homelands in turn in the slow American advance and stubborn Japanese defence. Here it was so peaceful, so beautiful. A playground for dolphins, a stage for the ballet of flying fish. I felt excitement that we were heading for Hawaii and then on towards other islands of the Pacific. They held a romantic place in my imagination.

I did not think about the tragedy that was befalling islands of such paradise. I thought of their beauty, which I was to be allowed to see, and not of the rape of them that war was bringing; neither did I think of their sordid ravage in the Japanese advance, nor the utter destruction of their loveliness in the shellfire and bomb blasts of their 'reclamation' by the Americans. And how very certain it was that any islands to which we went must expect to be laid waste, to become a crater-pocked no-man's-land. For if the Japanese were now fighting a rearguard action devastating to the islands that they were having to retreat from, the fury of their reaction would be even greater when it was known, as soon it would, that they must prevent a base being built for enemy bombers who would rain down fire and high explosive out of the night sky on Japanese cities as had destroyed German ones. There would be no shortage of heroes who would delight to hurl themselves in suicidal sacrifice against a foe who dared to attack their homeland. There would be no shortage of kamikaze volunteers whose unstoppable propulsion head-on into a night bomber stream would blow many of those bombers to smithereens and send them to a Japanese Valhalla of eternal heavenly reward.

But as I stood on the boat deck and watched the ship lifting gently out of each sea-hollow on to the next smooth blue mound of ocean, it was an uncomplicated unspoilt world of blue sea, blue sky, warm golden sunshine, dolphins and flying fish. All was peace and tranquillity. The war was another world away.

We entered Pearl Harbor. Sheltering green hills surrounded us on three sides as we passed through the graveyard of ships that was the memorial to American unreadiness at the time of the Japanese attack. Gaunt grey bows or sterns still stood upended out of the blue water. Rusting superstructures pointed crazily, as though accusingly, at one another. We berthed. We went ashore. Provision was made for the men of Shield Force to go ashore to clubs and places of recreation, and unlike Colon, there was an atmosphere of universal welcome.

Aboard the *Empress of Australia* once more, the dolphins came to play with us again, the shoals of flying fish performed their ballet beside us, and the hot sun demanded generous use of sun cream bought in Honolulu. I was very brown and feeling very well. I had learned nothing in Pearl Harbor about our probable future, except an American idea, probably optimistic, that Operation *Olympic*, the invasion of Japan, was imminent. There were also people who thought that with the facilities that Shield Force had for aerodrome building we would soon be called to put down an airstrip on a bloodily won bridgehead on the mainland. John did not take this idea very seriously, for we were there to prepare for the strategic heavy night bombardment of targets on the Japanese mainland and not for short-term tactical use.

On 6 or 7 August we were south-west of Eniwetok, about 2000 miles from our expected destination of Okinawa, which lies to the south of Japan (and we were about the same distance from Tokyo) when we heard on the radio news of a bomb. It was a single bomb, which had been dropped on the Japanese city of Hiroshima and virtually wiped it out. About four days later another was dropped on the city of Nagasaki with comparable effects. The rumour weavers were frantic. Surely now the Japanese would sue for peace. Reactions aboard were more muted than later would be expected, for no one knew about the horrors of 'Fall Out', or of the fate that even as much as four years hence would befall large numbers of people living near to the two cities even if they had somehow survived the explosion. But we were astonished at the magnitude of the bomb and wondered if our 17,000 or so mile journey would now be found to have been unnecessary. If the Japanese sued for peace because of this sudden and unexpected development where would Shield Force go? Home again? We doubted if we would now be required to fulfil the purpose for which we had come, but we had heard before of the enemy being 'expected to sue for peace', and it was unlikely that outlying contingents of Japanese would even know that they should stop fighting.

Our course was now more southerly because our destination was now Manus, the largest island in the Admiralty Islands, to the north of Papua New Guinea.

The ship arrived at Manus very early in the morning. We were having breakfast when an envelope was brought to John, which contained a signal to him from the Joint Chiefs of Staff in London.

'Come on Peter, let's go and look at this.' The two of us went along to his cabin. And so with a rackety fan to eavesdrop, we read that the War had been ended by the Japanese surrender. The signal told him additionally to go at once in person and to get in touch with the Admiral Commanding the Battle Cruiser Squadron at Leyte in the Philippines.

It was not known of course what the future held for any of us, but there must now be a waiting period while the *Empress of Australia* was refuelled and provisioned for proceeding in any direction that might be ordered. It would be a day or two before the Liberty Ships that contained all our heavy equipment arrived to join us, but John left the ship immediately.

Going ashore, he called on an American general and told him of his urgent need to get to Leyte.

He joined the 1st Battle Cruiser Squadron commanded by Rear Admiral Daniels, which included *Anson* and several light cruisers, with a flotilla of destroyers. To the north of the Philippines they joined up with the 1st Carrier Squadron commanded by Rear Admiral Harcourt, comprising *Indomitable*, *Venerable*, and two other carriers, together with more destroyers. This fleet then proceeded north towards Hong Kong.

Admiral Daniels called John to his cabin and John showed him the signal that he had received. The Admiral asked him what he read into it, and said that he too had received signals from London. Members of his staff were called in for a discussion and together it was decided that obviously the British Chiefs of Staff were quite determined that they had to prevent the Americans getting to Hong Kong first, because there was a belief that if that happened they would lose the Colony for good.

The intelligence that they had was that the Japanese, who were still in charge in Hong Kong, were quite prepared to defend the place.

The Colony comprised several islands. Victoria, the administrative centre of Hong Kong, was the second largest and was about 6 miles by 6. It is separated from the mainland, the New Territories, which have a much bigger area than the islands (perhaps 20 miles by 16), by a channel of sea of an average width of about one mile, though the complicated shape of Victoria island and of the shoreline of the New Territories, with their many headlands and inlets, make these measurements very approximate. Although at that time there were several villages in the New Territories between their boundary with mainland China and their southern deeply indented coast opposite the island of Victoria, between their complex western and eastern coasts, there was only one town, Kowloon.

John was on the bridge of *Anson* as the fleet approached Hong Kong. Upon arrival the Carrier Squadron stood outside while *Anson* and *Swiftsure* and attendant destroyers came into the channel. *Swiftsure* lay off the jetty on the island side while *Anson* lay in the straits between the island and the mainland.

The first thing that happened was that a flotilla of motor boats came out at speed from the Kowloon side. It was believed that they were kamikaze boats. If indeed they were, they had only a forward gear and the bow was packed with high explosive. They were no-going-back boats.

Anson was not prepared to take any chances. She promptly opened up with what was called light armament, which is everything from 6 inches and below. The water boiled. When the surface cleared there was no sign that there had ever been any boats there at all. There was no further problem of that kind.

John then went ashore on the Kowloon side with a party of sailors, the matelots under the command of a Lieutenant-Commander. They went ashore to the aerodrome of Kai Tak and formed up the Japanese there into a hollow square. The Japanese commander handed over his sword to John. They then hauled down the Japanese flag and hoisted in its place a Royal Navy white ensign.

Meanwhile on the island of Hong Kong, Victoria, Admiral Harcourt took the surrender there. John took up residence in the convent on the steep hillside overlooking Kai Tak airfield. He set about completing his plans, begun in *Anson*, with a large-scale map of Kowloon provided by Admiral Daniels, of how to deploy his troops in order to secure and maintain order in Kowloon and the New Territories immediately the *Empress of Australia* should arrive.

CHAPTER TWENTY-FOUR

Hong Kong

While these events were taking place, I and the complement aboard the *Empress of Australia* waited in Manus for the arrival of the eight Liberty Ships before we too were ordered to proceed to Hong Kong. There were on board many Sten guns and ammunition. One of John's orders before he left was that the few of us who had the necessary knowledge should see that the troops, almost none of whom had been combat troops, became trained in how to handle and use the Sten gun. This we did, and I was impressed by the enthusiasm with which these men of the aerodrome construction units, and their officers who were mainly civilians in uniform, fell to their task, particularly as no one knew how they would be employed, or what they would find waiting for them upon their arrival. If it was one surprise after another opening up for John, we who were privy to nothing of the unfolding of events simply had to accept and act upon whatever should arise.

Our passage to Hong Kong coincided with a typhoon.

I had flown over thousands of miles of sea at low level when in 233 Squadron, both in the approaches to the Norwegian coast and in the Bay of Biscay and in the NW and SW approaches to the British Isles. I had learned to estimate wind strength by observing the 'wind lanes', the lines of white foam combed back by the surface wind from the breaking waves that hurry before it. The wind lanes are faint and few in a light breeze, and increasingly conspicuous in stronger winds. From Leuchars on the east coast of Scotland I had flown (and somehow landed, I thanked God) in a windspeed estimated at about 90 mph, when the sea I flew above looked like dirty cream, white wind lanes masking most of the grey-green colour of the spray-blown tortured sea.

Now, as we tried to make our way through the South China Sea towards Hong Kong, what little we could see of the sea's surface was like that. It seemed as if the great *Empress of Australia* was being tossed about like a fisherman's unsecured marker dan in a storm. She buried her nose in each great rolling wave and threw it over her decks. She pitched so that her propellers must sometimes have been out of the water. In the old days her helmsman would have been fighting with the wheel to try to keep her into the wind and seas and never to broach side-on to roll over and under. Of course, no one could go on to her decks; the foredeck was green water, the boat deck would have meant certain loss overboard and even her promenade decks were funnels of gale-blown water and spray; her portholes were no clearer than if they had been of frosted glass. Apart from those on the bridge, no one knew the direction in which the ship pointed or if she made any forward progress or just kept station against the wind. We were greatly delayed, having a far greater windage, less power, and frankly the *Empress of Australia* was not built to maintain any forward speed in these conditions as the sleek grey naval warships could do.

At last the storm eased and we made progress. Finally we threaded our way between the islands of Hong Kong and came into a long deepwater berth by a jetty to the west of the ferry terminal on Kowloon side. The diminutive figure of John was waiting on the quay below us on our starboard side, his every gesture expressing a mixture of impatience and delight. He came aboard and we held a short briefing. A small beginning had been made of getting a few British people out of Shamshipo, one of the Japanese internment camps. Most important among them to Shield Force was Geoffrey Wilson. Until the Japanese invasion of 1941 he had been the senior policeman of Kowloon and the New Territories.

Soon after we had docked, I was standing at the heads. The man in the urinal beside me was an Englishman whom I had not seen before. His face was lean, his clothes hung loosely about him, and as we both turned away and moved towards the door the man gave me a friendly smile.

'God, I'm glad to see you chaps. I've been shut up in Shamshipo since the Japs overran the Colony about four years ago. My name's Geoffrey. Geoffrey Wilson.'

'And I'm Peter. Peter Russell. Good to meet you. Very glad to see you're a free man again. Welcome aboard!'

'I thought that's who you were. Your most excellent CO, Group Captain Barker, told me that I should look out for you.'

'So you've met John? "Excellent" is right – I've got a very high opinion of him. I gather that we are to report to him at the Peninsula Hotel. Doubtless you know your way there. Let's walk together.'

That short walk, with Geoffrey pointing out the many landmarks on the way, was the beginning of a friendship between us. We were to spend a lot of time together. Here was a man who knew intimately the town of Kowloon, through whose dockside area we were now walking. It was the part of the town, close to the waterside, which runs from the jetty where the *Empress of Australia* lay berthed, past the ferry terminal to the Peninsula Hotel. His wide parish had included all of the New Territories, a largely rural district with many villages, bigger even than the island across the water which was the seat of government of the Colony. There was almost no traffic, and we saw no other western people. Chinese peasants in faded blue trousers and shallow conical coolie hats hurried past us. Some of them, a pole on their shoulder, carried at its ends baskets that contained every kind of produce – but always heavy, so that they made their way along the road at a little short-paced run, which presumably eased the burden of such heavy weights.

The ground beside the road on each side of us was fairly open, and dotted with simple huts and other often delapidated buildings. As we passed the Ferry Terminal we saw people who were not coolies, but perhaps businessmen in grey gown-like garments, and women in thin trousers and shirts, like very light-weight pyjamas, perhaps shop assistants or office workers. There was a stream of such people now hurrying among the crowds of coolies, mostly disembarking from one of the ferries that lay alongside the pier of the terminal, or eager to reach the other ferry, which was rapidly filling up to make the crossing to Hong Kong island.

Soon we were approaching a large building facing the water, which I assumed to be the Peninsula Hotel. On each side of the main entrance a wing jutted forwards to enclose gardens and a central driveway. The middle one of the three stories of rooms had balconies in front of some of the windows.

We went into the hotel and were immediately greeted by another very thin bearded Englishman. Geoffrey greeted him warmly.

'Peter, this is Jack Diamond. Jack, Peter Russell. Before the war Jack was manager of this great hotel. Judging by the look of him he is now unarguably manager of it again. He built it up to be recognised as one of the finest hotels in the Far East.'

'This is a happy day. Something tells me I shall be seeing a lot of both of you. Group Captain Barker has requisitioned it as the headquarters of you chaps who will now be running this side of the Colony. He's in the Dining Room. Through those doors over there.'

There were many tables spread throughout the room, each surrounded by bent-wood chairs, but not yet many people. John stood at one of them, holding the back of one of the chairs, and grinned as Geoffrey and I walked among the tables to join him.

'So you two have met? Good. You've met Jack Diamond too, I expect Peter.'

More of Shield Force officers were now arriving. With little more than a nod and gesture John directed them to the chairs. He ascended a dais and the spatter of conversations fell quiet.

You left Britain with a job to do. To prepare for a strategic night bombing offensive of the Japanese mainland by Tiger Force. That job is now redundant. We have therefore been redeployed here. We have a new job. It is to re-establish the British presence and to be responsible for law and order here in Kowloon and probably in due course in the New Territories, an area to the north of us. In area terms by far the largest part of the colony of Hong Kong.

While waiting for you in the *Empress of Australia* to make your way here through the very rough weather, I have drawn up a plan for the division of Kowloon into areas. Each area will be garrisoned by a squadron of you chaps. I'm sorry to disappoint those of you who were looking forward to the task of laying down airstrips. In Kai Tak we've already got one.

Admiral Harcourt has been made acting Governor of the Colony. His headquarters is in Government House in Victoria. He has arranged that one of his Carrier Squadron, *Indomitable*, will lie alongside the Kowloon shore. There are enough men aboard her to give us assistance if this should prove to be necessary. But I hope it will not. We are not expecting any trouble from the Japanese, though across the water there two days ago in the Typhoon Junk Harbour there were those who in spite of their leaders' surrender made a last stand of defiance. It was stormed and flushed out by the Navy in good old-fashioned pistols and cutlasses style.

When the British and Chinese Internees were released from Shamshipo – they are still being released – many were physically in very poor condition. You may have heard stories of the shocking conditions of that place. Those who wish or need to are being given the opportunity to return to Britain in the *Empress of Australia*, which you are now vacating. Some of them, however, have, remarkably and most commendably, survived their ordeal of the last four years in a state of health which we must admire.

We, in Shield Force, are very fortunate that one of these is Chief Superintendent Wilson. Before the occupation he was chief-of-police in all of this part of the Colony for which we are responsible. He is already re-forming his civilian police force, and meantime is himself playing a vital role in helping us to begin our task of bringing British law and order to the town of Kowloon. He speaks Cantonese, he knows where everything is and who everyone is. I ask him now to stand up so that you can all see him and be able to recognise him in future. [Geoffrey drew himself to his feet and nodded to the acknowledgement of those around him.]

'Thank you. I should now like Wing Commander Jenkins and the Squadron Leader commanders of the units of our aerodrome construction people to come over here so that with Chief Superintendent Wilson I can show you on the map the areas of Kowloon for which each squadron will be responsible. He has arranged that you and your men will be guided to your proposed headquarters in those areas. You will march there from the ship in a manner that will show the local population and any Japs who may be around what a fine body of men are now here. Men who will, justly and fairly, bring peace to their lives.

My headquarters will be here at the Peninsula. You are to report to me here at once any problem you may be faced with for which you require help or advice. I shall also instruct my officers to call upon you regularly to discuss with you any way in which we at headquarters can be of assistance.'

It was a tribute to John's planning and to Geoffrey Wilson's energetic efficiency, so quickly regained in spite of four years in prison camp, and to the discipline of the squadrons of aerodrome builders, that each section came ashore and marched through the trafficless streets of the sprawling town of Kowloon without mishap.

Although John requisitioned the Peninsula Hotel as his headquarters, it also continued to be a hotel for civilians as it had been before. Doctors turned the convent on the hillside above Kai Tak airfield, where John had billeted himself until the arrival of the *Empress of Australia*, into a hospital, where they were given competent and enthusiastic assistance by the nuns.

The ground floor of the forward-projecting wing on the left at the front of the hotel was an arcade, previously of shops, hairdressing saloons and cafes. One of the rooms in this arcade was John's office. Mine was next to it. The windows of both rooms commanded a view of the main entrance.

Those first few days were hectic. Everyone was on their toes and prepared for trouble of nobody knew what kind. I made rounds of the command posts of the units who were keeping order in various parts of the town. I received a number of complainants who had come to the office to argue that requisitioning, particularly of furniture, had been over-enthusiastic. I was broadly sympathetic but it was only once that I insisted on its return, for the units generally speaking were well-behaved and considerate in their dealings with the local people.

There was great uncertainty about the likelihood of trouble from the Japanese. In spite of their leaders' surrender, there had been that defiant action of a few of them in the Typhoon Junk Harbour. Geoffrey explained to John and me that his chief concerns lay elsewhere.

'I am not expecting trouble from the Japanese so much as I am from Chinese brigands. They are now lying low in Kowloon and beyond in the New Territories. They will try to take advantage of any unreadiness during the transitional period from Japanese to British rule of the Colony, particularly on our Kowloon side. I know that there are some Chinese who favour a terrorist approach to achieve ambitions of power in local communities who have got hold of arms, and it is not unheard of for more peace-loving citizens to be terrorised by such characters with hand grenades.'

Because the young British workmen-in-uniform had never been trained to fight or to kill, their natural horror of using their Sten guns made very unlikely an unintentional escalation of violence. The local people, after years of dreading the armed Japanese, treated the peacekeepers of this new situation with respect, and stood in little danger of being shot by a trigger-happy sentry.

Once in those early days two young Chinese girls came into my office. Their slim bodies were flauntingly displayed in their skin-tight cheongsam dresses slit on one side of the thigh up to the hip, and their red lips beneath their dark glasses were calculated to allure. Whatever the professed purpose of their visit, it was more likely to be in order to try out the strength of their feminine charm on the new administration of law and order and to seek any advantage or privilege that it might bring them. Perhaps it was because they were attractive that my eye followed them from the window as they walked out into the sunshine, so that I saw a Chinese man run towards them and begin to rough up one of the girls. A sentry, one of the airfield construction chaps, shouted his command for the man to stop, but it was ignored. Perhaps because the man's knowledge of English was minimal, but probably because in his rage for revenge or whatever emotion filled him he did not care, he took no notice. The sentry, who stood quite near my window, shouted again. The girl's attacker still ignored him and was beating the girl to the ground. So he fired a shot, the man fell, and the two girls made good their escape.

The sentry was clearly horrified at what he had done, and appealed to me in an agony of contrition. Others were attending to the wounded man and I called the sentry to my window and told him that he had done right.

'We are here to maintain order and this attack on a girl, for whatever reason, was inexcusable. You gave warning twice, and whatever was the reason for non-compliance it does not alter the fact that you acted correctly to protect the girl in the only way open to you.'

This was not a Hong Kong of full employment and relative plenty, but a place in which there was great poverty and undernourishment. The British requisitioning of buildings, necessary to house those whose policing would in time create an environment in which the Colony would be able to re-attain stability and prosperity, exacerbated an already bad housing situation. Large numbers of people lived on the pavements, including many poor creatures whose matchstick limbs and beriberi abdomens showed them to be near to death and probably too far gone to save. But the attitude of the people towards the new garrison troops was tolerant, even friendly. People quickly realised that they had no intention of acting in the grimly sadistic manner that had become the reputation of the Japanese. When the Japanese had occupied the Colony in 1941, they had swept down through the New Territories against very little opposition. Their commanders had designated whole areas, Happy Valley on Hong Kong Island for one, into which they turned loose their soldiers to rape, pillage and kill to their hearts' content for many days unchecked, in an orgy of carnal licence. Right up to the time of the British arrival, police methods of interrogation were often brutal. 'Water Treatment', when water was poured down a tube into the victim's mouth until they almost drowned, was a favourite for men and women alike.

In those first days, more and more British and Sino-British internees were being released from the camps, to be housed in the *Empress of Australia* as she lay in her berth, or upon their preference, finding accommodation in the Peninsula and other hotels in the Colony. Geoffrey, with more of his inspectors, sergeants and constables coming back to him and taking up their previous duties, was re-establishing a police presence throughout the town of Kowloon. Often I went around with him, for there was necessary overlap between the police stations and the command posts of the men of Shield Force. Many Chinese members of the Hong Kong Police who had worked under Japanese authority continued to work under Geoffrey's command, but some had established a reputation with the local communities that made them unemployable with credibility and they were replaced. No doubt, as always in such conditions, replacement was sometimes unjust. It was very difficult for Geoffrey and his more trusted lieutenants to check how much truth there was in the tangled evidence of wrongdoing and how much was the repayment of old scores and the perpetuation of old feuds.

But progress was being made every day and at least the alarming crime of destroying buildings by ripping up floors or pulling down beams in a search for fuel was stopped.

On instructions from Admiral Harcourt, the Acting Governor of the Colony, Jas Eccles, the captain of the carrier *Indomitable*, which lay alongside on the Kowloon shore, set up a small naval shore headquarters in the Peninsula Hotel. He and John clearly shared a mutual respect and worked well together.

CHAPTER TWENTY-FIVE

Geoffrey Wilson

W e had been in the colony for about a week. Disarming of the Japanese garrison troops in Kowloon was well under way. It was decided that the people, and Japanese units, in the villages in the country districts of the New Territories should have it confirmed to them – if the Japanese command had not yet done so sufficiently – that the British were now in charge again. There were, as yet, no Army units in the Colony, only officers and men of those ships of the Naval fleet who still remained in Hong Kong waters. John's RAF Shield Force, who though doing an excellent job, were not combative troops or men likely to be very credible in a show of strength.

Geoffrey spoke fluent Cantonese and knew every corner of the New Territories. In addition to his other invaluable work he was the obvious man to do the job of showing the flag among the villages. I was delighted when he asked me to go with him. We draped a union flag over the bonnet of an open Jeep and the two of us set off along the Nathan Road northward out of Kowloon to make a two-day tour of the villages and settlements of the New Territories, which I, of course, had not yet seen.

'You should know, Peter, that the Chinese disrespectfully call the Japs "Lo-Bar-Tow", though not in their hearing. It means Turnip Head, and I don't know if it refers to their cranial form or to the level of their intelligence.'

Each time we came to a village Geoffrey would stand up in the Jeep and immediately, so it seemed, the entire population of villagers would gather closely round. Sometimes there was also a unit of Japanese soldiers, in those early days still armed, and they also surrounded the Jeep, a study in curiosity, while Geoffrey spoke. Probably not all of them understood Geoffrey's Cantonese, certainly it was the Chinese members of his audience who reacted most positively to him, and always he quickly had them laughing. He would sing, loudly and with credit, to the tune of 'Who's afraid of the Big Bad Wolf?'

Bin-su pow (who's afraid) lo-bar-tow, lo-bar-tow, lo-bar-tow, Bin-su pow lo-bar-tow etc. Perhaps the temerity of just two British who had come among them and were happy to sing insults in front of armed Japanese soldiers was sufficient demonstration that these newcomers were in some way superior and unneedful of any back-up, sufficient to convince these country folk that the rumour that they had heard, that British warships, with just one short burst of gunfire a few days ago had indeed returned to the Colony and retaken the place that four years ago they had given up to the Japanese invaders with only a token of resistance. As well as singing, Geoffrey of course told them that the British were indeed now in charge, that the Japanese would now very soon be sent away, and that British law and justice was now in force.

This performance he repeated in different places to different audiences, and with always the same result: delighted laughter from the Chinese peasants; sullen silence, perhaps lack of understanding, from the Japanese soldiery.

One of my happiest memories of that trip came when we called at an isolated orphanage. It must have been the time of the midday meal because at each of about twenty tiny tables, each no more than 2 feet by 2 feet and no more than 15 inches high, sat four little girls. They all appeared to be aged under six years, and they were tucking into their bowls of rice. The place was run by three or four Chinese women, possibly of some religious order. Oh so much would I have loved to have had sufficient Cantonese to learn more about those tiny tots! Geoffrey said that they were unwanted female children, but what happened to them after they were six years old? Perhaps the orphanage was no older than that and it had been their policy to take in only infants. I should never know. Geoffrey told me that the women assured him that they had had no trouble from the Japanese soldiers, so here was a contradiction to the awful stories we had heard in the town of their atrocities. Who paid to keep such a place going? Who supplied the rice for all these little mouths? I never knew, and I was sorry to leave them (smiling, well-looking, busy with their chopsticks in their bowls) and go on to our next stop.

From the first night I had had a room on the first floor of the Peninsula Hotel. It had a bathroom and a double bed over which hung a mosquito net, and it was all very comfortable. The hotel faced the harbour, looking across an area of laid-out flower beds and across the road and a hedge and what looked like a disused railway line and then to the shore. In those hedges wild hibiscus grew, and though if one went to the right one came to the busy terminal of the ferry that ran across the straits – or harbour – to the island of Hong Kong and its town of Victoria and other smaller conurbations across the island, one could walk to the left, beside an old railway line, in surroundings that one could almost call country. Windows on the right-hand side of the hotel, as one looked towards it, looked on to Nathan Road, which climbed slowly up at right angles to the shore towards the New Territories and a real countryside of rice fields and then hills that stretched away to the Chinese border. My bedroom was on the left-hand side of the hotel and looked on to a road that ran inland parallel to Nathan Road. Up there was a big market of canvas-roofed stalls, and further on you came to Shamshipo.

Of course John and Geoffrey, too, had rooms in the Peninsula Hotel, as did most of those officers who were not with their men in command posts about the city or based at the hospital or at Kai Tak airfield. And so did a number of the 'Old China Hands'. These were collectors' items for the student of human nature. Each in his way, before the Japanese had come in 1941, had wielded power in his own sphere. Now after four years of internment, weak but getting stronger, thin but getting fatter, and with growing confidence, they relived old times among themselves or to anyone else who would listen. As time went on I was to see almost all of them give up the unequal struggle, or after having made a tremendous contribution in spite of their weakness, return to England for a well-deserved convalescence, whence some of them would return and take up again their former lives and previous jobs.

One of this last category was James Norman, who before the war had worked in the prison at Stanley on the other side of the island, of which his father had been governor. There was Alf Bennett, a 1941 Wing Commander who spoke Japanese, who having just got out of Japan before he was interned, was unable to repeat that happy escape when he arrived in Hong Kong. Mark Evans had had a job in the Colony whose detail I did not properly understand, but it had clearly been a job that rewarded him well financially and in influence. Kenneth, with his straggly beard, had been manager of Kai Tak airfield. He had a dog-like adoration of Madame Chiang Kai-shek, wife of the Kuo Min Tang leader and daughter of the renowned Sun Yat Sen. Her name was always on his lips and if he had ever met her she had certainly had a remarkable effect on him. Jack Diamond, already back managing the Peninsula Hotel, came into a different category, like Geoffrey Wilson, but they were both Old China Hands indeed, and very good friends of mine. Da Silva was a senior lawyer probably of Portuguese origin, and a power in the Colony. Patrick Thaxter was there but I did not know what his line had been pre-war. And there were women too, Yvonne, Lucia, and Mrs Evans, who came into my life at that time.

As these ex-internees fattened and flourished and their strength returned, they mostly began to look around for the red meat of companions of the other sex, which either their own weakness or the weakness of their closest playmates in the camp had denied them. Better food seemed to go straight between the legs of Pat Thaxter. In prison camp the quietest fellow, his appetite for sex now grew tremendously. But it was not the still-pallid ladies from the camp who appealed to him, it was Chinese prostitutes – he could not have enough. Not surprisingly he soon admitted that he had caught a dose of clap, though that did not seem to deter him for long. James Norman, for whom all said that Yvonne had most openly shown her adoration during the uneventful years in Shamshipo, and who could now do more than he ever could before to satisfy her adoration, found that he had lost her to any of the red-blooded males who had now come into the Colony. His puzzlement grew into such a pitiable state that it seemed that his heart would break.

These good people who had suffered so much and who now at last were free, loved to gather together in the room of one of them and talk about old times, and they were indeed collectors' items to anyone the Americans would call a 'People Watcher'. I enjoyed listening to them. Sometimes John, too, was there. He, who after all his many experiences was understandably a raconteur par excellence, would sit listening, putting his head first on one side and then on the other, as was his wont.

I very much enjoyed the police work I was doing with Geoffrey or with his number one, Fraser, one of the few of his more senior old staff who had come out of prison fit enough to be effective. There was some 'rounding up' to be done – Chinese with Mafia-like ambitions of power, and also some Japanese who rightly believed that they might have to answer to British justice for their sadistic behaviour. There were tip-offs about the whereabouts of such men and most of our activities were at night. We carried out activities like raiding houses in better residential parts of Kowloon and getting over garden walls, etc., often to do no more than frighten some poor wife or even child, the bird we were after having flown. But there was some success.

At the time of the Japanese invasion in 1941, some atrocities had been committed. It was reported from several sources that one unit in particular had taken pleasure in such actions, which had included the capture of a group of six airmen, pouring petrol on them and setting them alight. Fourteen men of that unit had, on a tip-off, been captured in a successful raid in which I had been involved. As they could be expected to have indulged in other bestial acts, members of the public and of the Police Force, and even airmen of Shield Force, could well have decided to take retributive action. We therefore were hoping that news of their capture would not become widely known. In fact, the Governor, hearing of it, instructed his Flag Lieutenant to tell John to have them sent across to the Island for safer custody. John asked Geoffrey to take them across, but he was very busy. He asked Fraser to do it and Fraser reported to John for instructions.

'Take one of my launches and take them across this afternoon.'

'If you don't mind Sir, I think it would be better to go across at night. There are several people gunning for them and it might be safer.'

Next morning John's telephone rang. It was the Admiral's Flag Lieutenant.

'The Governor's compliments Sir and he wishes to know where the Japanese prisoners are whom he asked you to send across.'

'They should be with you. They came across last night in my launch.'

'Well Sir, we have seven of them but the Governor had understood that there were fourteen. The Governor asks you to look into it and report to him.'

John sent for Fraser and asked for an explanation.

'We took them across, Sir, but on the way over there was a bit of a scuffle when the prisoners tried to take over the ship and we had to restrain them.'

'And then?'

'Well Sir, in the scuffle some of the prisoners went over the side, and as it was dark it would not have been possible to recover them.'

'Indeed. And were there any shots fired?'

'Well yes, Sir. I think there were a few shots.'

John went across to the Island and reported to the Governor who listened in silence to John's account.

'I think, John, that it would be better if we forget about the whole incident, don't you?'

*   *   *

In those days the appearance of the Colony was entirely different from how it was to become. There was only one tall building, the Hong Kong and Shanghai Bank, on the Island side (and that was later taken down to make way for bigger ones). On Kowloon side there were *no* tall buildings; all, except for the Peninsula Hotel, were single storey or two or three storey, comparable with an average-sized town in pre-war Britain. There were no tourists, no expensive shops, very few hotels, almost no places for entertainment, even hardly any restaurants. But there was an unprepossing little eating house in Nathan Road called the Sun Sun where the food was very good but not expensive and there Geoffrey and I quite often had supper together. There it was that I first learned to eat with chopsticks.

'Hold them higher up. Don't have your fingers down nearly on the plate!'

I also learned how to drink from my little tea bowl with my fingers politely positioned and without lifting it up so high as to show its bottom. There I learned that 'birds' nest soup' is more of an invalid food, like calf's foot jelly – though delicious – than an epicurean delicacy; that sharks' fin soup, on the other hand, is both. I learned that 'rice birds' are angels' food if your conscience does not rebel against eating a plateful of the tiny walnut-sized mouthfuls, whole little birds complete apart from their feathers and feet, knowing that they have been caught in their thousands in nets as they fly over the rice fields. Apart from ourselves I never saw a Westerner in there, for, apart from a few Naval and Shield Force men and those few Old China Hands who had not gone to the Empress, there were no Westerners.

One evening Geoffrey and I, on our way home after eating at the Sun Sun, called in at one of the police stations. An excited Chinese police sergeant came quickly up to Geoffrey, spoke to him and immediately all three of us were hurrying out and along the street. Geoffrey explained the urgency as we ran.

'One of our wanted chaps has been seen to go to ground in an opium house.'

It was a rough wooden building on a bit of waste ground behind the shops or dwellings that lined the street and there was a rather insecure-looking flight of steps leading up to a door in the end of the building on the upper floor. Geoffrey had been talking in Cantonese to the sergeant as we had hurried along. The sergeant began climbing up to the door. Geoffrey turned to me.

'Follow me!' The two of us ran round to another door and up a stairway from an inner room, which ended in a small landing and a closed door. Geoffrey's voice sank to a whisper.

'He's got a good place to hide. Bloody difficult in these places to know who's paralytic and who's shamming. I'll go in and wake a few of them up. You stand just inside the door. If anyone tries to bolt towards you that's our man, shoot him. Or he'll shoot you.'

With that he burst into the door with me behind him. I closed the door, unbuttoned my leather holster and pulled out my father's Luger and released the safety catch. It was my first visit to an opium den. It was a long room with certainly no attempt at decoration, with small open cubicles on each side of a wide corridor, which was divided into two by a line of benching down the middle. Most of the cubicles had an occupant. Every occupant was male. They were mostly thin, pathetic-looking things, lying on the low wooden table, which appeared to be the only furniture in each of them, and there were one or two ragged creatures sitting slouched on the central benching.

Considering the haste of our entrance there was virtually no reaction from anyone. Even the two or three little girls who were attending to the customers, presumably filling the clay pipes with a small pill of opium and holding it in the flame of a candle till it began to melt and turn brown, looked up at us with little curiosity. They had seen such interruptions frequently. Geoffrey began to walk down the space between the left-hand lot of cubicles and the benching, looking searchingly at each customer. One hand held his Colt revolver and with the other he sometimes roughly prodded a sleeper or actually pushed one off his wooden bed with his foot so that he rolled senselessly on to the floor. I noticed that the police sergeant had positioned himself inside the closed door at the other end of the room. He was dressed in the ordinary cotton trousers and jacket of any one of a thousand Kowloon citizens, not, like Geoffrey or me, in any sort of uniform. He looked more like a newly arrived customer taking stock of the room before coming in and sitting down and calling for a pipe, than a police sergeant whose observant perception had started this search, this inter-ruption in tonight's indulgence by these rather pitiable creatures in their probably fatal addiction.

Geoffrey had now nearly reached the end of the room down the left-hand side of the central aisle. I expected him to walk round the far end of the benching and begin to walk towards me up the right-hand side, rather like a beater driving game birds in ground cover. But perhaps something caught his eye so that he wanted to check again one of the supposed sleepers whom he had already passed. He turned and began to come back towards me on the same side.

He had hardly begun to walk back when suddenly a figure, which had been covered by a blanket in one of the right-hand open cubicles, sprang up and bolted towards the further door. It was a creature in ragged clothing and it collided with the man who stood by the door. It happened so quickly. I heard the crack of the sergeant's fist, though it could have been something metal in his hand, on the man's jaw and the thud as his other fist punched into his stomach. In a second the man's arm was twisted up behind his back and he was on the floor at the sergeant's feet. Geoffrey was on him in a second; he was cuffed and pulled to a standing position. But there was no fight left in him. He was gasping for breath and then he was vomiting.

We all walked back to the police station, the man handcuffed to the police sergeant and dragging his feet drunkenly as he came. My head was spinning from the fumes of the opium smoke, the violence I had witnessed and the adrenalin that now flowed as I realised I might have had to shoot someone at close quarters.

CHAPTER TWENTY-SIX

Macau

The population of Hong Kong at that time was about half a million, not the many millions that there would later be. Then the refugees were not flooding across the border fleeing from the revolution in China. The packed-together upended dominoes of high rise buildings were not yet needed to house, layer on top of layer, the teeming millions that were to come. In time there would not be enough land on which to build. Whole areas of land would be added to the Colony by dumping rock and soil into the sea.

But to me even then there seemed to be a lot of people about. Pavement vendors and stalls narrowed the streets where rickshaw coolies ran between them pulling their big-wheeled creaking vehicles. Parties of labouring coolies, barefoot and stripped to the waist, their once-blue trousers bleached almost colourless by the sun, shaven-headed or wearing their traditional coolie hats, running awkwardly and bent kneed under their heavy loads, seemed never to rest. Especially near to the terminal of the two-deck paddle-wheeled ferry, which wove its ceaseless journeys back and forth carrying the crowds of office girls and shopgirls in their cotton pyjama suits and business men in pale grey lustre gowns from Kowloon to Hong Kong or from Hong Kong to Kowloon, there was an ant-like continuous movement of people. Here and there among the crowd or walking gracefully alone all in black under her black-covered breadbasket hat with its black fringed pelmet almost obscuring her face, a Hakka woman from the New Territories, sometimes beautiful when she tilted her head so that I could see her features, added a spice of enigma to the scene.

Even on the broad band of sea that separated Kowloon from the Island it was busy. Junks with stiff, brown, layered sails plied their way through the Straits. Hundreds of small flat sampans, each a home for a family as well as a moving means of livelihood as taxis, freight carriers, work places, tossed in the careless wake of every bigger boat that passed them. It sometimes looked as though but for the straw-plaited canopy, which arched like a beehive over part of their deck, all their belongings would be tipped into the water.

If there were half a million people crowded into the small area of the Colony, there were at least as many, perhaps more, who lived on the water. The junks carried merchandise of every kind up and down the coast. Most of them did. But some of them were pirates preying on the traders, having as their base one or other of the many islands to which the Law of Britain did not yet extend.

And the sampans, in addition to all their other occupations, fed off the junks, loading, unloading and supplying them and being tenders to them. Soon I and some of the others were to venture again on to the water where the cut-throat strong-arm lawlessness of these sea traders held sway in a precarious balance of power.

In the very early days it had been brought to John's notice that there was an interesting-looking boat lying off the jetty at Kai Tak. She was about 40 feet long, a low sleek motor launch with a long cabin top generously glazed to give her a light and airy cabin. She boasted good teak decks and a bow shape and sheer that suggested she might be a reasonable sea boat in moderate conditions. David Mitchell-Smith, with whom I had spent time at Hawaii, the senior Transport Officer, had a penchant for marine engines and he adopted her, tinkered with her powerful diesel engine and soon reported that he now considered it reliable. Opinion was that the timber of her hull was sound and she had been lying in the water, not out of it for her planking to dry and open up, and was making only a little bit of water in her bilges.

David's report coincided with a remark to John by the Governor, Admiral Harcourt, that he thought it would be a good thing if somebody made the journey across to Macau, the Portuguese colony on the far side of the mouth of the Pearl River, to see how things were with them there, to issue an invitation to the Governor there to come on a visit to Hong Kong, and perhaps to receive thereby an invitation for him, Admiral Harcourt, to visit Macau.

Both of John's powerful launches had temporarily been lent to the Navy, but the Governor seemed to think that John was the man who should make this exploratory visit and present the Admiral's compliments to whomsoever was Governor of Macau. John was pleased with this idea and developed the notion that the Kai Tak launch should be the means of getting him there.

Of course he would take David Mitchell-Smith and Geoffrey Wilson, and he had in mind one or two others. Perhaps because he had a disproportionate idea of my boat-handling abilities, knowing of my enthusiasm for sailing before the war and of my more recent experience in County Down, he delighted me by asking me to come too. Understandably he thought it would be polite to invite someone from the Navy, and asked Captain Dalmeyer, commander of *Venerable*, if he would like to accompany us. Dalmeyer refused. Probably it was pride. Perhaps as a Captain in the senior service he did not want to accompany a Group Captain in the junior service who would not only be his host but, in the circumstances, skipper of the vessel and the one bearing the Governor's compliments to the senior personage in Macau. As a professional, though not guilty of that sin, John would understand, but did not comment. But amateurs like me, unable to believe real the absurd jealousies we saw senior officers sometimes display, thought that the refusal was because he did not wish to risk his person in a small and vulnerable boat on a pirate- and shark-infested sea. Be that as it may, John now asked Basher Watkins, captain of the destroyer *Wager*, to come with us, and he enthusiastically agreed. Basher was a man with a most attractive personality whose nickname had been earned by his prowess as a boxer in the Navy. He was the sort of man you would want to have on your side rather than on the other.

The distance from Kowloon to Macau was about 40 miles. It was perhaps a little more than it would be by crow's flight as we had decided to pass outside Lantau, an island rather bigger than Hong Kong. To pass between it and the mainland, the south-western part of the New Territories, would have been like an insectivorous lizard ambling along the flight board of a beehive. Lantau was a veritable hornets' nest of pirates. We were expecting a passage of about five hours. It was a very beautiful bit of coastline, with almost no buildings on the islands or anywhere along the shore.

Our course took us quite close to several junks, and it was interesting to see them at close hand. I was familiar only with sails made of canvas cloth, supple enough to make an aerofoil shape to drive into the wind and which one reefed and stowed by folding their pliable material. The rigid material of junk sails, of necessity made up of layers or panels joined into a common area with poles along their edges, was quite new to me. Whether or not they were all peaceful traders or if any were predatory pirates we fortunately did not have to discover.

It was a lovely day. The sea was calm with only a little movement on the water, and the launch was behaving like the elegant lady her shape promised. It was delightful to be on the water and close to the water, not perched so high above it as we had been on the decks of the *Empress of Australia*. Soon we were beginning to cross the mouth of the Pearl River or whatever name is claimed by the wide estuary mouth that is the escape to the sea for several rivers that run down out of the vast hinterland of China at that point along her coast. There was plenty of seagoing traffic as some miles up at the head of the estuary was the teeming city of Canton, or Kwangtung.

Apart from any tidal consideration, the volume of water flowing out to the sea there makes a very powerful current, and now our progress became slower. Macau lies beyond the big estuary that we were crossing, tucked in among several smaller islands near the seaward side of a complicated delta, and thither we were now heading, albeit slowly and with some deflection by the current. At last we were moving into the approach to the port and towards a long quayside faced with baulks of timber where we came alongside and made fast.

The buildings now facing us presented a very beautiful and paintable scene. It was unquestionably an oriental port, but many of the house fronts were colour-washed as though they had been transported from the Mediterranean: pale blue, soft green and cream. Such was the happy marriage of Chinese and Portuguese architecture.

Though there was plenty of evidence of them, the Japanese had not occupied the tiny colony of Macau as they had Hong Kong. Perhaps they thought it more valuable as a neutral port for espionage, for it was reported to be swarming with spies. The Portuguese had a frigate there, which, except when it was near to high water, sat on the mud. Her teeth had been drawn by dispensing with the armament on her superstructure and replacing it with a most luxurious wardroom.

There did not appear to be a governor. John was told that the most senior dignitary was the Bishop, which is credible as it was a devoutly Roman Catholic country. So after we had booked ourselves in at the principal hotel and had a wash and change, John set off for the Bishop's palace. He paid his respects and handed the Governor's letter to His Lordship.

We were all invited to dinner in an imposingly porticoed house. On entering the building we seemed to step back almost into the last century. We were seated at a long banqueting table very luxuriously appointed and I found myself between two charming Portuguese ladies who spoke excellent English. The lady on my left wore a pale mauve silk dress and had, around her neck, an exquisite jade adornment. The lady on my right was in crêpe de chine of corn colour with a necklace of jet. She told me that I must not fail to go to Portugal, so beautiful, especially in the spring. We were drinking a wine in which small cherries hung, rather than floated, in the glass, and she assured me that I should find Portuguese wines most interesting.

CHAPTER TWENTY-SEVEN

Encounters with Communists

Police information was that there was a unit of the communist Red Army patrolling the northern border of the New Territories with China. They had not wasted much time in the 'race to move into Japanese-held territory'. Geoffrey decided to pay them a visit, and I was very pleased that he wanted me to go with him.

We set off again, just the two of us in an open Jeep up the Nathan Road towards the New Territories. This time we did not make ourselves conspicuous with a union flag draped over the bonnet. At that time you came out of the town and into open country quite soon. But first, over on our right, inland from the small airfield that then was Kai Tak, we passed the bare ochre-coloured terraced hill that was one of the largest Chinese burial sites. At short intervals along each one of its many terraces were the stone surrounds of the Chinese family tombs, some seeming at that distance to be backed by a small cave; it was not a particularly lighthearted sight though I realised how much they resembled the rows of front doors of a still-in-construction hill-town of oriental Hobbits. Thereafter the country on each side of us was greener, for the rice was now well grown but had not yet begun to show the splashes of gold that herald its change to the yellow fields of harvest.

'That is the golf course.' The area Geoffrey indicated, looked, in its post-war rags of neglect, no different from any other area of scrubland. Coarse tufty grass was overgrown with thickets of thorns and little wild shrubs. The road climbed and dipped and we saw no other traffic except for a very occasional antediluvian lorry piled high with vegetables. But we did see many bicycles, hung with panniers full of farm produce, and small groups of people walking, mostly women, each under a wide straw hat, except the Hakka women – they were all in black including the black-fringed lampshades on their heads. All the walkers were barefoot, moving with little hurrying steps under their heavy loads. Of course there were other roads in and out of the Colony, and a great traffic of sampans by water, but it would need many ant-like columns of human porters in those days of scarcity of vehicles to supply the needs of Hong Kong.

The New Territories are a strange shape – a badly misshapen triangle whose southern tip points across the straits to the Island. Kowloon then was wedged into that tip. The long northern side is the border with China and its eastern and western sides look out over water, deep wide bays where the South China

Sea encroaches into the land mass of Kwangtung province. Looking westward to our left it was too far to glimpse the sea that is the great wide estuary of the Canton river, which anyhow is hidden by the hills. But looking east to our right from the vantage of any higher ground on our road, we could see glinting blue in the morning sun the many-miles-wide inlet of Port Shelter, wherein are many islands and lobes of land stretching into it like short fat fingers, creating sheltered havens for the villages of the fishermen and seamen who make their living along that part of the coast.

Later we saw the first of the lakes, reservoirs of water for the Colony, and I realised that Hong Kong is no fortress, in spite of all its hills and all the moats surrounding it, which the sea makes. An enemy coming down towards it from China would only have to cut off the water supply that pours down from those reservoirs. From one place we could look down on Tai Po and on Geoffrey's house of the years before the war, whence four years ago his wife had with bravery, fortitude and suffering made her way, with her two small children, across the mountains to Kunming and so eventually to Burma, India and England. Since the start of that long journey Geoffrey of course had not seen them. But he showed no inclination to turn off the road and go down the hill to take a closer look; after four years of Japanese occupation there would be nothing left; better the memory than the reality. So we drove on; the hills, particularly on our left, rose in ridges, more blurred towards the distance and the north-west, and quite devoid of trees.

'They've cut down anything that they could burn for fuel these last few years,' explained Geoffrey.

Miles later we came to the border. It was vaguely indicated by a wire fence, but as the Japanese had been in control on both sides of it there was no need for demarcation. We turned left and soon there were men waving us down and Geoffrey stopped. Two of the men climbed on to the vehicle and pointed the way he must follow. At a small group of huts there were more men, dressed in cotton shirts and trousers and mostly with some sort of belt or bandoleer to carry a gun. We alighted and were pointed towards one of the huts, then one of them made it clear that we should take off our belts. Geoffrey had a .45 revolver slung in a holster, which was partly cut away for a quicker draw, while mine bore my Luger with its conveniently available Sten gun ammunition. I felt made rather naked by this confiscation, though in the company in which we now found ourselves, armed or unarmed would have made little difference to our safety.

We went into the hut. The man who rose to greet us similarly handed his gun to one of his aides, which was a polite gesture if nothing else. He was about Geoffrey's age, probably early forties. He looked lean, hard and fit – really a rather impressive creature. At his bidding, the two of us sat down on the two stools that were brought into the hut so that the three of us sat at a rough trestled table. Three mugs of blackish tea were brought in and put before us with a bowl of sugar. I stared at the sugar bowl. I expected it to be white sugar and at first I thought that the bowl was very full. As it stood on the table its contents were black. Then as we each in turn put a spoon into it much of the blackness moved and was disturbed as many of the mass of flies rose in protest before settling back on to the sugar.

As the two men talked I watched them. They looked well matched. Everyone else had left the hut and of course I could not follow their conversation in the language in which they spoke. Afterwards Geoffrey told me that the man was a colonel, pretty senior in the Red Army, unlike in the Nationalist Army with whom I would later come in contact wherein Chiefs almost seemed to outnumber Indians. He wore no uniform or badge of rank, and yet he was a man whose appearance commanded respect without the necessity of such trappings. I learned afterwards that he had wanted assurances that the Colony would not be a refuge for any of those whom he counted as enemies of the Communist movement that he served. Geoffrey was happy to tell him that the Colony had problems enough without having them added to by troublemakers and that for his part he would be grateful for assistance in preventing large numbers of refugees flooding into Hong Kong over the border. What else they spoke of I did not know, but I had the impression that there was mutual respect and that Geoffrey felt the time to have been well spent.

On the way back, having been reunited with our belts, I learned something about the country people through whose villages we passed, people whom Geoffrey liked and respected after his work among them before the war. We turned off left after a while and drove down to a small cove where we took off our clothes and swam in the sea; it was warm yet refreshing and calm up here in the shelter of islands and headlands. It was a conversation we had had before and Geoffrey knew that I had a growing conviction that a life in the Hong Kong Police was what I wanted for myself now that my time in the Air Force was obviously coming to an end. It was an idea in which Geoffrey encouraged me greatly, and I now began to ask him what steps I should take to further my wish.

'Most importantly you must persevere with the language. You cannot interrogate a Chinese through an interpreter, it will be the opinion of the interpreter that you will hear.'

'How did you learn? It seems appallingly difficult and presumably there are no schools in which I can learn.'

'Of course not, and there is only one way to learn a language, and that is to live with someone who cannot speak yours. It would be a bit impractical at the moment, but before the war we all learned the same way. We came out here from England, not knowing a word of Cantonese. It's Cantonese you want here in Hong Kong, not Mandarin. Very soon we went off to Canton, on our own – no good trying to learn while you're living among other people speaking English – and we picked up some attractive little Chinese girl, made an arrangement with her, or with her parents, and you learned Cantonese. You had to. She could not speak any English and you needed her company. And you were expected to study the written language too, and to go back to Hong Kong about once a fortnight and take some sort of exam and show that you were doing some work and not just fucking all the time. Which it was a temptation to do.' He smiled.

'Have you had a Chinese girl?' I told him of my non-consummated experience in Macau.

'They've not got long film star's legs but they're tiny, enthusiastic, and with only about five hairs at the place where you least want a girl to be tickly.'

'It sounds like Heaven.' I in my innocence could not help wondering if Geoffrey's Cantonese teachers had all been schoolgirls.

'But how do I go about it when I can't go to Canton?'

'Have to make some sort of arrangement here in Hong Kong, I suppose. I don't imagine there's anything against it in the rules of your service. After all, you'll not be trying to draw marriage allowance!'

It would be quite untrue to say that I thought no more about it. I thought a great deal about it, but I made no further progress with the idea. Though there was one incident which had me thinking.

At about this time I sometimes went out in the evening with one of the Old China Hands called Mark. He had been interned and his wife with him, but she had gone back to England and Mark was kicking over the traces quite a bit. He had fixed himself up with an attractive little Chinese girl, Lee, with whom he was living and several times we went to a restaurant together, usually on the Hong Kong as opposed to the Kowloon side. We would go over on the ferry and wherever we went it was clear that Mark had quite a pull. Restaurant proprietors and the like were especially obsequious. His girlfriend had a good singing voice and sometimes at the table she would sing Chinese folk songs. It was usually not long before people at other tables abandoned their conversation and turned in their chairs to listen to her, while Mark looked at her with a mixture of pride and longing on his face. Though very many years his junior I thought that she was genuinely fond of him, and not only because he was her bread and butter.

CHAPTER TWENTY-EIGHT

Wu

John was not long at Kai Tak. He flew one of the Hurricanes that were sent there, spotting pirate hideouts on islands like Lantau. They had also a couple of Halifaxes, but to bring one of those in to land on the small airfield, coming in towards the sea, losing height down the face of the hill behind, with an up-current upsetting one's judgement, must have been a tricky operation. A squadron of Spitfires arrived, and using five incendiary bullets to one (instead of the usual one to five) the pirate junk menace was much reduced. I sincerely hoped the identification-intelligence was good before each sortie of these 'sitting duck' operations, because decent families also sailed those trading junks. Those Spitfires also, Spitfire 20s, were difficult to bring in to land on the old, hill-backed, Kai Tak airfield, because of their tendency to 'float'.

I felt sad that Shield Force had indeed broken up. By then some of the Peninsula Hotel's European former Hong Kong citizens had gone home. Others of these who can be called Old China Hands still remained. James Norman took me over to see the Prison at Stanley where he had some position and where in former days his father had been Prison Governor. I saw there some of the Japanese internees. One, a fat man who had held senior rank and against whom charges of many war crimes were stacked awaiting his trial, crouched like Shelob in his solitary confinement cell. I did not see the man from the opium den, perhaps he was one of those who 'went over the side' from the launch.

James was all right that day, but some days he was in an almost suicidally depressed state. His depression took the form of an unrequited longing for Yvonne. In the internment camp she had, everyone said, loved him dearly, while he had returned her interest only a little. Now, while he wore his heart on his sleeve, she did not deign to notice it, which excited his passion all the more. It was nearly the last straw when she went off on an extended dirty weekend to Calcutta with Squadron Leader Chadwick – he who had painted my portrait aboard the *Empress of Australia*.

Those who were James' friends tried to persuade him to go back to England and take a holiday, but he would not go unless Yvonne went with him, of which there seemed to be little chance. Several times, thinking that he had agreed to go, a seat in an aeroplane was reserved, but at the last moment he refused to leave.

Finally, Geoffrey decided that he must go home. He had not seen his wife or children for over four years and had done a magnificent job in Hong Kong; his contribution had been truly enormous. I was going to lose a very good friend and during the last week of his time in the Colony we went out together every evening. Some afternoons we went to Big Wave Bay on the far side of the Island and bathed.

He had introduced me to several Chinese friends of his on the Kowloon side and on the Island side who would stand me in good stead. He urged me to ask for an appointment with the Police Commissioner, Sansom, and make it clear to him that after I had been called back to England and been demobilised I wanted to return to Hong Kong and join the Hong Kong Police, rather than being only seconded to them (and that entirely unofficially) from the Air Force as now. He stressed once more the importance of learning Cantonese.

With the imminence of Geoffrey's departure my need to find a girlfriend was greater. Though there had been exceptions, I had always preferred a girl, rather than men, for company. I was seldom one to stand at a bar in all-male company, though sometimes it went with the job.

It was Mark who made the next step in my search for a girlfriend. Partly it was kindness and partly because he wanted a more reliable foursome for our evenings together. He was very enamoured of his charming little girl with the pretty singing voice. It was clear that he had influence. People seemed to want to please him.

'We shall go tomorrow to meet two business friends of mine,' he said. 'I have told them that in England you have a family business and they are keen to seek the opportunity of being appointed as your agents for the Hong Kong market when you return to England to be demobbed. You need not be worried. They cannot hold you to it on your return if it does not prove to be possible and anyhow they are anxious to get some business which I can put their way, so they will put their best foot forward.' Next day in the afternoon he and I went to a house in Central District, Hong Kong, and in an upstairs room were received by his two friends. After introductions and pleasantries and a little time to become acclimatised to the situation, looking out of the windows down at the busy street below, I saw the door opened and two Chinese ladies entered. They wore the grey silk cheongsam dresses of better class Chinese and stood demurely by the door awaiting an instruction from the two men. Then the door opened again and a Chinese girl came into the room. She was tiny, she was slim, and it was obvious she was desperately shy. Her little face was so painted with rouge and make-up and whitened with dead white powder that I could not tell if she was pretty or ugly. My face betrayed my disappointment as the painted doll paraded before me. Within a moment I had regained a friendly smile but the damage had been done. I saw her lip quiver as she interpreted that first reaction as rejection. I felt mortified.

Oh, I would have given a year of my life to have had those moments again and controlled the expression that must have shown on my face. If it was horror, little girl, please forgive me. Terrified enough already, what must it have meant to her? I could not speak her language. I could make no apology or amends. It had to be through first Mark and then the Chinese men, with awful delay, that at last she received my apology and my request that she allow me to see her without make-up. It had been a terrible beginning. And so we stood about, I without any of the poise I hoped I had displayed on our arrival. The two Chinese men, and Mark too whose many years among orientals had taught him to hide the indications of his emotions, showed not a trace of acknowledgement that anything untoward had occurred. The two ladies and the girl had left the room, walking with little steps on black felt shoes.

My thoughts were a jumble of self recrimination and embarrassment. 'Please God they are not being unkind to her in another room, not blaming her, the most guiltless of us all, for my ignorance of their customs, for the nakedness of my thoughts upon my face. Did they see it there, as you did then, my disappointment, little girl? Give me please another chance for kindness!'

It seemed an age while we waited, watching the traffic below us and the dawning of coloured tube-light signs over shop fronts and business houses, large Chinese characters in red and blue and green now dominating the bunting that hung above the street, as the short tropical twilight began to fall. But at last they came back into the room, the two ladies followed by the girl. Her kimono was the same, but it was the face of a different girl. Considering the trauma of recent minutes she looked controlled, serene. But it was admiration for more than that alone that my eyes spoke out to her. Cleared of the coloured paint and chalk white powder she was pretty, and because of my guilty conscience that I had caused her pain I looked at this brave tiny person with stirrings of a deeper affection than so short an acquaintance justified. I had not heard her voice, I knew nothing of her as a person, but I had to break the expectant silence of that room.

'She's lovely,' I whispered to Mark. The Cantonese version of my words reached her from the lips of the two men, whose accent she probably understood better than Mark's. Until now she had looked at the floor, but now she lifted her childlike face and looked at me, and I liked to think a fleeting smile played about her mouth and brightened her eyes as she left the room.

The two ladies stayed and though they did not speak they sometimes nodded assent as the men spoke the words they had already decided. Mark relayed to me the terms that I must agree if this woman was to become my companion and my teacher. The terms were within my means and our business was done. The transaction agreed, I learned that the men could speak very reasonable English – there was now no need for mystique. Her name was Wu, they said, she was seventeen and her young Chinese husband had been killed by the Japanese. How, they spared me from knowing, but I understood that it had been about a year before.

At a word from Mark the ladies left the room after much bowing and smiling between the two parties. We four men talked of this and that and nothing in particular. I thanked them for a happy conclusion. Wu came in again. She had left her kimono behind and now wore a cotton pyjama suit and there was no trace at all of all the make-up that had hidden her beauty. We said goodbye to the two men.

'I told Lee to wait for us at the Green Dragon,' said Mark. 'Bring your new little friend. I think we can get into one rickshaw. She'll not take up much room.'

At the Green Dragon Restaurant Lee was excitedly waiting for us. Mark continued to direct everyone else.

'Lee, darling, take her shopping, but don't be too long. I'm hungry. Give Wu some money, Peter. Two or three hundred dollars should do for tonight. Peter and I will wait here but if you're not back in an hour I'll smack both your bottoms!' Though Lee's English was improving, it was probable that Wu understood not a word of what he said, but she smiled happily and the two girls hurried off hand in hand.

'Now tell me what you think,' said Mark.

'I can't believe my luck. I think she's gorgeous. Did you choose her?'

'No, but I told them what to look for. I've noticed, and so has Lee, the sort of girl your eyes have followed across the room a hundred times.'

'Bless you Mark, I don't know how to thank you.'

'No need my friend. I shall be glad not to see that hungry look on your face any more! And it will help her, because a widow here dependent for every dollar on her family is not allowed much self-respect; in fact they almost treat her as their slave. She'll still spend as much time with her family as she wishes, whenever you don't want her, but she'll have gained a lot of face.'

Mark and I sat at the round table as the time ticked by, sometimes cracking a melon seed between our teeth from the porcelain bowl between us. Mark told me many things I did not know and I was grateful for his friendship. Nothing was said about the make-up and I was glad. More people came into the restaurant, almost all Chinese, and each time anyone arrived our glances to the door betrayed how important to us was the return of our partners. Finally the women returned. What their purchases had been neither man knew, but I understood that Wu was set up for the immediate future. Now the meal was ordered and Mark was ravenous, but neither Wu nor I ate much. I was too excited to be hungry. At the end of supper Mark said

'Now, it's Saturday evening. We'll not meet tomorrow. Better to leave you two together. But on Monday night we'll meet here at seven. That all right?' I said that it most certainly was.

I did not know where the other two went, but Wu and I walked out and down to the waterfront and the ferry terminus and took our seats together on the upper deck under a starlit sky. The paddle wheels churned, the phosphorescent splashes flickered on the black harbour water, oil lamps on sampans and other boats made ladders of rippling light towards us. Behind us the dark cone of the Peak was shaped against the night sky by the lighted windows of its houses above the brighter base of streets in Central and Wanchai, and the ferry pointed its bows towards the less bright carnival that was Kowloon. I was only dimly aware of the picturesque scene. My attention was consumed by the young girl on the seat beside me whose small hand I took in mine.

Most people can remember that as children they knew the magic that can be made by a space within a space. A circle of chairs in the nursery made real a 'pretend game'. The game had to begin again if the circle was broken. For me, the strongest magic was made under the nursery table, where one or two could go to a land of make-believe undreamt of in the open spaces of the house or garden. It is the same with a mosquito net. A mosquito net is a cube of space that excludes mosquitoes and encloses happiness, evoking the old magic that I knew beneath the nursery table. In my room in the Peninsula Hotel the mosquito net covered the area of the bed, suspended from its four upper corners to reach the floor with perhaps one extra cord from the centre of its ceiling to stop it sagging. One entered its magic space between the overlapping curtains of one of its sides.

I had watched Wu undress and seen her beauty plain. Now she went in first on hands and knees and I followed her between the entrance curtains, following that small bare bottom, which led the way. Inside, she sought quickly and with a practised eye for any mosquito that might already be within, clapping her little hands together in the upper corners of the net. Then she knelt in the centre of the bed and looked at me. She was so beautiful. Slowly and very gently I worshipped every detail of her loveliness and then I took her in my arms. Everything that Geoffrey had said was true, but now he was very far from my mind.

CHAPTER TWENTY-NINE

Wu's Temple

A s I drove up the Nathan Road towards the New Territories I reflected on
how wonderfully lucky I was. I was not a charred and twisted corpse
lying undiscovered, except by wild pigs, in a German forest's under-
growth, as probably some of my friends were. I was not on a Pacific island alert
to hear the siren's wail and the scream of Japanese suicide dive-bombers, as I
had expected that by now I would be. I was driving towards the countryside
with this delicious young girl beside me, because against expectation I had got
a Jeep. We had reached the outskirts of the town, shops and houses and the few
small blocks of flats built just before the war were thinning out, well spaced now
with plots of cultivated ground between them. The late morning sun behind us
enriched the colours, greens and soft browns, of the hills and fields towards
which we were heading.

It was a warm and gorgeous day, but our unhurried progress blew a fresh
breeze in our faces and put her dark brown hair in pretty disarray. Wu looked
happy. A holiday, which this was, had not come frequently in her short life.
That it was Sunday made not a bit of difference to the many country people we
passed on the road walking with their sacks and panniers into town or back
again. Every day for them, each week, each year, was a day of toil, as it was for
millions like them throughout the Far East, whether they were country people
or townsfolk.

We drove on towards the hills, then turned right along a track that I had
bumped along with Geoffrey. We got out of the Jeep and walked uphill and on
to a ridge. Yes, it was where I thought we were, and in front of us the land fell
away towards the sea, and the view before us was a patchwork of rice fields and
low hills. They were rice fields wherever it was low enough to flood, centuries-
old paddies now taken for granted where each rainy season the plankton-rich
water would flow quietly in through the small gaps left in the little low mud
walls that divided up the rice field into squares. But once, long ago, it would
have been the scene of great labour and digging, probably involving the whole
family.

From where we stood we could see a coolie-hatted peasant walking along
those tiny dividing walls, a long-handled net on his shoulder and a little pear-
shaped basket at his waist. We could see him stoop and pick up something in
his fingers and transfer it to the basket, probably a small freshwater crab. He

stooped to pull out a weed and lay it on the narrow path the wall made, to wither in the sun. The ground was drying out now; soon the crabs would all have burrowed down into the mud to await the coming of the rain again. The low hills too were mostly cultivated. There were fields of sugar cane and the fresher green of maize, sometimes beans, and on some hillsides vertical stripes of yellower green showed where ginger had been planted. Beneath the soil of those hand-heaped ridges, divided by shallow runnels to drain away the surplus rain-water, the tubers of ginger swelled like dahlias.

Wu stood in front of me, leaning against me, her head against my chest. We looked out across the countryside.

'Mei,' I said. She turned her head a little to look up at me. She nodded and echoed my word, 'Mei'. The scene was indeed beautiful. But to my eyes it was her face that was beautiful.

'M-hai, Wu mei,' I corrected, and the smile with which I was rewarded made me long to know more words to do justice to my admiration.

But that would come later, for now I must be content just to be with her, to be allowed to touch her. My fingers were gently massaging the base of her neck, where her hair, glinting a little in the sunlight, fell about her shoulders. They were graceful, sloping shoulders, not the square strong shoulders of a girl who since she was a little child had had to work in the fields.

A mile or two away a junk was reaching up the channel of Hebe Haven, making towards an anchorage just off a village that nestled in the curve of a finger of land protruding into Port Shelter Bay. We watched her come about and lie her course on to her buoy. I was conscious of a great happiness. It was enough at this moment just to be with Wu. At that distance the sounds we were conscious of were more imagined than heard as we saw the junk swing to the wind, secure on her mooring and saw her crew running along her deck about their routine tasks. Something else caught my eye; it was a small group of trees on another hill like the one on which we stood. Groups of trees were not common here where almost all had been cut down for fuel. I signed to Wu, my eyebrows raised in question, if we should walk over there to investigate. Laughing, she took my hand in hers and pulled me down the slope towards the other hill.

At the bottom we had to cross the rice field, and I followed her as she ran nimbly along the tops of the little banks that divided the rice field into reticulate squares. We were like knights crossing a chessboard, turning an endless succession of right angles in order to go straight on. A foot or so down from our shoes the tufts of rice plants grew out of soft mud, and in some places there was still standing water. The rice was quite tall, its oat-like ears reaching nearly to her shoulders so that when she had turned a corner I could only see her head bobbing up and down as she ran. I hoped that neither of us would slip on the short grass that covered the banks. We didn't, and soon we had reached the further side and were ascending the slope that was crowned with the little group of trees. We reached it laughing and a little breathless, and as we approached we saw that the trees almost hid a small stone building.

Its roof was of old ceramic tiles, many of them broken, and creepers were invading where once a door had hung and sending green-leafed fingers into the squared holes in the masonry that served as windows. We stepped inside, our feet printing the dust that lay thick on the floor. There was almost nothing to prove the purpose of the place, the few bits of broken stone littering the floor gave no clue, but the expression on Wu's face and the reverent way she walked showed me that she knew it was a temple. I assumed she was probably a Buddhist but I had no reason to be sure, and then as I stood there she went down on her knees and put the palms of her hands together against her breast and waited. Then she stretched out her arms and put her hands palms down in front of her, bowing her forehead to touch the dusty ground. Three times she did this, for Buddhism too has a Trinity, and I knew that she knew that this little building, neglected and probably vandalised, was a sacred place. She looked back at me and I had no choice but to go and kneel beside her. I did not make obeisance, but kneeling there I felt the warmth of her faith flowing into me. When she stood up and with a gentle pull of her hand asked me to rise and stand beside her I knew in my heart that silently we had made intercession together to the Spirit of some Good Power whose influence still resided in that place. Holding hands and happy we walked out into the dappled sunlight beneath the trees.

A dry narrow path led down from there to join the track on which we had left the Jeep, now visible from this far side of the little temple, and from there we could see that several people were standing around it, people in the faded blue clothes and coolie hats of country villagers. We walked together down the path, shielding our eyes from the brightness of the lowering sun, which shone straight at us, and also by reflection from the burnished band of light that was the sea. As we approached we saw that there were two men, several women and even more children, though the similarity of their coolie hats, their trousers and their rough cotton blue shirts left us in a little doubt until we were among them. A vehicle was a rarity in those days, especially in the countryside of the New Territories of Hong Kong, and word must have come to the village or to people working in the fields and brought this little party of curious investigators. Now we too were being investigated, and a little boy with a runny nose stood close to me and screwed his head round to look up at me. No doubt I was very much taller than anyone of the boy's previous experience. The others were questioning Wu, or telling her something, and then I noticed that on the seat of the open Jeep lay the small collection of my weekly sweet ration, which I had left there when we had abandoned the vehicle to climb to the top of the ridge. They were poor people and the baby looked very undernourished, its stick-like limbs quite inadequate to its round tummy. It was the baby who Wu was examining, and the young woman who looked younger than the 17-year-old Wu, was talking quickly and urgently. Wu turned to me.

'A-so-tsai yau-peng. M'yau yeuk-t'soi.' She put her hand into my pocket. I did not need much Cantonese to understand her urgent request. The baby looked ill, perhaps with beri-beri, the scourge of the undernourished there in those early days. I knew m'yau meant 'no have' and it hardly mattered if the rest meant food or medicine. I took all the paper notes I had on me from my pockets and gave them to Wu. I was not looking to see if she gave them all to the mother or made a distribution, and we should never know if a share-out was later demanded by the others, who may or may not have been of her family, but, sadly, there was not very much. Then I pulled out the pocket-linings and laughed at Wu at this demonstration of our now impecunious state. The little boy was disbelieving and put his hand in my pocket as Wu had done. They were poor people, made poorer no doubt by the heavy hand of Japan, and yet my unprotected sweet ration was intact on the seat. I heaped the collection of Fry's cream bars into the boy's hands and watched a grin spread across his face, which threatened to join his ears.

We said goodbye to them all. It was neither the first nor the last time that I wished that I had trained as a doctor instead of going into a business before the war. I wished fervently to have been more use to them than to offer money and chocolate but my gifts were probably as generous as anything they had ever received before.

We had had no lunch, and as far as I remember no breakfast, and the afternoon of that happy day was well advanced. It did not matter that we had no money. We stopped at the Sun Sun in the Nathan Road and after a delicious meal I signed a little piece of paper. This custom of trust was a left-over from before the War, but perhaps it did not last much longer. Soon after that I was shown a chitty signed 'LAC I-never-come-back', presumably the iniquity of an airman, and a little later I saw a similar atrocity by someone who, if the rank could be believed, was of the Army. Unkindnesses like this made me more and more prefer the ordinary Chinese whose land this was to my fellow countrymen whose actions so often made me ashamed. 'Marry a Chinese girl? You won't get far in the service if you do that old man!'

Those two days – no, those forty eight hours, for it was not only the days that were so full of happiness – went so quickly, and then it was time for us to cross to the Island and join our friends again. We had thought to cross by hiring the services of a sampan, but a little last-minute shopping had taken longer than expected, as shopping always does, and there was not enough time so we went by ferry. We found Mark and Lee already in the Green Dragon at the corner table they liked to have. We were earlier than usual and there were many more bent-wood chairs than customers. Mark's raised eyebrows made his spoken question almost superfluous.

'Well?'

'Delicious, quite delicious,' I responded. Mark was a man who liked the correct use of words. He was weighing my reply with his head on one side, and obviously he approved it.

'You look very happy. That hungry look has gone.'

'But is Wu happy?' I asked. Sitting together on the other side of the table, Wu was showing Lee her little purchases, but they heard this question and looked across at us.

'Is she? Wu foonhay la?' asked Mark, smiling.

This set the two girls talking together in Cantonese, a conversation much interrupted by shy giggling. Then a pause and then Wu leaned closer to her friend and said something to her behind her hand, which made both of them dissolve into paroxysms of giggling.

'What did she say?' I asked Mark. I could feel a blush rising to my cheeks – sensing I was being teased in a way I could not understand. Both girls were watching our faces, first Mark's to imagine his reply and then mine to watch my reaction, but it was Lee who tried to conquer her laughter.

'She say muchee time . . . ' No good, her laughter was uncontrollable.

'She say for vellee long . . . ' But she could manage little more, and Wu was holding on to her arm as though wanting her to tell us and yet overcome with embarrassment lest she should. A large grin filled Mark's face as he turned towards me while still watching Wu out of the corner of his eye.

'Your teenage widow says she has had to sleep alone for a long time but now you have – how shall I put it – cured her sexual frustrations. Yes, she is very happy.'

His obvious delight in being able to say this and the joy on my face to hear it said was too much for the girls. Hiding their mouths behind their hands in an involuntary reaction to their happiness and embarrassment they fell into each other's laps. I stumbled my embryonic Cantonese.

'Wu foonhay, Peter foonhay. Toh-tse darling.'

Even in two days I had learned a few Cantonese words. It is a difficult language because it is tonal. Alter the pitch of your voice and you change the meaning of the word. The same monosyllable said in a high voice with a rising inflexion or a falling inflexion, or again, in a lower tone, will mean four different things. In Cantonese there are nine tones. And because there is clearly no way in which these differences of tone and inflexion can be written in our inadequate twenty-six-letter alphabet, there is no way in which we can write down a phonetic version of their picture writing and thereby more easily remember a word visually.

Wu was a good teacher, with infinite patience, and she never made the common mistake of correcting me too frequently. As the days and weeks sped by in that little girl's company I learned more and more of a basic core of Cantonese.

About a week later came the day appointed for my interview with the Commissioner of the Hong Kong Police, Sansom. I made my way to his Headquarters on the island and I was shown into his office. The man behind the desk had a strong face, with short grey hair and eyes that looked to have seen men's iniquities in many forms and yet to have retained an optimism essential for the conduct of his job. He motioned me to sit down and for a while did not speak but studied me closely.

'I met your commanding officer, Group Captain Barker, before he went home. I understand that he thought well enough of you to ask for you to be appointed to his staff, and though the original intention of Shield Force did not materialise I have not heard that he came to regret his decision.'

I wondered if this had been a chance meeting or if Sansom had intentionally made inquiry having heard, probably through Geoffrey Wilson, of my interest.

'He was a good friend to me, whom I admired as my squadron commander and then also in his execution of his task here. It was an open-ended, play-it-by-ear assignment, full of unknowns even before we set off and its requirements changed continually as a quite unexpected situation developed.'

'You have a DFC. Tell me about it.'

'There is nothing to tell, except that it is one more demonstration of my extreme good fortune. I was a member of a good team and we survived.'

'You certainly had good fortune to survive two tours of operations, but do you think that you were less deserving because you led a good team that survived?'

'I think that if an All-Seeing Eye wrote all our citations, most awards would be posthumous.'

Sansom looked thoughtful, digesting the meaning of what I had said. I wondered if he had perhaps himself lost a son in one of the services.

'What was your entry?'

I told him that it was through RAFVR, a weekend and summer camp form of Territorial Service, but that a broken knee had caused me to have little of the training I had expected to have by the time we were mobilised just before the outbreak of war. The Commissioner asked me for a quick resumé of the years of my service and he was interested to hear that I had been in the first course through wartime Cranwell, of which a third had been amateurs like myself.

'Why do you want to join the Hong Kong Police?'

'I was fortunate to see a little of its activity while I was with Superintendent Wilson, and I find that I like John Chinaman.'

'It is important that you should, but police work is not only the excitement of chasing villains in narrow streets. You have much that you must learn of our procedures. But we need new men. I wish they could all be as good as Wilson. He was one of the best of all my officers. I am fortunate to have been back to England since you arrived here, and I have come back sooner than I expected. There have been many changes in recent years and we have new political masters. I hope that we can change some of our attitudes and yet retain the best of our traditions. Your Service is too new to have acquired traditions out here and that is something in your favour. Why do you think that I believe that?'

I believed it too, and I hoped my reason was the same as Sansom's.

'I have seen the divisions that exist here, even in the social life of the Colony. The Army, the Navy, the Police, the Civil Administration, the Business Community, they keep their own company and do not intermingle; they are like shingle between breakwaters stretching out to sea. I think that because of too much tradition different parts of the Administration are in danger of seeing themselves as something which is an end in itself. They can forget that the purpose of our being here is to make and maintain conditions in which all the people of the Colony, Chinese and British alike, will prosper within a just administration. And I am surprised at the separation of Chinese and British.'

'You are right, it is something that a new attitude must remedy – the Business Community has made the most progress in that direction, others must follow. Those of us who have served in India have seen an administration moving towards its own destruction, a colonial attitude, not helped by its womenfolk, which has produced a huge army of clerks but no elite of administrators – except hostile ones. But do not decry tradition too much, we need both, the old and the new. Perhaps that is why I have been returned here. Out of the old comes a dedication that is essential. And nowhere more than here. The power of money is frightening; opportunity for corruption is very great, especially in the police force. If our pay were increased tenfold it would be but a tiny barrier against the limitless temptations of bribery. If it should be lacking, the outcome is too dreadful to contemplate.'

In such a vein our conversation continued. I was grateful that his questioning was friendly, but sometimes I realised that his shrewd inquisition included questions to which my answers would tell him much. My answers must come from the honesty of my heart and I must hope that my thoughts, formulated during my weeks and months there, were as far as possible the right ones. If they were not, then it were better I did not pursue this ambition, for I had no intention of adopting a less radical outlook.

During recent years I had attended interviews, but not since RAF Cranwell had I felt the same respect for the intellect of my interviewer, but of course the Commissioning Board at Cranwell were not men chosen lightly, nor would this man have risen to a position of this responsibility without being held in considerable esteem. Sansom brought the interview to a close.

'If, as I hope, you continue with your wish to join us, you must of course, after your demobilisation in England, apply to the Colonial Office. But they will have before them a report from me, and I have authority to appoint some of my new intake from among applicants here. Indeed it would be a lost opportunity to the service if I could not take advantage of the reservoir of potential officers who are currently collected here. Then after you have been here for a further three months and have continued with your endeavour to master a sufficient knowledge of Cantonese and an intelligent grasp of our procedures, in view of your six years of RAF service and your good fortune of having worked with Wilson – who you must realise may not return here, for his experience and seniority may be required in other forces – I shall be happy to confirm you in the rank of Chief Inspector. And I wish you the best of luck and happiness among us.'

The interview had gone better than I had hoped, and it was with a light heart that I met my friends, and Wu, that evening.

'Tonight,' said Mark, 'Lee and I will let you into our secret.'

After supper we took two rickshaws and were borne up the lower slopes of the Peak, then branched off left-handed where the houses had thinned out. We paid off the coolies and walked under a full moon across a hillside, which then was turfed with tufted grass, loud with the high-pitched string-music of crickets. We followed a dry sandy path. Below us to our left lay the harbour, the straits between Hong Kong island and the New Territories. Lights of many ships at anchor on its waters gleamed like stars, each one seeming to grow on a stalk of brightness that was its reflection, and across the water, hanging full above the dark silhouette of the land, the moon sent a brilliant band of light towards us. The rickshaws had gone. We were alone. Our surroundings were almost colourless in the moonlight, but when we came to a gate and passed through, silver discs of night flowers, sometimes attended by hovering moths, tried hard to show that they were sulphur yellow in a green boskage. It was a neglected garden. The path, now tiled, led up to the dark shadow of a house and a door for which Mark produced a key. My face must have voiced a question, which Mark felt prompted to answer.

'It belongs to friends of mine. It is our hideout, away from the censorship of curious eyes and prattling tongues. If there is a danger here we think it worth it.'

He struck a match and the soft orange light of an oil lamp illuminated a room sparsely furnished. Lee went into another room with Wu and came back with coffee, which we sat and drank, happy as naughty children, with a subconscious feeling of shared conspiracy. Mark pointed to a doorway.

'There's a bed and a mosquito net in there. We shall stay in here.'

He handed a second oil lamp to us, and with our movements mimicked by our shadows on the wall, we entered and found pallets on the floor in a corner hung with a welcoming net whose hem was tucked under the simple mattress. Perhaps the occasional scuffling cockroach might have deterred less eager lovers, but certainly none of the four of us.

A cool breeze off the sea blew through the house, but cuddled together under the net this was a welcome improvement to the Damocletian circling of a revolving electric fan. There was no sound of traffic or human voices, only the shrill song of grasshoppers who serenaded us from the turf and bushes outside. There was only the occasional hooting of an owl or the muted soft-feathered downbeat of wings when a large night-flying bird passed our shuttered window, quartering the land around the house to watch the twilit ground for the little creatures who must betray their presence by their movement in their nightly search for food.

I awoke before Wu and quietly opened up the shutters and lifted the mosquito net, bunching its curtains together and tying them with a handkerchief, to let the early morning light fall on her sleeping form. I lay watching her. I marvelled at the beauty of the Chinese girl's face asleep. The high cheekbones made a setting for the soft dark brushes of her eyelashes. The pale complexion of her faultless skin showed the delicate moulding of her nostrils. Her lips were slightly parted, the porcelain perfection of her teeth just visible where in the night my tongue's tip had touched. Her little breasts were rising and falling imperceptibly as she breathed the morning air and perhaps dreamed.

Somewhere a cock crowed. Another, younger bird responded, each crow preceded by the sound of a beating of wings, but the second was a strangled cock-a-cuck while the older cockerel's greeting to the morning was a full triumphant cock-a-doodle-doo.

I ought not to wake her, yet I longed to hold her in my arms again. The towelling coverlet had slipped aside. The creamy light of dawn fell on her thighs, and on the mound that in the dark her hips had lifted up to meet my kiss.

The cock crowed again, and as the sun peeped over the horizon to our east, the colour flowed back into the landscape. Leaves were green again. Flowers changed their night attire of silver to yellow, reds and blues. In the garden about the house bougainvillaeas planted several together of different colours made rainbow fountains of beauty in this pretty place, a quiet and unspoilt countrified oasis on the edge of town. The sea now was blue again, ships great and small swung to their anchors on the change of tide or held steady between their moorings, junks sailed to and fro about their business and doubtless in sheltered places the crowded population of sampans had already begun the day with the smells of cooking and the clickety click sounds of Cantonese conversation.

Wu was awake, and the other couple too. Someone made coffee before we emerged into the daylight garden. It was still early. We would meet no acquaintances, and we made our way down into town.

CHAPTER THIRTY

Farewell to Hong Kong

Unimportant assignments came my way out of the Colonel's office and I was kept busy enough. Most days Wu returned to one or another branch of her family and we met again by arrangement, sometimes to be together with our friends, sometimes joined by others who knew not Mark and Lee's secret, sometimes just the two of us, and usually we repaired at bedtime to our room at the Peninsula Hotel. Occasionally she asked me for the price of some item like a pair of shoes, though for all I knew it could have been to pay for some family improvement or small emergency. She was never demanding or extravagant. All the time my Cantonese vocabulary grew, and with it knowledge of how to string words together, to emphasise, and to ask questions, for in a tonal language one cannot do this by altering the modulation of one's voice as in a European language. It is done by adding words special for the purpose, for the rise and fall of one's voice does not make a statement become a question, it alters the actual meaning of a word. More and more I avoided Mess life and company, rejoicing in every opportunity to spend my time among the native people of the Colony.

One day I received a message to contact Da Silva, and I went to his chambers in Hong Kong. He was asking me, and S\Ldr Hollis with whom I had shared a cabin in the *Empress of Australia*, to join him to form a triumvirate of judges in the High Court. It was a murder case. Da Silva sat between us on the dais of Hong Kong's highest courtroom while counsel for the prosecution and counsel for the defence produced their witnesses and argued their cases. We were shown some particularly gory photographs, for the victim had been hacked to pieces with an axe. As the dramatic tale of violence and hate unfolded before us I could see that in spite of the likelihood of the defendant's guilt, there was much missing from the prosecution's case, which circumstantial evidence could not replace. Quite simply, the police could not produce enough proof of the man's guilt, and although muscular and handcuffed, tattooed and shaven-headed, he looked a bruiser indeed, I doubted if we could bring in a verdict of guilty. I felt particularly sorry for some of the witnesses, for as they testified to acts of butchery without much to convince the judges that they did so except out of hatred for the defendant, I realised that they too could become victims of the man's axe if he was discharged. He did not look like a man who would forgive. And discharged he was, Hollis and I having first given our opinion, which Da

Silva confirmed wholeheartedly. The man went free, and that night in over-crowded tenements poor men must have lain sleepless, hearing in each creak and footfall on old wooden staircases a warning of the revenge to come. Such seemed to be British justice, which amateurs such as myself were there to uphold. For me it was a new experience to be a judge, a judge without benefit of a knowledge of the Law.

I was also concerned in a piece of police work on the Island side, and as the police officer in charge, a Scot, had very little Cantonese I saw at first hand the danger of a miscarriage of justice when decisions are made on the word of an interpreter, particularly as this one seemed to be in some way concerned in the case.

I had a good room boy on my part of the first floor in the Peninsula Hotel. He had at first seemed hostile to Wu, and I never knew his reasons, but having had a suitcase made for me for ridiculously few dollars I thought that I was unlikely to want again one of the tin trunks I had and I gave it to him. A man un-accustomed to privacy or to any security for his possessions, I might have given him the earth, he was so thrilled. After that he could not do enough for me or for Wu.

Jack Diamond's favour continued, and sometimes I sat with him and some of his cronies in his beautifully furnished office in the mezzanine curve of the main stairway. It was as though he directed much of his gratitude for his release from Japanese prison camp to John Barker and to me, though why I should be so equally included I did not know. He had given to John and to me one each of a pair of Chinese rugs, which displayed the figures of the seven Taoist Immortals, the deep, washed pile cleverly cut so that their figures stood out in relief from their background, and even their noses from their faces.

One of Jack Diamond's cronies was the manager of the Hong Kong Hotel on the Island side. He said that he still had a few rooms there that had not yet been converted back from the way in which Japanese officers had preferred them, and he invited me to go and try one. Wu met me there and we were shown our room. It was small, perhaps one normal hotel room divided into two or four, and its floor, walls and ceiling were panels of woven reeds, natural straw-coloured and quite unadorned. There was no furniture except a neck bolster and a coverlet to pull over us. The floor surface had some resilience but I would have preferred a mattress. Yet we slept well enough and no Japanese ghosts disturbed us, and though some had committed hara-kiri at the time of the surrender, we encountered no disembowelled spectres.

I was very happy to have a companion, and one with whom more and more I could converse in a simple, limited way. It was an advantage too that she knew her way about the island, or at least could ask. My own geography was better in Kowloon. Together we sampled Chinese theatre. We went to Repulse Bay and took tea in a palm-filled, glassed-in verandah, a place legendary in the annals of old Hong Kong, which soon afterwards was pulled down. We went

to Deep Water Bay and Big Wave Bay and others on that side of the island and
made our way down to the water's edge through breaks of evergreens, which
gave us enough privacy to get into bathing costumes and we bathed together in
the sea. At about that time a police sergeant had his leg torn off by a shark, but
was brought to shore by friends. He had been fishing on some rocks and he had
cleaned and gutted two big fish and fastened them to his belt to make his way
back to the beach when the shark attacked him. It was said that they attack only
if they smell blood in the water surrounding a bather, but attendance by
swimmers at Big Wave Bay fell off for a while afterwards.

At about that time I helped in an almost forced repatriation of James
Norman. His yearnings for Yvonne were no less, but her indifference towards
him was even greater. One evening some of us got him packed and got him fairly
drunk, and at about five in the morning, while it was still dark, I went with him
in a taxi to Kai Tak and persuaded him on to an aeroplane.

Across in the mainland of China battles were being fought between the
Nationalist Army of the Kuo Min Tang of Chiang Kai Shek and the Red Army
of the Communists, despite an attempt at reconciliation, but news was scarce.
One day a large contingent of Kuo Min Tang arrived in the Colony and
bivouacked beside the road on Kowloon side. They were not, poor things, an
impressive sight. They were poorly equipped and looked listless and dis-
interested. It would be another four years before Chiang Kai Shek would give
up his military struggle for China and take his army and their camp followers
into the island of Formosa, which would be called Taiwan. I did not know why
those soldiers had arrived among us, stayed a day or two and then been shipped
off. But I vaguely believed it was part of an American interference, they seeking
to move some of Chiang's troops from the south of China to the north, an area
more vital to Chiang it is true but also where a force of Chinese not hostile to
America, albeit dispirited, might be some deterrent to a Russian entry
into north-east China. The men gave no trouble but the colonel with whom
Geoffrey had conferred across the border would have been displeased.

I had had no news of my own return to England for demobilisation to enable
my return to Hong Kong to take up my commission in the police.

My father, because he was older than most servicemen, had been demobilised quickly after VE Day. He had been able to recommission his *Nancy
Blackett* after nearly six years in a mud berth at Pin Mill, and he sailed all that
summer among the creeks and estuaries of those parts long before the buoyage
had been reintroduced, often going aground on sandbanks for his pains. They
were waters he had known since boyhood, but channels had changed in six years
and he had to relearn navigation marks and check the reliability of the few
fishermen's withies that remained. For him it was a happy time, reuniting with
old cronies and making new friends among the 'dirty shirt' yachtsmen who were
the coterie of enthusiasts in their little boats or in the friendly bars of Essex and
Suffolk waterside pubs. How distant seemed that estuarine idyll – so far
removed from the bustle of the Nathan Road.

The Japanese advance into the Colony in 1941 by way of the New Territories had been swift and overwhelming, but there had been a resistance and I often heard tales of men of a local defence force of Hong Kong citizens who had suffered in that attack. While more and more of the Colony's housing was being taken over for the accommodation of British servicemen, many of the new arrivals now being men of no battle experience, there seemed to me to be an unjust neglect of Hong Kong's own veterans: they were receiving no acknowledgement at all. Much I learned from among NCOs of the Hong Kong Police. An Inspector Thompson, with whom I was working, who had been in the Colony in 1941, more than anyone else fired me to do something about it. There was a great backlog of building repair work needing to be undertaken. Little or nothing appeared to be being done, and among the Chinese veterans of the 1941 local defence force were craftsmen of many kinds who, it seemed to me, could make a useful contribution. So, firmly pulling on my 'Energetic Stupid' hat, I began to gather about me those who seemed to be able reasonably well to establish a claim to authenticity, and I appointed NCOs among them. My Colonel agreed to what I was doing, and I received support from many quarters. The Equipment people were sympathetic, and I issued my growing band with footwear and what passed for uniform. Greatly daring, I commandeered the stable block of the sacrosanct Pony Club of Hong Kong. Here I made my headquarters and a reasonable standard of discipline was established by members of my 'Force' who were jealous to see the project prosper and to avoid any false steps that might jeopardise any of their support. There were enough among them who could speak sufficient English for me to promulgate orders. Of course there were interlopers, a Chinese brand of nepotism saw to that, but so long as they were the exception and so long as they were competent craftsmen – carpenters, builders, plumbers, etc. – the idea of collecting together a disciplined unit of men who would in my eyes be less parasitic than the majority of British servicemen who were cluttering up the Colony remained intact. The idea found favour with the police with whom I continued to work, it was acceptable to my Colonel to whom I was accountable, and there seemed to be nobody in the old Shield Force who had not gone into the aerodrome building business or to the hospital or to Kai Tak who appeared to claim any jurisdiction over me. My NCOs were anxious to retain the goodwill and patronage of 'Major Lussun' (which was about as near as they got to pronouncing my name) and my private life was impinged upon very little during this period of forming a convincingly disciplined unit of men.

Suddenly came the news that my repatriation for demobilisation was imminent. I was to report to a collecting unit in Bombay. My Colonel was helpful in arranging for an Army captain to take over the commitment I had started, and I introduced him to them and sought their loyalty to him. The stage had now been reached when these Chinese enthusiasts should be put to useful tasks. Salesmanship of potential abilities was what was required now, and I hoped the young man made a success of it. As an embarrassingly generous gesture of thanks to me, I was presented with a bronze image of the Buddhavista

Sankajai, circa 1750. God knows where it came from, but the Navy took it home to England for me.

I now began to worry about what would happen to Wu. It might take quite a long time to return to England, attend whatever interviews the Colonial Office might require and prepare myself to come back to Hong Kong and take up my appointment. In my leisure time she was my constant companion, night and day, but many of the nights were sleepless in anxiety. She knew about my probably fairly imminent departure and the necessity of it, but she knew that I would do whatever was best for her. I thought of Jack Diamond.

'Jack, I think you know that I have a very dear Chinese companion.'

'I do Peter. My spies reported to me long ago that Room 276 was a love nest. How can I help?'

'I wonder, Jack, if you could employ her here in the Peninsula? She is intelligent, reliable and attractive.'

'My dear Peter, you know that I have always looked upon you and John as the people – representatives of the people if you like – who restored me to a proper life and enabled me to begin again where I had left off. If you have now thought of a way in which I can express a little of my gratitude I should be delighted. Bring her along to me as soon as you like.'

So I did, but first I took Wu to the tall building that dominated the central district of Hong Kong, the Hong Kong and Shanghai Bank. I opened an account in her name and put into it a quite large sum of money that would be her nest egg and something to fall back on if she should have troubles when I was not there to look after her. Jack showed her every consideration and respect, and a modest but adequate remuneration was agreed. I – and Wu too – were much happier. That evening I told Mark what I had done, and he approved.

'If she is in any trouble please ask her to come to see me.'

'She my flend, I look after her,' said Lee.

We four companions had several more evenings together, but in due course the sad dawn arrived of my penultimate day. On that, our last night, Mark was once more the organiser.

'Tonight we shall all go to the Hide-out. You two will spend your last bitter-sweet cuddle in the most romantic surroundings we are able to offer. It is a lovely fine evening.'

CHAPTER THIRTY-ONE

Grief

Although I had been told to get to Bombay, I had not been told the way I should go. I had sufficient friends in the Colony to choose my way. This was to hitch-hike. I was convinced that it would take no longer; it would probably be quicker. There was a Short Sunderland flying boat going to Singapore, and they took me with them.

From Singapore I found a flying boat leaving for Madras, and flew over Sumatra and many small flooded islands, mangrove swamps. I stayed at a hotel where the dining room was oval, like being inside a large hollow egg, with a gallery running round its walls high up. My bedroom was cooled with a fan and well shaded by trees, with a large balcony where, among potted plants, chipmunks entertained me, stuffing their cheek pouches with any food they found. Climbing into bed that night I realised how much Wu had become part of my life, part of my happiness, but this was a journey that had to be undertaken.

From Madras I crossed India by train, having a compartment to myself whose seat converted to a bunk, with a small washroom off it. I kept my doors locked, as the crowds of Indian people waiting at railway stations would have swamped me. I could not feel in myself the friendliness, affection almost, that I felt towards Chinese people in Hong Kong. It was a dull journey, dry and brown and bare, and though I had hoped to see fauna of many kinds, I only saw a few bands of baboons hurrying away from the train's noise.

In Bombay the machine that was the Air Force movements system began to catch up with me, but I visited the Yacht Club and one or two of the places I had heard of. I was accommodated in one of several flat-roofed buildings, property of the Air Force, near the sea shore, and during my enforced stay there took on a mahogany tan, for I was already well coloured by the Hong Kong sun and by my long sea voyage.

I returned to my billet one afternoon to find a letter from Jack Diamond. Longing for news of Wu, I slit open the blue envelope with shaky hands.

Dear Peter,
    Thank you for your letter. Yes, Wu appears to have settled down very well. We are beginning now to get quite a lot of guests from Singapore, many of whom were good customers before the war. She speaks an educated Cantonese and some

Mandarin, so I have put her into Reception. She is making a little progress also with English.

I am glad that you enjoyed your brief stay in Singapore, and had the good fortune to meet with some hospitable Dutchmen. Get your business completed in England as soon as you can and get back to us here. I, or Mark, will keep you posted about Wu.

I crossed Bombay harbour to the *Isle de France* in a liberty boat, and as I learned that she was apparently too large to go through Suez and must go round the Cape, I knew that I would have at least five weeks of a dull journey. Of course, I looked forward to seeing some of those in England, but there was not the anticipation of adventure of my voyage in the *Empress of Australia*. Our complement was mostly returning servicemen but there was a sprinkling of women – wives accompanying their husbands who had been in India before the war – and with them one or two children.

I found that there was a letter waiting for me aboard and hurried to read it. It was from Mark.

Dear Peter,

As Jack has so recently written to you, it has fallen to me to write to you and give you some very bad news. Last Tuesday evening your Wu, having finished her turn of duty at the Peninsula, had left the hotel and was beginning to walk towards the Ferry Terminal. You will remember that her family lived Island side. No one is very sure what happened, but it is believed that a motorcycle, being erratically driven, mounted the pavement and knocked her down. The motor cyclist did not stop. A passer-by found her lying on the ground and believed that she had hit her head against the kerb. He hurried to the Peninsula and those who came back with him carried her into the hotel. One of the Air Force doctors was there and attended her, attempted resuscitation, but I am so very sorry to have to tell you Peter that he pronounced her dead. He gave it as his opinion that she would have died instantly. The man who found her saw the accident rather as it had just happened. He did not see the impact and did not get the number of the motorcycle, though moments before he had been conscious of one being driven very dangerously and had himself had to move quickly aside. He thought that the driver may have been drunk. He thought that it could have been a soldier from one of the units up in the New Territories but this was only his supposition and he could have been mistaken, though as you know hardly anybody of the local population has a motor vehicle.

Needless to say, Lee is heartbroken, and I too am very unhappy that we have lost our little friend. Jack also is appalled, knowing what a loss this will be to you, and he says also that the hotel has lost a member of staff who had already shown that she would become increasingly valuable

What can I say to you? Lee and I know that you loved her dearly, as she obviously did you. To send you our sympathy is so inadequate in a loss so great as this. We hope that you can find a little compensation and comfort in the knowledge that in her last months you made her happier than she had probably ever been before. She knew that she had found someone who wanted to take care of her, someone to whom she could give her love, and that her life would thereafter be without the hardship and anxiety to which she had been accustomed . . .

I felt strangled by the enormity of my grief. She was the girl with whom I had expected to make my life in Hong Kong, the anchor to which I would make fast my emotions and longings: my companion, my comfort, and the recipient of every instinct and desire to protect of which I was capable. Dear little girl, how awful that this terrible fate should strike someone so young, so sweet and caring, so guiltless as Wu.

I knew the number of the cabin to which I had been allocated and I made my way there with head bowed, my eyes dimmed by tears, walking like a zombie.

We were overcrowded and it was hot, twenty or more to a cabin in two-tier iron bedsteads. The last to arrive, I put those few belongings that did not have to be stowed in the ship's hold onto the only bed, a lower bunk, which had not yet been claimed. Around me was the noisy laughter of the other men. I realised that I would now have to live for about five weeks in their company with little to fill my thoughts except my loss. Lying on the bed I stared unhappily up at the lower surface of the bunk above me, longing for sleep to drift me away from the cabin's noise, longing for the touch of Wu's body beside me.

The only solace was provided by an airman who at the request of Dame Myra Hess was being sent home for early demobilisation, Colin Pritchard. Every day and through much of the day he played most beautifully on the piano in the officers' wardroom, the only instrument in the ship. It was a large room, perhaps the liner's ballroom in peacetime, and as there were nowhere near enough chairs, I sat on the stairs or anywhere I could to listen to him. Music was something of which I had heard very little in recent months, and being without friends it was my only form of companionship, something to help the dragging time to pass until I could be again in the companionship of my family.

Berthed among a crowd of men among whom sadly I found no one with whom I felt I had anything in common, the thing to which I most looked forward was the time I could sit listening to Colin Pritchard. Perhaps it was unfortunate that the first time I walked into the large room and heard the piano playing, Colin was playing Schubert's A Minor Sonata, perhaps the bleakest and most anguished of them all. Was it perhaps because Schubert, only in his mid-twenties, was conscious of the first manifestations of the disease that only five years later would kill him? As Colin played, I felt Schubert's despair. It was too much for me. I had to leave the room and walk about on the boat deck. But I knew that I must persevere, and I returned to the room in which the piano was playing. Colin had changed to another Schubert Sonata, the B Flat Major, and the lovely tranquil almost hymn-like theme brought calm and solace to my nervous misery.

It was the piano music that as time went by gradually brought me out of my melancholy. Sometimes what Colin played brought back my despondency, and

I sat there with my head in my hands in black despair. But at other times the music washed over me and sluiced away my memory of my loss.

Sometimes I sat on the boat deck in the sunshine, or lay reading lazily in the shadow of a lifeboat, just conscious of the hum of the ship's engines and of her gentle rise and fall, like a giant breathing, on the slowly curving swell of the Indian Ocean. So time drifted by.

I relived in memory incidents of recent months: exciting hours working with Geoffrey, and happy intimacies in the company of Wu. Those I sadly knew could never come again. But increasingly now my thoughts searched forward to England and home, my parents and Tiled Cottage and the garden sloping up into the beech woods of Westbrook Hay. *Nancy Blackett* too, was now re-comissioned and sailing in English waters from one happily remembered anchorage to another. More and more I realised that my enthusiasm for returning to Hong Kong and police work was waning. It would be so different now.

I recalled Geoffrey's courage and sense of fun, which had made his company so thrilling and so enjoyable. However, Sansom had said that it was very unlikely that he would be returning to Hong Kong. The Colonial Office would want to use his experience and seniority in other parts of the Empire. It was amazing that he was a man who had only just walked away from four years' internment in a Japanese prison camp. He was a remarkable man. I knew that I had been so fortunate to have worked with him and known his friendship.

Though my time with her had been so tragically short, how wonderful it had been to meet Wu and earn her love. I lifted my eyes and gazed unseeing out across the blue sea. Where was that little girl now? Surely that bright spirit could not be extinguished! In her own Buddhist faith she would have known confidently that her spirit would live on, returning recycled to someone of similar vitality born soon after her own death. Living with her, I had begun already to share that faith.

What would it be like to live again in England? If I did not return to Hong Kong and the appointment I had been offered, what would I do? In my self confidence I did not dwell on the details of that question, but I realised that there were two possible reactions.

For some years now – quite a large proportion of my life – I had led an adventurous life. Without the stimulation of rapidly changing experience, without the moments of danger and physical anxiety, would life be too bland, too dull?

Or would it be that living among people who had come to terms with the changed priorities of peacetime life, I would feel a need to put down roots, to marry and to try to build something that wartime had delayed? Shutting out the spacious enormity of my present surroundings I reached again in my mind, as I had thought so often before the war, for my idyll: a little cottage in a village, prettily furnished with old things, low beams and horse brasses and near to woodland full of birdsong and dappled sunlight. I could find that only in England.

There was no doubt that Geoffrey and Wu had shaped my ambition to live in Hong Kong and work in the police. Enthusiasm waned for a Hong Kong without them.

There was another consideration. A jab of conscience pricked me when I admitted that it should have figured sooner and with greater priority in my thoughts. What would be the feelings of my parents if they knew that I was planning to live so far away from them for the rest of their lives? Though my mother had initially not known that I was on operations in Bomber Command, when she had learned that fact she must have been disappointed that I was then and immediately about to go to the Far East and continue with dangerous work. My father had borne the worry of knowing what I was doing, perhaps daily expecting the fateful telegram. He would be disappointed that his son was not coming back to share his company and sail with him in *Nancy Blackett*.

CHAPTER THIRTY-TWO

Return to Pin Mill

F ather was delighted to see me.
'I've missed my crew. What about going down to *Nancy Blackett* next weekend? I've got her at Walton at present.'

Walton, where aeons ago the sea invaded the land that lies behind the sheltering headland called the Naze. It is a swampy saltmarsh of mud, grown over by samphire and other green, saltwater-loving weeds. When the tide is high, it is an intricate network of little creeks. When the tide falls the water drains away and the creeks are only soft slimy mud. Sometimes, therefore, the creeks are navigable in a dinghy, but at other times the saltmarsh is a place only for birds: redshank and curlew, terns and oystercatchers. The flooding water of Dovercourt Bay flows into the Walton creeks through a broad channel between sea walls, older than memory. You can walk along the walls, their grassy banks falling down to the channel on one side or to the marsh on the other. It is a lonely but a beautiful place to walk, your feet stepping carefully to avoid treading on wild flowers, the air about you loud with the wheeling calls of gulls and waders. But it is a place loved by many people, unspoilt, never noticeably changing, and in the clear sea air you can often see for miles, lifted up there on the wall.

Out of the main channel from the sea up to the back of the little town of Walton, tucked behind the Naze and with its beach and breakwaters and pier on the seaward side, here and there a broader creek floods twice each day or night through the saltmarsh, perhaps to an isolated farm on higher ground. One of these broad creeks is called the Twizzle. *Nancy Blackett* lay at anchor just inside the Twizzle.

It would be more convenient to lie nearer to the top of the main channel, best of all, some might think, right up at the clubhouse. But up there there would be water to float *Nancy Blackett* only just before and just after high water time. At low water she would stand in only a trickle of water. Unless she was shored up she might fall over sideways! And in the Twizzle, there was that peace, that unspoilt beauty, which my mood required. Sitting in *Nancy Blackett*'s cockpit, perhaps with a cup of tea, we would watch other boats sailing in, to find their moorings or to anchor. My father recognised most of them and told me who they were. Happily we would plan the next day's voyage, north, or south, according to how the tide would serve, to another happily remembered anchorage along the Suffolk or Essex coast. At some states of tide there was a place not far from us where we could get ashore in the dinghy, and walk along the sea wall, the sunny green turf at our feet, the desolate but beautiful salt-marsh, patterned with a glinting filigree of tiny creeks, stretching away from us into the distance.

In the last of the ebb I pulled the dinghy perhaps half a mile from the club-house out to *Nancy Blackett*.

When we had stowed our gear, we hoisted sail, threw our mooring over the side, and threaded our course out between the other boats to the Pyefleet, to Dovercourt Bay and Harwich Harbour, up the Orwell Estuary and so to Pin Mill. There, bobbing in the water among other moored or anchored boats, was the red marker-buoy of our mooring. Father sailed on to it and with our boathook I pulled it up and made it fast on the fore deck. We lowered the sails, stowed them tidily, and I looked around me at this well-loved place.

I had come a long way since I had sailed out of Pin Mill nearly seven years ago on that lovely last weekend of peacetime England. I had travelled right round the world. I had loved, and lost. But now the shingled hard, part-covered by the rising tide, reached out to greet me from the Butt and Oyster, where Mr Watts, my father told me, was still the landlord. And near it in the sunshine, against the green hill, was Alma Cottage, where Miss Powell still lived. This time it was again a halcyon day, but in 1939 she had been so right, it had been indeed 'a weather breeder' . . .

Index